INDIAN LANGUAGES AND TEXTS THROUGH THE AGES

Essays of Hungarian Indologists in Honour of Prof. Csaba Töttössy

Edited by
Csaba Dezső

MANOHAR
2007

First published 2007

ISBN 81-7304-749-9

Published by
Ajay Kumar Jain for
Manohar Publishers & Distributors
4753/23 Ansari Road, Daryaganj
New Delhi 110 002

Typeset by the editor in 'Computer Modern' and Velthuis' Devanāgarī using LaTeX and Peter Wilson's 'memoir' class.

Printed at
Lordson Publishers Pvt Ltd
Delhi 110 007

Contents

Preface

Some people are born great, others acquire greatness, yet others have greatness thrust on them. Similarly my long experience in teaching suggests that some are born teachers, others become teachers by training, yet others have the profession of teaching thrust on them by circumstances. Professor Töttössy obviously falls into the first category. *Pædagogus nascitur non fit.* This was the feeling I got on the very first day I attended his class and each passing day further reinforced this feeling.

He is a challenging and charismatic personality whose influence one can not remain impervious to. He is a personality who invokes intense feelings; one can not remain indifferent towards him.

For Prof. Töttössy life means teaching and teaching means life. His character, his whole has merged with the notion of Syntax—Latin, Ancient Greek or Sanskrit—for generations of his students. We, his students are closely acquainted with his individual "Socratic" method of teaching. He is not a professor who only declaims his theories or ideas which one can accept or reject but—being led by his questions—we discover ourselves the possible solutions of a problem. He teaches not only the subject matter but first of all the way of scholarly thinking. He does his best endeavors to launch students not only on the already discovered paths of the grammatical system, but also accompanies them in the process of exploring new territories together.

He taught us to question the generally excepted truths, as he himself always makes a thorough examination of the subject he deals with. It was his intellectual ability to conceive an entirely new system of syntactical analysis which establishes beyond doubt his linguistic genius.

We are deeply influenced by his fascinating and colorful, at the same time severe and demanding personality. His highly respected and favorite professor, Árpád Szabó used to say that a teacher must be an actor to attract attention and fascinate the students. Prof. Töttössy certainly listened to this advice, but most likely he had already been born to be uniquely entertaining and captivating. In the moment he opened the door of his room, and ceremonially invited us in saying "Could you please come inside?", we found ourselves in another world. It was as hot as in India, usually about 30 °C. He used to be late in starting the class, in spite of having a watch on each of his wrists and a third one in his pocket. His lectures are unforgettable. He has a treasury of illustrative sentences which have become maxims. They have been handed down for several decades among the students.

Prof. Töttössy finds his ultimate happiness in the success of his students. As he says, a teacher must be a ladder for the students on which they can ascend. He always takes the needs of the students into consideration, and many times he submitted his own personal interest to the department's demands.

This humble attitude can be observed in his activities in the field of organization of scholarly work. He was member of several academic organizations. Since 1958, as the youngest member of the management in the Society of Classics (Ókortudományi Társaság) he took part in the administrative work for more than three decades. In 1985 he became the vice-president of the Society. So his name has become inseparable from the activities of the Society.

All of us are also inspired by his example, how to work hard with sincere devotion, with *ekāgratā* and enthusiasm. We learned from him how to deal with a text with utmost respect and accuracy, sometimes even up to a scrupulously exact way.

He had a dream to become a university professor, and he fulfilled this dream. He has never been eager to get awards or higher and higher position in life; he wanted to remain a professor, a *teacher*, because in his eyes there is nothing more one can achieve in life. So he one of those few people who can feel satisfied when they look back upon the path of their lives.

While offering these *"Pāṭhāntarāṇi"* ("variant", or rather "varied readings" of Indian culture) as a variegated garland of article-flowers to our respected Guru, we would like to thank him with this small volume his work, devotion, his solicitude and all his kind help at the first steps we made.

Mária Négyesi

Prof. Csaba Töttössy

Professor Csaba Töttössy was born on the 6th of July, 1931, in Budapest. His father, himself a self-made man, was a grammar school teacher until his retirement in 1935; he provided a fairly good financial background as well as excellent education for all of his children. The discussions with his friends and the atmosphere of his father's library gave Csaba Töttössy the first inspiration to become a teacher. When one of his elderly friends told him that the highest rank a teacher could achieve was that of a university professor, he made a vow to become a full professor.

His father died in 1943, and in 1945 the secure background disappeared. The Second World War raged in Europe. On the last day of the siege of Budapest, on 11th February 1945, their villa, with the library inside, was reduced to ashes, and they survived the war with almost nothing.

The young Töttössy attended the Szent Imre Grammar School of the Cistercian order in Budapest (which became the Szent Imre State Grammar School in the last year of his studies), where he passed his A level finals with distinction. At this time, the best mark was "seven" and he had sevens throughout these years as well as at the finals. He started teaching when he was still a secondary school student—between 1945 and 1948 his income was the only support of his family, that is his mother, sister and younger brother, since his mother's pension had been withdrawn by the new political regime. (Even later he never stopped to fulfil his responsibilities towards his family.)

It was at this time that he decided to become a teacher of Latin and Greek. After his school leaving examination, in autumn

1949, he was admitted to the Faculty of Humanities of Pázmány Péter University (today Eötvös Loránd University), in the subjects of Classics (Latin and Ancient Greek) and Hungarian language and literature. From his third year he persued his studies only in Classics. He managed to obtain "A"-s with distinction in most semesters, and in 1953 he obtained a degree and a teacher's diploma in Classics. He also obtained an award for his thesis at the Faculty Competition.

Immediately after his university studies, on the 15th of July, 1953, he was appointed to the post of professor's assistant at the Department of Indo-European Studies, where he worked for more than half a century, until his retirement. In September 1956 he was given an independent tenure, but it was withdrawn when his brother, who had taken part in the anti-Soviet revolution in 1956, was committed to prison. The tenure was given back to him only in spring 1962, and he did his PhD preliminary examinations by the 30th of June in the same year. After handing in his PhD thesis in Sanskrit studies on the *Śukasaptati* at the end of 1962, he defended it on the 31st of May, 1963. He was given the doctoral title in linguistics by the Board of the Academy on the 6th of June, 1963, before his 32nd birthday.

The confirmed assistantship was given to him only on the 1st of September, 1963, since—as the head of the department was told—the dean did not dare to give this title to him immediately after his PhD because of his brother's involvement in the political affairs of 1956. He was appointed as a tenured reader (Dozent) on the 1st of July, 1970. The Ministry of Domestic Affairs objected to it already that year. The then head of the department, Professor János Harmatta had already suggested that he should have been considered for the appointment for professorship, but he did not get this appointment. He became so deeply engaged in studies on syntax (based on Latin, with references to Greek, Sanskrit and comparative Indo-European syntax) that he started to regard this as the main field for his future research.

He was the Head of the Department of Indo-European Studies between 1987 and 1996. In 1993 he was elected as the head of the Institute for the Study of the Ancient World, which included the Departments of Indo-European Studies, Latin, Ancient Greek, Egyptian Studies, Assyrian and Hebrew Studies. In 1996 he was appointed to a full professorship. Then he also succeeded in enlarging the department. On 31st December 2001—past the official age of retirement—he retired on a pension, but continued teaching until June 2002. These days he regularly comes to the department and takes interest in the research and teaching work of the staff, advises and evaluates their efforts, and remains an inspiring force for all members of the department who were selected by him in the past.

He started his university teaching practice by participating in teaching at the Department of Latin, and he lectured on Latin syntax from that time. In the beginning he taught Latin to non-specialist students, too, and had such excellent students as Professor László Kákosy and Professor Géza Alföldi. He also taught Latin historical linguistics, the history of the Latin language, and Indo-European comparative linguistics to students with Latin major. He also conducted seminars on Latin textual analysis for students of Latin and on Greek syntax and textual analysis for students of Ancient Greek.

In 1956, the Ministry of Education commissioned the Department of Indo-European Studies to teach Indian studies, though without giving any possibility for further appointments at the department, which consisted of two persons at that time. Young scholars could only join the department as late as in 1971 and 1981. First György Karsai was appointed as an assistant lecturer, and later Mária Négyesi as a PG student who became specialised in Hindi Studies. Before then it had been entirely Töttössy's task to teach Sanskrit language and litarature, since the head of the department, Prof. Harmatta had to lecture on Indo-European comparative linguistics and Iranian studies.

Töttössy himself started learning Sanskrit and studying the appropriate fields only after being appointed at the department (1953). He could not study Sanskrit as a university student because Sanskrit was not taught at the university. In spite of this fact by 1956 he obtained a fair knowledge of Sanskrit so he could start teaching this difficult and wonderful language. Therefore it can be regarded as a considerable achievement that he managed to launch Indian studies as early as 1956. He published a Hungarian translation of such a difficult text as the *textus ornatior* of the *Śukasaptati* in 1962, while he handed in his PhD thesis the same year without going on sabbatical. In Sanskrit Studies, in addition to teaching the language, textual analysis and text reading, he also lectured on linguistics, on the history of Sanskrit literature, and on the history, religions and philosophies of India. He always gave a great variety of lectures and seminars, teaching thirteen or fourteen hours per week, and he always did it with great enthusiasm and tried to utilise the results of his research in teaching.

When Indian studies were started, Professor Harmatta, the then head of the department entrusted him to organise completely the whole field, so it was his task to determine the way in which teaching should be done in the subject. The basic principle of the system he introduced is that everything should be based upon the proficiency in the language, and philological research should be done on this firm basis. Indology is a very difficult major, and although there are twenty to thirty students applying each year, there are not more then thirty altogether who have graduated so far. It should be noted that three of them are heads of departments at various universities and many of them are excellent scholars. Since 1987, when Dr Mária Négyesi was appointed as a senior lecturer, Hindi studies have also been successfully organised.

Initially Töttössy started doing research in the field of Greek philology, at the time when the periodical *Studies on the Antiquity* was first issued. Being interested in Aristophanes, he wrote a paper on the Lysistrate in this journal. Later he held lectures abroad on various topics in linguistics, partly based on the texts of Aristophanes. Although he still plans to write some more studies on Greek topics, he turned from Greek philology towards Sanskrit, since he had gained great enthusiasm for this fields from the department and from the teaching he was doing there.

His job at the department always required experience and knowledge in a wide range of different fields, so his works cover a wide range, too. The first field he studied was the linguistic relations between Greek, Latin and Sanskrit, and later between Sanskrit and Ancient Iranian. In 1956 an excellent study by Prof. Tarn inspired him to find a better explanation for the Indian name of the Greeks. He showed that the form "*yauna-*" in Old Persian goes back to the uncontracted form "*iaones*", the Prakrit borrowing of which gives the form "*yona-*", which was the name of Greeks in India, while the Sanskrit name "*yavana-*" is only a Sanskritization of the Prakrit form "*yona-*", and not a borrowing of the word "*iavones*". Moreover, the prakrit form "*Yonaka-*" is not the result of borrowing from Greek—as it had been thought by Prof. Tarn and even by Prof. Altheim—but was an indigenous Indian Prakrit development. In addition to linguistic data, he considered the historical evidence of the relation, too. Greeks were named after the Ionians in other ancient languages he considered in his study. The fact that Prof. Mayrhofer recognized these results and included them in his *Kurzgefasstes etymologisches Wörterbuch der Altindischen* made him very enthusiastic, being a young researcher at that time, and he continued dealing with the subject of Indo-Iranian and Greco-Latin, and later Greco-Latin and Indo-Iranian linguistic relations and borrowings even in later studies and lectures at international conferences. These borrowings etc. developed through trade relations, and many present names of gems and spices originate from India.

His second major field concerns mainly, although not exclusively, the *Śukasaptati*, which raised considerable interest among European scholars largely because of his contribution (at least as far as the German and Russian translations are concerned). He has shown that this work, which had been considered to be a collection of tales, represents a new genre, the book of short stories. It is not accidental that some of these stories occur in the Decameron by Boccaccio who is regarded the founder of the European short story as a literary genre. This beautiful work, enjoyable from the European point of view as well, was discovered by an excellent German scholar, Richard Schmidt, without whom Indians would not know even about the existence of this piece of art. Richard Schmidt maintained that the *textus ornatior* was later than the *textus simplicior*, but with detailed argumentation and textual evidence Töttössy has shown that the *textus ornatior* is closer to the original work, and that it is the older and more reliable version. In another study, he proved that the author of the *textus ornatior* is indeed Cintāmaṇibhaṭṭa. He has also dealt with the relation of the variants to each other and to the *Pañcatantra*-variants. Furthermore, in opposition to the view of R. Scmidt and Hertel, he has shown that the author of the original work was not a Jain monk, only the author of the *textus simplicior*. Though after defending his PhD thesis he worked on this topic for several years and presented papers on it at various international conferences, he has not yet published all his results collected in one volume.

He has also published book reviews, translations from and studies in the field of Greek, Ancient Persian and Sanskrit, but his main interest remained Latin syntax. It is of great value for him in this field that he cannot help considering Greek and Sanskrit parallels even if Latin is in the focus of his research. Moreover, his knowledge of some modern European languages also helps him significantly, and being a native speaker of a Finno-Ugric language, he can view the characteristics of these languages from a distance, maybe in a somewhat better way than a native speaker of German or English could.

It might be appropriate to mention a few of his works and results at this place. When he wrote a university textbook on Latin syntax in 1957, he already knew that the accusative with the infinitive *(accusativus cum infinitivo)* could not have developed in the way it is described in the *Lateinische Grammatik* by Stolz-Schmalz-Leumann-Hofmann-Szantyr, and that the solution of Hermann Hirt also lacks syntactical coherence. Nevertheless, he published his solution to the problem only in 1975. According to this, it was not the *verba iubendi* beside which this construction evolved, but the *verba sentiendi et dicendi*, and in these cases the accusative is the object of the *verba sentiendi et dicendi*. The theory can be tested in the following way: when we put this verb in the passive, this accusative becomes the passive subject of it in the nominative with the infinitive, and then the infinitives ending in *-e* and deriving from locative *-i* ending (as Greek infinitives) function as adverbials of state. So originally they meant something like "I see my father in joy" *(video patrem gaudere)*. He also called attention to the neglected fact that it is only beside the *verba sentiendi et dicendi* that Latin has three actions for the accusative with the infinitive, while Greek has four. In this case, the Greek *infinitivus aoristi* is antecedent, just as its indicative aorist is posterior.

There is another reason why the accusative with the infinitive could only evolve beside this type of verb requiring a system of infinitives of various actions, namely that the *verba iubendi* can have an accusative with the infinitive with one action only in Latin, and with only two in Greek. In this case, the Greek *infinitivus aoristi* is not antecedent, but is like the imperative of the aorist. The concordance with the *imperativus aoristi* shows that some kind of desire is also expressed here. In these constructions of the accusative with the infinitive with one or two actions, the infinitive is not an adverbial of state, but—according to Töttössy's system and naming—an "adverbial of end", such as in the following sentence: "I order you to leave" *(iubeo te abire)*. In this adverbial function, the *-i* ending of the dative infinitive can be used, which corresponds to the Greek infinitives ending in *-ai*. This accusative with the infinitive construction of the "adverbial of end" is too clear to develop into the accusative with the infinitive. Here the task was to explain how the original infinitives of locative and dative endings developed into cases of nominative and accusative. This explanation had been missing so far. He has also shown how the Latin active infinitive of dative became *imperfectus passivi*. The explanation is that after a certain time the original case values of these infinitives became obsolete, although we can still find the old forms in Vedic Sanskrit.

In another paper he argued that constructions of adjectives with participles—which he calls reversed adjectival constructions—are indeed reversed adjectival constructions in Latin, Greek and Sanskrit, and the whole problem is not only a matter of translation technique. Töttössy was pleased to learn at a conference in Turin (Italy) that the renowned Sanskritologist, Prof. Gonda accepted his theory concerning Sanskrit.

In other papers he demonstrated the way in which different cases of the gerundive are used in various functions. He tried to solve the old problem whether the gerundive or the gerund is the more ancient form. He pointed out that the view that considers the gerundive to be *instans actio* goes back to the mistake of Priscian, who projected the usage of his time onto the classical language, just as he did in the case of the *praeteritum* and *futurum perfectum indicativi*, with the exception that this latter mistake did not have an influence on our views of grammar.

Prof. Töttössy has been a member of the Committee of Classical Philology of the Hungarian Academy since 1967, and also was its secretary from 1970 till 1990. He has been a member of the editorial board of the *Studies on the Antiquity (Antik Tanul-*

mányok) since 1965, and he was its managing editor between 1975 and 1990. Between 1991 and 2004 he was a member of the editorial board of the *Acta Antiqua Hungarica*, in whose editing he participated for the 1977 and the 1978 issues. He was the editor of the periodical *Annales Universitatis Scientiae Budapestiensis, Sectio Classica* between 1970 and 1974 and in the year of 1979. From 1972 till 1987 (throughout 5 periods) he was the secretary of the Doctoral Committee of the Faculty of Humanities, and between 1987 and 1989 he was also a member of the Doctoral Committee of ELTE University. He was also a member of the Academic Committee of the Faculty in 1983 and 1984. He was elected as a member of the Committee of Classical Philology of the Ministry of Education, and had worked as a secretary for the forerunner of this committee (from 1971). He has been a member of the Committee of Oriental Studies at the Hungarian Academy since 1991. He became a member of the managing board in the Society of Classics (Ókortudományi Társaság) already in 1958 (as the youngest member at that time), and he took part in the administrative work for thirty-three years, from 1985 as vice-president. Organizing this society demanded a great amount of work and time, since it was not only financial matters he had to deal with, but practically he did all the organising work for many years. He also organised several conferences and congresses, such as the seventh International Congress of Classical Studies (FIEC) in 1978 in Budapest.

The first time he was abroad was in 1964, sponsored by the Hungarian Academy, when he attended the International Conference on the History of Religion in Strasbourg. He held a lecture in 1972 at the First Sanskrit World Conference in Delhi, and then he went on a lecturing tour in India. In autumn, the same year, he participated in the Eiréné Conference of Classical Philology in Cluj (Rumania). His lectures in Delhi and in Cluj have been published abroad. In 1973 he took part and lectured at the Congress of Oriental Studies in Paris, and then he spent three weeks of research and study in Switzerland at the Hardt Foundation in Geneva. After this, he participated in and lectured at the following conferences: in 1974 in Dubrovnik (Yugoslavia) at the Eiréné Conference of Classical Philology, in 1975 in Berlin (GDR) at the Sanskrit World Conference, in 1975 in Turin (Italy) at the Second

Sanskrit World Conference, in 1976 in Moscow at the Conference of Soviet Indologists and then in Yerevan (the then Soviet Union) at the Eiréné Conference of Classical Philology, and in 1977 in Paris at the Third Sanskrit World Conference. Between the 27th of June and the 26th of July 1977 he was on a research trip to the Hardt Foundation again in Geneva. He also lectured in 1978 in Nesebar (Bulgaria) at the Eiréné Conference of Classical Philology, in 1979 in Weimar (GDR) at the Fourth Sanskrit World Conference, in 1981 in Varanasi (India) at the Fifth Sanskrit World Conference, and then in 1987 in Leiden (Holland) at the Seventh Sanskrit World Conference, after which he again spent some weeks in Switzerland at the Hardt Foundation to do research.

Professor Töttössy did not give up his academic work after his retirement. Currently he is busy with summing up his life work: he is finalising his *magnum opus*, a Comprehensive Latin Syntax. He also plans to publish some articles in the field of Ancient Greek Studies.

In the light of Professor Töttössy's *curriculum vitæ* it is evident that his fist love towards Latin and Ancient Greek Studies prevails up to his old age. Nevertheless as a university professor he educated generations of Sanskrit scholars. He established a school of Indologists who are deeply and with all heart involved with Indian Studies and continue on the way opened up by their beloved professor.

List of Publications

'Review of V. Ehrenberg's *The People of Aristophanes*' in *Antik Tanulmányok* Vol. I, 1954, pp. 184–185.

'Jegyzetek [Notes]' in Aristophanés, *Három komédia [Three Comedies]*. Budapest: Szépirodalmi Könyvkiadó, 1954.

'The Name of the Greeks in Ancient India' in *Acta Antiqua Hung.* Vol. III, 1955, pp. 301–319.

'Megjegyzések Aristophanés Lysistratéjához [Some Remarks on Aristophanes' Lysistrate]' in *Antik Tanulmányok* Vol. II, 1955, pp. 60–67.

'A görögök neve az ókori Indiában [The Name of the Greeks in Ancient India]' in *Antik Tanulmányok* Vol. III, 1956, pp. 69–81.

'Review of K. Marót's *A görög irodalom kezdetei [The Beginnings of Greek Literature]*' in *Antik Tanulmányok* Vol. III, 1956, pp. 285–287.

'Review of V. N. Gyakov - N. M. Nyikolszkij's *Az ókori világ története [The History of Ancient World]*' in *Antik Tanulmányok* Vol. III, 1956, pp. 295–296.

'Jegyzetek [Notes]' in Thomas Mann's *Elcserélt fejek [Die vertauschten Köpfe / The Transposed Heads]*. Budapest: Magyar Helikon, 1957, pp. 221–235.

'Latin mondattan és stilisztika [Latin Syntax and Stylistics].' Budapest: Felsőoktatási Jegyzetellátó Vállalat, 1958, pp. 94–186.

'Review of J. Schmidt's *Pancsatantra azaz ötös könyv* [Pañcatantra (tr. from original Sanskrit)]' in *Antik Tanulmányok* Vol. VII, 1960, pp. 97–98.

'India története (Ókor és középkor) [History of India (Ancient and Mediaeval)].' in Új Magyar Lexikon [New Hungarian Encyclopaedia]. Vol. III, Budapest: Akadémiai Kiadó, 1960, pp. 387–388.

'Thukydidés: A hatalom filozófiája (Az V, 84–116 fordítása) [Thukydides: The Philosophy of Power (Transl. of V, 84-116)].' in A demokrácia bölcsője (Összeállította Sarkady János) [The Craddle of Democracy (Ed. by János Sarkady)]. Budapest: Gondolat, 1960, pp. 174–185. = A méloszi dialógus (Thukydidés V, 84–116 fordítása) [The Melos Dialogue (Translation of Thukydides V, 84–116)].' in Görög történetírók (Vál. és szerk. Ritoók Zsigmond) [Greek Historians (Selected and ed.

by Zsigmond Ritoók)]. Budapest: Európa Könyvkiadó, 1988, pp. 324–333.

'A latin versek magyarra fordítása és a latin szövegek sajtó alá rendezése [Translation and Editing of the Latin Texts].' in Vörösmarty Mihály Összes Művei. I. Kisebb költemények. (Kritikai kiadás) (szerk. Horváth Károly) [Collected Works of Vörösmarty Mihály. I. Minor Poems (Critical edition) (Ed. by Károly Horváth)]. Budapest: Akadémiai Kiadó, 1960.

'A Magyar Tudományos Akadémia és az Ókortudományi Társaság Klasszika-filológiai Konferenciája [Conference on Classical Philology Organized by the Society of Ancient Studies and the Hungarian Academy of Sciences].' in *Magyar Tudomány* Vol. LVIII (VI), 1961, pp. 117–119.

'Sukaszaptati (Az "ékesebb szöveg" fordítása szanszkrit eredetiből, tanulmány és jegyzetek)[Śukasaptati (The Translation of "textus ornatior" from Sanskrit, study and notes)].' Budapest: Magyar Helikon, 1962. pp. 249.

'Lysistrate and the Oligarchic Coup d'État.' in *Acta Antiqua Hung.* Vol. X, 1962, pp. 273–282.

'A Śukasaptati változatai viszonyának kérdéséhez [The problem of the relation between the Śukasaptati's different recensions].' in *Antik Tanulmányok* Vol. X, 1963, pp. 155–165.

'India (Bevezetés és Kauṭilya Arthaśāstra-jából fordítások szanszkrit eredetiből) [India (Introduction and translations from Kauṭilya's Arthaśāstra)].' in A hadművészet ókori klasszikusai. (Szerk. Hahn István) [Classics of the Ancient Art of War (Ed. by István Hahn)]. Budapest: Zrínyi Katonai Kiadó, 1963, pp. 191–201.

'Dareios Naqš-i Rustam-i B és suezi felirata, Xerxés daiva-felirata (Fordítások óperzsából) [Inscriptions of Dareios at Naqš-i-Rustam B and at Suez (Translations from Ancient Persian)].' in Ókori keleti történeti chrestomathia (szerk. Harmatta János) [Chrestomathia of Ancient Eastern History (Ed. by János Harmatta)].' Budapest: Tankönyvkiadó, 1964[1], (1993[4], 1996[5], 1997[6]). pp. 321–322, 328.

'Manu törvényeiből és Kauṭilya Arthaśāstra-jából (Bevezetések és fordítások szanszkritból) [Introductions and Excerpts from Manu's Laws and Kauṭilya's Arthaśāstra].' in Ókori keleti történeti chrestomathia (szerk. Harmatta János) [Chrestomathia of Ancient Eastern History (Ed. by János Harmatta)]. Budapest: Tankönyvkiadó, 1964^{1}, (1993^{4}, 1996^{5}, 1997^{6}). pp. 370–377.

'A L'Association Internationale d'Histoire des Religions strasbourgi kollokviuma (1964. szeptember 17–22.) [Colloquium of the L'Association Internationale d'Histoire des Religions in Strasbourg (17–22. September 1964)].' in *Antik Tanulmányok* Vol. XII, 1965, pp. 313–316.

'The Problem of Internal Frame Stories of the Śukasaptati.' in *Acta Orientalia Hung.* Vol. XVIII, 1965, pp. 227–240.

'A Śukasaptati-változatok és a jaina szerzőség kérdése [The Śukasaptati Variants and the Jaina Authorship].' *Antik Tanulmányok* Vol. XIV, 1967, pp. 249–253.

'A Śukasaptati elbeszéléseinek jellege és műfaja [Character and Genre of the Stories of the Śukasaptati].' in *Antik Tanulmányok* Vol. XV, 1968, pp. 221–228.

'The Śukasaptati Variants and the Jaina Authorship.' in *Acta Antiqua Hung.* Vol. XVI, 1968, pp. 447–454.

'A latin gerundivum [The Gerunde in Latin].' in *Antik Tanulmányok* Vol. XVI, 1969, pp. 205–208.

'Character and Genre of the Stories of the Śukasaptati.' in *Acta Antiqua Hung.* Vol. XVII, 1969, pp. 433–441.

'A Sukaszaptati 19. meséje (Fordítás szanszkrit eredetiből) [The 19th Tale of the Śukasaptati (Translation from Sanskrit)].' in A világirodalom legszebb elbeszélései. [The Best Short Stories of the World Literature].' Budapest: Európa Könyvkiadó, 1971^{1} (1973^{2}, 1973^{3}), Vol. I. pp. 220–223 (180–182, 195–198).

'The System of the adiectivum verbale in the Latin Language.' in *Annales Univ. Sci. Budapest. Sectio Classica* Vol. I, 1972, pp. 69–76.

'Sanskrit Literature and Indology in Hungary.' in *Cultural Forum* New Delhi: Vol. 15/1, 1972, pp. 55–58.

'The Dates of the Variants of the Śukasaptati.' in *Acta Antiqua Hung.* Vol. XXI, 1973, pp. 273–279.

'A Śukasaptati és a Pañcatantra.' in *Antik Tanulmányok* Vol. XXI, 1974, pp. 59–64.

'The Development of the Greek and Latin acc. and nom. c. inf.' in *Annales Univ. Sci. Budapest. Sectio Classica* Vol. II, 1974, pp. 9–16.

'Eastern Elements in the Technical Vocabulary of Graeco-Roman Trade.' in Actes de la XIIe Conférence Internationale d'Études Classiques "Eirene", Cluj-Napoca 2-7 Octobre 1972. Ed. Acad. Rep. Soc. Rom. – Adolf M. Hakkert, B. V. Bucuresti — Amsterdam: 1975, pp. 153–157.

'Aziánus nyelvek. Megfejtetlen ókori nyelvek. Indoeurópai nyelvcsalád. Baszk nyelv. [Ancient Near-Eastern Languages. Undechiphered Ancient Languages. Indo-European Language Family. Basque Language].' in Zsebenciklopédia. Budapest: Gondolat, 1975, pp. 240–243, 244.

'A görög és latin infinitivus-os szerkezetek [Infinitive Structures in the Ancient Greek and Latin].' in *Antik Tanulmányok* Vol. XXII, 1975, pp. 13–19.

'The participium absolutum in the Greek, Latin and Sanskrit.' in *Annales Univ. Sci. Budapest. Sectio Classica* Vol. III, 1975, pp. 11–16.

'The 16th Story of the textus ornatior of the Śukasaptati.' in *Acta Antiqua Hung.* Vol. XXIV, 1976, pp. 285–296.

'Cintāmaṇibhaṭṭa szerzősége [The Authorship of Cintāmaṇibhaṭṭa].' in *Antik Tanulmányok* Vol. XXIII, 1976, pp. 223–232.

'Indo-iráni elemek a görög–római kereskedelmi szókészletben [Indo-Iranian Elements in the Trade Related Vocabulary of the Greek and Latin Languages].' in *Antik Tanulmányok* Vol. XXIII, 1976, pp. 242–245.

'The participium absolutum in the Sanskrit, Greek and Latin.' in *Indologia Taurensia* (Official Organ of the International Sanskrit Studies) Vol. III–IV: Proceedings of the Second World Sanskrit Conference (Torino, 9–15 June 1975). Torino: Edizione Sereno, 1976, pp. 477–482.

'Graeco-Indo-Iranica.' in *Acta Antiqua Hung.* Vol. XXV, 1977, pp. 277–288.

'A latin, görög és szanszkrit participiumos szerkezetek [Participial Structures in Latin, Greek and Sanskrit].' in *Antik Tanulmányok* Vol. XXIV, 1977, pp. 221–224.

'Görög és latin elemek az indo-iráni nyelvek szókészletében [Greek and Latin Elements in the Vocabulary of Indo-Iranian Languages].' in *Antik Tanulmányok* Vol. XXIV, 1977, pp. 1–6.

'Bibliography of the Scholarly Works and Papers of J. Harmatta.' in *Acta Antiqua Hung.* Vol. XXV, 1977, pp. 11–22.

'Bemerkungen zur Geschichte der Śukasaptati [Some Remarks on the History of the Śukasaptati].' in *Annales Univ. Sci. Budapest. Sectio Classica* Vol. VII, 1979, pp. 29–36.

'The Variants of the Frame Story of the Śukasaptati.' in *Acta Antiqua Hung.* Vol. XXVIII, 1980, pp. 437–453.

'Ó- és középind nyelvek [Ancient and Middle Indian Languages].' in Keleti nevek magyar átírása (Főszerk. Ligeti Lajos) [Transliteration of Eastern Names (Gen. ed. Lajos Ligeti)]. Budapest: Akadémiai Kiadó, 1981, pp. 291–293.

'A papagáj hetven meséje (Fordítás szanszkrit eredetiből) [The Parrot's Seventy Tales (Translation from the Original Sanskrit)].' in Mesefolyamok óceánja (Válogatás a szanszkrit elbeszélésirodalomból) [The Ocean of the Rivers of Tales (Selected Stories from the Sanskrit Story Literature)]. Budapest, Európa Könyvkiadó, 1982, pp. 285–496.

'A Śukasaptati-változatok papagájtörténetei [The Parrot-Stories of the Śukasaptati Variants].' in *Antik Tanulmányok* Vol. XXIX, 1982, pp. 199–212.

'Az Indoeurópai Nyelvtudományi Tanszék története és a tanszéken folyó szanszkritológiai tudományos és oktató munka [The History of the Department of Indo-European Studies and its scholarly and teaching work].' in India magyar szemmel (Szerk. Bethlenfalvy Géza és Puskás Ildikó) [India through Hungarian Eyes (Ed. by Géza Bethlenfalvy and Ildikó Puskás)]. Budapest: Indiai Nagykövetség, 1987, pp. 62–69.

'Harmatta János hetven éves [János Harmatta's 70th Birthday]. in *Archeológiai Értesítő* Vol. 114–115, 1987–1988, pp. 124–125.

'Marót Károlyné közérdekű meghagyása (Marót Károly Alapítvány) [Bequest of Marót Károlyné (The Marót Károly Foundation)].' (Co-authors: J. Harmatta, Zs. Ritoók) in *Antik Tanulmányok* Vol. XXXIII, 1987–1988, pp. 74–75.

'Az 1985. évi Ábel Jenő Emlékérem (Maróti Egon) [Ábel Jenő Commemorative Medal (Egon Maróti)].' in *Antik Tanulmányok* Vol. XXXIII, 1987–1988, pp. 76–77.

'Az indicativus "irrealis" a latinban [The Indicativus "Irrealis" in Latin].' in *Annales Univ. Litterarum et Artium Miskolciensis* Vol. I, 1991, pp. 139–145.

'A coniunctivus bizonyos használatai a latin főmondatokban [Some Usages of the Coniunctivus in the Latin Main Clauses].' in *Annales Univ. Littorarum et Artium Miskolciensis* Vol. II, 1992, pp. 197–202.

'A latin gerundivum használatának alakulása [The History of the Usage of the Latin Gerundivum].' in *Annales Univ. Litterarum et Artium Miskolciensis* Vol. III, 1993, pp. 137–146.

'Indogermán -tṛ nomen agentis képző a latin inf. és part. instans activi-ban [Indo-Germanic -tṛ suffix in the Latin Inf. and

Part. Instans Activi].' in *Annales Univ. Litterarum et Artium Miskolciensis* Vol. IV–V, 1995, pp. 130–133.

'A latin (valamint a görög és a szanszkrit) egyszerű mondat (főmondat) és részei (állítmány, alany, tárgy) [The Latin (Greek and Sanskrit) Simple Sentence and its Parts (Verb, Subject, Object)].' in *Annales Univ. Litterarum et Artium Miskolciensis* Vol. IV–V, 1995, pp. 134–138.

'A latin (valamint a görög és a szanszkrit) mondat részei II. (a határozók stb.) [The Latin (Greek and Sanskrit) Sentence and its Parts II. (Adverbs, etc.)].' in *Annales Univ. Litterarum et Artium Miskolciensis* Vol. VII, 1997, pp. 4–14.

A latin igerendszer instans alakjainak kialakulása [The Development of the Instans Forms of the Latin Verb System].' in Saxa Loquuntur. A József Attila (korábban Szent Imre) Gimnázium évkönyve [The Yearbook of the József Attila (former Szent Imre) Gimnázium], Budapest 1997, pp. 248–254.

'The Development of the Usage of the Latin Gerundive.' in *Acta Antiqua Hung.* Vol. XXXVIII, 1998, pp. 381–389.

'Origin and Development of the Forms of the Latin Future Active Infinitive and Participle.' in *Acta Antiqua Hung.* Vol. XXXVIII, 1998, pp. 253–259.

A latin instans actio és eredete [The Instans Actio in Latin and its Origin].' in *Antik Tanulmányok* Vol. XLIII, 1999, pp. 115–121.

'A latin gerundivum és gerundium. Kialakulásuk és szerkezeteik [The Gerundivum and Gerundium in Latin. Their Rise and Structures].' in *Antik Tanulmányok* Vol. XLIII, 1999, pp. 123–131.

'A latin perfecta actio kialakulása [Development of the Perfecta Actio in Latin].' in *Antik Tanulmányok* Vol. XLIV, 2000, pp. 59–71.

'The Development of Actio Perfecta in Latin.' in *Acta Antiqua Hung.* Vol. XL, 2000, pp. 459–469.

'Töttössy Csaba (Autobiográfia) [Autobiography].'in *Napút* 2000 / 10, pp. 85–86.

'The Latin Supine and the Sanskrit Infinitive; Priscian.' in *Acta Antiqua Hung.* Vol. XLV, 2005, pp. 337–342.

List of Conference Papers

'Sanskrit Literature and Indology in Hungary.' First World Sanskrit Conference, New Delhi, 26–31 March 1972.

'A Comparison of Bocaccio's Decamerone and the Śukasaptati.' Kurukṣetra University (India), 6 April 1972.

'Eastern Elements in the Technical Vocabulary of Graeco-Roman Trade.' XXIIe Conférence Internationale du Comité "Eirene", Cluj (Romania), 2–7 October 1972.

'The Śukasaptati and the Pañcatantra.' XXIXe Congrès International des Orientalistes, Paris, 16–22 July 1973.

'Typology of Nominal Structures in Classical Languages.' XIIIe Congrès International des Études Anciennes du Comité "Eirene", Dubrovnik, 7–12 October 1974.

'Remarks on the History of Śukasaptati.' Internationale Sanskrit Konferenze. Sprache und Kultur im Alten Indien, Berlin, 19–21 March 1975.

'The Participium Absolutum in the Sanskrit, Greek and Latin.' Second World Sanskrit Conference, Torino, 9–15 June 1975.

'The Rise of the Sanskrit Short Stories.' Congrès of the Soviet Indologists, Moscow, 4–11 January 1976.

'Graeco-Indica.' XIVe Congrès International des Études Anciennes du Comité "Eirene", Jerevan (Sovietunion), 7–24 May 1976.

'The Author and the 16th Story of the textus ornatior of the Śukasaptati.' Third World Sanskrit Conference, Paris, 20–25 June 1977.

'The Character of the Scythes in Aristophanes' Thesmophoriazousai.' XVe Congrès International des Études Anciennes du Comité "Eirene", Nesebar (Bulgaria), 3–8 October 1978.

'The Variants of the Frame Story of the Śukasaptati.' Fourth World Sanskrit Conference, Weimar (DDR), 23–30 May 1979.

'Indian and Graeco-Roman Linguistic Contacts.' Fifth World Sanskrit Conference, Varanasi (India), 21–26 October 1981.

'The Internal Frame Stories of the Śukasaptati.' Seventh World Sanskrit Conference, Leiden (Holland), 23–29 August 1987.

Mária Négyesi

One

Remarks on the Periphrastic Constructions with the Verb 'To Make, To Do' in Sanskrit, Greek and Latin

Máté Ittzés*

Introduction

Periphrastic constructions like German *zur Aufführung bringen*, *einen Unterschied machen* (in place of *aufführen, unterscheiden*), for which in German linguistics[1] the term *Funktionsverbgefüge*[2]

---

*I dedicate this paper to Professor Csaba Töttössy, from whom I have studied Sanskrit and who also elucidated to me many aspects of the syntax of Latin and Greek. I also would like to thank to my colleagues Dr. Mária Négyesi, Dr. Balázs Déri and Dr. Csaba Dezső for their helpful comments on different parts of this paper.

[1]See e.g. BUSSMANN 1990: 259–260; HENTSCHEL–WEYDT 1990: 78–80; LEWANDOWSKI 1990: 329–330; ENGEL 1991–92, I: 407–408, II: 869; WEINREICH 1993: 1052–1058, etc. See also the references in HOFFMANN 1996.

[2]Various English terms have recently been used for this phenomenon (e.g. *"light-verb-construction"*, *"collocational verb construction"*, *"stretched*

(henceforth FVG) was coined, frequently occur in other Indo-European languages as well, although the term itself had not been widely used until recently by the grammarians of the particular languages:[3] see e. g. English *to make use of, to make allowance for*; Russian *держать речь* 'to give a speech'; French *prendre garde à qc, prendre part*; Italian *dare una lavata*[4] and so on.

As for a definition, the *Funktionsverbgefüge* is the connection of a verb (*Funktionsverb*, henceforth FV) and a noun (*Fügungsnomen* or *Funktionsnomen*, henceforth FN) with or without a preposition, in which the lexical or conceptual meaning of the construction is conveyed by the FN, while the FV, almost entirely deprived of its original lexical meaning, functions first and foremost as the exponent of grammatical features and categories. The FN is a noun denoting action, typically a deverbal nomen actionis,[5] so the principal function of the FV is very similar to that of the word formative denominal suffixes. Note e. g. the mechanism in Lat. *quaestiō* 'searching, examination, investigation' →

---

verb construction"), but none of them seems to have yet gained ground. In French, the term *"verbe support"* is now generally used, which was transferred e. g. into Portuguese (*"[construções com] verbo-suporte"*), English (*"[construction with] support verb"*) and even into German (*"Stützverb"*).

[3]Previously, they had usually been dealt with within the framework of phraseology. For instance, many typical Russian FVGs are found in DERIBAS 1983. In French their name earlier was *"locution verbale"* (cf. GREVISSE 1949: 447; KELEMEN 1985: 263), in English *"verb + noun phrase + prepositional phrase idioms"* (QUIRK et al. 1992: §12.64) or *"verb + noun + preposition collocations with delexical verb"* (ASHER /ed./ 1994: 3169 s. v. *phraseology*). But cf. already the remark by ESAU 1976: 151: *"English, another language which uses FVG..."* In the last two or three decades the term *Funktionsverbgefüge* (or its translation) has been applied to these constructions in different languages (English, Dutch, Italian, Portuguese, French, Spanish, Russian, Czech, Slovakian, Chinese, Korean, etc.) and important attempts have also been made to describe thoroughly their characteristics.

[4]RENZI–SALVI 1989: 79–82 (with the term *"espressioni idiomatiche ... con ... verbi supporto"*). But see recently also PFLEIDERER et al. 2000.

[5]This approach takes *Funktionsverbgefüge* in a slightly narrower sense than it is usually done. It must be noted, however, that the very category of FVG is neither homogenous nor easy to delimit from the free word-combinations and collocations on the one side and from the idiomatic units on the other. There are criteria with which we can select the FVGs (e. g. in contrary to free collocations, in a FVG the FN normally can not be pronominalized or questioned, cf. HENTSCHEL–WEYDT 1990: 79), but exceptions always remain.

[Late Lat.] *quaestiōnāre* ≈ *quaestiōnem pōnere/habēre* 'to examine, investigate'.[6] Here the FV (together with the case ending *-em*) is equivalent to the word formative *-ā*-suffix of *quaestiōnāre*: *quaestiōn-* + {*-ā-re*} ≈ *quaestiōn-* + {*-em pōn-ere*}.

But beside word formative functions, the FV also does the duty of other suffixes, since it has to express other grammatical categories too (number, person, mood, tense; aspect, manner of action [Aktionsart], voice). According to the difference of the last three categories FVGs often form a pair or even series (e. g. difference of voice: German *zur Aufführung bringen* [active] ↔ *zur Aufführung kommen* [passive]; difference of manner of action: *zur Ruhe bringen* [terminative] ↔ *in Ruhe lassen* [durative], etc.). The FVG is a syntactic and semantic unit which, though looking like an ordinary syntagma (VP → V + NP/PP), functions as a simple verb (usually as the complex nominal predicate of the sentence) and can thus very often be replaced by the verb underlying, or derived from, the FN (cf. above e. g. *zur Aufführung bringen* ≈ *aufführen*).[7]

FVGs are common in every strata of modern languages, but particularly in the official usage and the media, what is due chiefly to a strong inclination for nominal style. In spite of their unquestionable advantages the stylistic evaluation of FVGs in modern western languages is often a subject of debate, because their great number in a text may yield that its language loses its natural vividity and gets too abstract. But as Hoffmann rightly emphasizes,[8] the FVG is in the first place not a stylistic, but a grammatical category and has to be approached as such.

Funktionsverbgefüge are widely used in non Indo-European languages, as well. In Hungarian, where the phenomenon seems to have appeared first in Middle Age translations from Latin and later, in the 17–18th century, from German as a syntactic calque, the most striking example nowadays is the verb *kerül* 'to come/get to' in constructions with nomina actionis (itself probably a calque from the German type *zur Aufführung kommen*) as a substitution of the practically lost passive voice: e. g. *eladásra kerül*, which lit-

---

[6]Cf. also HOFMANN 1965: 756 and 297.

[7]For a useful description of the general characteristics of FVG with regard to Latin see HOFFMANN 1996: 200–204.

[8]HOFFMANN 1996: 203.

erally means 'is getting to (the state of) being sold' (something like Skt. *krītatvaṃ* [or *krīyamāṇatvaṃ*] *gacchati*), instead of the regular, but by now obsolete, passive form *eladatik* 'is being sold'. This kind of expression, however, gets more and more common not just in the written language and the official usage, but also in everyday conversation, what gives plenty to think and worry about for manuals of correct Hungarian usage.

In this paper I am dealing with some questions concerning the FVG in three ancient Indo-European languages, Sanskrit, Greek and Latin.[9] Although there are many verbs that can appear as lexically empty FV,[10] I choose the most typical one: the verb 'to make, to do' (Skt. √*kṛ*, Gk. ποιέομαι, Lat. *faciō*),[11] which in my view makes up the very core of the category *Funktionsverb*. The frequency and importance of FVGs are changing during the history of the individual languages, so I will attempt to deal with not just synchronic, but also diachronic aspects of our present topic.

Let us take first an example from Sanskrit and see how a typical FVG actually works. The root *pra+*√*viś* 'to step into, penetrate into, enter' is in the first step transformed into a deverbal noun *praveśa-* 'entering, penetration into'. Now, in order that this word with the lexical meaning of expressing the action in an abstract way might be able to form the predicate of a sentence, it has to form a phrase with a finite verb that indicates all the necessary categories such as person, number, tense, mood, aspect, voice: *praveśaṃ karoti* (3rd sing. pres. ind. act.). The FV functions here in fact as if it were merely a complex of denominal suffix, modal, temporal suffixes and personal ending. It can be

---

[9] As far as I know, the term *Funktionsverbgefüge* has not yet been applied to the constructions in question in Sanskrit and Greek. As to Latin, see HAPP 1976: 454–455 (and e.g. 500 note 74–75) and especially HOFFMANN 1996 (and his references). The same construction is dealt with under the name *"accusative-passive periphrasis"* by ROSÉN 1983: 198.

[10] It need not be emphasized that *Funktionsverb* is not the same kind of grammatical category as noun, verb, etc. are, but only a particular employment of verbs that tend to lose their lexical meaning (process of desemanticization, cf. HOFFMANN 1996: 206). E.g. Skt. √*kṛ*, though frequently used as FV, can also mean 'to prepare, make, accomplish'. Sometimes it is hard to decide whether we are dealing with a FVG or not (see later).

[11] Cf. MW s.v. √*kṛ*; LSJ s.v. ποιέω A II 5; OLD s.v. *faciō* 23.

clearly seen that the lexical meaning is concentrated in *praveśam*, while the grammatical features in *karoti*.[12] It seems as if the FVG were a totally redundant construction in place of a simple verb (*praveśaṃ karoti* = *praviśati*). Many times, like here, it certainly is, but as we will see it later, other FVGs can often have a surplus as opposed to the verb related to the FN.[13]

---

[12]Cf. RENZI–SALVI 1989: 79: *"la parte lessicale è concentrata sul nome..., la parte grammaticale sul verbo..."* See also THUMB–HAUSCHILD 1959: §685: *"...der Bedeutungsinhalt [scil. des Prädikats] wird gern in ein Abstractum gelegt, während ein Verbum finitum oder Participium nur das formale Prädikat bildet."* Monier-Williams (s. v. √kṛ, p. 301) is not completely right in saying that *"the senses of √kṛi may be variously modified or almost infinitely extended according to the noun with which this rt. is connected."* The meaning of the root is not extended, but rather reduced, because in FVG it does not in fact have a lexical meaning at all! It is only in English that it has to be translated with different words. It is true, however, that not all of his examples are FVG.

[13]New Persian, too, has a verbal periphrase of the same kind, called usually *"compound verbs"*, but termed, quite adequately, as *"syntagmatische Verben"* ('syntagmatic verbs') by the Hungarian scholar, Zs. TELEGDI (1955: 69). Here, too, the most frequently used verb is 'to make', i. e. *kardan* (e. g. *ḥisāb kardan* 'to count [lit. make counting]', *qabūl kardan* 'accept [lit. make acceptance]'), which also can form verbs from loan-words (especially from Arabic): e. g. *qaṣd* (< Arabic 'intention') *kardan* 'to intend', *taškil* (< Arabic 'formation') *kardan* 'to form', etc. (TELEGDI 1950–1951: 321; 1973). In Persian, a language that is poor in verbs, the great majority of these periphrastic constructions have no simple verb counterpart, which means that in the system they function in fact as finite verbs (TELEGDI 1950–1951: 317–318). This is also facilitated by the absence of nominal inflection, which makes the original syntagmatic relation between the noun and the verb obscure. One can also recall the various constructions of the same (or similar) kind in the Hindī language, first of all the so called "denominative verbs" with active transitive *karnā* (like Persian *kardan*, cf. above) and intransitive *honā* (e. g. *nāś karnā* 'to destroy' ~ *nāś honā* 'to be destroyed'), which also serve as a productive device for forming "verbs" from loan-words (e. g. *pās* [< English] *karna* 'to pass [an exam]'; *kharīd* [< Persian] *karnā* 'to buy'). See e. g. GATZLAFF-HÄLSIG 1978: 111–115. The properties of FV (i. e. the function of expressing grammatical categories) can also be compared to those of the "explicator" (or "vector") verb part of the so called "compound verbs" in Hindī (e. g. *khānā* 'to eat' ~ *khā jānā* 'to eat up, devour': here the explicator verb *jānā*, which originally has the lexical meaning 'to go', simply modifies the manner of action), about which — under the name *"verb basis/stem syntagmata"* — see recently KOSTIĆ 1999 (esp. 60–107 and the *"possible diachronic view"* 111–113).

Sanskrit

Within Old Indian it is necessary to make a distinction between the Vedic and the Classical Sanskrit period. It is a well known fact that the verbal system of the Vedic language is much more extensive and complex than that of the later period. The expansion of the nominal compounds and the appearance of infinite verb forms in the function of the predicate in the later language is obviously connected with the loss of certain verbal categories and so with the diminishing complexity of the system of practically used verbal forms.[14] Parallel to this process periphrastic forms appeared, two of which, the periphrastic future and the periphrastic perfect, even acquired a position in the verbal paradigm.

The constructions of the agent noun (nomen agentis) with the verb 'to be' in older Vedic literature do regularly not have the function of expressing futurity (this is common only since the times of the Brāhmaṇas). It is more often the idea of accomplishment that is given prominence. These enunciations contain a communication about the future in the form of a mere statement, while the tendency of anticipation is clearly perceptible.[15] Thus the meaning of expressing a real future,[16] and consequently the appearance of what we can really call a periphrastic future, is just a relatively later development.

We can observe the same process in the case of the periphrastic perfect, as well. Its development is clearly parallel to the spread of FVGs with √*kṛ*. As far as the so called periphrastic perfect is concerned, its first example appears in the Atharvaveda (AV XVIII, 2, 27 *gamayāṃ cakāra* ← causative *gamayati* 'to cause to go, send, impart'), and this is actually its only occurrence in the mantra parts of the Saṃhitās. Later, since the time of the Brāhmaṇas, it is getting more and more often used, and in the

[14]KRAUSE 1925: 214–219. Cf. also SPEIJER 1886: 228: *"The history of the syntax of the Sanskrit verb is a history of decay."*

[15]GONDA 1975 (with many examples). About the two kinds of agent nouns in Vedic (i. e. the one with hysterodynamic inflection and situative meaning and the other with acrostatic inflection and general meaning) see also TICHY 1992a and 1995.

[16]About the special function of the periphrastic future (cf. P. 3, 3, 15: *anadyatane luṭ*), which seems to have replaced the prospective subjunctive, see also TICHY 1992b.

later literature it becomes current as the exclusive perfect formation for certain groups of verbs (derivative conjugations, roots beginning with a vowel in a heavy syllable, etc.). It is significant that at first only the verb √*kr̥* was used as auxiliary,[17] and it is only later that √*as* and √*bhū* appeared in this function (first in AB 7, 14, 8: *āmantrayām āsa* ← *āmantrayate* 'to address, speak to'). Later √*as* became the most commonly used auxiliary, while √*bhū* remained always rare.

Regarding the prominent role of the transitive verb √*kr̥* at the beginning of the process, I think it is without question that originally the form in -*ām* was the accusative of a deverbal noun being syntactically the direct object of the verbal element.[18] When the nominal element in -*ām* was frozen in this construction and its origin and nature was no more transparent, the root √*as* (and √*bhū*), though intransitive, could replace √*kr̥*. Furthermore, since √*as* is the most often used auxiliary (and copula) in Sanskrit, it acquired the chief role in the formation of the periphrastic perfect, as well.[19]

It is important for the present purpose to note that in early literature the deverbal noun in -*ām* is sometimes connected with other forms of √*kr̥* too, not just with its perfect *cakāra*. There occur e.g. aorists as *vidām akran* (← √*vid* 'to know') TS 3, 5, 10, 2; *abhyutsādayām akaḥ* (← caus. *abhy-ut-sādayati* 'to cause to set out towards') MS 1, 6, 5; imperatives as *vidāṃ kurvantu* cf. P. 3, 1, 41, etc.[20] This makes clear that the periphrastic perfect of Sanskrit is only a remnant of a greater linguistic variety: it was

---

[17]Note that Pāṇini (3, 1, 40) mentions only this root (Kātyāyana and Patañjali the verbs √*as* and √*bhū* as well). Some scholars consider √*kr̥* in this *sūtra* as a *pratyāhāra* for √*kr̥*, √*as* and √*bhū* (e.g. VASU 1988: 365). Against this view see e.g. SPEIJER 1886: 251; RENOU 1930: §362; DEBRUNNER 1954: 256, etc.

[18]So, among many others, DELBRÜCK 1888: 426–427, DEBRUNNER 1954: 252–259; THUMB–HAUSCHILD 1959: §533; POHL 1979: 347 and 360 note 9, etc. For other views see e.g. BRUGMANN 1892: 1265, §896 (instrumental case); JACOBI 1899 (a special absolutive formation), etc.

[19]Cf. THUMB–HAUSCHILD 1959: §533; DEBRUNNER 1954: 259. According to Debrunner it is not clear, "*wieso ein Ersatz* [sc. for √*kr̥* by √*as* and √*bhū*] *nötig war.*" I think it was not a *necessity* that caused this change, but the analogical function of the verb(s) 'to be' in other analytic constructions.

[20]DEBRUNNER 1954: 252–253; THUMB–HAUSCHILD 1959: §533; WHITNEY 1993: §1073, etc. Cf. P. 3, 1, 41–42.

incorporated into the verbal paradigm, while the other constructions consisting of a noun in *-ām* and some other form of $\sqrt{}$*kṛ* had gone out of use by the classical period. The reason for the survival of the perfect form is that this was the one that was in fact needed: in this way a special perfect could be formed even to those verbs (derivatives, roots with long vowels as $\sqrt{}$*īkṣ*, $\sqrt{}$*ās*, reduplicated presents as *bibharti* etc.) for which the formation of the regular reduplicated perfect was originally impossible or caused difficulties.

Parallel to this is the tendency to use other types of deverbal nouns too in periphrastic constructions. These constructions can involve practically any form of the verb $\sqrt{}$*kṛ*. But while the periphrastic perfect after having been frozen has been integrated into the verbal paradigm, the latter are just occasional formations, not grammaticalized units. The proper term for them is *Funktionsverbgefüge*, just as $\sqrt{}$*kṛ* should be properly called *Funktionsverb* (and not auxiliary),[21] because in spite of its primarily grammatical meaning (i. e. its function of expressing in fact only grammatical categories) syntactically it is a member of an ordinary and real syntagma (VP → V + NP /direct object/). *Cakāra* and *āsa*, however, in the periphrastic perfect can be adequately termed auxiliary, because the construction is frozen and the original syntactic relations are no more perceptible.

Let us now have a look at some examples of FVG with $\sqrt{}$*kṛ* (apart from those constructions which later became the periphrastic perfect). As a survey with the help of the article $\sqrt{}$*kṛ* in Grassmann's lexicon[22] has shown, in the oldest Vedic texts such periphrases are extremely rare.[23]

[21] As e. g. SPEIJER 1886: 233 calls it.

[22] GRASSMANN 1955: cols. 332–345

[23] In the major part of the occurrences the root has its original conceptual meaning ('to make, to accomplish' etc.) and it stands very often with double accusative ('to make, to render'), e. g. *kṛdhí mā devávantam* 'make me one who is guarded by gods' RV VI, 47, 10 etc. This observation (i. e. that $\sqrt{}$*kṛ* is very rarely a FV in the RV) might be helpful when interpreting the hymns.

[1] *sáṃ yád ā́naḷ ádhvana ā́d íd áśvair vimócanaṃ kr̥ṇute* 'wenn sie [sc. die Sonne, Sūrya] ihre Wege vollendet hat, dann macht sie mit den Rossen Ausspann'[24] RV III, 30, 12;

[2] *ayám agne tvé api yáṃ yajñáṃ cakr̥mā́ vayám* RV II, 5, 8;

[3] *svā́hā yajñáṃ kr̥ṇotana índrāya yájvano gr̥hé* RV I, 13, 12;

[4] *yajñéna yajñám ayajanta devā́s* RV I, 164, 50 = X, 90, 16;

[5] *etáṃ vāṃ stómam aśvināv akarma* RV X, 39, 14;

[6] *tápo yé cakriré máhas tā́ṃś cid evā́pi gachatāt* 'die die Kasteiung zu ihrer Herrlichkeit gemacht haben, auch zu diesen soll er (der Tote) gelangen' RV X, 154, 2;

[7] *śruṣṭíṃ cakrur bhŕ̥gavo druhyávaś ca* 'die Bhr̥gu's und Druhyu's leisteten willig Folge' RV VII, 18, 6;

[8] *ádhvaryavaḥ kártanā śruṣṭím asmai* RV II, 14, 9;

[9] *yáthā devā́ ásureṣu śraddhā́m ugréṣu cakriré* 'wie die Götter bei den mächtigen Asura's sich Glauben verschafft haben' RV X, 151, 3.

In [1] the case is fairly clear morphologically (the deverbal neuter noun *vimócana-* is obviously from *vi+√muc*) as well as semantically (*vimócanaṃ kr̥ṇute = vimuñcáte*). We might, but in fact need not, assume that *vimócana-* has shifted its meaning ('unyoking' → 'stopping for rest', thus *vimócanaṃ kr̥ṇute* with the instrumental meaning 'is stopping for rest together with /his horses/'), we can rather think that *áśvair vimócanaṃ kr̥ṇute* should be interpreted as *áśvānāṃ vimócanaṃ kr̥ṇute* ('is making the unyoking of his horses'),[25] the construction being thus a genuine FVG.

At first sight it could be tempting to see a FVG in examples like [2]. But the correct interpretation is to consider the verb *√kr̥*

[24] Translations of RV passages, unless indicated otherwise, are from GELDNER 1951.

[25] This is the single occurrence of *vimócana-* in connection with the root *√kr̥*.

here as having its original conceptual meaning (cf. Geldner: '[sei] dieses Opfer in deiner Hut, o Agni, das wir bereitet haben').[26]

Passage [3] and [4] are at first sight a bit ambiguous. If we interpreted the expression in [3] in a similar way as the one in [2], i. e. 'to prepare a sacrifice', then it would not be a FVG. But if we, rightly, follow Geldner ('vollziehet mit Svāhāruf das Opfer für Indra im Hause des Opferers!'), then it is a FVG indeed *(yajñáṃ kr̥ṇómi = yájāmi)*.[27] In example [4] we can find instead of √*kr̥* a triple figura etymologica, which is definitely a more poetical expression. This sentence could mean 'by means of sacrifice the Gods accomplished their sacrifice'[28] (with a cognate accusative), but Geldner translates it as 'mit Opfer opferten die Götter dem Opfer', and in the latter interpretation *yajñám ayajanta* is obviously not equivalent to *yajñám akr̥ṇvata.*

The same as in relation to [2] can be said about [5]. *Stóma-* 'praise, laud' is from √*stu*, but not a nomen actionis, and √*kr̥* has here its original meaning 'to prepare, make' ('dies Loblied haben wir für euch, Aśvin, gemacht'). There is no FVG in [6] either, because √*kr̥* stands here with double accusative ('make sg sg; etw. zu etw. machen').[29] A true FVG appears with all probability in [7], where *śruṣṭíṃ cakrur* could be replaced by some verbal form of the root √*śruṣ* 'to listen, attend to, obey', a collateral form of √*śru*.

Another example with *śruṣṭí-*, example [8] is highly remarkable. Geldner translates it similarly as above, ('Adhvaryu's! Erweiset ihm Gehorsam!'), while Grassmann's interpretation runs otherwise: 'O Priester, schaffet euch Gehör bei diesem!'. The problem could be solved if we were able to tell who the agent of the action involved in *śruṣṭí-* is. If it were the same as the agent of √*kr̥*, then it would be clearly a FVG and Geldner's translation

[26]This is evident also because the noun could be, and actually is, pronominalized: *ayám ... tvé ..., yáṃ yajñáṃ cakr̥mā́ vayám = ayáṃ yajñáḥ ... tvé ..., yáṃ cakr̥mā́ vayám.* Cf. note 5.

[27]That this is the correct interpretation is also shown by the fact that *svāhā* was uttered while *carrying out* the sacrifice and making the oblation and not while *preparing* it. Cf. also that e. g. *ā́huti-* f. never occurs with √*kr̥* whenever meaning the 'action of the oblation'.

[28]This is the translation of GRIFFITH 1995.

[29]It is also interesting that *tápas-* (orig. 'warmth, heat') has the meaning 'penance, observance' only in the latest R̥gvedic hymns.

would be correct, if not, then Grassmann's interpretation would be preferred. In [7] the case is entirely clear (the two agents are one and the same, so it is a FVG) as it is also in [9], where the agents are different.

Hoffmann, too, speaks about the difference of the two agents in connection with Latin "desemanticized" *adferre* '(lit.) to take/carry (sg to a place)'. He takes *adferre* as a FV with grammaticalized causative meaning.[30] On the other hand, he also rightly emphasizes that in certain kinds of analytic forms *facere* is not a FV, because it does not undergo the process of desemanticization. The same may be said with regard to √*kr̥*. I hesitate to consider √*kr̥* as a FV in *śruṣṭíṃ kr̥ṇóti* + dat. 'sich Gehör schaffen bei jemandem', because it seems to me to retain a great part of its lexical meaning here ('to bring about, effect').[31] The action of *śruṣṭí-* here is in fact the result of the action of *kr̥ṇóti*, while in a typical FVG we do not have two separate actions. The FN is rather a certain kind of inner object *("inneres Objekt")* of the FV, even if they are not related etymologically.

A more detailed survey may tinge the picture sketched above, but the general tendency in the R̥gveda-saṃhitā, which can be clearly seen here, is to avoid constructions with √*kr̥* as a FV. In the later Vedic literature,[32] in epic Sanskrit and, especially, in classical Sanskrit the number of FVGs with √*kr̥* increases considerably and it remains always a very popular and frequent construction.

---

[30] HOFFMANN 1996: 204-207 (e. g. *mors ... est finita omnibus, / quae generi humano angorem nequicquam adferunt* 'death is end for all the things, / which bring vexation in vain to the race of men' Cic. Tusc. 3, 59; transl. after J. E. King). Note that the translations of Greek and Latin passages are usually cited from the respective volumes of the Loeb Classical Library and with the translator's name only. Translations without translator's name are mine.

[31] A corresponding Latin expression is *audientiam facere* + dat.: e. g. *exsurge, praeco, fac populo audientiam* 'Crier! Rise and bid this crowd give ear! (lit. bring about listening in the crowd)' Plaut. Poen. 11, transl. P. Nixon. Cic. div. in Caec. 42 is different, because here the dative expresses the beneficiary of the action of listening, not the agent: *iam nunc mente et cogitatione prospicio ... quantam denique audientiam orationi meae improbitas illius factura sit* 'even now I picture to myself ... the keen attention which his misconduct will direct to the speech I make against him' transl. L. H. G. Greenwood.

[32] Cf. the examples from the *Atharvaveda* by HOFFMANN 1976: 583. See also HOFFMANN 1976: 579–580 for the interpretation of *karóti / kuruté* as allegro variants of *kr̥ṇóti / kr̥ṇuté* originating from the frequent use of √*kr̥* as "faktitive Kopula", "Allerweltswort" and "Funktionswort".

Since this kind of periphrastic construction is far too well known to everybody reading Sanskrit texts, I will only cite a handful examples from different sources.

[10] *bhagavan hi kṛtā rakṣā tvayā sarvā viśeṣataḥ* 'the whole protection, o venerable sir, was indeed made by you excellently' (in a passive construction) MBh. 3, 187, 27;

[11] *sa kṛtvā niścayaṃ rājā ... yaṣṭuṃ samupacakrame* 'the king having made a decision ... began to sacrifice' R. 1, 37, 24;

[12] *Kapilo ... roṣeṇa mahatāviṣṭo huṃkāram akarot tadā* 'Kapila ... filled with a great anger made the utterance (lit. the making) of hum' R. 1, 39, 27;

[13] *teṣveva nityam śuśrūṣāṃ kuryāt* 'he should always render service unto them' transl. G. Jha, Mn. 2, 235;[33]

[14] *kṣatriyeṇa ... sarvasyāsya yathānyāyaṃ kartavyaṃ parirakṣaṇam* 'the protection of all this shall be done according to law by the Kṣatriya' transl. G. Jha, Mn. 7, 2;

[15] *putre rājyam samāsajya kurvīta prāyaṇaṃ raṇe* 'making over the kingdom to his son, the king shall bring about his departure in battle' transl. G. Jha, Mn. 9, 323.

[16] *atra yaḥ salile praveśaṃ karoti sa me bhakṣya iti* 'he who enters (lit. makes entering into) the water here shall be eaten by me' Pañc. (textus simpl.) 5, 10;

[17] *sarve ... araṇyavāsino bhayavyākulitacitrāḥ samantāt palāyanakriyāṃ kurvanti* 'all the forest-dwellers, with hearts overtaken by fear, run away (lit. make the action of fleeing) in all direction' Ibid. 1, 10;

[18] *tanmadhye kasyacid rājño 'ntaḥpuraṃ ... jalakrīḍāṃ karoti* 'in its middle the ladies (the harem) of a certain king are playing with water (lit. are making playing with water)' Pañc. (textus orn.) 1, 6;

[33] Note that $\sqrt{}$*kṛ* stands here with the accusative of a deverbal -*ā*-stem noun as in the periphrastic perfect (see earlier).

[19] *aṇḍajo ... aham asamartho māṇuṣaiḥ saha virodhaṃ kartum* 'being a bird ... I am unable to struggle (lit. make a struggle) with men' Ibid. 1, 6;

[20] *kim punar asya durātmano mahāśatror upāyena vadhaṃ kariṣyāmi* 'how much more am I to kill (lit. make the killing of) this great wicked foe with a trick' Ibid. 1, 5;

[21] *sūkareṇāpyāgatya pralayaghanaghoragarjanaṃ kr̥tvā sa vyādho muṣkadeśe hataśchinnadruma iva papāta* 'and hurt in the region of the scrotum by the boar, who ran there with a roar (lit. making a roaring) terrible as the cloud of dissolution (of the world), the hunter fell down as a riven tree' Hit. 1, 7;

[22] *yasya vacasi tvayā viśvāsaḥ kr̥tas tasya phalametat* 'this is a reward from that person in whose words trust was put (lit. made) by you' (with passive participle) Ibid. 1, 9;

[23] *kusumāvacayaṃ karomi* 'I am gathering (lit. making the gathering of) flowers' Mr̥cch. 9, 28b.[34]

The preference for FVGs is often an idiosyncrasy of a particular author's style, so it was possible for Divekar to use their frequency as one of the distinguishing factors between the two authors of the *Kāvyaprakāśa*. One of the writers, Alaka (Alaṭa), the author of the vr̥tti, uses it quite often (e.g. ... *ityupadeśaṃ karotīti* 'thus he teaches/instructs (lit. makes the teaching)';[35] ... *iti nāsya bhedalakṣaṇaṃ kr̥tam* 'thus there has been made no indication of its being divided', etc.), while in the portions written by Mammaṭa it does not occur.[36]

One can find FVGs in Buddhist Hybrid Sanskrit texts, as well, e.g.:

[34]Cited by GAWROŃSKI 1907: 21.

[35]In *Vetāla* (ed. Uhle, p. 62, line 7) the same words are found: *yadā mamopadeśaṃ na kariṣyasi* 'when you will not teach me (lit. make my teaching)'. Another FVG from the same text (p. 54, line 37): *viṣam ānīyatām yathāham ... prāṇatyāgaṃ karomi* 'let poison be brought here in order that ... I may make the abandonment of life'. Both passages cited by BLOCH 1906: 70.

[36]DIVEKAR 1927: 519.

[24] *dūrato evāgacchantaṃ dr̥ṣṭvā Bhagavantaṃ kriyākāraṃ karonti* 'having caught sight of the Buddha approaching from afar, they make an agreement (lit. make the making of a decision)' Mv III, 329, 3;

[25] *tato rājā ... nagare ghaṇṭāvaghoṣaṇāṃ kārayati sma* 'after that the king made in the town a proclamation by bell ringings' LV 186, 28;

[26] *kathāṃ kr̥tvā* 'having said sg (lit. having made a speech)' LV 409, 1, etc.[37]

One could enumerate the examples ad infinitum. But I think it is more important to put the question instead, whether the use of this type of periphrastic construction has any special grammatical, semantic, etc. function whatsoever or it is a mere pleonasm instead of an entirely synonymous simple verb. To answer this question with certainty a much greater corpus of texts and a complete list of *Funktionsverbe* should be thoroughly examined. However, some points and tendencies can still be emphasized even at this stage of research.

As far as the *Funktionsverbgefüge* with √*kr̥* is concerned, the periphrase can ordinarily be replaced by a simple verb, i. e. the two expressions are in fact synonymous in all respect. E. g. [14] *kṣatriyeṇa ... sarvasyāsya ... kartavyaṃ parirakṣaṇam* = *kṣatriyeṇa ... sarvam idam ... parirakṣitavyam,* [16] *yaḥ salile praveśaṃ karoti* = *yaḥ salile praviśati,* etc.[38]

But even if there is no general semantic difference, we can still recognize some obvious stylistic reasons that lead an author to use a FVG instead of the simple verb. I think the most important among these is a tendency to use as elaborate a language as one can. This means that beside other devices, chiefly nominal composition, the authors also make use of complicated periphrastic

[37] EDGERTON 1953; cf. also in Pāli: RHYS DAVIDS–STEDE 1989: s. v. *karoti.*

[38] Theoretically, however, the deverbal abstract noun can undergo a semantic change so that the whole expression has a meaning different from the simple verb. A difference of meaning may also mean a difference of aspect or Aktionsart. (I have not yet found clear Sanskrit examples for these phenomena.)

constructions. Furthermore, in many cases the two devices, nominal compound plus FVG, can combine in a highly characteristic way, giving a possibility for the author to use a nominal compound or a longer compound as he could do if using a simple verb, since the nominal element (FN) can readily serve as the last member of a tatpuruṣa compound (cf. above e. g. [18] *jalakrīḍāṃ karoti* instead of *jale krīḍati*, [23] *kusumāvacayaṃ karoti* instead of *kusumāny avacinute*, etc.). This tendency is apparently connected with the strong preference for nominal style in classical Sanskrit (especially in scientific literature),[39] which is a clear sign of the abstract and artificial character of this language.

Some minor points may be added. If the deverbal noun is formed of a transitive verb, the FVG makes it possible to omit the object, while beside a simple verb it would be indispensable (e. g. [26] *kathāṃ kṛtvā* in contrary to *kathayitvā*, beside which we would expect at least a pronoun like *tad, etad*, etc. or a clause with *iti*). But if the original direct object of the simple verb is not omitted in the FVG, there are different possibilities. It can be transformed into the first member of a tatpuruṣa compound (e. g. [23] *kusumāvacayaṃ karomi*). Often it is transformed into the objective genitive governed by the FN (e. g. [20] *asya ... mahāśatror ... vadhaṃ kariṣyāmi*). Sometimes the FVG is regarded as a single lexical unit and governs an accusative as if it were a simple verb: e. g. *anyāṃ vivāhaṃ kuryāt* 'should marry (lit. make the marrying of) another woman' VaikhS. 6, 2; *vedam adhyayanaṃ karoti* 'studies (makes the studying) the Veda' Ibid. 8, 3.[40] If the underlying simple verb stands with another case than the accusat-

---

[39]The term "nominal style" (i. e. the preference for nominal elements, compounds, etc.) is not synonymous with the "use of nominal sentences". The latter means that kind of sentences where there is no verb predicate, just „nomina" and the optionally occurring copula ($\sqrt{as}$). But regarding the primacy of the verb in Indo-European languages we can, following Professor Töttössy, speak even in these cases of a verb predicate (which is the copula even if missing) plus a predicative attribute or noun. About "nominal sentences" in Indo-European see MEILLET 1906; in Sanskrit: JACOBI 1903; BLOCH 1906; BLOCH 1934: 303–305; HARTMANN 1955; GREN-EKLUND 1978; BREUNIS 1990. None of them, of course, mentions the FVGs with $\sqrt{kṛ}$, for strictly speaking it is not "nominal", i. e. it involves also a verb (mostly finitum, but cf. the gerundive without *asti* in [14]). But cf. THUMB–HAUSCHILD 1959: §684–685.

[40]Cited by DEBRUNNER 1954: 258. About the same construction in Greek see e. g. KÜHNER 1898: 322.

ive, the FVG generally retains it unchanged, e. g. [19] *māṇuṣaiḥ saha virodhaṃ kartum* (cf. *vi* - $\sqrt{}$*rudh* + *saha* + instr.); [16] *salile praveśaṃ karoti* (cf. *pra* - $\sqrt{}$*viś* + loc.); [22] *vacasi* ... *viśvāsaḥ kṛtas* (cf. *vi* - $\sqrt{}$*śvas* + loc.).

Greek

In ancient Greek, the FVG as a construction consisting of a nomen actionis and the verb ποιεῖσθαι is equally common, and its characteristics are generally speaking the same as in Sanskrit. Just a handful of examples will now be listed here:[41]

[27] αὐτοὶ ἐπανέπλεον ἐπὶ τοὺς βαρβάρους, ἀπόπειραν αὐτῶν ποιήσασθαι βουλόμενοι τῆς τε μάχης καὶ τοῦ διεκπλόου 'themselves advanced their ship against the foreigner, desiring to put to the proof (make trial of) his fashion of fighting and the art of breaking the line' Hdt. 8, 9, transl. A. D. Godley;

[28] ἣν συναναμνησθεὶς ὑμῖν ἐγὼ κοινῇ τὴν ἀπόκρισιν ποιήσομαι 'reminding ourselves of which I, along with you, will make answer' Plat. Nomoi X, 897E, transl. R. G. Bury.

[29] ποῖ τὴν καταφυγὴν ποιήσεται ἄλλοθι ἢ πρὸς ὑμᾶς καὶ τὸ δίκαιον; 'where else will he find refuge (lit. make / take flight) than with you and with justice?' Antiph. 1, 4;

[30] ἐπίδειξιν μὲν τῆς ἑαυτῶν δυνάμεως ποιούμενοι 'making a display of their own power' Lys. 14, 21;

[31] ἄκακον κόρην μόνην ἀφεὶς ἐν ἐρημίᾳ / ἐᾷς, φυλακὴν οὐδεμίαν, ὡς προσῆκον ἦν, / ποιούμενος 'you leave an innocent girl all alone, / in isolation, and without her due / protection (lit.

[41] It seems that in poetry other verbs are more often used. E. g. ἔχω 'to have' in ἓν μὲν πρῶτά σοι μομφὴν ἔχω 'first, one reproach have I for thee' Eur. Or. 1069, transl. A. S. Way (μομφὴν ἔχω governing an accusative, i.e. regarded as a single lexical unit); τίθημι 'to put, to set' in οἵαν μ' ἄρ' ἔθου λώβαν 'what a ruin have you brought (lit. put) upon me' Soph. Trach. 996, etc.). But see e. g. καταφυγὰς ποιούμενοι / εἰς τέκνα 'finding refuge with (lit. making flight to) sons' Eur. Or. 567–568. A statistics should be made covering a much greater corpus of texts in Greek (and Sanskrit and Latin) literature to have a thorough and complete picture.

making no protection as is proper)' Men. Dysk. 222–224, transl. W. G. Arnott;

[32] Κικέρων ... πολλὴν μὲν ἐπίδειξιν ὑπεροψίας χρημάτων ἐποιήσατο, πολλὴν δὲ φιλανθρωπίας καὶ χρηστότητος 'Cicero gave many proofs (lit. made much display) of his contempt for wealth, and many of his humanity and goodness' Plut. Cic. 52 (Synkr. 3, 3), transl. B. Perrin;

[33] οἱ δὲ δὴ ἄλλοι ... ἐς ... τὰ ἐρυμνὰ ἀναφυγόντες ἐκεῖθεν ὅπη παρείκοι καταδρομὰς ἐποιοῦντο 'and as for the others ... took refuge in the mountain fortresses, from which they made vaiding expeditions whenever the chance offerred' Cass. Dio 55, 30, 6, transl. E. Cary.

There is a great number of examples in Thucydides (transl. C. F. Smith), e. g.:

[34] οἱ παρὰ θάλασσαν ἄνθρωποι μᾶλλον ἤδη τὴν κτῆσιν τῶν χρημάτων ποιούμενοι βεβαιότερον ᾤκουν 'the dwellers on the sea-coast now began to acquire (lit. making the acquiring of) property more than before and to become more settled in their homes' 1, 8, 3;

[35] οὐ ῥᾳδίως τὴν διάγνωσιν ἐποιοῦντο ὁποῖοι ἐκράτουν ἢ ἐκρατοῦντο 'it was not easy ... [for the Corinthians] to determine (lit. to make the determination of) just who were conquering and who were being conquered' 1, 50, 2;

[36] καὶ οἱ Κορίνθιοι ἀποτραπόμενοι τὴν διάλυσιν ἐποιήσαντο 'whereupon the Corinthians put their ships about and broke off (lit. made the breaking off) the action' 1, 51, 2;

[37] ἔκπλουν ποιεῖται λαθὼν τὴν φυλακὴν τῶν Ἀθηναίων 'he sailed out (lit. is making the sailing out), unobserved by the Athenian guard' 1, 65, 1;

[38] καρτερεῖν δὲ χρὴ καὶ ἄλλων παίδων ἐλπίδι, οἷς ἔτι ἡλικία τέκνωσιν ποιεῖσθαι 'but those of you who are still of an age

to have offspring (lit. to make the begetting [of children]) should bear up in the hope of other children' 2, 44, 3,[42] etc.

It is easy to recognize in these examples the characteristics we have seen in Sanskrit, apart from the nominal compounds, which are not used in Greek as a productive way of expression. The authors often use the FVG in order to form subtle parallelisms (e. g. [32]), the grammatical and logical connection between the complements (ὑπεροψίας χρημάτων, φιλανθρωπίας, χρηστότητος) governed by the same noun (ἐπίδειξιν) being stronger than it would be if depending on a verbal predicate on a higher level. It is obvious, however, that many times the FVG is only a sophisticated and complicated periphrase.

It is parallel to Vedic that in Homer such constructions are extremely rare and they spread only in later times.[43] Let us have a look at some passages with ποιέω in the Iliad and the Odyssey (transl. A. T. Murray):

[39] Τρώων αὖτ' ἀγορὴν ποιήσατο φαίδιμος Ἕκτωρ 'then did glorious Hector make a gathering of the Trojans' Il. 8, 489 (cf. Il. 8, 2);

[40] ἀλλ' οὐδ' ὧς ἐδύναντο φόβον ποιῆσαι Ἀχαιῶν 'even so they could not put the Achaeans to rout' Il. 12, 432;

[41] ἡ δ' οὔτ' ἀρνεῖται στυγερὸν γάμον οὔτε τελευτὴν / ποιῆσαι δύναται 'she neither refuses the hateful marriage, nor is she able to make an end' Od. 1, 249–250 = 16, 126–127;

[42] οὐδέ τιν' ἄλλην / μύθου ποιήσασθαι ἐπισχεσίην ἐδύνασθε, / ἀλλ' ἐμὲ ἱέμενοι γῆμαι θέσθαι τε γυναῖκα 'nor could you find any other plea to urge, save only as desiring to wed me and make me to wife' Od. 21, 70-72;

[43] ἀλλ' ἄγε νῦν ῥήτρην ποιησόμεθα 'but come now, let us make a covenant' 14, 393.

[42] Cf. the remark in Classen's commentary (1889: ad loc.): "*nach der überwiegenden Neigung des Thukydides zur Umschreibung der einfachen Verba.*"

[43] On the evidence of MINTON 1976 there is no FVG with the verb ποιέω, ποιέομαι in Hesiod either.

In [39] we find e. g. ἀγορὴν ποιεῖσθαι, but it is not a FVG, because it does not mean 'to have an assembly, to assemble', but 'convoke an assembly', in which the verb basically retains its lexical meaning ('to make' → 'to bring about' → 'to convoke'). The same is true for φόβον ποιεῖν 'to excite anger' (and not 'to be angry') in [40]. In the Odyssey, in [41] we have e. g. τελευτὴν ποιῆσαι 'to bring to an end, to accomplish' (= τελευτῆσαι), which is clearly a FVG. Another possible candidate may be the expression in [42], where ἐπισχεσίη 'pretext' comes from ἐπέχω 'to hold out, present, offer' with a semantic change. Elsewhere, in [43] we find ῥήτρην ποιεῖσθαι, which is a hapax[44] in Homer. But it is not a FVG, because the noun ῥήτρη, though deverbal (from the root *ῥη-: cf. ῥήτωρ 'rhetor', ῥητός 'stated, specified, spoken of', ἐ-ρρή-θην suppletive aor. of the verb 'to say, to speak', etc.), is not a nomen actionis, but a nomen acti.

As to the question of the origin of these FVGs, Schwyzer thinks[45] that in these constructions the verb ποιεῖσθαι is a substitute for the verbal element of a figura etymologica with a so called cognate accusative, e. g. ἀπόπειραν ποιεῖσθαι (in [27]) for ἀπόπειραν ἀποπειρᾶσθαι. Thus the FVG as a type of construction would in fact be a simplification of a more elaborate expression. However, I think that these constructions should rather be opposed to the simple verb of which the noun is formed (or to which it is related), and considered not a "simplification", but rather a "complication": a sign of the effort to make use of complicated and abstract constructions. It is then not surprising that Thucydides and the Attic orators show such a great number of them.

Since FVGs appear in a great variety also in non-literary papyri,[46] scholars thought that their origin should rather be sought in the popular speech or the vernacular, from where it had been transferred to higher literature by quite an early date.[47] But regarding the complex and artificial characteristics of these periphrastic expressions I consider it more probable that the process

---

[44] Cf. GEHRING 1891: s. v.

[45] SCHWYZER 1950: 78.

[46] Cf. MAYSER 1926: 123–130.

[47] Cf. MAYSER 1926: 123.

was precisely the opposite.[48] The language of the documentary papyri, which stands between the vernacular and the written language of high literature, borrowed the FVG as such from the latter, especially from the historians and the orators, whose language shows other similarities with non-literary official usage, as well (first of all in terms of vocabulary).

Another interesting point within Greek is the voice of the FV. In genuine FVGs we can find the middle almost everywhere, while the active is used if the construction is not a periphrase and the verb has its original conceptual meaning ('to make, bring about, effect'): cf. e.g. the difference between ναυμαχίην ποιήσασθαι 'to fight (lit. make) a naval battle' Hdt. 8, 70, 1 (= ναυμαχήσασθαι → FVG) and πόλεμον ποιήσει Thuk. 1, 40, 2 'will bring about war (for others), will involve in war' (≠ πολεμήσει → no FVG).[49] See also examples [44] and [45] with the verb in the active:

[44] ὑπὸ δὲ ἑνὸς ἀνδρὸς ἀποθνήσκων οὔτ' ἀνέκραγεν οὔτ' αἴσθησιν οὐδεμίαν ἐποίησεν οὔτε τοῖς ἐν τῇ γῇ οὔτε τοῖς ἐν τῷ πλοιῷ; 'was a man who was struck down by but one assailant not going to shout out or attract the attention of those on shore or on board (approx. to make them observe him)?' Antiph. 5, 44, transl. K. J. Maidment;

[45] ὀλίγοι δέ τινες νεκροὺς ἐς αὐτὴν τὴν φλόγα ἐμβαλόντες, καὶ δίοδόν σφισι δι' αὐτῶν καθάπερ ἐπὶ γεφύρας ποιήσαντες, διέφυγον 'but some few escaped by casting corpses into the flames and making a passage for themselves by using the bodies as a bridge' Cass Dio 56, 11, 6, transl. E. Cary.

In [44] the active voice indicates that the construction is not a FVG in the narrower sense adopted by us. This is corroborated semantically by the fact that the agents of the actions expressed by ἐποίησεν and of αἴσθησιν are different: the agent of ἐποίησεν is

---

[48] I agree at this point with Frisk, who in his review on Mayser's book says (Gnomon 5 [1929]: 38): *"Daß die Umschreibungen eines einfachen Verbums durch* δίδωμι ['to give'], ἔχω ['to have'] *usw. mit Objekt in erster Linie volkstümlich seien, ist wenig wahrscheinlich. Vielmehr scheinen diese Ausdrücke gewählter zu sein als die einfachen Verba und eine gewisse Hebung des Stils hervorrufen zu wollen."* Against Frisk: HOFMANN 1965: 755.

[49] There are of course exceptions, e. g. Hom. Od. 1, 249–250 with the active.

the person dying, the agents of αἴσθησιν are the people on shore and on board, ἐν τῇ γῇ καὶ ἐν τῷ πλοιῷ. The construction thus has in fact a kind of causative meaning.[50] In [45] the meaning of δίοδον ποιήσαντες is clearly not 'going through, making the crossing of' but 'preparing a passage' with ποιέω in its original sense. It must also be added that δίοδος is not even a deverbal noun.

Generally speaking, the middle is always a sign of the agent's interest in an action. Rijksbaron is quite right in saying that *"in these cases* [in what we call FVG] *the Agent's interest in the verbal action is one of an active participation: he is the Agent of the action denoted by the noun rather than the Beneficiary; when, on the other hand, the active of* ποιῶ *is construed with a verbal noun the Agent need not be actively involved in the action denoted by that noun."*[51]

Latin

Finally, we can turn to Latin and list a couple of examples in chronological order. The first examples seem to be [46] and [47]:[52]

[46] *si nox furtum faxsit* (codd. *factum sit*), *si im occisit, iure caesus esto* 'if [somebody] has done theft by night, if [the owner] kills him, [the thief] shall be held lawfully killed' Lex XII tab. 8, 12 (Macr. Sat 1, 4, 19), transl. E. H. Warmington;[53]

[50]Quite similarly to the Latin example *(angorem afferre)* quoted by HOFFMANN (see note 30) and regarded by him as a FVG.

[51]RIJKSBARON 1984: 141–142. About the voice cf. also KÜHNER 1898: 106; STAHL 1907: 53–54 (with lots of examples); against Stahl, however, see e. g. SCHWYZER 1950: 232. It can be observed that later, in New Testament Greek, where FVGs with ποιεῖσθαι are also very common, the active is used almost as often as the middle. See BLASS–DEBRUNNER 1975: 163; BAUER 1958: s. v. ποιέω I. 1. b. d.; II. 1.

[52]Cf. ERNOUT 1957: 120–121.

[53]Cf. Gell. 11, 18, 7–8 (and also the passive 11, 18, 13: *scriptum est ... non hominum tantum neque rerum moventium ... sed fundi quoque et aedium fieri furtum* 'there is ... written ... that thefts are committed not only of men and moveable objects ... but also of estate and of houses' transl. J. C. Rolfe). See also *si iniuriam alteri faxsit* 'if he has done simple harm to another' Lex XII tab. 8, 4 (Gell. 20, 1, 12), transl. E. H. Warmington; which is probably not a FVG, because there is no related verb (cf. *furtum* ~ *furor*). *Iniuriam facere*

[47] *si servus furtum faxsit noxiamve noxit* 'if slave shall have committed theft or done damage' Lex XII tab. 12, 2a (Ulp. ad Dig. 9, 4, 2, 1), transl. E. H. Warmington.

This legal term had been borrowed ([48], [49]) by Plautus (transl. P. Nixon), who uses other FVGs, as well (about Plautus' usage of FVGs see also later):

[48] *furtum ego vidi qui faciebat* 'I saw a person commit (lit. make) a theft' Rud. 954 (cf. the pass. in Rud. 958);

[49] *et praedicabo quomodo furta faciatis multa* 'and I'll lay bare the way you constantly commit robbery (lit. make many thefts)' Poen. 1245;

[50] *immo, hospes, magis cum periclum facies, magis nosces meam / comitatem erga te amantem* 'ah, well, my dear boy, the more you test (lit. make trial of) me, the more you'll be convinced of my good will toward you in your affair' Plaut. Mil. 635-636;

[51] *per tua te genua obsecro, / ne indicium ero facias meo* 'by your knees, sir, I beg you, don't give away (lit. make denouncing) to master!' Plaut. Most. 743–744;[54]

[52] *sed ecquid meministin here / qua de re ego tecum mentionem feceram?* 'but you—do you remember that matter I mentioned (lit. made mention of) to you yesterday?' Plaut. Persa 108–109;

---

is a popular expression in the comedies, e. g. Plaut. Mil. 548; Ter. Hec. 256, 692; Ad. 148, etc. It must be noted, however, that it is often very difficult to decide if an expression is a FVG or not. See e. g. the interesting fact that the FN of *furtum facere* is pronominalized in Plaut. Rud. 955: *noram dominum, id cui fiebat* 'I knew the owner against whom it [the theft] was comitted'.

[54]Cf. also Plaut. Aul. 188, 671, Capt. 1014, Cist. 678, Mil. 306; Cic. Verr. II, 1, 150; in pass.: Cic. div. 2, 46. Cf. the same FN (and two more) with another FV *(habere)*: Cic. [?] ep. ad Oct. 2: *Illud vero, quod et praesentis doloris habet indicium et praeteritae iniuriae testimonium et absentium sensus significationem, non praetermittam* 'but that thing which reveals (lit. has the revealing of) present grief, bears (lit. has) witness to past injury and gives (lit. has) indication of the feelings of absent friends I shall not omit'.

[53] *dum ludi fiunt, in popinam, pedisequi, / inruptionem facite; nunc dum occasio est, / nunc, dum scriblitae aestuant, occurrite* 'lackeys, while the show is on, storm the bakeshop! Now while you have the chance, now while the tarts are hot, charge!' Plaut. Poen. 41–43.[55]

Periclum appears in [50] as a nomen actionis in its original sense 'testing, inquiry, experiment' (← *perior*), not 'risk, danger'.[56] *Mentionem facere* 'to make mention' found in [52] is an extremely frequent phrase.[57] The verb underlying the noun *men-tio* occurs in the present tense in a weakened form as *-min-iscor*, but only with preverbs (*comminiscor*, perfect part. *commentus* 'to think up', *reminiscor* 'to recollect', cf. also *me-min-i* 'to remember'). In various prose works we can also find a considerable number of FVGs, some of which are listed below:

[54] *at ille ... ita, uti censuerant Italici, deditionem facit* 'but he ... makes surrender in the way the Italians have recommended' Sall. Iug. 26, 2;

[55] *cum his Adiatunnus eruptionem facere conatus...* 'with these men Adiatunnus tried to make a sortie...' Caes. Gall. 3, 22, 4, transl. H. J. Edwards;

[56] *est boni iudicis parvis ex rebus coniecturam facere uniuscuiusque et cupiditatis et continentiae* 'it is the part of a competent judge to infer (lit. to make an inference) from trifling circumstances how far a man will indulge or restrain his passion for this thing or that' Cic. Verr. II, 4, 34, transl. L. H. G. Greenwood;

---

[55] Cf. the impersonal passive formulation in Cic. Manil. 15. See also Caes. Gall. 7, 70, 2: *ne qua subito inruptio ab hostium peditatu fiat* 'so that there may not be any sudden inrush on the part of the enemy's footmen' transl. after H. J. Edwards.

[56] The same FVG e.g. Plaut. Asin. 617, Bacch. 63, Cist. 504; Cic. Verr. I, 1, 34: *eos velle meae fidei diligentiaeque periculum facere, qui innocentiae abstinentiaeque fecissent* 'that the people who had made trial of my integrity and self-control were willing now to make trial of my good faith and energy' transl. L. H. G. Greenwood. In this example it is interesting that the FN is omitted in the subordinate clause. Cf. also Cic. prov. 35.

[57] E.g. in Cicero: Quinct. 37, 39; Verr. II, 2, 46; Cael. 56; Phil. 2, 19, etc.

[57] *has in sententias meas si consules discessionem facere voluissent* 'if the consuls had been willing to vote (lit. to make a "going apart" = voting) on my proposals' Cic. Phil. 14, 21;

[58] *Helvetii sine dubio sunt in armis excursionesque in provinciam faciunt* 'the Helvetii are undoubtedly in arms and making raids on our province' Cic. Att. 1, 19, 2, transl. E. O. Winstedt;[58]

[59] *anceps proelium Romanos circumsteterat incertos, in quem potissimum hostem quamve in partem conferti eruptionem facerent* 'the Romans found themselves between two battles, uncertain against which enemy and which direction they should choose to break through (lit. make a breaking through) in a mass' Liv. 25, 34, 11, transl. F. G. Moore;[59]

[60] *hoc quoque, si inclusum est, aeque fugam quaerit et cum sono evadit, ac modo universam eruptionem facit eoque vehementius intonat, modo per partes et minutatim* 'if inclosed, this, too, seeks an outlet and escapes with a noise. Sometimes it makes a total eruption and thunders all the more vehemently; at other times it escapes in parts, little by little' Sen. nat. 2, 54, 2, transl. T. H. Corcoran;

[61] *C. Iulius Proculus auctionem faciet rerum supervacuarum* 'C. Iulius Proculus is going to hold (lit. make) an auction of his superfluous property' Petron. 38, 16;

[62] *cum hac quoque divortium fecit* 'divorced (lit. made a divorce with) her also' Suet. Aug. 62, transl. J. C. Rolfe;

[63] *sin autem ventus interpellaverit et motionibus lineae non potuerint certam significationem facere...* 'but if the wind disturbs and, owing to their movements, the lines cannot

---

[58] See also Caes. Gall. 2, 30, 1.

[59] But cf. Liv. 40, 21, 8: *sed non solum parendum patri, sed etiam adsentiendum erat, ne invitum parere suspicionem faceret* 'but he had not only to obey his father, but also to agree with him, so as not to give rise to suspicion of obeying unwillingly'. About this type of causative construction with different agents of *facere* and of *suspicio*, and hence probably not to be regarded as FVG, cf. earlier (in connection with *śruṣṭiṃ karoti*).

give (lit. make) a certain indication ...' Vitr. 8, 5, 2, transl. F. Granger.

Remarkably enough at first sight, a huge number of FVGs occur in Late Latin texts:

[64] *fecimus ergo et ibi oblationem et orationem impensissimam* '(lit.) so we made there, too, an expensive offering and prayer' Aeth. 4, 3;[60]

[65] *faciens denuo mansiones aliquot per Palestina regressa sum in Helia* 'again, after a journey of a couple of days (lit. making a couple of remainings / sections of journey) in Palestina, I returned to Helia' Aeth. 9, 7;

[66] *unus ex diaconibus facit commemorationem singulorum* 'one of the deacons makes a commemoration of each of them' Aeth. 24, 5;

[67] *sanguinis emissionem facies ex temporibus aut ex ipsa facie* 'you should make blood-letting from the temples or the face itself' Mul. 3, 117 (but cf. *sanguinem emittito de cervice* 'you should let blood from the neck' 3, 126);

[68] *cave ne ei calido detractionem sanguinis facias* 'take care that you should not make blood-letting when he [sc. the animal] is warm' Mul. 3, 158 (cf. Veg.[61] 1, 38, 8: *cave ne sanguinem calido detrahas* 'be careful not to let blood when he is warm');

[60]In Christian context, like here, these expressions in fact have special meaning (*oblatio* 'offering → the Holy Communion', *oratio* 'speech → prayer'), LÖFSTEDT 1911: 39, 97.

[61]Vegetius (4–5th c. AD) wrote his handbook of veterinary science by using the previous works about the same topic (Pelagonius, the *Mulomedicina Chironis*, etc.) and "cleaned off" some of their Vulgar Latin characteristics. VÄÄNÄNEN 1963: 16. Cf. SCHANZ 1914: §847 (citing Veg. 1, prol., 2: *Chiron vero et Apsyrtus diligentius cuncta rimati, eloquentiae inopia ac sermonis ipsius vilitate sordescunt* 'but Chiron and Apsyrtus, although they have examined carefully all the relevant subjects, are still dirty because of lack of eloquence and their low style itself').

[69] *aliis tumores in capite, in temporibus collectiones faciunt* 'in others the swellings make gatherings/collections on the head and on the temples' Mul. 3, 184;

[70] *adiectionem cibariae paulatim facies* 'you should make the adding of food little by little' Mul. 3, 254 (cf. Veg. 2, 6, 11: *ad cibaria ipsius aliquid per partes semper adiunges* 'you should always add something gradually to his food');

[71] *odore et gusto cognitionem eorum* [sc. *piscium*] *facere* 'to make the identification of them [sc. the fishes] on smell and taste' Orib. 4, 14 (but in another recension: *cognosci debent* 'should be identified');[62]

[72] *sacrarum scripturarum facite lectionem* 'you should make a reading aloud of parts from the Holy Script' Did. ap. 61, 14 (with FVG also in the Greek version: τὴν ἀνάγνωσιν ποιούμενοι).[63]

All these Latin constructions show essentially the same grammatical, semantic and stylistic peculiarities as the Sanskrit and Greek examples. There is, however, one thing that can be demonstrated here particularly clearly. It has already been mentioned that, compared to the verb underlying, or sometimes derived of, the FN, the FVG often makes a semantic shift, which means that the two expressions are not synonymous in all respects. Thus, e. g., *excursiones faciunt* [58] is more than *excurrunt*, for the former is a military term, the same way as is *inruptio* (cf. Cic. Manil. 15, 1; Caes. Gall. 7, 70, 2 in note 54; and see also Cic. Phil. 11, 7), a fact Plautus was very much aware of, for he used it as a source of humour in [53], an exhortation for attacking—a cookshop! The *Fügungsnomina* of the FVGs in the Mulomedicina Chironis (*emissionem, detractionem facere sanguinis*, etc.) are technical terms of veterinarian science and seem thus to have a special meaning that is not so transparent in the "emendations" of Vegetius with simple verbs (*emittere, detrahere sanguinem*, etc.).

Finally, *furtum facere*, being probably the earliest FVG in the extant documents of the Latin language (Lex XII tab. and later

[62] SVENNUNG 1935: 451, note 1.
[63] TIDNER 1938: 117.

in comedy, see [46]–[49]) is evidently a legal term. It shows particularly clearly that the valency of the simple verb and the related FVG need not be the same: the FVG often has a *"detransitivizing force"*.[64] In contrast to *furor, furtum facere* need not be complemented, which gives the opportunity for not having to mention the thing stolen. This fits the language of law, where general formulation is necessary.[65] The same difference in terms of valency can be observed in [63], where *significationem facere* has no objective genitive, while the transitive *significo* should obviously have a direct object.[66]

Example [73], though not with *facere*, contains a FVG that shows another peculiarity of this type of construction, namely that it can express a special 'Aktionsart' in contrast to its simple verbal counterpart.

[73] *voluptatem capio maximam cruciari te tua culpa* 'I take a great pleasure in that you are tormented because of your sin' Afranius, frg. 356.[67]

Capio as a FV is generally a suitable exponent of the terminative-ingressive Aktionsart. Though synchronically there is no verb underlying the verbal substantive *voluptas*, the construction *voluptatem capio* might still be regarded as a FVG, because, except for its 'Aktionsart', it is synonymous with *gaudeo* or some other durative verb meaning 'to be glad, to be delighted'. Its being a FVG is also indicated by its valency properties, for it can take an accusative with infinitive as its complement, the normal construction with simple verba affectuum (*maximam voluptatem capio* + a.c.i. ≈ *maxime gaudeo* + a.c.i.).[68]

---

[64] ROSÉN 1983: 198 and *"absolute, univalent employ of periphrasis as against transitive multivalent verb"* (ibid.).

[65] Cf. ROSÉN 1983: 198: *"the verbal noun lends the syntagma a colouring of indefiniteness."*

[66] Cf. ROSÉN 1992: 22–23 *("valenzreduzierende Periphrase")*.

[67] Cited by MOELSBERGER 1989: 223. Cf. also Cic. fam. 3, 2, 2.

[68] A similar case is Enn. Tel 272: *Aiacem cui tu obsidionem paras* 'Ajax, against whom you (lit.) are preparing a siege/attack' (cited by MOELSBERGER 1989: 179), in which *obsidionem parare* seems to be the terminative-ingressive counterpart of durative *obsidere*. One has to admit, however, that the typical loss of the conceptual meaning of the FN is far from being complete in this case.

One of the vexing problems concerning the Latin FVGs is, from which stratum of the language these periphrastic constructions originate. Scholars usually think that they come from the popular speech, the vernacular or the spoken language, the "Umgangssprache".[69] The reason for this assumption is that allegedly we meet them in a great mass in Late Latin texts and in those which show peculiarities of Vulgar Latin, so it would actually be straightforward to regard them as one of these characteristics.

I suggest to make a distinction between two types of construction with *facere*. In the first type the direct object of *facere* is a deverbal nomen actionis (e. g. *inruptionem, emissionem*, etc. *facere*), or at least a noun denoting action generally, while in the second one it is (synchronically) an ordinary noun (e. g. *verba, iter*, etc. *facere*).[70] In the latter group *facere* seems to be a replacement for other verbs with a more complex meaning. This construction with *facere* is thus a sort of "simplification" by means of a general verb ("Allerweltsverbum"[71]). In the first type, however, the periphrastic constructions are a more elaborate way of expressing approximately the same content as a simple verb. In my view, it is only the first type that can be regarded as FVG.

The popular speech and the spoken language in general ("Umgangssprache") usually tends to make use of constructions that are

---

[69] Cf. LÖFSTEDT 1911: 163–164; SALONIUS 1920: 382; SVENNUNG 1935: 451, note 1. As to my knowledge, it is only R. Hoffmann who does not regard them as such (see note 74). ROSÉN 1983: 203 ascribes them *"generally to non literary style."* See also J. B. HOFMANN 1965: 755 *("im wesentlichen familiär und umgangssprachlich")*, who thinks that the constructions with other verbs (*dare* 'to give', *capere* 'to take', etc.) seem rather to be urbane. I suppose that all these verbs behave essentially the same way.

[70] E. g. *certumnest celare, quo iter facias, pessuma?* 'do you intend to keep your destination (lit. where you make your way) dark, you vile female?' Plaut. Persa 221, transl. P. Nixon; *verba quidem haud indocte fecit* 'she did not actually speak (lit. make words) entirely pointless' Ibid. 563; *iter fecimus semper inter vineas* 'we made our journey all the time among vine-stocks' Aeth. 9, 4, etc. Cf. also Cicero often in his letters, but seemingly not so often in his prose works: *iter facere* e. g. fam. 3, 5, 4; Att. 8, 12c, 1; Cic. div. 1, 73; *verbum / verba facere* e. g. fam. 8, 8, 1. On the other hand, nominal style with many abstract nouns prevails in Cicero's theoretical writings. See ROSÉN 1983: 209.

[71] HOFMANN 1926: 8; cf. also MAROUZEAU 1935: 176.

not complicated,[72] while the written language, the higher prose literature and the official (legal, etc.) usage often do the opposite.[73] Therefore I think that the periphrastic FVG constructions with the verb *facere* appeared first in the written language of the educated people, the literary language and, last but not least, the legal and other kinds of technical usage.[74]

Many times their occurrence had a special grammatical (or semantic or stylistic) reason. E. g. *habere* 'to have' as a *Funktionsverb* with a deverbal noun often functions as the missing passive of a deponent verb:[75] *admirari* 'admire' (act. meaning) ↔ *admirationem habere* (pass.; in [74] this FN is followed by other nouns in

---

[72]It uses many conventional formulas: cf. HAPP 1967: 75–76 *("Basic Latin")*; HOFMANN 1926: 165. Hofmann (VIII), however, regards the expression of affection and emotion as its most important characteristic *("Die Umgangssprache ist in erster Linie Affektsprache.")*.

[73]Cf. the observation of M. A. Stewart (cited by MOELSBERGER 1989: 27), who pointed out that *"in respect to the use of substantives at least, classical prose is as abstract, or even more so, than the popular speech."* Hans-Jürgen Moelsberger, the author of a monograph (MOELSBERGER 1989) on abstract expressions in Old Latin, takes a point of view totally different from ours. Since he takes an expression (verbal substantives, too) into account in as far as it is exponent of mental abstraction and since he defines abstract nouns as *"Substantive ..., durch die etwa Zustände, Qualitäten oder Vorgänge auf den Begriff gebracht werden"* (48), he necessarily excludes from his examination the constructions of the type *inruptionem facere* (Plaut. Poen. 42), because they are not generalizing statements, but merely the periphrastic expressions of the content of a simple verb which refer to a single action: *"Das Substantiv erscheint hier kaum als Ausdruck einer besonders hohen sprachlichen und gedanklichen Abstraktionsleistung etwa im Sinne der Zusammenfassung eines komplexen Geschehens oder zum Ausdruck einer vom einzelnen losgelösten Generalisierung. Es bezeichnet vielmehr einen einmaligen und als gegenwärtig vorgestellten Zustand oder Vorgang."* (57). Cf. the sections on nouns derived from verbs in Plautus (56–58) and Terence (109–111).

[74]According to LÖFSTEDT (1911: 165) it is not so common in the best classical prose, which in fact might be true as far as *facere* is concerned. But the FVG as a general type of periphrase is common in the higher prose literature, as well. Cf. the examples given by HOFFMANN (1996: 203–204) from Cicero's *De natura deorum*, book 1 (and his just remark *"gegen die verbreitete stilkritische Zuordnung der lateinischen FVG zur sog. Umgangssprache"*).

[75]Cf. MENGE 2000: §124; ROSÉN 1983: 199 n. 75. About *adferre* as a FV that, according to Hoffmann's wider concept of FV, forms FVG with causative sense see HOFFMANN 1996: 201–210. Other motivations might be parallelism, omission of the direct object, generalization, etc.

parallel construction); *misereri* 'to feel pity for' (act.) ↔ *misericordiam habere* (pass. in [75]).

[74] *at viri saepe excellentis ancipites variique casus habent admirationem, exspectationem, laetitiam, molestiam, spem, timorem* 'but the uncertain and varied fortunes of a statesman who frequently rises to prominence give scope for surprise, suspense, delight, annoyance, hope, fair' Cic. fam. 5, 12, 5, transl. W. G. Williams;

[75] *misericordiam spoliatio consulatus magnam habere debet, una enim eripiuntur cum consulatu omnia* 'we should feel deep compassion for loss of the consulship; for with the consulship all else is lost' Cic. Mur. 87, transl. C. Macdonald.

On the other hand, FVGs often were redundant periphrases of a simple verb. The less educated people might have taken them over into their own language, probably because they regarded them as a specific sign of elaborate and artistic speech. This process was facilitated by the fact that *facere*, in the other type of construction (with *facere* as "Allerweltsverbum"), had already been a frequently used element of their language. It was therefore probably only in a second step that the FVG, with its increasing frequency, became a conspicuous element of the Vulgar and Late Latin texts.[76] We can thus speak about a certain kind of syntactic "hypercorrection".[77]

This suggestion can be confirmed by examining the language of Plautus. It is a well known fact that in the language of Plautus' comedies we can distinguish between two strata: that of the iambic senars, which were spoken ("Sprechverse"), and that of the recited and sung portions ("cantica"). The former shows many characteristics of the spoken language ("Umgangssprache"), while the latter is much more artistic and has a higher style.[78] If the FVGs were characteristic of the spoken language, we would expect them to

[76] There appeared of course new constructions following the existing models.

[77] This is exactly what is happening with the FV *kerül* in Hungarian, which is more and more frequently used by less educated people too, whenever they want to speak, or seem to speak, the educated speech.

[78] Cf. HAFFTER 1934; HAPP 1967.

appear in a great mass in the senar portions. But the situation is in fact the opposite.

The most typical kind of FVG consists of the accusative of a nomen actionis in *-(t)io* or *-(t)ura* with *facere.* I have found only 30 such constructions in Plautus (I have not counted the occurrences with *fio*). The examples from senarportions are marked with an asterisk: *mentionem* 'mention' Aul. 204, 685*; Cist. 134*; Most. 813; Persa 109*; Trin. 976, 1069; *coniecturam* 'inferring, conclusion' Cas. 224; Cur. 246*; Men. 164; Poen. 91*; Rud. 771; *auctiones* 'auctions' Epid. 235; *auctionem* 'auction' Men. 1153; Poen. 411*, 1364*, 1421; Stich. 201*, 218*, 384; *revorsionem* 'return' Bacch. 296*; *reversionem* 'return' Truc. 396*; *suppositionem* 'placing underneath = the fraudulent introduction (of a child into a family)' Cist. 144*; *excidionem* 'destruction' Cur. 534; *seditionem* 'going apart, rebellion' Mer. 124; *inruptionem* 'bursting in, inroad' Poen. 42*; *ascensionem* 'climbing up' Rud. 599*; *legerupionem* 'law-breaking' Rud. 709; *mercaturam* 'trade, commerce' Rud. 931;[79] *censionem* 'assessing or rating in a census' Rud. 1273.

There are only 14 such FVGs altogether in the senarportions and 16 in the recited or sung parts. I think that a similar, or even clearer, ratio would work out on the basis of all *Funktionsverbgefüge.*[80] *Indicium facere*, e. g., occurs 9 times in Plautus (Aul. 188, 671; Capt. 1014; Cist. 678; Mil. 306; Most. 744; Rud. 428, 429; Trin. 675), but only once in iambic senar (Aul. 671)! Moreover, the expression is the borrowing of a legal term as are e. g. *furtum facere, auctionem facere.* If we leave these borrowings out of consideration, there remain only a handful of examples of FVG proper. Other expressions with *facere*, which are not FVG (e. g. *facinus, iter, verba facere*, etc.), are of course very frequent in Plautus in the senarportions, as well. All these facts corroborate our assump-

[79]Cf. also the synonymous FVG *in mercatura verti* 'to occupy onself, be active (lit. to move about) in trade' in Most. 639.

[80]A quick survey of this kind on the basis of three comedies (Poen., Pseud., Mil.) makes me think that one would find about two or three times more FVG proper in the other portions than in the iambic senars. If this turned right it would be significant, even if we bear in mind that the amount of the recitatives and arias is almost three times bigger than that of the senarportions. Cf. HAPP 1967: 88. Other possible sources for everyday Latin usage (e. g. Petronius, Cicero in his letters, etc.) do not show a great number of genuine FVGs either.

tion that FVG as such is in the first place not “umgangssprachlich” in Latin, neither in Greek or Sanskrit.

Conclusory remarks

Finally, we can shortly answer the question, if these constructions are a common heritage of the three languages from Proto-Indo-European or an independent innovation. Considering that at the earliest phases of Old Indian, Greek and Latin *Funktionsverbgefüge* were rare and their number was increasing only in the course of time and that the verbs used by the particular languages (Skt. √*kṛ*, Gk. ποιέομαι, Lat. *facio*) are not related etymologically,[81] it is obvious that we have to do with an independent innovation. Desemanticization and the gradual transition from synthetic to analytic types of linguistic forms can be observed in the independent Indo-European languages in other cases, too.[82] Moreover, we have to bear in mind that *Funktionsverbgefüge* as such, and the development towards analytic forms in general, is common in other, non Indo-European languages as well, which means that both the phenomenon and the process are probably morphosyntactic universals.[83]

Abbreviations

Skt.: Sanskrit; Gk.: Greek; Lat.: Latin

Dictionaries and lexicons:

LIV²: H. Rix et al. (ed.), *Lexikon der indogermanischen Verben*, zweite erweiterte und verbesserte Auflage, Ludwig Reichert Verlag, Wiesbaden, 2001.

---

[81] LIV²: 139–140 *$d^h eh_1 k$- ‘machen, herstellen’ /> Lat. *facio*/; 378–379 *$k^u ei̯$- ‘sammeln, schichten’ /> Gk. ποιέομαι/; 391–392 *$k^u er$- ‘abschneiden, schnitzen’ /> Skt. √*kṛ*/. It is also clear that none of these verbs had the general meaning ‘to do, to make’ in Proto-Indo-European!

[82] See e. g. KOSTIĆ 1999: 112–113 and note 55.

[83] The ideas presented in this paper should be regarded as preliminary remarks on the subject, which call for further investigation covering a greater corpus of texts and all the possible *Funktionsverbe* in all the three languages.

LSJ: H. G. Liddell–R. Scott–H. S. Jones, *A Greek–English Lexicon*, with a revised supplement, Clarendon Press, Oxford, 1996.

MW: M. Monier-Williams, *A Sanskrit–English Dictionary*, new edition with the collaboration of E. Leumann and C. Cappeller, Motilal Banarsidass, Delhi, 1999 (repr. of 1899).

OLD: P. G. W. Glare (ed.), *Oxford Latin Dictionary*, with corrections, Clarendon Press, Oxford, 1996.

Sanskrit authors and texts:
AB: Aitareya-Brāhmaṇa; AV: Atharvaveda; Daś.: Daśakumāracarita; Hit.: Hitopadeśa; LV: Lalitavistara; MBh.: Mahābhārata; Mn.: Mānavadharmaśāstra; Mṛcch.: Mṛcchakaṭikā; MS: Maitrāyaṇī-Saṃhitā; Mv: Mahāvastu; P.: Pāṇini; Pañc.: Pañcatantra; R.: Rāmāyaṇa; RV: Ṛgveda; TS: Taittirīya-Saṃhitā; VaikhS.: Vaikhānasa-Saṃhitā

Greek authors and texts:
Antiph.: Antiphon; Cass. Dio: Cassius Dio; Eur.: Euripides (Or.: Orestes); Hdt.: Herodotos; Hom.: Homeros (Il.: Ilias; Od.: Odysseia); Isokr.: Isokrates; Lys.: Lysias; Men.: Menandros (Dysk.: Dyskolos); Plat.: Platon; Plut.: Plutarchos (Cic.: Vitae parallelae, Cicero); Soph.: Sophokles (Trach.: Trachiniai); Thuk.: Thukydides; Xen.: Xenophon (An.: Anabasis)

Latin authors and texts:
Aeth.: Peregrinatio Aetheriae; Caes.: Caesar (Gall.: De bello Gallico; civ.: De bello civili); Cic.: Cicero (Att.: Epistulae ad Atticum; Cael.: Pro M. Caelio; div.: De divinatione; div. in Caec.: Divinatio in Q. Caecilium; ep. ad Oct.: Epistula ad Octavianum; fam.: Epistulae ad familiares; Manil.: Pro lege Manilia de imperio Cn. Pompei; Mur.: Pro L. Murena; Phil.: In M. Antonium oratio Philippica; prov.: De provinciis consularibus; Quinct.: Pro Quinctio; Tusc.: Tusculanae disputationes; Verr.: In Verrem); Did. ap.: Didascalia apostolorum; Enn.: Ennius (Tel.: Telephus); Gell.: Gellius; Lex XII tab.: Lex duodecim tabularum; Liv.: Livius; Macr.: Macrobius (Sat.: Saturnalia); Mul.: Mulomedicina Chironis; Orib.:

Oribasius; Petron.: Petronius; Plaut.: Plautus (Asin.: Asinaria; Aul.: Aulularia; Bacch.: Bacchides; Capt.: Captivi; Cas.: Casina; Cist.: Cistellaria; Cur.: Curculio; Epid.: Epidicus; Men.: Menaechmi; Mer.: Mercator; Mil.: Miles gloriosus; Most.: Mostellaria; Poen.: Poenulus; Pseud.: Pseudolus; Rud.: Rudens; Stich.: Stichus; Trin.: Trinummus; Truc.: Truculentus); Sall.: Sallustius (Iug.: Bellum Iugurthinum); Sen.: Seneca (nat.: Naturales quaestiones); Suet.: Suetonius (Aug.: Vita divi Augusti); Ter.: Terentius (Hec.: Hecyra; Ad.: Adelphoe); Ulp.: Ulpianus; Veg.: Vegetius; Vitr.: Vitruvius

References

ASHER (ed.) 1994: *The Encyclopedia of Language and Linguistics*, editor-in-chief R. E. Asher, coordinating editor J. M. Y. Simpson, Pergamon Press, Oxford–New York–Seoul–Tokyo.

BAUER, W. 1958[5]: *Griechisch–deutsches Wörterbuch zu den Schriften des Neuen Testaments und der übrigen urchristlichen Literatur*, Verlag Alfred Töpelmann, Berlin.

BLASS, F.–DEBRUNNER, A. 1975: A *Greek Grammar of the New Testament and Other Early Christian Literature,* transl. and rev. by R. W. Funk, University of Chicago Press, Chicago & London (repr. of 1961).

BLOCH, J. 1906: *La phrase nominale en Sanskrit*, MSL 14, 27–96.

— 1934: *L'Indo-Aryen (du Veda aux temps modernes)*, Paris.

BREUNIS, Andries 1990: *The Nominal Sentence in Sanskrit and Middle Indo-Aryan*, E. J. Brill, Leiden–New York–København–Köln.

BRUGMANN, K. 1892: *Grundriss der vergleichenden Grammatik der indogermanischen Sprachen*, II, Karl J. Trübner, Strassburg.

BUSSMANN, H. 1990: *Lexikon der Sprachwissenschaft*, Alfred Körner Verlag, Stuttgart.

CLASSEN, J. 1889[4]: *Thukydides*, erklärt von J. Classen, II. Band: Zweites Buch, besorgt von J. Steup, Weidmannsche Buchhandlung, Berlin.

DEBRUNNER, B. 1954: [J. Wackernagel–]B. D., *Altindische Grammatik*, II 2: *Die Nominalsuffixe*, Vandenhoeck & Ruprecht, Göttingen.

DELBRÜCK, B. 1888: *Altindische Syntax*, Halle. (= *Syntaktische Forschungen* 5.)

DERIBAS, V. M. 1983: *Устойчивые глагольно-имменые словосочетания*, Moscow.

DIVEKAR, H. R. 1927: *The Dual Authorship of the Kavya-Prakasa*, JRAS 1927, 505–520.

EDGERTON, F. 1953: *Buddhist Hybrid Sanskrit Reader*, Yale University Press, New Haven.

ENGEL, U. 1991–92: *Deutsche Grammatik*, I–II, Julius Gross Verlag, Heidelberg.

ERNOUT, A. 1957: *Recueil de textes latins archaïques*, Klincksieck, Paris.

ESAU, H. 1976: *Funktionsverbgefüge revisited*, FoL 9, 135–160.

GATZLAFF-HÄLSIG, M. 1978: *Grammatischer Leitfaden des Hindi*, VEB Verlag Enzyklopädie, Leipzig.

GAWROŃSKI, A. 1907: *Sprachliche Untersuchungen über das Mṛcchakaṭikā und das Daśakumāracarita*, Diss. Leipzig.

GEHRING, A. 1891: *Index Homericus*, Teubner, Leipzig.

GELDNER, K. F. 1951: *Der Rig-veda*, I–III, übers. und komm. von K. F. Geldner, Harvard University Press, Cambridge, MA.

GONDA, J. 1975: *A Critical Survey of the Publications on the Periphrastic Future in Sanskrit*, in: *Selected Studies*, III, E. J. Brill, Leiden, 69–90.

GRASSMANN, H. 1876–77: *Rig-Veda*, übers. von H. Grassmann, F. A. Brockhaus, Leipzig.

— 1955³: *Wörterbuch zum Rig-Veda*, Harrasowitz, Wiesbaden.

GREN-EKLUND, G. 1978: *A Study of Nominal Sentences in the Oldest Upanisads*, Uppsala. (Acta Universitatis Upsaliensis, Studia Indoeuropaea Upsaliensia 3)

GREVISSE, M. 1946⁴ (1986¹²): *Le bon usage. Grammaire française*, Paris.

GRIFFITH, R. T. H. 1995: *The Hymns of the R̥gveda*, transl. and comm. by R. T. H. Griffith, revised ed. by J. L. Shastri, Motilal Banarsidass, Delhi (repr. of 1973).

HAFFTER, H. 1934: *Untersuchungen zur altlateinischen Dichtersprache*, Weidmannsche Buchhandlung, Berlin.

HAPP, H. 1967: *Die lateinische Umgangssprache und die Kunstsprache des Plautus*, Glotta 45, 60–104.

— 1976: *Grundfragen einer Dependenz-Grammatik des Lateinischen*, Vandenhoeck & Ruprecht, Göttingen.

HARTMANN, P. 1955: *Nominale Ausdrucksformen im wissenschaftlichen Sanskrit*, Carl Winter, Heidelberg.

HENTSCHEL, E.–WEYDT, W. 1990: *Handbuch der deutschen Grammatik*, Walter de Gruyter, Berlin–New York.

HOFFMANN, K. 1976: *Ved. karóti*, in: *Aufsätze zur Indoiranistik*, II, Ludwig Reichert Verlag, Wiesbaden, 575–588.

HOFFMANN, R. 1996: *Funktionsverbgefüge im Lateinischen*, in: *Akten des VIII. Internationalen Kolloquiums zur lateinischen Linguistik*, ed. A. Bammesberger und F. Heberlein, Carl Winter, Heidelberg, 200–212.

HOFMANN, J. B. 1926: *Lateinische Umgangssprache*, Carl Winter, Heidelberg.

— 1965[2]: *Lateinische Grammatik*, II: *Lateinische Syntax und Stilistik*, neu bearbeitet von A. Szantyr, Beck'sche Verlagsbuchhandlung, München.

JACOBI, H. 1899: *Über das periphrastische perfekt im Sanskrit*, KZ 35, 578–587.

— 1903: *Über den nominalen Stil des wissenschaftlichen Sanskrits*, IF 14, 236–251.

KELEMEN, J. 1985: *Grammaire du français contemporaine*, sous la direction de J. Kelemen, Budapest.

KOSTIĆ, S. 1999: *Verb syntagmata in Hindī. Structure and Functions*, Univerzita Karlova v Praze, Nakladatelství Karolinum, Praha, 1999. (Acta Universitatis Carolinae Philologica. Monographia CXXX)

KRAUSE, W. 1925: *Altindische und altnordische Kunstpoesie, ein Vergleich ihres Sprachstiles*, KZ 53, 213–248.

KÜHNER, R. 1898: *Ausführliche Grammatik der griechischen Sprache*, II: *Satzlehre*, neue Bearb. von B. Gerth, 1. Band, Hahnsche Buchhandlung, Hannover–Leipzig.

LEWANDOWSKI, Th. 1990: *Linguistisches Wörterbuch*, Quelle & Meyer, Heidelberg–Wiesbaden.

LÖFSTEDT, E. 1911: *Philologischer Kommentar zur Peregrinatio Aetheriae. Untersuchungen zur Geschichte der lateinischen Sprache*, Uppsala–Leipzig.

MAROUZEAU, J. 1935: *Traité de stylistique appliqué au latin*, Les Belles Lettres, Paris.

MAYSER, E. 1926: *Grammatik der griechischen Papyri aus der Ptolemäerzeit*, II: *Satzlehre*, 1: *Analythischer Teil*, Walter de Gruyter, Berlin–Leipzig.

MEILLET, A. 1906: *La phrase nominale en indo-européen*, MSL 14, 1–26.

MENGE, H. 2000: *Lehrbuch der lateinischen Syntax und Semantik*, völlig neu bearbeitet von Th. Burkard und M. Schauer, Wissenschaftliche Buchgesellschaft, Darmstadt.

MINTON, W. W. 1976: *Concordance to the Hesiodic Corpus*, E. J. Brill, Leiden.

MOELSBERGER, H. J. 1989: *Abstrakter Ausdruck im Altlatein. Form und dramatische Funktion abstrakt-begrifflichen Sprechens in der altlateinischen Bühnensprache,* Athäneum, Frankfurt a. M.

PFLEIDERER et al. 2000: B. Pfleiderer–M. Raffa–C. Stromboli, *Funktionsverbgefüge im Italienischen*, Philologie im Netz 13, 73–107. (http://www.fu-berlin.de/phin/phin13/p13t4.htm)

POHL, H.-D. 1979: *Methodische Fragen bei der Erklärung von Neubildungen im Bereich des Tempussystems,* in: *Sprachtheorie und Sprachenpraxis. Festschrift für Henri Vernay zu seinem 60. Geburtstag,* hrsg. Walter Mair, Edgar Sallager, Günter Narr Verlag, Tübingen, 343–363.

QUIRK et al. 1992: R. Quirk–S. Greenbaum–G. Leech–J. Svartvik, *A Grammar of Contemporary English*, Longman, London.

RENOU, L. 1930: *Grammaire sanscrite*, I–II, Adrien-Maisonneuve, Paris.

RENZI–SALVI 1989: *Grande grammatica di consultazione*, I, a cura di L. Renzi e G. Salvi, Il Mulino, Bologna.

RHYS DAVIDS, T. W.–STEDE, W. 1989: *Pali–English Dictionary*, Munshiram Manoharlal, New Delhi (repr. of 1921–23).

RIJKSBARON, A. 1984: *The Syntax and Semantics of the Verb in Classical Greek. An Introduction,* J. C. Griben, Amsterdam.

ROSÉN, H. 1983: *The Mechanisms of Latin Nominalization and Conceptualization in Historical View,* in: *Aufstieg und Niedergang der römischen Welt,* II, Band 29/1, hrsg. Wolfgang Haase, Walter de Gruyter, Berlin–New York, 178–211.

ROSÉN, H. B. 1992: *Die Periphrase. Wesen und Entstehung,* Innsbruck. (IBS Vorträge und Kleinere Schriften 57)

SALONIUS, A. H. 1920: *Vitae Patrum. Kritische Untersuchungen über Text, Syntax und Wortschatz der spätlateinischen Vitae Patrum (B. III, V, VI, VII),* Lund.

SCHANZ, M. 1914²: *Geschichte der römischen Litteratur,* IV/1: *Die Litteratur des 4. Jahrhunderts,* Beck'sche Verlagsbuchhandlung, München.

SCHWYZER, E. 1950: *Griechische Grammatik,* II: *Syntax und syntaktische Stilistik,* vervollständigt und hrsg. von A. Debrunner, Beck'sche Verlagsbuchhandlung, München.

SPEIJER, J. S. 1886: *Sanskrit Syntax,* E. J. Brill, Leiden.

STAHL, J. M. 1907: *Kritisch-historische Syntax des griechischen Verbums der klassischen Zeit,* Carl Winter, Heidelberg.

SVENNUNG, J. 1935: *Untersuchungen zu Palladius und zur lateinischen Fach- und Volkssprache,* Uppsala.

TELEGDI, Zs. 1950–1951: *Nature et fonction des périphrases verbales dites "verbes composés" en persan,* Acta Orient. Acad. Scient. Hung. 1, 315–334.

— 1955: *Beiträge zur historischen Grammatik des Neupersischen. I. Über die Partikelkomposition im Neupersischen,* Acta Ling. Acad. Scient. Hung. 5, 67–183.

— 1973: *Remarques sur les emprunts arabes en persan,* Acta Ling. Acad. Scient. Hung. 23, 51–58.

THUMB, A. HAUSCHILD, R. 1959: *Handbuch des Sanskrit,* II, Carl Winter, Heidelberg.

TICHY, E. 1992a: *Zur Rekonstruktion der Nomina agentis auf *-tér- und *-tor-,* in: *Rekonstruktion und relative Chronologie. Akten der VIII. Fachtagung der Indogermanischen Gesellschaft, Leiden, 31. August–4. September 1987,* hrsg. R. Beekes et al., Innsbruck.

— 1992b: *Wozu braucht das Altindische ein periphrastisches Futur?*, ZDMG 142, 334–342.

— 1995: *Die Nomina agentis auf -tar- im Vedischen*, Carl Winter, Heidelberg.

TIDNER, E. 1938: *Sprachlicher Kommentar zur lateinischen Didascalia Apostolorum*, Stockholm.

VÄÄNÄNEN, V. 1963: *Introduction au latin vulgaire*, Paris.

VASU, S. Ch. 1988: *The Aṣṭādhyāyī of Pāṇini*, I–II, ed. and transl. by S. Ch. Vasu, Motilal Banarsidass, Delhi (repr. of 1891).

WEINREICH, H. 1993: *Textgrammatik der deutschen Sprache*, Dudenverlag, Mannheim–Leipzig–Wien–Zürich.

WHITNEY, W. D. 1993: *Sanskrit Grammar*, Motilal Banarsidass, Delhi (repr. of 1924).

Two

Proto-Indo-European Cultural Lexicon: Traces of an Afro-Asiatic Substratum

Gábor Takács

Introduction

The present paper, dedicated to my teacher, Prof. Töttössy with honour and thanks, represents a minor contribution to the much debated question of language contacts in the obscure early history of the Proto-Indo-European population.[1]

It has long been well known and accepted that certain words in the cultural vocabulary (fauna, flora, agriculture, and so forth) of Proto-Indo-European and Proto-Semitic coincide due to borrowing. These loans in these two proto-languages have been recently thoroughly examined by V. M. ILLIČ-SVITYČ (1964), Th. GAMKRELIDZE & V. V. IVANOV (1984, 871–876), I. M. DIAKONOFF (1985), and A. B. DOLGOPOLSKY (1987; 1989). This high

[1]I express my warm thanks to the Alexander von Humboldt Foundation (Bonn) for supporting my linguistic research in Frankfurt in 1999–2000.

number of cultural borrowings in Proto-Semitic and Proto-Indo-European can be explained only if we suppose a certain period, when speakers of these two proto-languages were in areal contact. The group of Sumerian loans in Proto-Indo-European has also been long well known (cf. e.g. AUTRAN 1925; SCHOTT 1936, 83; GI 1984, 876–877). At the same time, a great deal of convincing parallels have been proposed in the Proto-Kartvelian vs. Proto-Indo-European cultural vocabulary esp. in the works by G. A. KLIMOV (from the 1960s–1990s), some of which, however, should be treated with reservations. Then, in the 1980s, S. A. STAROSTIN (1988) demonstrated the presence of cultural borrowings in Proto-Indo-European and Proto-North-Caucasian. V. BLAŽEK (1992 MS *passim*) lexical parallels to Proto-Indo-European terms for mammals in the surrounding Near Eastern language families, while the joint paper by V. BLAŽEK & C. BOISSON (1992) presented agricultural *Wanderwörter* All these results point to Proto-Indo-European as neighbour to several Near Eastern populations around the 5th and/or 4th mill. B.C. This is the time depth, to which the aforesaid Near Eastern proto-languages (Proto-Semitic, Kartvelian, North Caucasian, Sumerian) are usually dated back.

My paper deals not with this period, but with one preceding that. Namely: presence of Afro-Asiatic (Semito-Hamitic) cultural terms in Proto-Indo-European, which cannot be explained directly from the Proto-Semitic lexicon. The Afro-Asiatic macrofamily is divided in 6 branches: Semitic, Egyptian, Berber, Cushitic, Omotic, and Chadic. Of all these branches, five are spread in North and East Africa, while alone Semitic can be found partly in Asia, partly in Ethiopia. The common ancient homeland of these languages is disputed. The approximate latest time level of the disintegration of the supposed Proto-Afro-Asiatic parent language and population has been estimated by relatively safe glottochronological calculations to around the 8th mill. B.C. (DIAKONOFF 1975; 1981) vs. 11th–9th mill. B.C. (MILITAREV 1983, 106; 1989, 128; MILITAREV & ŠNIREL'MAN 1984, 35; MILITAREV & PEJROS & ŠNIREL'MAN 1988, 32, 34). The lexical evidence presented below speaks for a very old Afro-Asiatic substratum in the Near Eastern region, much before the Proto-Semitic and Proto-Indo-European era, which would support the theory on the Asiatic homeland of Proto-Afro-Asiatic. A definite judgement about these hypotheses lies, of course, well beyond the limits of this etymological contribution.

Fauna

IE *g^{w}ow- 'Rind' [IEW 482–483; GI 1984, 565; cf. LAROCHE 1967–1968, 46f.; KOROLEV 1969, 36–44; 1976, 73]: cf. AA *g[a]w- 'bull' [GT]: MEg. gw 'Art Stier' (MK, Wb V 159, 5) = '(wilder) Stier' (GHWb 896) ||| NBrb.: (?) Sus a-ɣu ~ a-ɣɣu ~ a-ɣwi [ɣ- < *g- irregular] 'taureau, boeuf, veau' [Mercy quoted by COHEN, not so apud Dst. 1938] ||| NOm.: (?) Kafa gaû ~ gō 'bull' (sic) [IS, source unnamed] = gáo 'buffalo' [Cecchi apud Rn.] = gā́hō [-h- obscure] 'Büffel' [Rn. 1888, 284] = gāhō 'buffalo' [Crl. 1951, 442] ||| CCh.: Gude ngwia 'buffalo' [Mch.]. Here might eventually belong Sum. gu_4 (unless the stem was gud) 'boeuf' [LABAT 1976, 137, #297].

Lit. for the AA comparison: COHEN 1947, #169;. The relationship of IE *g^{w}ow-, Eg. gw, and Sum. gu_4 was discussed by HOMMEL 1904, 109; IPSEN 1923, 175f; WÖLFEL 1955, 58; IS 1964, 3, #2; CASTELLINO 1984, 18; GI 1984, 575; 1984a, 112; BOISSON 1990 MS, 21–22; Blz. 1992 MS, 154–155.

NB1: V. É. Orel & O. V. Stolbova (HSED #905) compared Eg. gw to ECh.: Tumak guūy 'bull' (sic), which is perfectly mistaken. In his dictionary J.-P. CAPRILE (1975:66) gives in fact Tumak gù̄ùy 'os'!

NB2: Beside AA *g[a]w-, a PAA variant root *kVw- [GT] can be pointed out on the basis of NAgaw: Qwara kuwā & Agawmeder kewā 'Büffel' [Rn. 1885:90] ||| WCh.: Bole kwō 'buffalo' [Meek apud Pls. 1960:110, #42] = kwɔ̄ [Meek in JI] || CCh.: Glavda káwa [k- irregular?] 'buffalo' [RB 1968] (Ch.: JI 1994 II, 51).

NB3: There is an old misunderstanding around Eg. gw, defended even recently by Th. GAMKRELIDZE and V. V. IVANOV (l.c.), according to which MEg. gw would be connected to OEg. ng 'Art grosse Rinder mit langen Hörner' (OK, Wb II 349, 1) which is certainly a different stem. OEg. ng has sometimes been mentioned in a wider North African perspective together with WSudanic: Ful nagge 'Rind', Wolof nag, Serer nak 'Rind' (cf., e.g. MUKAROVSKY 1957:131; 1959:17, #28; DIAKONOFF 1981:54, note 89).

IE *Hel- (?) → Gmc. *ēlo- 'eel' [ZALIZNJAK 1963:130]: cf. AA *ʕul- '1. eel, 2. leech' [GT]: Eg. ʕnʕr.t [act. *ʕlʕl.t] 'Art Wurm oder kleine Schlange, auch im Wasser lebend: ob Aal (?)', cf. also ʕnʕr.t n.t znf 'bildlich: ʕnʕr.t des Blutes: Blutgerinnsel' (Med., Wb I 191, 15–17) = 'ein Wurm der in Wasser lebt: ein Borstenwurm' (Ebbell apud Deines-Grapow 1959:96–97) = '1. ein Wurm

im Wasser lebend, 2. Blut-Gerinnsel' (GHWb 143) ||| LECu.: Somali ʕolāʕol (f) 'leech' [Rn.], Oromo ulanul-a 'leech' [Tutschek] ||| NOm.: Haruro ul-o 'leech' [CR] (HECu.-NOm.: Dlg. 1973, 141).
NB: There have been a few attempts to affiliate the Germanic term within Indo-European. J. KATZ (1995) identified it with Hitt. ellu-eššar- 'hole of snake (?)' (hapax) [Watkins, Münchener Studien zur Sprachwissenschaft 45, 1985, 251, 255, n. 11] and Gk. ἔλλυες "creatures living in the river Smaragdos" [Hesykhios], Ἐλλερο-φόντης "killer of ἔλλερος" [KATZ] = "kind of snake" [WATKINS] (probably haplology, from *Ἐλλερο-οφι-φόντης "killer of the eel-fish"). In addition, independently from each other, both V. BLAŽEK (1993:33) and J. KATZ (1995) have identified the second component of PIE *ang^{w}h-el(lu)- 'eel' with PIE *Hel- 'eel'. For the first part cf. IE *ang$^{w(h)}$- 'snake, worm' [IEW 43–45]. Thus, the PIE compound may have actually meant 'snake-eel', to be interpreted as a reverse ***nīlotpalam*** compound of comparison in the OIndic terminology (e.g. OInd. ***puruṣa-vyāghra-*** 'tiger-man'). Besides, earlier, Germanic *ēlo- was considered to be isolated within IE, and supposed to be of substratum origin (VERNER 1991:44; POLOMÉ 1992:51).

IE *Howi- 'sheep' [GI 1984:577; LAROCHE 1967–1968:46ff.; KOROLEV 1969:36–44; 1976:73]: cf. AA *Haw- 'sheep' [GT]: SCu.: Asa hāw 'sheep' [Flm. 1969:12, #22]. The same substratum word seems to have been preserved in Sum. $^{(udu)}u_8$ (= us_5) 'ewe' [BORGER 1978:183, #494] = 'brebis adulte' [LABAT 1976:217, #494].
NB: Any connection to Eg. ʕw.t 'Kleinvieh (i.a. Schafe und Ziegen)' (OK, Wb I 170–171) = 'small cattle (i.e., sheep and goats)' (FD 39)? In this case, we should assume AA *ʕaw- 'sheep' [GT]. Note that Eg. ʕw.t and IE *Howi- have been combined already by A. R. BOMHARD (1984:265) and C. T. HODGE (1990:372; 1990:644, #4B), although not as areal parallels. Cf. also BLAŽEK 1992 MS, 114, 234.

IE *k^{w}el- (or ***kel-**) 'bitch' [KLUGE 1975:850–851; ONIONS 1982: 1001; PARTRIDGE 1983:802]: cp. CCh.: Bura-Pela kıla [Meek] | PKotoko *kelew 'dog' [GT]: Logone kle [Mch.] = gəléw [Bouny] = kəlè [Lks.] = kalee [Nct.], Buduma kəle [Cyffer] = keli [Lks.], Kuseri kẹlẹ & kéle [Slk.], Afade kléw [Slk.], Ngala kĕlē & kĕllä & kĕlĕ [Slk.], Makeri kẹlẹo̱ & kíllĕu [Slk.], Shoe kelo [Slk.] (Ktk.: Slk. 1967; Prh. 1972:20) | Higi kĕllĕ́ & Kapsiki kĕlĕ [Str. 1922–1923].

IE *k̑won- ~ *k̑un- 'dog' [IEW 632–633]: cf. AA *kan-/*k^{w}an- 'dog' [GT] = *k^{w}n̥ [Djk.]: Guanche: Gran Canaria cuna [*kuna], Tenerife cancha ~ cuncha [*kWn-ča] 'dog' (Guanche: Wlf. 1965 apud Mlt. 1991:250, #18.5) ||| NOm. *kan- 'dog' [Bnd.] (Om.: Flm. 1974:88; Bnd. 1988:145) ||| ECh.: WDangla kànyà 'dog' [FÉDRY 1971] | Jegu kány 'Hund' [Jng. 1961:113]. A special isogloss

(perhaps AA *k^{w}aHn- [GT]?) is represented by ECu.: Yaaku kwe-hen 'dog' [Hobley & Grb. apud Dlg. 1973:71, not found in HEINE 1975] ||| WCh.: Fyer k^{w}éeŋ (m), kumù (f) 'dog' [Jng. 1970:389].
Lit. for the AA comparison: COHEN 1947, #189; Dlg. 1968:104–105; IS 1971, #238; Djk. etc. 1986:44; OS 1992:207; Blz. 1992 MS, 121; OREL 1995:105, #78; HSED #1425, #1498, #1511.

IE *lew- 'lion' [GI 1984, 507; Neu 1974:103]: cp. eventually AA *raw- 'wild cat, lion' [GT]: OEg. rw 'lion' (PT, Wb II 403:8) ||| CCh.: PMasa *raw 'cat' [GT]: Masa ra̩w [Mch.], Zime-Batna ráw ~ mé-ráw [Jng.] = mé-riāo [Scn.] || ECh.: Kera kíi-ríw 'leopard', cf. also *tə-raw 'cat' [Ebert], Kwang-Mobu ku-rú 'leopard' [Jng.] | Lele ki-rwe 'leopard' [Gowers] | Tumak ərəw 'leopard' [Cpr.] | Mubi òrṹwà 'lion' [Lks. 1937:184] = ʔórúwà [Jng.] (Ch.: JI 1994 II:65, 223).

Lit.: for the AA comparison see MÖLLER 1921:195; CALICE 1936, #66; COHEN 1947, #34; Grb. 1963:59; HODGE 1976:11; OS 1992:183; OREL 1993:43; JI 1994 II:227. The similarity of the AA and IE stems has been discussed already by V. M. ILLIČ-SVITYČ (1971, #238) and V. BLAŽEK (1992 MS, 70).
NB1: Not clear whether Sem. *ʔarw- [prothetic *ʔa-] 'lion' [GT] = 'animale selvatico' [Frz. 1968:292, #5.43] also belongs here, cf. esp. Hbr. ʔări 'Löwe' [GB 65], Syr. ʔaryō 'lion' [Frz.].
NB2: Th. GAMKRELIDZE and V. V. IVANOV (1984:507–510) have emphasized that the IE word for 'lion' is a 'migration term'. Following a wrong tradition in their monograph, the two outstanding linguists connected PIE *lew- with a number of different "Mediterranean" (Kartvelian, Egyptian, Semitic) terms for 'lion', which have clearly nothing to do with each other because of the significant phonological differences. It is evident that the words like Krt. *lom- 'lion' [GI, not found in KLIMOV 1964 or ĘWKS], Sem. *labiʔ- 'lioness' [Frz. 1968, 281], and Eg. rw 'lion' (OK, Wb) cannot be related. It may be rather misleading to be so generous with phonology as GAMKRELIDZE and IVANOV are in this case, esp. e.g. to allow a change *-m ~ *-b ~ *-w in the auslauts. *Pro primo*: in the case of PKrt. *lom- 'lion' (Georg. lom-, Svan löm), we may not exclude an ancient Near Eastern *Wanderwort*, which might have its ultimate source in the Afro-Asiatic substratum, cp. AA *lum- ~ *rum- 'lion' [GT]: LEg. 3m [*lm/*rm] 'Löwe (als Name des Gottes oder Königs)' (GR, Wb I 10, 6) ||| WCh.: Diri ʔɪrɪmì 'leopard' [Krt.], Polchi yirim 'leopard' [Krf.] || CCh. PMasa *lum- 'lion' [GT]: Zime-Batna lúm [Jng.] = lúm [Scn.], Lame lúmú [Krf.], Lame-Peve lum [Krf.] || ECh.: Migama á:rúm 'lion' [Jng.] (Ch.: Krf. 1981, #159 & #162; JI 1994 II:227). For this Eg.-Ch. etymology see HODGE 1992:219; OS 1992:183; HSED #2134. *Pro secundo*: Sem. *labiʔ- 'lioness' [Frz. 1968:281] = *labʔ- 'lion' [Djk. 1970:473, fn.96] = *labiʔatu or *libʔatu 'lioness' [Hml. 1879, 401] derives from AA *lVb(?)- 'lion', [GT], cf. Eg. 3bj [*lbj] 'Panther' (XVIII., Wb I 7-14) ||| NAgaw *yib- [*yi- < *li-] 'panther' [GT] || LECu.: Saho & Afar lubák 'lion' [Rn. 1886, 874] | PSam *libāḥ- 'lion' [HEINE 1978:67]. For the AA comparison see COHEN 1947, #7; Djk.

1965:50; 1975:126, note 36 (mistakenly including Eg. rw); HODGE 1966:44; 1976:18, #18; 1992:218; Dlg. 1983:124; OREL 1993:43.

IE *sk̑ego- 'goat' [Blz.]: IA *chaga- ~ *chagana- ~ *chagalá- 'goat' [TURNER]: cf. esp. Vedic chā́ga- (m) 'he-goat' (IA: KEWA 406; TURNER 1960–1966, #4958 & #4961 & #4963) || Osset.: Digor säɣä 'goat' [Abaev] = sāɣ 'Ziege' (sic) [KEWA] | Pamir: Vakhan čēɣ̌ 'goat' [PAHALINA 1975:193] ||| OHGerm. schege 'goat' [SCHRÖDER, IF 22:195] (IE: Blz. 1992 MS, 35): the PIE initial complex *sk̑- may correspond to an anlaut affricate in Afro-Asiatic (such phoneme being absent in PIE), cf. AA *[č̣]iK- 'goat' [GT]: NOm.: Zayse ciegā 'goat' [Mkr.] ||| WCh. *čikan 'goat' [Stl. 1987: 193] || CCh.: (?) Sukur ǯuk 'goat' [Meek] || ECh.: Somray čágé 'goat' [Jng.] (Ch.: JI 1994 II:166–167; Mkr. 1987:193). Cf. also Mande *sVgV 'goat, sheep' [GT]. The same ancient Near Eastern *Wanderwort* may be preserved in Sum. $^{\text{si-iq-(qa)}}$šeg$_9$ 'Wildschaf, Schabock' [AHW 88] = 'jeune bouquetin' [LABAT 1976:229, #551] and NCauc. *čekV 'goat, kid' [NCED 1094].

Lit. for Zayse-Ch.: Mkr. 1987:193. For the AA-NCauc. etymology see Mlt.-Sts. 1984:38. For IE-AA-Sum.-NCauc.: Blz. 1992 MS, 35.

Apiculture

IE *b^{h}ey- 'Biene' [IEW 116]: cf. AA *b[i]y- 'bee' [GT]: Eg. bj.t 'Biene' (OK, Wb I 434:1–5), bj.t 'Honig' (OK, Wb I 434:6–12) ||| Bed. wiyu [w < *b possible] wíyu 'Biene' [Rn. 1895, 240].

Lit. for the Eg.-Bed. etymology: C. BROCKELMANN (1932:806), E. ZYHLARZ (1932–1933:167), and G. TAKÁCS (1998:152, #10). For the IE-Eg. etymology see GI 1984, 610-611; 876; 1985, 19; 1985:178–179; HODGE 1983:44; 1987:95; 1988:274; 1990:649; BOMHARD 1986:237; TAKÁCS 1998:152, #10.
NB: The Afro-Asiatic etymology of the Egyptian counterpart has been debated. For a detailed discussion of these problems see EDE II:307–309.

IE *Hap- (?) [GT]: Lat. apis 'bee' (apparently lacking IE cognates, cf. GI 1984:602), cf. AA *ʔ/ʕaf- 'bee' [GT]: Eg. ʕfj 'bee' (NK, Wb I 182:10) ||| SCu.: PRift *[ʔ]af- 'natural beehive' [Ehr.]: Burunge afa | Asa ʔafo-tok (Rift: EHRET 1980:377, #1).

Lit.: for the Eg.-SCu. etymology see BLAŽEK 1991:53, #33. To the best of my knowledge, this IE-Eg. parallel has not yet been noticed in the literature

except for BRUNNER (1969:23, #42).
NB: Due to phonological reasons, we cannot speak about a late borrowing from some North African source into Italic. Lat. apis must date back to some earlier period of the Indo-European language history (perhaps PIE?), where a borrowed AA *-f- might have become PIE *-p- for the simple reason that the PIE consonantism seemingly lacked *f.

IE *med^{h}u- "honey" [WP II, 261; GI 1984, 604]: cf. AA *maT- "bee, honey" [GT]: NOm.: Wolayta matt-ā, "ape" [Crl. 1938 III, 172] = matt-a "honeybee" [Alm.], Gofa matt-a "honeybee" [Alm.], Gamu mað-a "honeybee" [Alm.], Dorze mað "honeybee" [Alm.], Shinasha mað "honeybee" [Alm.], Dawro mātt-a "honeybee" [Alm.] (NWOmt.: Alm. 1993, 6) | Kafa maṭ-i "bee" [Hyw. 1988, 284] | Hozo & Sezo mati ~ bati "bee" [Bnd. 1990, 605, # 212; 1988, 148] ||| WCh.: presumably Hausa máḍì "a sweet drink made from juice of sugar-cane and various trees" [Abr. 1962, 630] | Grnt. m^{w}aḍami "sweet" [Jgr. 1989, 188] || ECh.: Mkl. máddé "Biene" [Lks. 1977, 219] = máddé "1. abeille, 2. miel" [Jng. 1990, 136] = màddè "1. honey, 2. bee" [Jng. in JI 1994 II, 19 & 191]. Lit.: for Mkl.-NOm. see Dlg. 1998, 64, # 79. The IE-AA etymology, to the best of my knowledge, has not yet been published.

IE *mel-it- & *mel-n- "sweet, honey" [GI 1984, 603]: cf. AA *mal-/*mul- "1. sweet, 2. honey" [GT]: SCu.: Ma'a mál-a "beer" [Ehret] | Dhl. mól-a "(honey) mead" [EEN 1989, 38] = mól-a "mead" [TOSCO 1991, 143] (SCu.: EHRET 1980, 154) ||| NOm.: Gamu malˀ- "to be taste well", malˀ-o "sweet" [SOTTILE 1999, 430, 440].

NB: Cf. also Eg. mnḥ [*mlḥ] "(bee)wax" (XVIII., Wb II 83, 4) ||| ECu. *malab- "honey" [Sasse 1979, 14]. Extended by suffixes -ḥ and *-b, resp.?
Lit.: TAKÁCS 1998, 153, # 11 (IE-AA).

Agriculture

IE *Har- "to plough", *Har-H̥-tro-m (n) "plough" [GI 1984, 687-688; Mann 1984-1987, 31, 35]: cf. AA *ḥ-r (perhaps *ḥar-) "1. to scratch, 2. to scratch earth → to plough" [GT]: Sem.: (?) Ar. ḥrr II "5-6. écrire" [BK I 400] (originally *"to scratch"?) ||| ECu. *ḥarˀ-/*ḥaˀr- "to scratch" [Sasse]: i.a. Burji harˀ- "to plough, till land" [SASSE 1982, 92] ||| WCh. *Har [GT]: Angas eer "to scratch, farm, hoe" [Flk. 1915] = "возделывать землю" [OS]. Cf. perhaps also

PDrv. *ar-ay(-kkV) "plough": Malto are "plough", Tamil araka- "a plough with bullocks etc." (Drv.: GUROV 1987, 27; BONGARD-LEVIN & GUROV 1988).

Lit.: for Angas-IE cf. OS 1990, 15, # 6. For IE-ECu. cf. BOMHARD (1984, 281-282, # 311; 1986, 249), followed by BLAŽEK & BOISSON (1992, 24, # 5).

NB: Because of the significantly different root vowel, it is highly obscure whether the same ancient Near Eastern term is preserved in Sum. uru_4 = ur_{11}(.ru) "to plough" [SALONEN 1968, 430; YOSHIKAWA 1968, 410; THOMSEN 1984, 321], perhaps Krt.: Georgian ur- "bebauen etc." (its basic meaning and the underlying PKrt. source are still questionable) [FÄHNRICH 1981, 92, # 20], Drv. *uṟu- "to plough" [BURROW-EMENEAU 1961, # 688; MCALPIN 1981, 133].

IE *Hars- [GT] → Hitt. ḫarš- "to spade, hoe, harrow" [STURTEVANT 1936, 45] = "aufreißen, beackern" [FRIEDRICH 1952, 59] = "обрабатывать землю на посев (to till the earth for sowing)" ≈ Hitt. teripp- "to plough" (Gk. δρεπάνη "sickle") [GI 1984, 687]: related to Sem. *ḥrṯ "to plough" [GT] = *-ḥruṯ- "arare" [Frz.]: Akk. erēšu "1. Feld bestellen, 2. besäen mit Saatpflug" [AHW 238] || Ug. ḥrṯ "pflügen, das Feld bebauen" [WUS #980], Hbr. ḥrš qal "1. einschneiden, in eine Tafel schneiden, 2. bearbeiten, 3. pflügen (v. Rinde)" [GB 263] || Ar. ḥaraṯa "labourer la terre, cultiver la terre" [BK I 403] || ES *ḥrs "to plow" [GT]: e.g. Geez ḥarasa "to plow, cultivate land" [Lsl. 1987, 243] (Sem.: Aro 1963, 475, #1; Frz. 1969, 310, #6.23; TYLOCH 1975, 58, #20). The underlying ancient Near Eastern *Wanderwort* is to be found also in NCauc. *HVrəc·c·u "wooden plow, plough" [Sts. 1985, 81, #35] vs. *=ērƛ'V "to plough, sow" [NCED 416] and Burushaski hərṣ̌ "plough", Werchikwar dialect harc̣ "plough" [Berger].

Lit.: PUHVEL in JAOS 74 (1954), 86-88 (Hitt.-Sem.); Mlt.-Sts. 1984, 36 (ECauc.-Sem.); BLAŽEK-BOISSON 1992, 25, #5 (IE-AA-NCauc.-Burushaski).

NB1: Hitt. ḫarš- has been traditionally explained directly from IE *Har- "to plough", extended by a root complement *-s- (cf. e.g. TISCHLER 1977, 182; GI 1984, 687). At the present it seems much more probable that Hitt. ḫarš- belongs to the group of the above listed Near Eastern terms for "plough(ing)" with the third consonant as a sibilant instead of being directly derived from IE *Har-, which, however, does not exclude an ultimate common origin.

NB2: A. B. DOLGOPOLSKY (1988, 631-632, #26) tried to demonstrate that ECu. *ḥarˀ- "to scratch" [Sasse] is cognate to Sem. *ḥrṯ treating the third root consonant *ṯ as a Semitic innovation.

IE *seg- "säen" [IEW 887]: cf. AA *S-k ~ *S-g "to sow" [GT]: Eg. sṯj [< *skj] "to sow, säen" (PT, Wb IV 346-347) = "to strew, scatter" (FD 255) ||| NOm. *šok- "seed" [Bnd. 1994, 1157, #70]: Janjero (Yemsa) sik- "(sich) zerstreuen" [Lmb. 1993 Yms., 372] | Kefoid *šōk- "to sow" [GT]: Kafa šok "seminare" [Crl. 1951, 496] = "to sow seeds" [Flm.], Mocha šȍkki-yé "to seed" [Lsl. 1959, 50], Shinasha-Bworo bok "to sow" [Crl.] = šōk-a "seed" [Flm.], Shinasha-Dangur šő́ka "seed" [Flm. 1990, 28], Wombera šok-a "1. seed, 2. to plant" [Flm.], Beke šōk-o "seed, fruit" [Flm.] (Kefoid: Flm. 1987, 151, #2) ||| WCh.: Hausa šúúkà "to sow" [Abr. 1962, 815] || CCh.: Chibak ŝəgátì [s̱-], Bura ĉika [thlika] "to sow" (BM: Hfm. 1955, 135) | MM *ẑigay "to sow" [Rsg.]: Mada ẑìgé, Muyang ẑìgé, Muktele ĉkáy [tl-], Gisiga ẑəgá, Mofu ĉəké [tl-] (MM: Rsg. 1978, 332, #674) | Pus sukí ~ soká "faire le trou avant de semer" [Trn. 1991, 60], Mbara čók "to sow" [TSL 1986, 256], Vulum súkí "faire le trou avant de semer" [Trn. 1978, 309; TSL 1986, 197]. Here might belong Drv.: PKurukh *cāk- "to sow" [DED #2431].

Lit. for the AA etymology: BEHNK 1928, 140, #50; Mlt. 1983, 101; 1989, 130; 1990, 77; BLZ.-BOISSON 1992, 26, #8; OS 1992, 176; 1992, 198. Cf. also BLAŽEK-BOISSON 1992, 26, #8 (Drv.-AA); Skn. 1996, 246 (AA-PIE); Blz. 2000 MS, 22, #118 (AA-PIE-PDrv.).

Abbreviations of languages

AA: Afro-Asiatic (Semito-Hamitic), Akk.: Akkadian, Ar.: Arabic, BD. Book of the Dead, BM: Bura-Margi, Brb.: Berber, Cauc.: Caucasian, Ch.: Chadic, Cpt.: Coptic, CT: coffin texts, Cu.: Cushitic, Dem.: Demotic, Dhl.: Dahalo, Drv.: Dravidian, E: East, Eg.: Egyptian, ES: Ethio-Semitic, Germ.: German, Gk.: Greek, Gmc.: Germanic, GR: Ptolemaid & Roman period (in Egypt), Grnt.: Guruntum, Hbr.: Hebrew, Hitt.: Hittite, IA: Indo-Aryan, IE: Indo-European, II: Indo-Iranian, Krt.: Kartvelian, LE(g.): Late Egyptian, Lit.: literary texts (or literature), M: Middle, Med.: medical texts, MK: Middle Kingdom, Mkl.: Mokilko, MM: Mafa-Mada, N: New or North, NE(g.): New Egyptian, O: Old, OHGerm.: Old High German, OInd.: Old Indic, Om.: Omotic, Osset.: Ossetic, P: Proto-, PT: pyramid texts, S: South, Sem.: Semitic, Sum.: Sumerian, Syr.: Syriac, Ug.: Ugaritic, W: West.

Abbreviations of authors' names

Abr.: Abraham, Alm.: Alemayehu, BK: Bieberstein & Kazimirsky, Blz.: Blažek, Bmh.: Bomhard, Bnd.: Bender, Brk.: Brockelmann, Chn.: Cohen, Clc.: Calice, Cpr.: Caprile, Crl.: Cerulli, Djk.: D'jakonov (Diakonoff), Dlg.: Dolgopol'skij (Dolgopolsky), Dst.: Destaign, EEN. Ehret & Elderkin & Nurse, Ehr.: Ehret, Flk.: Foulkes, Flm.: Fleming, Frz.: Fronzaroli, GB: Gesenius & Buhl, GI: Gamkrelidze & Ivanov, Grb.: Greenberg, GT: Takács, Hfm.: Hoffmann, Hml.: Hommel, Hyw.: Hayward, IS: Illič-Svityč, Jgr.: Jaggar, JI: Jungraithmayr & Ibriszimow, Jng.: Jungraithmayr, Krf.: Kraft, Lks.: Lukas, Lmb.: Lamberti, Lsl.: Leslau, Mch.: Mouchet, Mkr.: Mukarovsky, Mlt.: Militarev, OS: Orel & Stolbova, Pls.: Pilszczikowa, Prh.: Porhomovskij, RB: Rapp & Benzing, Rn.: Reinisch, Rsg.: Rossing, Skn.: Skinner, Slk.: Sölken, Snr.: Šnirel'man, Ss.: Sasse, Stl.: Stolbova, Str.: Strümpell, Sts.: Starostin, Trn.: Tourneux, TSL: Tourneux & Seignobos & Lafarge, Wlf.: Wölfel, WP: Walde & Pokorny, Zhl.: Zyhlarz.

Literature

ABRAHAM, R. C.: *Dictionary of the Hausa Language.*[2] London, 1962., University of London Press.

AHW = Soden, W. von: *Akkadisches Handwörterbuch. I-III.* Wiesbaden, 1965-1981., Otto Harrassowitz.

ALEMAYEHU, A.: "Ometo Dialect Survey—A Pilot Survey Report" = Survey of Little-Known Languages of Ethiopia (S.L.L.E.) Reports 4 (1993), 1–10.

ARO, J.: "Gemeinsemitische Ackerbauterminologie" = *Zeitschrift der Deutschen Morgenländischen Gesellschaft* 113/3 (1964), 471–480.

AUTRAN, Ch.: *Sumérien et indo-européen. L'aspect morphologique de la question*, Paris, 1925, Paul Geuthner.

BEHNK, F.: "Über die Beziehungen des Ägyptischen zu den hamitischen Sprachen" = *Zeitschrift der Deutschen Morgenländischen Gesellschaft* 82 (1928), 136–141.

BENDER, M. L.: "Proto-Omotic Phonology and Lexicon" = Bechhaus-Gerst, M. & Serzisko, Fr. (eds.): *Cushitic-Omotic. Pa-*

pers from the First International Symposium on Cushitic and Omotic Languages, Cologne, January 6–9, 1986. Hamburg, 1988., Helmut Buske Verlag, pp. 121–159.

BENDER, M. L.: "The Limits of Omotic" = Hayward, R. J. (ed.): *Omotic Language Studies*, London, 1990, SOAS. Pp. 584–616.

BENDER, M. L.: "The Mystery Languages of Ethiopia" = Marcus, H. (ed.): *New Trends in Ethiopian Studies*, Vol. 1. Lawrenceville, 1994., Red Sea Press, pp. 1153–1174.

BLAŽEK, V.: "Honey in Cushitic and Omotic Languages" = *Afrikanistische Arbeitspapiere* 26 (1991), 37–66.

BLAŽEK, V.: *Historická analýza indoevropské zoologické terminologie (savci)*. Kandidátská disertace. MS. Brno, 1992.

BLAŽEK, V.: "Po stopách indoevropské pravlasti" = *Slovo a Slovesnost* 54/1 (1993), 31–40. An abbreviated English version has been published in *Mother Tongue* 20 (1993), 40–41.

BLAŽEK, V.: *The New Dravidian-Afroasiatic Lexical Parallels. Full version.* MS. Paper presented at the Conference "Problemy izučenija dal'nego rodstva jazykov na rubeže tret'ego tysjačeletija" (Moscow, 29 May – 2 June 2000). 26 p.

BLAŽEK, V. & BOISSON, C.: "The Diffusion of Agricultural Terms from Mesopotamia" = *Archív Orientální* 60 (1992), 16–37.

BOISSON, C.: *Additions to "Sumerian/Nostratic/Sino-Caucasian Isoglosses (Version 3.16)"*, Version 0.4, MS. Lyon, 1990.

BOMHARD, A. R.: *Toward Proto-Nostratic. A New Approach to the Comparison of Proto-Indo-European and Proto-Afroasiatic*, foreword by P. J. Hopper, Amsterdam-Philadelphia, 1984, John Benjamins.

BOMHARD, A. R.: "Common Indo-European/Afroasiatic Roots: Supplement I" = *General Linguistics* 26 (1986), 225–257.

BONGARD-LEVIN, G. M. & GUROV, N. V.: "Drevnejšaja étnokul'turnaja istorija narodov Indostana: itogi, problemy, zadači issledovanija" = *Drevnij Vostok. Étnokul'turnye svjazi*. LXXX. Moskva, 1988, Nauka, pp. 58–111.

BORGER, R.: *Assyrisch-babylonische Zeichenliste*, Neukirchen-Vluyn, 1978, Verlag Butzon & Bercker Kevelaer.

BROCKELMANN, C.: "Ägyptisch-semitische Etymologien" = *Zeitschrift für Semitistik* 8 (1932), 97–117.

BRUNNER, L.: *Die gemeinsamen Wurzeln des semitischen und indogermanischen Wortschatzes. Versuch einer Etymologie*, Bern, 1969, Francke Verlag.

BURROW, T. & EMENEAU, M. B.: *A Dravidian Etymological Dictionary*, Oxford, 1961, Clarendon Press.

CALICE, F.: *Grundlagen der ägyptisch-semitischen Wortvergleichung*, Wien, 1936, Selbstverlag des Orientalischen Institutes der Universität Wien.

CAPRILE, J.-P.: *Lexique tumak-français (Tchad)*, Berlin, 1975., Verlag von Dietrich Reimer.

CASTELLINO, G. R.: "Relazione introduttiva" = *Atti della Terza Giornata di Studi Camito-Semitici e Indoeuropei*, Roma, 1984, Università degli Studi "La Sapienzia", pp. 8–18.

CERULLI, E.: *Studi etiopici. III. Il linguaggio dei Giangerò ed alcune lingue Sidama dell'Omo (Basketo, Ciara, Zaissè)*. Roma, 1938, Istituto per l'Oriente.

CERULLI, E.: *Studi etiopici. IV. La lingua caffina*, Roma, 1951, Istituto per l'Oriente.

COHEN, M.: *Essai comparatif sur le vocabulaire et la phonétique du chamito-sémitique*, Paris, 1947, Librairie Ancienne Honore Champion.

DED = Burrow, T. & Emeneau, M. B.: *A Dravidian Etymological Dictionary*, Oxford, 1961, Clarendon Press.

DEINES, H. & GRAPOW, H.: *Wörterbuch der ägyptischen Drogennamen*, Berlin, 1959, Akademie-Verlag.

DESTAING, E.: *Vocabulaire français-berbère (tachelḥit du Soûs)*, Paris, 1938, Éditions Ernest Leroux.

D'JAKONOV, I. M.: *Semitohamitskie jazyki. Opyt klassifikacii*, Moskva, 1965, Nauka.

DIAKONOFF, I. M.: "Problems of Root Structure in Proto-Semitic" = *Archív Orientální* 38 (1970), 453–480.

D'JAKONOV, I. M.: "Lingvističeskie dannye k istorii drevnejbih nositelej afrazijskih jazykov" = *Africana. Afrikanskij Étnografičeskij Sbornik* 10 (1975), 117–130.

DIAKONOFF, I. M.: "Earliest Semites in Asia. Agriculture and Animal Husbandry According to Linguistic Data (VIIIth–IVth Millennia B.C.)" = *Altorientalische Forschungen* 8 (1981), 23–74.

DIAKONOFF, I. M.: "On the Original Home of the Speakers of Indo-European" = *Journal of Indo-European Studies* 13/1–2 (1985), 92–174.

DIAKONOFF, I. M. (with assistence by MILITAREV, A. Ju. and STOLBOVA, O. V.): *Proto-Afrasian and Old Akkadian*, MS. Leningrad, about 1986.

DOLGOPOL'SKIJ, A. B.: "Drevnie korni i drevnie ljudi" = *Russkaja Reč'* 2 (1968), 96–108.

DOLGOPOL'SKIJ, A. B.: *Sravnitel'no-istoričeskaja fonetika kubitskih jazykov*, Moskva, 1973, Nauka.

DOLGOPOLSKY, A. B.: "Semitic and East Cushitic. Sound Correspondences and Cognate Sets" = Segert, S. & Bodrogligeti, A. J. E. (eds.): *Ethiopian Studies Dedicated to Wolf Leslau*, Wiesbaden, 1983, Otto Harrassowitz, pp. 123–142.

DOLGOPOLSKY, A. B.: "The Indo-European Homeland and Lexical Contacts of Proto-Indo-European with Other Languages" = *Mediterranean Language Review* 3 (1987), 7–31.

DOLGOPOLSKY, A. B.: "Semitic and East Cushitic: Word-Initial Laryngeals" = Taddese, B. (ed.): *Proceedings of the Eighth International Conference of Ethiopian Studies*, University of Addis Ababa, 1984. Volume 1. Addis Ababa, 1988, Institute of Ethiopian Studies, Addis Ababa, pp. 629–637.

DOLGOPOLSKY, A. B.: "Cultural Contacts of Proto-Indo-European and Proto-Indo-Iranian with Neighbouring Languages" = *Folia Linguistica Historica* 8/1-2 (1989), 3–36.

DOLGOPOLSKY, A. B.: *The Nostratic Macrofamily and Linguistic Paleontology*, Cambridge, 1998, The McDonald Institute for Archaeological Research.

EDE II = Takács, G.: *Etymological Dictionary of Egyptian. Volume Two: b-, p-, f-*, Leiden, 2001, E. J. Brill.

EHRET, Ch.: *The Historical Reconstruction of Southern Cushitic Phonology and Vocabulary*, Berlin, 1980, Dietrich Reimer Verlag.

EHRET, Ch. & ELDERKIN, E. D. & NURSE, D.: "Dahalo Lexis and Its Sources" = *Afrikanistische Arbeitspapiere* 18 (1989), 5–49.

EWKS = Fähnrich, H. & Sardschweladse, S.: *Etymologisches Wörterbuch der Kartwel-Sprachen*, Leiden, 1995, E. J. Brill.

FÄHNRICH, H.: "Das Sumerische und die Kartwelsprachen" = *Georgica* 4 (1981), 89–101.

FD = Faulkner, R. O.: *A Concise Dictionary of Middle Egyptian*, Oxford, 1962, Clarendon Press.

FÉDRY, J. (avec la collaboration de KHAMIS, J. & O/NEDJEI, M.): *Dictionnaire dangaleat (Tchad)*. Thése de 3ème cycle, Institut National des Langues et Civilisations Orientales, Lyon, 1971, Afrique et Langage.

FLEMING, H.: "Asa and Aramanik: Cushitic Hunters in Masai-Land" = *Ethnology* 8/1 (1969), 1–36.

FLEMING, H.: "Omotic as a New Afroasiatic Family" = *Studies in African Linguistics. Supplement* 5 (1974), 81–94.

FLEMING, H. C.: "Proto-Gongan Consonant Phonemes: Stage One" = Mukarovsky, H. G. (ed.): *Leo Reinisch. Werk und Erbe*, Wien, 1987, Verlag der Österreichischen Akademie der Wissenschaften, pp. 141–159.

FLEMING, H.: "Omotica, Afrasiana and More: Ethiopia as the Ever-Flowing Vase" = *Mother Tongue* 12 (1990), 22–30.

FOULKES, H. D.: *Angass Manual. Grammar, Vocabulary*, London, 1915, Kegan Paul, Trench, Trübner and Co.

FRIEDRICH, J.: *Hethitisches Wörterbuch*, Heidelberg, 1952, Carl Winter Universitätsverlag.

FRONZAROLI, P.: "Studi sul Lessico Comune Semitico. V" = *Rendiconti delle Sedute dell'Accademia Nazionale dei Lincei. Classe di scienze morali, storiche e fililogiche*, ser. VIII, vol. XXIII, fasc. 7–12 (1968), 267–303.

FRONZAROLI, P.: "Studi sul Lessico Comune Semitico. VI" = *Rendiconti delle Sedute dell'Accademia Nazionale dei Lincei. Classe di scienze morali, storiche e fililogiche*, ser. VIII, vol. XXIV, fasc. 7–12 (1969), 285–320.

GAMKRELIDZE, T. V. & IVANOV, V. V.: *Indoevropejskij jazyk i indoevropejcy*, Tbilisi, 1984, Izdatel'stvo Tbilisskogo Universiteta.

GAMKRELIDZE, T. V. & IVANOV, V. V.: "The Ancient Near East and the Indo-European Question. Temporal and Territorial Characteristics of Proto-Indo-European Based on Linguistic and Historico-Cultural Data" = *Journal of Indo-European Studies* 13/1–2 (1985), 3–48.

GAMKRELIDZE, T. V. & IVANOV, V. V.: "The Migration of Tribes Speaking the Indo-European Dialects from Their Original Homeland in the Near East to Their Historical Habitations in Eurasia" = *Journal of Indo-European Studies* 13/1–2 (1985), 49–91

GB = Gesenius, W. (bearbeitet von Buhl, F.): *Hebräisches und aramäisches Handwörterbuch über das Alte Testment*, Unveränderter Neudruck der 1915 erschienenen 17. Auflage. Berlin, Göttingen, Heidelberg, 1962, Springer-Verlag.

GHWb = Hannig, R.: *Großes Handwörterbuch Ägyptisch-Deutsch (2800-950 v. Chr.)*, Mainz, 1995, Verlag Philipp von Zabern.

GREENBERG, J. H.: "The Languages of Africa" = *International Journal of American Linguistics* 29 (1963).

GUROV, N. V.: "Dravidijskie élementy v tekstah rannih samhit" = *Literatura i kul'tura drevnej i srednevekovoj Indii*, Moskva, 1987, Nauka, pp. 26–42.

HAYWARD, R. J.: "Remarks on Omotic Sibilants" = Becchaus-Gerst, M. & Serzisko, F. (eds.): *Cushitic-Omotic. Papers from the International Symposium on Cushitic and Omotic Languages, Cologne, January 6-9, 1986*, Hamburg, 1988, Helmut Buske Verlag, pp. 263–299.

HEINE, B.: "Notes on the Yaaku Language (Kenya)" = *Afrika und Übersee* 58/2 (1975), 119–138.

HEINE, B.: "The Sam Languages. A History of Rendille, Boni and Somali" = *Afroasiatic Linguistics* 6/2 (1978), 23–115.

HODGE, C. T.: "Hausa-Egyptian Establishment" = *Anthropological Linguistics* 8/1 (1966), 40–57.

HODGE, C. T.: "An Egypto-Semitic Comparison" = *Folia Orientalia* 17 (1976), 5–28.

HODGE, C. T.: "Relating Afroasiatic to Indo-European" = Wolff, E. & Meyer-Bahlburg, H. (eds.): *Studies in Chadic and Afroasiatic Languages*, Hamburg, 1983, Buske Verlag, pp. 33–50.

HODGE, C. T.: "Lislakh Cluster Resolution" = *Anthropological Linguistics* 29/1 (1987), 91–104.

HODGE, C. T.: "Consonant Ablaut in Lislakh" = Arbeitman, Y. L. (ed.): *FUCUS. A Semitic/Afrasian Gathering in Remembrance of Albert Ehrman*, Amsterdam, Philadelphia, 1988, John Benjamins. pp. 267–276.

HODGE, C. T.: "The Multivalence of Hittite ḫ" = *The Seventeenth LACUS Forum 1990*, Lake Bluff, 1990, LACUS, pp. 368–374.

HODGE, C. T.: "The Role of Egyptian within Afroasiatic" = Baldi, Ph. (ed.): *Linguistic Change and Reconstruction Methodology*, Berlin, New York, 1990, Mouton, pp. 639–659.

HODGE, C. T.: "Tooth and Claw" = *Anthropological Linguistics* 34 (1992), 202–232.

HOFFMANN, C.: "Zur Sprache der Cibak" = Lukas, J. (ed.): *Afrikanistische Studien*, Berlin, 1955, Akademie-Verlag, pp. 118–143.

HOMMEL, F.: *Die Namen der Säugethiere bei den südsemitischen Völkern*, Leipzig, 1879, J. C. Hinrichs'sche Buchhandlung.

HOMMEL, F.: *Grundriss der Geographie und Geschichte des Alten Orients*, München, 1904, C. H. Beck'sche Verlagsbuchhandlung.

HSED = Orel, V. É. & Stolbova, O. V.: *Hamito-Semitic Etymological Dictionary*, Leiden, 1995, E. J. Brill.

IEW = Pokorny, J.: *Indogermanisches etymologisches Wörterbuch. Band I*, Bern-München, 1959, Francke Verlag.

ILLIČ-SVITYČ, V. M.: "Drevnejšie indoevropejsko-semitskie jazykovye kontakty" = Toporov, V. (ed.): *Problemy indoevropejskogo jazykoznanija*, Moskva, 1964, Nauka, pp. 3–12.

ILLIČ-SVITYČ, V. M.: *Opyt sravnenija nostratičeskih jazykov. Vvedenie. Sravnitel'nyj slovar' (b-Ḳ)*, Moskva, 1971, Nauka.

IPSEN, G.: "Sumerisch-akkadische Lehnwörter im Indogermanischen" = *Indogermanische Forschungen* 41/1–2 (1923), 174–183.

JAOS = *Journal of the American Oriental Society*

JAGGAR, Ph. J.: "Guruntum (gùrdùŋ) (West Chadic-B): Linguistic Notes and Wordlist" = *African Languages and Cultures* 2/2 (1989), 175–202.

JUNGRAITHMAYR, H.: "Beobachtungen zur tschadohamitischen Sprache der Jegu (und Jonkor) von Abu Telfan (Republique du Tchad)" = *Afrika und Übersee* 45 (1961), 95–123.

JUNGRAITHMAYR, H.: *Die Ron-Sprachen. Tschadohamitische Studien in Nordnigerien. Glückstadt*, 1970, Verlag J. J. Augustin.

JUNGRAITHMAYR, H.: *Lexique mokilko*, Berlin, 1990, Dietrich Reimer Verlag.

JUNGRAITHMAYR, H. & IBRISZIMOW, D.: *Chadic Lexical Roots. Volume II. Documentation*, Berlin, 1994, Dietrich Reimer Verlag.

KATZ, J. T.: *The Etymology of Hittite* $^{(MU\check{S})}$*illuyankaš "snake, serpent"*. Handout of the paper presented at the 205th Meeting of the American Oriental Society (Salt Lake City, 26 March 1995), 9 p.

KEWA = Mayrhofer, M.: *Kurzgefaßtes etymologisches Wörterbuch des Altindischen*, Band I-III. Heidelberg, 1956–1976, Carl Winter Verlag.

KLIMOV, G. A.: *Étimologičeskij slovar' kartvel'skih jazykov*, Moskva, 1964, Izdatel'stvo Akademii Nauk SSSR.

KLUGE, F.: *Etymologisches Wörterbuch der deutschen Sprache*, Berlin, 1975, Akademie-Verlag.

KOROLEV, A. A.: "Lykische Wörter und Namen" = *Archív Orientální* 37 (1969), 36–44.

KOROLEV, A. A.: "Hetto-luvijskie jazyki" = *Jazyki Azii i Afriki. I. Indoevropejskie jazyki*, Moskva, 1976, Glavnaja Redakcija Vostočnoj Literatury, pp. 13–93.

KRAFT, Ch.: *Chadic Wordlists I-III*, Berlin, 1981, Dietrich Reimer Verlag.

LABAT, R.: *Manuel d'épigraphie akkadienne*[5], Paris, 1976, Librairie Orientaliste Paul Geuthner.

LAMBERTI, M.: *Materialien zum Yemsa*, Heidelberg, 1993, Carl Winter Universitätsverlag.

LAROCHE, E.: "Comparaison du louvite et du lycien" = *Bulletin de la Société de Linguistique de Paris* 62 (1967–1968).

LESLAU, W.: *A Dictionary of Moča (Southwestern Ethiopia)*, Berkeley, Los Angeles, 1959, University of California Press.

LESLAU, W.: *Comparative Dictionary of Geʕez (Classical Ethiopic)*, Wiesbaden, 1987, Otto Harrassowitz.

LUKAS, J.: "Zentralsudanische Studien" = *Abhandlungen aus dem Gebiet der Auslandskunde, Hansische Universität*, Reihe B, Band 45, Band 24 (1937).

LUKAS, J.: "Tschadische Studien I. Beiträge zur Kenntnis des Mokulu" = *Afrika und Übersee* 60 (1977), 1–58, 182–229.

MANN, S. E.: *An Indo-European Comparative Dictionary. I-II*, Hamburg, 1984–1987, Helmut Buske Verlag.

MCALPIN, D. W.: "Proto-Elamo-Dravidian. The Evidence and Its Implications" = *Transactions of the American Philosophical Society* 71/3 (1981).

MILITAREV, A. Ju.: "Ob odnom obščeafrazijskom zemledel'českom termine. Novye lingvističeskie dannye o proishoždenii zemledelija" = *Vestnik Drevnej Istorii* 4 (1983), 97–106.

MILITAREV, A. Ju.: "Ešče raz o proishoždenii zemledelija po dannym praafrazijskoj (prasemitohamitskoj lingvističeskoj rekonstrukcii" = *Vestnik Drevnej Istorii* 1 (1989), 128–131.

MILITAREV, A. Ju.: "Evidence of Proto-Afrasian Cultural Lexicon (I. Cultivation of Land. II. Crops. III. Dwelling and Settlement)" = Mukarovsky, H. G. (ed.): *Proceedings of the Fifth International Hamito-Semitic Congress. Band 1.* Wien, 1990, Afro-Pub. pp. 73–85.

MILITAREV, A. Ju.: "Istoričeskaja fonetika i leksika livijskoguančskih jazykov" = Solncev, V. M. (ed.): *Jazyki Azii i Afriki. IV, kniga 2*, Moskva, 1991, Glavnaja Redakcija Vostočnoj Literatury, pp. 238–267.

MILITAREV, A. Ju. & PEJROS, I. I. & ŠNIREL'MAN, V. A.: "Metodičeskie problemy lingvoarheologičeskih rekonstrukcij étnogeneza" = *Sovetskaja Étnografija* 4 (1988), 24–38.

MILITAREV, A. Ju. & ŠNIREL'MAN, V. A.: "K probleme lokalizacii drevnejših afrazijcev (opyt lingvo-arheologičeskoj rekonstrukcii)" = *Lingvističeskaja rekonstrukcija i drevnejšaja istorija Vostoka. Tezisy i doklady konferencii. Čast' 3. Jazykovaja situacija Perednej Azii v X-IV tysjačeletijah do n.é.* Moskva, 1984, Nauka, pp. 33–43.

MILITAREV, A. Ju. & STAROSTIN, S. A.: "Obščaja afrazijskosevernokavkazskaja kul'turnaja leksika" = *Lingvističeskaja rekonstrukcija i drevnejšaja istorija Vostoka. Tezisy i doklady konferencii. Čast' 2. Lingvističeskaja i istoričeskaja rekonstrukcii (problemy interdisciplinarnyh issledovanij)*, Moskva, 1984, Nauka, pp. 35–53.

MÖLLER, G.: "Aegyptisch-libysches" = *Orientalistische Literaturzeitung* 24/9-10 (1921), 193–197.

MOUCHET, J.: "Vocabulaires comparatifs de quinze parlers du Nord-Cameroun" = *Bulletin de la Société d'Études Camerounaises* 29–30 (1950), 5–74.

MUKAROVSKY, H. G.: "Das "Sonnenrind" der Ful'be" = *Wiener Zeitschrift für die Kunde des Morgenlandes* 54 (1957), 130–140.

MUKAROVSKY, H. G.: "Altmediterranes Wortgut in Westafrika" = *Wiener Zeitschrift für die Kunde des Morgenlandes* 55 (1959), 1–48.

MUKAROVSKY, H. G.: *Mande-Chadic Common Stock*, Wien, 1987, Afro-Pub.

NCED = Nikolaev, S. L. & Starostin, S. A.: *A North Caucasian Etymological Dictionary*, Moscow, 1994, Asterisk Publishers.

NEU, E.: *Der Anitta-Text*, Wiesbaden, 1974, Otto Harrassowitz.

ONIONS, C. T.: *The Oxford Dictionary of English Etymology*, Oxford, 1982, Clarendon Press.

OREL, V. É.: "Mir semito-hamitov" = *Principy sostavlenija étimologičeskih i istoričeskih slovarej raznyh semej. Tezisy dokladov konferencii 8-9 nojabrja 1993 g*, Moskva, 1993, Institut Jazykoznanija Rossijskoj Akademii Nauk, pp. 37–44.

OREL, V. É.: "Semitohamitskij, sinokavkazskij, nostratičeskij" = *Moskovskij Lingvističeskij Žurnal* 1 (1995), 99–116.

OREL, V. É. & STOLBOVA, O. V.: "Iz semitohamitskih dopolnenij k nostratičeskomu slovarju" = *Konferencija "Sravnitel'no-istoričeskoe jazykoznanie na sovremennom étape" pamjati V. M. Illič-Svityča. 6-9 fevralja 1990 g*. Moskva, 1990, Nauka. pp. 15–16.

OREL, V. É. & STOLBOVA, O. V.: "Cushitic, Chadic, and Egyptian: Lexical Relations" = Shevoroshkin, V. V. (ed.): *Nostratic, Dene-Caucasian, Austric and Amerind*, Bochum, 1992, Brockmeyer, pp. 167–180.

OREL, V. É. & STOLBOVA, O. V.: "On Chadic-Egyptian Lexical Relations" = Shevoroshkin, V. V. (ed.): *Nostratic, Dene-Caucasian, Austric and Amerind*, Bochum, 1992, Brockmeyer, pp. 181–203.

OREL, V. É. & STOLBOVA, O. V.: "Position of Cushitic (Preliminary Report)" = Shevoroshkin, V. (ed.): *Nostratic, Dene-Caucasian, Austric and Amerind*, Bochum, 1992, Brockmeyer, pp. 204–224.

PAHALINA, T. N.: *Vahanskij jazyk*, Moskva, 1975, Nauka.

PARTRIDGE, E.: *Origins. A Short Etymological Dictionary of Modern English*, New York, 1983, (publisher unknown to me).

PILSZCZIKOWA, N.: "Le haoussa et le chamito-sémitique à la lumière de l'Essai comparatif de Marcel Cohen" = *Rocznik Orientalistyczny* 24/1 (1960), 97–130.

POLOMÉ, E. C.: "Germanic, Northwest-Indo-European and Pre-Indo-European Substrates" = *Recent Developments in Germanic Linguistics*, Amsterdam, 1992, John Benjamins.

PORHOMOVSKIJ, V. Ja.: *Istoričeskij konsonantizm jazykov kotoko*, Moskva, 1972, Institut Jazykoznanija Akademii Nauk SSSR.

RAPP, E. L. & BENZING, B.: *Dictionary of the Glavdá Language*. Frankfurt am Main, 1968, Bible Society Franfurt am Main.

REINISCH, L.: "Die Quarasprache in Abessinien. II. Quarisch-deutsches Wörterbuch" = *Sitzungsberichte der Kaiserlichen Akademie der Wissenschaften. Phil.-hist. Classe* 109/1 (1885), 3–152.

REINISCH, L.: "Die ʕAfar-Sprache II" = *Sitzungsberichte der Kaiserlichen Akademie der Wissenschaften. Phil.-hist. Classe* 113/2 (1886), 795–916.

REINISCH, L.: "Die Kafa-Sprache in Nordost-Afrika. II. Kafa-Deutsches Wörterbuch" = *Sitzungsberichte der Kaiserlichen Akademie der Wissenschaften. Phil.-hist. Classe* 116 (1888), 251–386.

REINISCH, L.: *Wörterbuch der Bedawye-Sprache*, Wien, 1895, Alfred Hölder Verlag.

ROSSING, M. O.: *Mafa-Mada: A Comparative Study of Chadic Languages in North Cameroun*. Ph.D. dissertation, Wisconsin, 1978, University of Wisconsin-Madison.

SALONEN, A.: "Agricultura Mesopotamica nach sumerisch-akkadischen Quellen" = *Suomalaisen Tiedeakatemian Toimituksia*, Sr. B. Tom 149 (1968).

SASSE, H.-J.: "The Consonant Phonemes of Proto-East-Cushitic (PEC)" = *Afroasiatic Linguistics* 7/1 (1979).

SASSE, H.-J.: *An Etymological Dictionary of Burji*, Hamburg, 1982, Buske.

SCHOTT, A.: "Indogermanisch-Semitisch-Sumerisch" = Arntz, H. (ed.): *Germanen und Indogermanen. Volkstum, Sprache, Heimat, Kultur. Festschrift für H. Hirt*. Bd. II. Heidelberg, 1936, Carl Winter Universitätsverlag, pp. 45–95.

SKINNER, N.: *Hausa Comparative Dictionary*, Köln, 1996, Rüdiger Köppe Verlag.

SÖLKEN, H.: *Seetzens Áffadéh. Ein Beitrag zur Kotoko-Sprachdokumentation*, Berlin, 1967, Akademie-Verlag.

SOTTILE, R.: "The Consonant System of Gamu" = Lamberti, M. & Tonelli, L. (eds.): *Afroasiatica Tergestina. Papers from the 9th Italian Meeting of Afro-Asiatic (Hamito-Semitic) Linguistics, Trieste, April 23-24, 1998*. Contributi presentati al 9° Incontro di Linguistica Afroasiatica (Camito-Semitica), Trieste, 23-24 Aprile 1998, Padova, 1999, Unipress, pp. 427–446.

STAROSTIN, S. A.: "Kul'turnaja leksika v obščesevernokavkazskom slovar'nom fonde" = Piotrovskij, B. B. & Ivanov, V. V.

& Ardzinba, V. G. (eds.): *Drevnjaja Anatolija*, Moskva, 1985, Nauka, pp. 74–94.

STAROSTIN, S. A.: "Indoevropejsko-severnokavkazskie izoglossy" = *Drevnij Vostok. Étnokul'turnye svjazi* LXXX, Moskva, 1988, Nauka, pp. 112–163.

STOLBOVA, O. V.: "Sravnitel'no-istoričeskaja fonetika i slovar' zapadnočadskih jazykov" = Porhomovskij, V. Ja. (red.): *Afrikanskoe istoričeskoe jazykoznanie. Problemy rekonstrukcii*, Moskva, 1987, Nauka, pp. 30–268.

STRÜMPELL, F.: "Wörterverzeichnis der Heidensprachen des Mandara-Gebirges (Adamaua)" = *Zeitschrift für Eingeborenen-Sprachen* 13 (1922–1923), 109–149.

STURTEVANT, E. H.: *A Hittite Glossary.*[2] Philadelphia, 1936, University of Pennsylvania.

TAKÁCS, G.: "Afro-Asiatic (Semito-Hamitic) Substratum in the Proto-Indo-European Cultural Lexicon?" = *Lingua Posnaniensis* 40 (1998), 141–172.

THOMSEN, M.-L.: *The Sumerian Language*. København, 1984, B. Stougaard Jensen.

TISCHLER, J.: *Hethitisches etymologisches Glossar*. Lieferung 1, 2, 3. Innsbruck, 1977, 1978, 1980, Institut für Sprachwissenschaft der Universität Innsbruck.

TOSCO, M.: *A Grammatical Sketch of Dahalo*. Hamburg, 1991, Helmut Buske Verlag.

TOURNEUX, H.: *Le mulwi ou vulum de Mogroum (Tchad). Langue du groupe musgu–famille tchadique*, Paris, 1978, Centre National de la Recherche Scientifique.

TOURNEUX, H.: *Lexique pratique du munjuk des rizières. Dialecte de Pouss*, Paris, 1991, Librairie Orientaliste Paul Geuthner.

TOURNEUX, H. & SEIGNOBOS, Ch. & LAFARGE, F.: *Les Mbara et leur langue (Tchad)*, Paris, 1986, Société d'Études Linguistiques et Anthropologiques de France.

TURNER, R. L.: *A Comparative Dictionary of the Indo-Aryan Languages. Fasc. I-XI.* London, 1962–1966, Oxford University Press.

TYLOCH, W.: "The Evidence of Proto-Lexicon for the Cultural Background of the Semitic Peoples" = Bynon, J. & Bynon, Th. (eds.): *Hamito-Semitica*, The Hague, 1975, Mouton, pp. 55–61.

VERNER, G. K.: "K probleme germano-enisejskih leksičeskih otnobenij" = *Slavistika. Indoevropeistika. Nostratika. Konferencija k 60-letiju so dnja roždenija V. A. Dybo. Tezisy dokladov*, Moskva, 1991, Institut Slavjanovedenija i Balkanistiki Akademii Nauk SSSR, pp. 42–46.

Wb = Erman, A. & Grapow, H.: *Wörterbuch der ägyptischen Sprache* I-V.[2] Berlin, 1957–1971, Akademie-Verlag.

WÖLFEL, D. J.: "Eurafrikanische Wortschichten als Kulturschichten" = *Acta Salamanticensia, filosofía y letras* 9/1 (1955).

WÖLFEL, J. D.: *Monumenta linguae Canariae. Die kanarischen Sprachdenkmäler. Eine Studie zur Vor- und Frühgeschichte Weißafrikas*, Graz, 1965, Akademische Druck- u. Verlagsanstalt.

WUS = Aistleitner, J.: "Wörterbuch der ugaritischen Sprache" = *Berichte über die Verhandlungen der Sächsischen Akademie der Wissenschaften zu Leipzig, phil.-hist. Klasse* 106/3 (1963).

YOSHIKAWA, M.: "The Marû and Ḫamṭu Aspects in the Sumerian Verbal System" = *Orientalia* 38 (1968), 401–416.

ZALIZNJAK, A. A.: "Materialy dlja izučenija morfologičeskoj struktury drevnegermanskih suščestvitel'nyh" = *Étimologija* (1963).

ZYHLARZ, E.: "Ursprung und Sprachcharakter des Altägyptischen" = *Zeitschrift für Eingeborenen-Sprachen* 23 (1932–1933), 25–45, 81–110, 161–194, 241–254.

Székesfehérvár (Hungary)
Institut für Afrikanische Sprachwissenschaften (Frankfurt)

Three

The Fertile Clash: The Rise of Philosophy in India

Ferenc Ruzsa*

Alien religion in the Veda

It is more or less an accepted fact that philosophy, at least in its earlier stages, is not independent of the religious background on which it grows. It is markedly so in the Indian tradition where all systems—except the little known *lokāyata* materialism—are aiming at salvation or release, *mokṣa, niḥśreyasa, apavarga, kaivalya* or *nirvāṇa*. The terminology may be different, but the fundamental idea, leaving the karmic cycle of transmigration for ever, is the same.

If this connection can be taken for granted it is natural to ask: how did religion influence philosophy? What might have been their connection "at the beginning"? Their contrast seems fairly obvious:

*An earlier version of this paper was read at the 35th International Congress of Asian and North African Studies, Budapest 1997. The underlying research received support from the OTKA fund (research projects T 21224 and T 043629).

religion is normally a relatively rigid, closed system manifested in typically public actions (i.e. ritual) of a community, whereas the very essence of philosophy is that it is an open-ended, private, theoretical enterprise. It is true of course that sometimes philosophy is completely subservient to religion—though in spite of the obvious technical similarities I would hesitate to call this kind of activity 'philosophy' at all. Sometimes philosophers elaborate on originally religious ideas giving them more depth or a more abstract character. And sometimes religion appropriates the philosophers' lines of thinking.

There is another, more interesting and fundamental possibility of contact: philosophy may react to religious conflict. A religion may grow old and get outdated; a typical philosophical reaction to this might be a general scepticism about the existence or at least the importance of the gods or the effectivity of the traditional rites. Something like this may have been going on in ancient India in the post-Vedic age: many people, young and old, left their homes for ever to become wandering religious seekers. This *parivrājaka* or *śramaṇa* movement culminating in the appearance of the Buddha has been seen in this light, i.e. that an essential motivation for their renunciation of the world and also its rites was the unsatisfactoriness of the aged, rigid Vedic ritualism.[1]

Long before that, already in the age of the *R̥g-veda* some people doubted the existence of Indra: "He about whom they ask, 'Where is he?', or they say of him, the terrible one, 'He does not exist', he who diminishes the flourishing wealth of the enemy as gambling does—believe in him! He, my people, is Indra."[2]

[1] RADHAKRISHNAN 147–149, 272–276, 352–360. Nowadays this oversimplified explanation is no longer tenable; cf. PANDE 258–261 and 315–338. For a more detailed account see e.g. OLIVELLE and BRONKHORST.

[2] R̥V II. 12, 5. O'FLAHERTY: 161. The original (Aufrecht's edition, Vol. I, p. 185): *yáṃ smā pr̥chánti kúha séti ghorám utém āhur naíṣó astī́ ty enam / só aryáḥ puṣṭī́r víja ivā́ mināti śrád asmai dhatta sá janāsa índraḥ //*

As this hymn is generally accepted to be quite old,[3] we cannot really think of the Vedic religion already being antiquated; perhaps we should look for another source of this scepticism. Although it seems impossible to prove it, the verse preceding this one seems to give us the clue: "He by whom all these changes were rung, who drove the race of the Dāsas down into obscurity, who took away the flourishing wealth of the enemy as a winning gambler takes the stake—he, my people, is Indra."[4]

The *Dāsás* or *Dásyus*[5] were the black-coloured, snub-nosed[6] people the Aryans found in India.[7] They were rich and civilised and had many cities or forts: "Indra and Agni [Fire], ye cast down the ninety forts which Dāsas held..."[8] Some of them must have been killed or driven out of their land: "For fear of thee forth fled the dark-hued races, scattered abroad, deserting their possessions, / When, glowing, O Vaiśvānara [Fire], for Pūru, thou Agni didst light up and rend their castles. ... Thou dravest Dasyus from

[3]In general the "family books" (II–VIII) are considered the oldest material in the *R̥g-veda-saṁhitā*; among them the VIII. is somewhat later (WITZEL 1997: 261–266).

[4]R̥V II. 12, 4. O'FLAHERTY: 161. In AUFRECHT (Vol. I, p. 185): *yénemā́ víśvā cyávanā kr̥tā́ni yó dā́saṃ várṇam ádharaṃ gúhā́kaḥ / śvaghnī́va yó jigīvā́ṁ lakṣám ā́dad aryáḥ puṣṭā́ni sá janāsa índraḥ //*

[5]On the somewhat vexing question of the relation of these two terms see HILLEBRANDT: Vol. II. 159–160. In general it seems that *dasyu* is used when difference in religion is in the focus, while *dāsa* may be the name of a (hostile) people or a designation of some tribes.

[6]This often repeated characterization (e.g. OLDENBERG: 82) rests upon a single occurrence (R̥V V. 29, 10) of the word *anā́s*, meaning either 'noseless' *(a-nā́s)* or 'mouthless' *(an-ā́s)*: "Thou slewest noseless Dasyus with thy weapon, and in their home o'erthrewest hostile speakers" (GRIFFITH: 249), *anā́so dásyūn̐r amr̥ṇo vadhéna ní duryoṇá āvr̥ṇaṅ mr̥dhrávācaḥ //* (AUFRECHT: Vol. I. 345.) Given the context, 'mouthless'—i.e. unintelligibly speaking—may be more appropriate (cf. HOCK: 156). For a comprehensive account of all the relevant passages on the *Dāsás* and *Dásyus* see MACDONELL–KEITH: Vol. I. 347–349 and 356–358, or, with all details quoted, HALE: 146–169.

[7]More recently Asko Parpola forwarded the theory that the *Dāsás* were not the indigenous black population but an earlier (ca. 2000 BCE) wave of Aryan immigration. For a summary see PARPOLA: 480–481. Hock questions that either *Dāsá* or *Dásyu* could ever be interpreted as racial terms. He tries to explain all references to their being black as having moral or ideological value only

[8]R̥V III. 12, 6. GRIFFITH. 167; in AUFRECHT: Vol. I. 220: *índrāgnī navatím púro dāsápatnīr adhūnutam /*

their home, O Agni, and broughtest forth broad light to light the Ārya."[9] Others were subjugated in great numbers: it is clearly shown by the word *dāsa* later meaning simply a slave or servant.[10]

The spiritual life of the *Dāsás* was markedly different from that of the invaders.[11] They were without rites and ordinances *(akarmán, avratá)*, made no offerings (*áyajvan* or *áyajyu*), said no prayers *(ábrahman)* and they had no gods (*ádeva* or *ádevayu*).[12] We cannot say whether the people who ask where Indra is and even say that he does not exist were these city-dwelling aboriginals

---

[9]R̥V VII. 5, 3&6. GRIFFITH: 336; in AUFRECHT: Vol. II. 6: *tvád bhiyā́ víśa āyann ásiknīr asamanā́ jáhatīr bhójanāni / vaíśvānara pūráve śóśucānaḥ púro yád agne daráyann ádīdeḥ // . . . tvám̐ dásyūm̐r ókaso agna āja urú jyótir janáyann ā́ryāya //*

[10]On this transition of meaning see HILLEBRANDT: Vol. II. 154–157.

[11]The word 'invasion' is highly suspect politically these days; something like migration (or infiltration or diffusion) would seem preferable to many. But I consider it a matter of principle to totally exclude politics from scholarly thinking. I see war and heroism in the *R̥g-veda*, later an Aryan-speaking ruling class in North India. A mere coincidence?

Archaeologists do not find traces of this invasion—nor of an immigration: "far from being an invading race, the Āryas of the Rigveda were a locally emerging ethnic group of northwestern India" (ERDOSY: 46). But I think traces of ancient migrations and invasions are particularly difficult to find (RATNAGAR). If the Aryans did not learn their Indo-European language from imported grammar books, then they did come in; they did meet earlier inhabitants; and they did become the rulers. (Somewhat more exactly: the rulers identified themselves as Aryans, spoke Aryan languages and confessed to practice Aryan religion.)

For some time (again quite implausibly, considering the evidence of the texts) it was thought that the Aryans entered an almost empty country, perhaps half a millennium after the collapse of the Indus Valley Civilization. But now it seems that the Painted Grey Ware (PGW) culture, generally considered to be the product of (late) Vedic Aryans, is in some areas (central Haryana) not separated by any gap from Late Harappan remains; of the 98 known PGW sites here, 34 are on top of Late Harappan sites. "[E]xcavations at Bhagwanpura... have demonsatrated that no chronological gap separates them. ... Thus, there is no 'Vedic night' (FAIRSERVIS 1975) separating the prehistoric/protohistoric from the early historic phases of South Asian culture history." (SHAFFER–LICHTENSTEIN: 255.) I have tried to show elsewhere that from at least late Vedic up to Middle Indo-Aryan *(Mahārāṣṭrī)* a continuous phonetic influence of a Tamil-like language can be demonstrated (RUZSA 2005), suggesting that Vedic Aryans were already in a fairly close contact with the major non-Aryan constituent of Indian culture.

[12]See e.g. R̥V VIII. 59 [=70], 11 or X. 22, 8. For a complete list see HILLEBRANDT: Vol. II. 159–160.

or some Aryans led to scepticism by contact with them. But it can be shown that their ideas did influence the new ruling class and later became a formative element of Hinduism.

First it is important to emphasise that the Dāsás were by no means materialists or atheists in any sense. Sometimes they are called *anyá-vrata*, 'having different ordinances' or performing alien rites;[13] and perhaps they are the enemies noted for their godless magic *(ádevī māyā́)*.[14] Magic[15] is the direct opposite of prayer: "down sink the sorcerer ['having *māyā́*'], the prayerless ['not having *bráhman*'] *Dasyu*."[16] Magic is disreputable, and associated with false gods or scepticism about the gods: "if I worshipped false gods, or considered the gods useless... Let me die at once, if I am a sorcerer [*yātudhā́na*], or if I have burnt up a man's span of life. ... The one who calls me a sorcerer, though I am not a sorcerer, or the one who says he is pure, though he is demonic [*rakṣás*]—let Indra strike him with his great weapon. Let him fall to the lowest depths under all creation."[17] Also the *Dāsá*s are not completely without gods—most scholars[18] would take the expression 'phallus-worshippers' *(śiśná-devāḥ)*[19] to refer to them.

That the 'godless' *Dāsá*s have their own religion is not that surprising. The expression *ádeva* should not be translated as god-

---

[13]R̥V VIII. 70, 11; X. 22, 8; and at V. 20, 2 without specifying that *Dāsá*s or *Dásyu*s are meant.

[14]R̥V VII. 1, 10; VII, 98. 5. At I. 117, 3 the dangerous magic of the *Dásyu (dásyor áśivasya māyā́)* is mentioned, while at VIII. 14, 14. appear "the Dásyus, who wanted to creep up by magic and climb up to the sky" *(māyā́bhir utsísṛpsata[ḥ]... dyā́m ārúrukṣataḥ... dásyūn̐r)*.

[15]By 'magic' I mean a technical manipulation of invisible supernatural forces, as opposed to sacrifice (or rather worship), that is a formal social behaviour towards invisible superhuman beings. The effect of magic is automatic; the consequences of the sacrifice depend on the will of the god. For an overview of the role and value of magic in Vedic society see OLDENBERG: 251–270.

[16]R̥V IV. 16, 9. GRIFFITH: 209; AUFRECHT: Vol. I. 288; *ní māyā́vān ábrahmā dásyur arta //*

[17]R̥V VII. 104, 14–16. O'FLAHERTY: 161; AUFRECHT: Vol. II. 78: (14) *yadi vahám anṛtadeva ā́sa móghaṃ vā devā́ṅ apyūhé agne / ...* (15) *adyā́ murīya yádi yātudhā́no ásmi yádi vā́yus tatápa pū́ruṣasya / ...* (16) *yó mā́yātuṃ yā́tudhānéty ā́ha yó vā rakṣā́ḥ śúcir asmī́ty ā́ha / índras tám hantu mahatā́ vadhéna víśvasya jantór adhamás padīṣṭa //*

[18]See e.g. KEITH: Vol. I. 129; ALLCHIN–ALLCHIN: 154.

[19]R̥V VII. 21, 5; X. 99, 3.

less, rather as having no *devás*. *Devás* are in the narrowest sense a group of Aryan deities, perhaps not even including the *ásuras*.[20] But even the widest meaning of the term never referred to all supernatural agencies; properly only the anthropomorphic, active 'force of nature' gods can be called *devás*, 'brilliant' or 'heavenly'. So the *Dásyus* were not irreligious at all. Their beliefs, as well as their rituals, fundamentally modified those of the conquerors. But how can we add to the rather meagre evidence we could extract from the *R̥g-veda* itself?

Further attempts at a reconstruction

(1) The most obvious way to reconstruct the non-Vedic source(s) of Indian religion is to deduce from the observable changes in the known beliefs and in the ritual. This may seem dangerously circular: we explain changes by supposing a source defined as the source of that change. The hypothesis will be in itself irrefutable and therefore meaningless. But if used with caution and compared with other information the method is valuable. Clearly not anything 'new' (i.e. undocumented in the Vedas) should be considered of foreign origin; but if the new element is not only missing from, but completely alien to the Vedic hymns, or even stands in direct opposition to their ideals, we can safely assume an external source.

(2) Another method is to use archaeological evidence. It seems pretty certain that the *Dāsas* were the inheritors of the Indus Valley Civilisation. Whether they were the originators of that culture is not that clear, but also not so important for the present investigation. As already the first excavator, Sir John Marshall, demonstrated,[21] there were significant motives in the Indus Culture that could not be found in the Vedas but reappeared much later in Hinduism.

---

[20]The *ásuras* seem to be an ancient, moral group of deities, guardians of order and possessors of magic power *(māyā́)*; many of them were also called *ādityás* (HALE: 2, 31–37). Beyond the well recognised difference between devás and ásuras, Oberlies speaks of three religions(!) of the Vedic people: "Die 'Āditya-', die 'Indra-' und die 'Agni-Religion'" (OBERLIES: 345–347).

[21]See ALLCHIN–ALLCHIN: 311–12.

(3) The last approach may seem rather antiquated and hopelessly shaky. Still it cannot be neglected. It consists of pure aprioristic speculation aided by a little comparativism: under the given situation what kind of beliefs must have been held by the people? And what do we find with peoples living in a similar way? Though speculation cannot be considered as data, it helps in understanding the historical processes involved and in explaining at least some of the urges for change. (Also it seems that most historians of ideas have their own speculative background, theoretical approach, interpretative model, set of preconceptions or whatever—then we may as well try to make these explicit rather than trying to hide them.)

If all three sources provide converging results that fit within the textual evidence of the Vedas we will at least have a working hypothesis. In what follows, I will try to show that it is so; and that starting from this hypothesis we can suggest a very basic motive for developing the concept of *Brahman*, the impersonal world-soul.

(1) Starting with the surprising religious developments, the most conspicuous is the appearance of the new gods (Śiva, Kr̥ṣṇa, Rāma, Durgā[22]). They do not belong to the *devas*. They are infinitely more powerful and have a practically monotheistic character. The older devas are almost totally forgotten: their role can be compared to that played by the Greek gods in Renaissance and Baroque art.

The older ritual, the *yajña* offering has been replaced by *pūjā*[23] worship. It was, in fact, a two-step process: first the *yajña* changed its meaning completely and only later went into oblivion. Origin-

[22]Even their names suggest their non-Aryan origin. Kr̥ṣṇa and Rāma, as well as Kālī (another name of Durgā) means simply 'black' (and in iconography they appear in strange —blue and green—, usually dark colours). The name Śiva is normally understood as euphemism (meaning 'benevolent') for the dangerous god Rudra, 'the Howler'; but it is equally possible to take Rudra to mean 'red', and that could be a rendering of the Tamil name of the god, Civa-, 'red / angry' (DEDR 1931). See CHAKRAVARTI: 28, WALKER: Vol. 2. 400.

[23]This name again appears to be Dravidian: Tamil *pūcu* 'besmear, anoint' (DEDR 4352); see BÜHNEMANN: 30. Or it might come from Tamil *pū* 'flower, menstruation' (DEDR 4345) + *cey* 'act' (DEDR 1957); see WALKER: Vol. 2. 252.

ally it was an offering: a call to the gods, an invitation for them to come and partake of the food and drink. It was an effort to win their friendship or at least temporary good-will, so that they would grant the fulfilment of their host's requests. Later, in the age of the *Brāhmaṇas*, it developed into a very complex magic, a purely mechanical technique, a manipulation of hidden forces, in which intentions—including the will of the gods—played no part. The gods were regarded as symbolic entities only.[24] It is extremely strange, perhaps unparalleled in the history of religions, that in spite of this radical change of function and interpretation the same ancient hymns of the *Ṛg-veda* continued to be used—no longer as invocations but rather as spells. In fact it was the perceived magical effect of their sound that lead to the exact preservation of these 3000 year old texts in a purely (and later mostly) oral tradition.

And though the later *pūjā* can be performed in a purely adorational spirit (partly under the influence of the devotional *bhakti* movement, partly in response to the challenges of Islam and Christianity), it has been shown that it originates from agricultural magic.[25] The essential ingredients offered at a *pūjā* are fruits, flowers, leaves, water (in many forms), incense and red powder or paste (symbol of female fertility). Although it is normally done in worship of a god, it is still definitely magical: the idol itself (unknown in the Vedas) is not a symbol only of the divinity, but the god actually enters the *mūrti* (through the *prāṇa-pratiṣṭhā*, 'establishment of life' ritual).[26]

The concept of sexuality in various aspects now totally pervades Hinduism. It is present in Kṛṣṇa's amorous sports with the shepherdesses, in the Śaiva phallus-worship, in the cult of the *yoni* as a symbol of female creative energy, in the appearance of the fearful mother-goddess (Kālī or Durgā), in the Tantric orgies (actual or symbolic) and in the concept of the world-process as the union of the cosmic male and female principles.

[24] KEITH: Vol. I. 257–264 and Vol. II. 379–401. A really surprising outcome of this tendency is that the standard exegetical and philosophical interpretation of the ritual, i.e. the *mīmāṁsā* school is proudly atheistic; see KEITH 1921: 61–64, 74.

[25] CHATTOPADHYAYA: 294–96.

[26] BÜHNEMANN: 52–54, 191–195.

The fate of man is now a beginningless cycle of transmigrations, with the mechanical (therefore impartial and just) system of karmic retributions. As a corollary, the highest aim of man is *mokṣa*, salvation, leaving this cycle and this world for ever. One—perhaps the most important—way to this goal is *yoga*, a rather specific technique of self-sanctification. *Karma* and rebirth motivate *ahiṁsā*, non-injury. Ideally this includes vegetarianism—whereas the Vedic Aryan prized meat above any other food, especially beef (by now an absolute taboo). A bull was also the best sacrifice for his *devas*.

It is clear that viewed through Vedic eyes, the modern Hindu is (like a *Dāsa*) *ayajyu*, *adeva* and *anya-vrata*: not offering (but using magic), not worshipping the *devas* (adoring instead the phallus) and performing different rites.

(2) The material from archaeological finds is most interesting. Though the Harappan script remains undeciphered, it is possible to interpret the material to an extent. Even the sceptical observer can notice[27] the mother-goddess cult: a very great number of clay figurines of women suggest their widespread use in household shrines,[28] and the notable sealing showing a female from whose womb a plant issues can be explained as representing Mother Earth giving birth to vegetation.[29] This can be connected to one form of Durgā, Śākaṁbharī, i.e. 'bearing vegetables'.[30] (The holy fig-tree was already sacred and seems to have been related to the goddess.) Priestly figures on the seals seem to be always female.

The famous proto-Śiva, appearing on several seals, has three faces and a horned headdress; he is sitting on a throne in a *yoga*-position, surrounded by animals worshipping him. His being also a fertility-god is shown by his ithyphallic character. Later Hindu

[27]This is an overstatement. Some cannot or will not. "The ideology ... is striking in the general absence of the pantheism associated with agricultural-village oriented societies. ... Instead, the religious attributes are strongly suggestive of a pastoral ideology." FAIRSERWIS: 63.

[28]"[M]other goddess figurines ... were ubiquitous in all ... centres of the Indus civilisation", except for Kalibangan. KULKE–ROTHERMUND: 24. "[P]resque chaque maison en possédait un exemplaire, qui avait dû être placé dans une niche, le dos au mur". SERGENT: 109.

[29]PIGGOTT: 201.

[30]*Devī Māhātmya* XCII. 43–44, quoted by CHATTOPADHYAYA: 293.

Śiva has four faces towards the four directions (of which only three are visible at a time);[31] he has no horns, but has the crescent moon on his head; he is the great *yogi (mahā-yogin)* and lord of animals *(paśu-pati)*. He is frequently described and shown with an erect phallus, especially by the *pāśupata-lakulīśa* sect.[32] The phallus (and very probably the female organ, in the form of stone rings of different sizes) was also object of separate worship. The bull[33] seems to have been already sacred, though of course it cannot be shown if it was already taboo or not.

Typological speculation

(3) The speculative model[34] starts from the assumption that peoples' beliefs are closely related to their way of life: the social organisation and the mode of production.[35] We know that the Aryans were nomadic herdsmen, while the prehistoric peoples they found in India typically relied on agriculture. Let's consider the possible effects of this difference on their respective religions.

As human infants need the milk and care of their mothers for several years, prehistoric women could survive only by gathering roots, fruits and seeds, while men did the hunting. So cattle-breeding could easily be an invention of men, agriculture that of women.[36]

a) On the grasslands a nomadic tribe can live prosperously on the milk and meat of the cattle, using wool for clothing. Shep-

---

[31]The *Mahābhārata* (I. 203. 20–26) relates the origin of his four faces in the legend of the beautiful maiden Tilottamā; see MANI: 789.

[32]WALKER: 194, CHAKRAVARTI: 124–142 and 164–169.

[33]In modern Hinduism besides the sacred cow/bull, the bull Nandin is Śiva's *vāhana* ('mount', emblematic animal).

[34]I follow loosely CHATTOPADHYAYA. A more recent account can be found in BHATTACHARYYA.

[35]This Marxist term, mode of production, covers the most general features of the way a society produces goods, distributes labour and the goods produced.

[36]Our hypothesis starts here, in the Neolithic. But ideas of a religious character are immensely older, as archaeology amply proves. Specifically the Great Goddess was widely worshipped in the Palaeolithic (GIMBUTAS: 316). Therefore the actual beliefs of the peoples we are trying to understand have already a very long and complex history and we must not expect to find anywhere the 'pure', abstract notional schemes outlined below.

herds or cowherds will be men only. They do the 'important' work and they own the cattle. They want their offspring to inherit their property, therefore a patrilineal lineage will be established – resulting in a strong patriarchal society with subordinate, insignificant women.

When the nomadic man looks at the world, he sees in it forces similar in character to himself. He will find there strong, lonely, impulsive and aggressive males (sometimes in small gangs): they are dangerous like fire on the steppes or the summer hail, but they can be friendly as the sun in spring or the camp-fire. Most of them will be divinities of the sky: Sun, Storm, Rain, Wind. If they have a father, probably it will be the Sky; if they have a king, it will be the one with the strongest weapon, the thunderbolt. When there are goddesses, they are mostly wives only. If the warrior hero has prospects of an after-life, it might be in the company of the gods and fathers, perhaps in heaven.

This is the homely polytheism of the Greeks, Germans, Celts and the Vedic Aryans. It is apt to develop a detailed mythology with lots of adventures, especially wars and robberies. The appropriate ritual is offering meat and wine into the fire which takes the food up into the sky. Its main objective is to win the friendship of the dangerous ones so that they will not harm the worshipper.

b) Where agriculture develops on some fertile land, it will be a far more reliable basis of existence than hunting. As long as it remains in the hands of the discoverer women, it will make them the ruling sex. They will do everything really important: work for food and give birth to the new generations of the tribe. A mother knows who her daughters are and therefore has no need for any strict form of marriage. In this strong version of matriarchy love may remain what it should be, having no economical consequences nor social constraints.

A woman in this society will look at herself and the world as embodiments of the same wonder—fertility. Mother Earth gives birth to the plants and thus supports daily life; women give birth to children and thus sustain the life of the tribe. Fertility is the only force we are concerned with, and it is markedly periodical. Besides the daily cycle of light and darkness (being active and inert in sleep), there is the monthly cycle of the Moon and the woman. The Moon gets round (as if pregnant) and bright, then disappears in darkness. A woman's menstrual blood is a sign of her fertility as well as a symbol of childbirth and also of (violent) death. The yearly cycle of darkness/cold and light/heat is also the life-cycle of the crop. It also approximates the time needed for humans and larger animals to bear offspring. The longest cycle seen is that of life; and there will be great hope of a new start after death, especially if the corpse is deposited into the womb of Mother Earth (possibly in the position of an embryo)—as it happens also with the seed. As the origin of the idea of rebirth is to be found here, also the speculations about larger cycles (world-ages) is also a natural extension of this all-important phenomenon.

As the essence of the whole view is the analogy of the fertility of women and of Nature, the ritual appropriate here is sympathetic magic.[37] In fact sowing itself is a purely magical act. The seed is 'shown' to the earth or rather put into contact with it, hoping that as a result fertile Earth will produce similar seeds. Also there is no-one to pray to. Fertility is an abstract idea. Even Mother Earth is not very personal. She is clearly female, but she does not resemble a human – she is too close, visible and tangible (and too big, in fact universal) to be anthropomorphic. The fitting symbols of fertility that can be used in this magic are woman (real or even rather abstract figurines), blood (or its colour, red), earth and plants.[38] It is only appropriate that the ritual itself is in the hands of women, and the specialists (healers, priestesses, midwifes) will also be females.[39]

This view of the world has certain accidental advantages. Philo-

---

[37]Magic based on the idea that different sorts of relations (similarity, contact, analogy, affinity, being a part of) express fundamental laws of the world. Manipulating one of the related entities, the effect will show on the other as well. Another type, the use of magical spells, starts from the assumption of an essential relation between the ('real') name and its reference.

[38]Many more could be added. Representations of the vulva—in its most abstract, but almost universally known form it is a triangle pointing downwards, sometimes with a dot (embryo or semen) in the middle. An egg or an egg / womb shaped object, e.g. a great nut. Holes and caves. Water, another obvious condition of survival and fertility (fertile earth as well as the female organ is damp). Also trees and snakes—both for their yearly renewal; but on account of their form they are able to represent masculine fertility as well. A very detailed treatment of the ancient European material can be found in GIMBUTAS (see especially 141–159, 316–321).

[39]Later, strongly patriarchal religions will be inclined to consider them

sophically its monism gives a unified picture of the world. The abstract goddess that has only symbols, not images in the strict sense, is more adaptable to later needs. Its magic is not yet very different from real technique and so not at all opposed to science: rather a source of it. (The will of gods can be incalculable, but the secret laws of Nature can be investigated. The strong sense of causality may also be the source of the idea of *karman.*) Also, psychologically it seems quite apt. Mother as the source of personal life; woman's womb as the dark place of birth, death and sexual joy seem to be eternal motifs of our character.

c) Of course men will not like the insignificant position they logically have in such a society. If they can, they will return to the centre. When they learn to use animals (their property) in ploughing, they will gain the upper hand. They will emphasize the role of the seed: woman or earth is only the material, the seed giving the form is the important thing. Without sowing, without the father, there is no reaping, no offspring. The proper child, a son, resembles the father as the crop resembles the seed sown. On the cosmic scale Mother Earth needs Father Sky to fertilize her with rain. His symbols are the phallus (of course: men are so proud of it) and the bull (not only a strong and fertile animal, but also the puller of the plough). The ritual that fits the picture is a real or simulated union of male and female, and the world will be seen as a cosmic sexual act. This is what we find in Tantrism, but traces of this view can be distinctly shown already in the *Brāhmaṇas.*[40] Anthropomorphism is more developed here, especially when the connection of the Great Mother to the earth slackens—then the Goddess will be considered first of all the wife of the far-away Lord.

Another version may be thought of as relatively archaic, on account of its transitional character. Here the maternal-material principle is still the prominent, active factor and quite autonomous. However, she is already considered subordinate to the passive male-spiritual entity whose interest and intentions she serves. This

witches, wielders of black magic, and purify them in the sacrificial fire of their heavenly gods.

[40]KEITH: 351, 476–477.

sort of *sāṁkhya*-type dualism may have originally been appealing especially for the non-working, male ruling class or intelligentsia.

From the point of view of agriculture only, the Indus Civilisation appears to be remarkably archaic. It exploited the yearly flooding of the Indus, and no animals were used in agriculture.[41] So quite possibly, it was still mainly the sphere of women. Therefore we could expect the Great Goddess to be very much in the foreground. But animal husbandry was also very important, and it had been so for the past four millennia. In the society of the cities men were quite probably the political rulers.[42]

As our results do converge, we will assume that the religion of the *Dāsa*s was of the fertility-type. Perhaps the Aryans first met more frequently with the relatively pure Mother Earth-only form: the godless people following alien rites. Later they also noticed the dualist form predominant among the higher strata of society 'whose god is the phallus' (we find only two references to them in the *R̥g-veda*).

Meeting of *Ārya* and *Dasyu*

The reaction of the Aryans to the fertility-religion of the subdued population was first a general rejection, which is what we see most often in the *R̥g-veda.* However, with time they themselves became settled and progressively dependent on agriculture instead of cattle-breeding only.[43] In response they had more need for agricultural magic[44] and less need for their most warlike gods. This accounts for many features of the development of Indian religion,

[41]"In modern practice such land is neither ploughed nor manured, nor does it require additional water." ALLCHIN–ALLCHIN: 260.

[42]The famous 'priest-king' sculpture has no female counterpart; the male god (proto-Śiva) is enthroned, while the goddess is not; the frequently depicted powerful animals are mostly emphatically male (the bull and the bovine 'unicorn' is always so).

[43]Vedic peoples did practise agriculture (e.g. they knew the plough and the sickle), but it was secondary and not highly valued for a long time. RAU: 205.

[44]As the *Dāsa*s became integrated into Aryan society, these rites were no longer practised by hostile peoples. Perhaps they were still not quite respectable in Aryan eyes, but a class fundamental for the survival of the whole community.

some of which were mentioned above; but we are now focusing on the origins of philosophy.

Some late Vedic seers must have perceived the greater explanatory strength of the single, unifying, all-encompassing creative principle, and they tried to import it. Coming from a strongly patriarchal society they abhorred the femaleness of the Fundamental, so they tried to change it into a male.[45] This might be the origin of the Jaina image of the world as a cosmic man.[46] Interestingly enough it is sometimes still conceived of as female.[47]

The same change of sex happened[48] in the famous hymn about

---

[45]Oberlies suggests that the concept of an androgynous primeval being was also formed (p. 380), but his Vedic examples are far from convincing. "Dies[e Welt] fürwahr ist [das Werk] dessen, der Stier und Kuh [zugleich] ist" seems an over-interpretation. *Tád ín nv àsya vṛṣabhásya dhenór ā́ nā́mabhir mamire sákmyaṃ góḥ* / (R̥V III. 38, 7; AUFRECHT: Vol. I. 251) is indeed somewhat obscure; Griffith translates it as "That same companionship of her, the Milch-cow, here with the strong Bull's divers forms they established" (p. 183). It could also mean that "they [the *gandharvas*] formed with names that nature (*sákmya*) of the cow, of the milch cow of this bull."

[46]ZIMMER: 241–248. Jainism is an ancient, non-Vedic religion. Vardhamāna Mahāvīra, who is frequently presented in handbooks as its founder was in all probability a contemporary of the Buddha (late 5th century BCE); but he was only an important saint *(tīrthaṁ-kara)* and reformer of a religion already well-established in East India.

[47]ZIMMER: 259.

[48]Some will object that the central idea of the hymn—the origin of the world from the parts of a primeval giant—is not new in the age discussed but inherited from Indo-European times, as the same is found in the story of the ice-giant Ymir in the old Norse (Icelandic) Edda. This has been excellently presented with plenty of comparative material from other Indo-European sources by Lincoln.

I have tried to show elsewhere (RUZSA 2006) that in spite of the very convincing appearance of the arguments they are inconclusive. The agreement in many details (body–earth, head–sky, eye–sun, bodily fluids–water, breath–wind, hair–plants) does not add to the strength of the argument, as they are just logical constituents of a single image: world – giant. This is (1) true intuitively, and (2) can be experimentally tested. Having asked children and university students, 'If the world arose from the body of a giant, which of his limbs became what?' their answers dominantly gave the details found in the myth. (3) The mythologem is found in other cultures as well (Aztec, native North American, Chinese, Tahitian, Finnish, Mongolian and Sumerian).

The earliest recorded variant of the myth is known from Mesopotamia: the creation of heaven and earth from the two halves of the sea-monster Ti'āmat, mother of all. On the other hand the idea does not appear in the earliest recorded Indo-European cosmogonies. In India, we find it only in the latest

the cosmic Man, the *Puruṣa-sūkta*: "It is the Man [*púruṣa*] who is all this, whatever has been and whatever is to be."[49] Through sacrificing this gigantic person "born at the beginning",[50] all the components of the ordered cosmos originate(d), including social order.

It is noteworthy that in this hymn there are also other signs of adaptation to the 'aboriginals'. Besides the much emphasized derivation of the four classes (*varṇas*),[51] it is clear that here the sacrifice is already magic and not an offering.[52] It is the *devás* who perform it with the cosmic Man, so there is no-one to offer it to;[53] and in fact they themselves are born in consequence of the sacrifice. The cyclicity of the fertility-cult is manifest at other places as well: the year is referred to,[54] and the perplexing 'from the daughter the father was born'-idea is put forward.[55]

Perhaps the same trend with progressive personification is visible in the later gods Prajā-pati, Lord of Offspring and Pitā-mahā, Great Father.

This effort, however, is fundamentally flawed. The high explanatory power of the Great Mother lies precisely in her being a female. By converting her into a Man, the image either becomes

---

stratum of the *Ṛg-veda*. So if the Puruṣa-myth is not an independent, local development, it could still be an (indirect) Mesopotamian import as well.

[49]ṚV X. 90, 2. O'FLAHERTY: 30; AUFRECHT: Vol. II. 377: *púruṣa evédáṃ sárvaṃ yád bhūtáṃ yác ca bhávyam* /

[50]ṚV X. 90, 7. O'FLAHERTY: 30; AUFRECHT: Vol. II. 378: *jātám agratáḥ*.

[51]Of which the lowest, the feet of the society-Man, the *śūdra* class is definitely non-Aryan, and remains excluded from Vedic ritual up to the present day.

[52]Perhaps it is not purely accidental that this Vedic hymn is still widely used in *pūjā* ritual (BÜHNEMANN: 68).

[53]Delighting in the paradox (quite appropriate to the transcendent): "With the sacrifice the gods sacrificed to the sacrifice." (ṚV X. 90, 16, O'FLAHERTY: 30; AUFRECHT: Vol. II. 378: *yajñéna yajñám ayajanta devā́s*).

[54]ṚV X. 90, 6: "When the gods spread the sacrifice with the Man as the offering, spring was the clarified butter, summer the fuel, autumn the oblation." O'FLAHERTY: 30; AUFRECHT: Vol. II. 378: *yát púruṣeṇa havíṣā devā́ yajñám átanvata / vasantó asyāsīd ā́jyaṃ grīṣmá idhmáḥ śarád dhavíḥ //*

[55]ṚV X. 90, 5: "From him Virāj was born, and from Virāj came the Man." O'FLAHERTY: 30; AUFRECHT: Vol. II. 378: *tásmād virā́ḻ ajāyata virā́jo ádhi pū́ruṣaḥ* / The gender of Virā́j, 'sovereign' is indeterminate. In the use of the word *ajāyata*, 'was born' the femineity (and especially the parthenogenetic power) of both principles is shown.

ridiculously incoherent or most of its force gets lost. But there is another, more difficult but fruitful way of solving the gender conflict, that of further abstraction: neither male nor female, an abstract principle of fertility or creation, the neuter and impersonal One.

The break with anthropomorphism

This is, in fact, what we find in the beautiful Hymn of Creation, the *Nāsadīya-sūkta* (R̥V X. 129). That One *(tád ékam)* coming into being *(ābhú)* was neither existent nor non-existent *(nā́sad āsīn nó sád āsīt)*; it was darkness hidden by darkness *(táma āsīt támasā gūḷhám)*, undistinguished water *(apraketáṁ salilám)* covered by void *(tuchyám)*—all carefully selected words of the neuter gender. But it is not the result of modern philosophical speculation; it is most closely tied up with the ancient fertility view. It is clearly alive: "That one breathed, windless, by its own energy";[56] "that One arose through the power of heat."[57] It was born *(ajāyata)*, desire *(kā́ma)* came upon it, and that was the first seed *(rétas)* of mind.

Also the dual-copulative vision of the world is detectable: "Was there below? Was there above? There were seed-placers; there were powers. There was energy beneath, there was impulse above."[58] The impulsive seed-placer above is an echo of the Sky-father; the power (*mahimán*, 'greatness') or energy (*svadhā́*, 'internal inclination') below is the maternal fertility of the Earth. Notably these two feminine fertility-expressions were already applied to the original neutral one (in verses 2 and 3). So this abstract entity here shows clear traces not only of being generally connected to the fertility-view, but especially of having been de-

[56] After MACDONELL: 208–210; AUFRECHT: Vol. II. 420: *ā́nīd avātáṃ svadháyā tád ékaṃ.*

[57] MACDONELL: 209; AUFRECHT: Vol. II. 420: *tápasas tán mahinā́jāyataíkam //*

[58] Combined from MACDONELL: 210 and O'FLAHERTY: 25. In AUFRECHT: (Vol. II. 421): *adháḥ svid āsí3d upári svid āsī3t / retodhā́ āsan mahimā́na āsan svadhā́ avástāt práyatiḥ parástāt //* (In the printed text the first *āsí3t* is without an accent *(āsī3d)* and the second *āsan* appears as *āsant*. Here I follow MACDONELL: 210).

veloped out of the feminine principle. The Aryan gods are insignificant compared to this One: "The gods came afterwards, with the creation of this universe."[59]

In the famous sixth chapter of the *Chāndogya-upaniṣad*, where Uddālaka Āruṇi teaches his son Śvetaketu the last truths, the Absolute is called Existent *(sat)* and One *(eka)*. That this is a material, fertile principle is shown by heat, water and food being born from it (both the masculine √*sṛj*, 'emit' and the feminine √*jan* 'be born' are used). These three forms *(rūpas)* together constitute everything in the world. They are rather alive: they determine the different ways of reproduction (from an egg, from a living being, from a sprout); and in man, they form flesh, blood and marrow, etc. They are also connected to the cyclicity of nature: they represent the hot, the rainy and the harvest-season, i.e.—taken together—the Indian year.[60]

The world is a modification *(vikāra)* of this One substrate, not an illusion. That interpretation, initiated by Śaṅkara, is based on a misunderstanding. The famous *vācārambhaṇaṁ vikāro nāmadheyam* does not mean: "the modification [is] only a name arising from speech",[61] rather that "speech grasps first the modification and uses this as name."[62] The Existent is alive, or rather it is life itself pervading all living beings. The simile, tellingly, is a tree, in which the life-sap pervades all branches. In the other agricultural illustration, that of the fig-tree, the emphasis is on the masculine seed-aspect. It is the invisible essence of the small seed that determines the structure of the gigantic tree.

Here we find a more conscious effort at overcoming the duality of the fertility-concept[63] and incorporating both its aspects, the material and the formal/spiritual into the One neuter principle that is called in other *Upaniṣads* the *Brahman*. This name itself shows the origin of the concept in the magical word-view. In the older texts *bráhman* means *mantra*, i.e. magical spell, and

---

[59] O'FLAHERTY: 25; AUFRECHT: Vol. II. 421: *arvā́g devā́ asyá visárjanena.*

[60] VAN BUITENEN: 91–92.

[61] RADHAKRISHNAN 1953: 446–447.

[62] A detailed argument can be found in RUZSA 2004.

[63] "There was only the existent, single, without a second" (*Chāndogya-upaniṣad* VI.2.1: *sad eva... āsīd, ekam eva, a-dvitīyam*), i.e. it had no mate.

the power of the sacrifice[64] (i.e. magical force). Also the term *upaniṣad* (and also *upāsanā*, 'meditative worship') originally denotes a fundamentally magical concept, homologization: connecting two items, one on the cosmic / divine, one on the personal / human plane.[65] In fact 'the central teaching of the *Upaniṣads*', the identity of *Brahman* and *ātman* is nothing but a full homologization of the cosmic and individual essence.

Conclusion

In what has been said above I have added many details, some of which may seem more probable than others, and some of which may need revision in the future. So it is perhaps not out of place here to re-state the central tenet of this paper that may still be accepted in spite of disagreement over many minor points of interpretation and analysis.

The origin of the abstract and universal philosophical concept of *Brahman* is not a linear internal development of the Vedic Weltanschauung: its roots are to be found in the deanthropomorphising of the (essentially non-Vedic) Earth Goddess. The motive for this change might have been the alienness of the fertility-cult and its image of the dominating Great Mother to the Aryans.

It is perhaps worthy of remark that in ancient Greece a similar process may have lead to the birth of philosophical thought. Indo-Europeans with a religion very similar to that of the Aryans conquered a people where the cult of the Great Goddess was still very much alive, and the interaction of the two religions is well documented in the historical records.[66] Is it possible that we found a key to the question: why is philosophy not present in most civilizations? Maybe because they did not have to face a similar conflict of these two basic types of religious understanding of the world?

1997–2005.

---

[64] Already in the *R̥g-veda*, see GRASSMANN: 916.
[65] OLIVELLE 1998: 24.
[66] GIMBUTAS: 318.

Bibliography

ALLCHIN–ALLCHIN: Bridget and Raymond ALLCHIN, *The Birth of Indian Civilization. India and Pakistan before 500 B.C.* Penguin Books 1968.

AUFRECHT, Theodor. *Die Hymnen des Ṛigveda*, Herausgegeben von –, Berlin, 1861-63.

BHATTACHARYYA, Narendra Nath. *The Indian Mother Goddess*, Delhi, 1977.[2]

BRONKHORST, Johannes. *The Two Sources of Indian Asceticism*, Delhi, 1998.[2]

BRONKHORST–DESHPANDE: Johannes BRONKHORST and Madhav DESHPANDE (eds.), *Aryan and Non-Aryan in South Asia. Evidence, Interpretation and Ideology*, Harvard Oriental Series, Opera Minora 3, Cambridge, 1999.

BÜHNEMANN, Gudrun. *Pūjā. A Study in Smārta Ritual*, Vienna, 1988.

VAN BUITENEN, J. A. B. "Studies in Sāṁkhya (III)" in: *Journal of the American Oriental Society* LXXVII (1957), pp. 88–107.

CHAKRAVARTI, Mahadev. *The Concept of Rudra-Śiva through the Ages*, Delhi, 1994[2], repr. 2002.

CHATTOPADHYAYA, Debiprasad. *Lokāyata. A Study in Ancient Indian Materialism*, Delhi, 1959.

DEDR: T. BURROW and M.B. EMENEAU, *A Dravidian Etymological Dictionary*, Oxford, 1984.[2]

ERDOSY, Erdosy. "The archæology of early Buddhism" in: N.K. WAGLE and F. WATANABE (eds.), *Studies on Buddhism in Honour of Professor A.K. Warder*, Toronto, 1993, pp. 40–56. (Quoted in Johannes Bronkhorst: "Is there an inner conflict of tradition?" (p. 48) in BRONKHORST–DESHPANDE, pp. 33–57.)

FAIRSERWIS, Walter S. 1975. *The Roots of Ancient India*, Chicago, 1975. (Quoted in SHAFFER–LICHTENSTEIN, p. 255.)

FAIRSERWIS, Walter S. "The Harappan Civilization and the R̥g-veda" in: WITZEL, pp. 61–68.

GIMBUTAS, Marija. *The Language of the Goddess*, Thames & Hudson, 1989 (repr. 2001).

GRASSMANN, Hermann. *Wörterbuch zum Rig-Veda*, Leipzig, 1873; reprint Delhi, 1999.

GRIFFITH, Ralph T. H. *The Hymns of the Ṛgveda*. Translated with a Popular Commentary by –. Edited by Prof. J. L. Shastri, Motilal Banarsidass, Delhi, 1973 (repr. 1995).

HALE, Wash Edward. *Ásura in Early Vedic Religion*, Delhi, 1986 (repr. 1999).

HILLEBRANDT, Alfred Hillebrandt. *Vedic Mythology*, Delhi, 1999.[3] (Originally *Vedische Mythologie*, Breslau, 1927–29.[2])

HOCK, Hans Heinrich. "Through a glass darkly: Modern 'racial' interpretations vs. textual and general prehistoric evidence on ārya and dāsa/dasyu in Vedic society" in BRONKHORST–DESHPANDE, pp. 145–174.

KEITH, Arthur Berriedale. THE RELIGION AND PHILOSOPHY OF THE VEDA AND UPANISHADS, Harvard Oriental Series XXXI-XXXII, 1925; reprint Delhi 1989.

KEITH, A. Berriedale 1921. *The Karma-Mīmāṁsā*, The Heritage of India Series, 1921; reprint Delhi, 1978.

KULKE–ROTHERMUND: Hermann KULKE and Dietmar ROTHERMUND, *A History of India*, Routledge, 1998.[3]

LINCOLN, Bruce. *Myth, Cosmos and Society. Indo-European Themes of Creation and Destruction*, Harvard U.P. 1986.

MACDONELL, Arthur Anthony. *A Vedic Reader for Students*, Oxford, 1917; reprint Delhi, 1995.

MACDONELL–KEITH: Arthur Anthony MACDONELL and Arthur Berriedale KEITH: *Vedic Index of Names and Subjects*, London, 1912; reprint Delhi, 1995.

The Mahābhārata, Text as Constituted in the Critical Edition. Vol. I, Poona, 1971.

MANI, Vettam. *Purāṇic Encyclopaedia. A comprehensive Work with Special Reference to the Epic and Purānic Literature*, Delhi, 1975, repr. 1998.

OBERLIES, Thomas. *Die Religion des Ṛgveda*, Wien, 1998.

O'FLAHERTY, Wendy Doniger. *The Rig Veda. An Anthology. One hundred and eight hymns, selected, translated and annotated by –*, Penguin Classics, London &c., 1981.

OLDENBERG, Hermann. *The Religion of the Veda*, Delhi, 1988. (Originally *Die Religion des Veda*, Berlin, 1916[2])

OLIVELLE, Patrick. *The Āśrama System. The History and Hermeneutics of a Religious Institution*, Oxford U.P. 1993.

OLIVELLE, Patrick 1998. *The Early Upaniṣads. Annotated Text and Translation*, Oxford U.P. 1998.

PANDE, Govind Chandra. *Studies in the Origins of Buddhism*, Delhi, 1995.[4]

PARPOLA, Asko. "From Archaelogy to a Stratigraphy of Vedic Syncretism: The banyan tree and the water buffalo as Harappan-Dravidian symbols of royalty, inherited in succesion by Yama, Varuṇa and Indra, divine kings of the first three layers of Aryan speakers in South Asia." in: Arlo Griffiths & Jan E.M. Houben (eds), *The Vedas. Text, Language & Ritual*, Groningen, 2004, pp. 479–515.

PIGGOTT, Stuart. *Prehistoric India*, Pelican Books, 1950.

RADHAKRISHNAN, S. 1994. *Indian Philosophy*, Repr. Delhi, 1994.

RADHAKRISHNAN, S. 1953. *The Principal Upanishads. Edited with introduction, text, translation and notes by –*, Oxford U.P. 1953; reprint Delhi, 1992.

RATNAGAR, Shereen. "Does Archæology Hold the Answers?" in: BRONKHORST–DESHPANDE, pp. 207–238.

RAU, Wilhelm. "The earliest Literary Evidence for Permanent Vedic Settlements" in: WITZEL, pp. 203–206.

RUZSA, Ferenc 2004. "The meaning of Āruṇi's promise." in: *Indologica Taurinensia* 30, 229–235.

RUZSA, Ferenc 2005. "A tamil nyelv és az indoárja hangfejlődés" [Tamil and the development of the Indo-Aryan sound system] in: Felföldi Szabolcs (ed.): *Abhivādana. Tanulmányok a hatvanéves Wojtilla Gyula tiszteletére*, Szeged, 265–273.

RUZSA, Ferenc 2006. "Puruṣa és Ymir" in *Keréknyomok* 1 (in press). (Also paper presented at the 13th WSC: "Is the Cosmic Giant an Indo-European myth?")

SERGENT, Bernard. *Genèse de l'Inde*, Paris, 1997.

SHAFFER–LICHTENSTEIN: Jim G. SHAFFER and Diane A. LICHTENSTEIN: "Migration, Philology and South Asian Archæology" in: BRONKHORST–DESHPANDE, pp. 239–260.

WALKER, Benjamin. *Hindu World. An Encyclopedic Survey of Hinduism*, Allen & Unwin, 1968, repr. Delhi 1995.

WITZEL, Michael. (ed.) *Inside the Texts, Beyond the Texts. New Approaches to the Study of the Vedas*, Harvard Oriental Series, Opera Minora 2. Cambridge, 1997.

WITZEL, Michael 1997. "The Development of the Vedic Canon and its Schools: The Social and Political Milieu" in: WITZEL, pp. 257–345.

ZIMMER, Heinrich. *Philosophies of India*, edited by Joseph Campbell, Bollingen Series XXVI (1951); Princeton, 1969.[4]

Four

A Curious Play (*kim api rūpakam*): Bhaṭṭa Jayanta's *Āgamaḍambara* in the Light of Classical Indian Dramaturgy

Csaba Dezső*

Considering the fact that fate was not merciful to such celebrated and outstanding plays as Viśākhadeva's *Devīcandragupta*, and that whole dramatic genres such as the *vīthī* survive only in meagre quotations (apart from its late 'reincarnation' in an altered form),[1] we should be grateful to the Jains of Gujarat who

*I gratefully dedicate this article to my first Sanskrit teacher, Prof. Csaba Töttössy. My heartfelt thanks go to my DPhil supervisor Professor Alexis Sanderson of All Souls College, who has been invariably generous in sharing his vast knowledge and his materials, and to Dr. Harunaga Isaacson, who tirelessly corrected my mistakes and helped me in every way both during and after the period of his supervision. I owe a debt of gratitude to many fellow Indologists for their contributions: Dr. James Benson, Dr. Dominic Goodall, Dr. Eivind Kahrs, Dr. Kei Kataoka, Dr. Somdev Vasudeva, Dr. Alex Watson.

[1] Cf. Raghavan 1978, pp. 872ff.

preserved, thanks to their commendable diligence and curiosity, a unique college-drama written by Bhaṭṭa Jayanta, the eminent ninth century Kashmirian *naiyāyika* philosopher, which gives a comprehensive picture of the contemporary religious debates as well as the 'Religionspolitik' of the royal court. The dramatic qualities of the *Āgamaḍambara*[2] leave much to be desired by classical Indian standards of dramaturgy. As Raghavan remarks in his introduction, 'when he [Jayanta] made his debut on the stage with this new play of his, he knew he was making the pandits of Nāṭya Śāstra prick their ears.'[3] In this paper we shall examine what makes Jayanta's play so unique and unorthodox. First we shall deal with the Prologue, which already reads as a parody of a traditional *prastāvanā*. A closer look will, however, reveal that although Jayanta was using the standard introductory devices in a novel way, his Prologue, in spite of all its strangeness, alludes elegantly both to the plot and the leading aesthetic relish of the play. Then we shall consider the phenomenon of 'philosophical plays' in the light of the discussions on the nature and relation of poetry and *śāstra*, doctrinal or scientific literature. Finally we shall study the predominant *rasa* of the *Āgamaḍambara*.

1.

Indian dramatists had an excellent means with which they could gently introduce the spectators to the world of the play. The prologue (*prastāvanā, sthāpanā* or *āmukha*) of a classical Indian play provides information about the author, the story, the characters, and the main sentiment or savour the audience is going to relish during the performance. In usual practice the Director (*sūtradhāra*) enters the stage after the preliminaries (*pūrvaraṅga*) are over and the initial benediction (*nāndī*) has been recited. In the Bhāsa-plays he is just about to make an announcement when a sound coming from off-stage interrupts him and at the same time

[2] A new critical edition of Jayanta's play prepared by the present author (see DEZSŐ 2004) is downloadable from the CSL website (www.claysanskritlibrary.org/extras.php). For an English translation see DEZSŐ 2005.

[3] *Āgamaḍambara (ed. pr.)*, p.viii.

introduces the first character who is about to enter the stage. In other plays the Director has a chat with an actress (*naṭī*), who is also his wife, or the comic actor (*vidūṣaka*), or an assistant (*pāripārśvika*) about the actual occasion of the performance, the qualities of the sponsor, the author, and the audience, then sometimes about domestic matters, which turn out to be similar to the story of the play. The end of the prologue is always linked in a more or less direct way to the plot: the Director infers from some noise that one of the characters is about to enter, sometimes because he has overheard (and misunderstood, as in the *Mudrārākṣasa*) the words of the *sūtradhāra*.

The prologue can be defined in semiotical terms as one of the 'rhetorical' or 'presentational' devices that draw the attention of the audience to the theatrical and dramatic realities, to the fact that what is going on is actually a performance. Although they appear outside the theatrical frame, in fact they confirm it 'by pointing out the pure facticity of the representation'.[4] To employ another method of analysis,[5] the prologue with the actor talking to another actor about the play to be performed and about (or to) the audience whose favour is to be gained, appears to belong to the actual world, as opposed to the world of the drama. At the end of the Sanskrit *prastāvanā*, the two worlds almost seem to merge: the action happening off-stage and already inside the drama-world, e.g. the crying of the *apsaras*es because the demons have kidnapped Urvaśī, is *audible* for the Director, just as the words said by the *sūtradhāra*, e.g. reciting a verse about the eclipse of the moon (*candrasya grahaṇam*), can be *overheard* by a character belonging to the world of the play. This proximity of the two worlds ensures the smooth transition of the audience between the actual and the fictitious worlds, but in a way that the two worlds are kept separate: the Director exits before the *apsaras*es or Cāṇakya enter.

'But surely', one might object, 'the Director, the Actress, and the Assistant all say the words contained in their script, they also play rôles, how could they belong to the actual world?' The ob-

[4] ELAM 1997, p. 90. Other 'presentational' devices are e.g. the epilogue, the induction, the play-within-the-play, the aside directed to the audience, etc.

[5] ELAM 1997, pp. 99ff.

jection is correct: the *prastāvanā* is certainly part of the play. In it the drama-world is disguised as the actual world. The *sūtradhāra* is a character just like Cāṇakya; he is never the actual referent but only a possible surrogate, even if he is played by the actual director.[6] Abhinavagupta has already observed this with his usual acumen in his commentary to the *Nāṭyaśāstra*. He observes that one of the obstacles to aesthetic experience is 'one's emotional response to pleasure and pain even if it is restricted to another person' (*paragatatvaniyamabhājām api sukhaduḥkhānāṃ saṃvedane*). The solution is the blurring of the actual identity of that 'other person': the costume and other theatrical conventions hide the 'actor-ness' of the actors, which has, however, been revealed in the preliminaries and the prologue (*pūrvaraṅgāniguhanena prastāvanāvalokanena ca ... naṭarūpatādhigamas*).[7]

So far so good. But why does Bharata describe the *prastāvanā* twice in the *Nāṭyaśāstra*: once as part of the *pūrvaraṅga*, and for the second time as part of the *bhāratī vṛtti* (the dramatic style in which the verbal aspect is predominant)? Abhinavagupta has the following answer:[8]

> *dvividhā prastāvanā bhavati—pūrvaraṅgasyāṅgabhūtā anyasya vā| tatra pūrvaraṅgāṅge *'syāṃ* (GOS : *'syāḥ* Parimal) *kavir udāsīnaḥ| sthāpaka eva svatantro nirmā*tāstv* (conj. : °*tā tv* eds.) *anyo vā kavir dhruvāgānādāv api|* (...) *sā dvitīyā yā vṛttibhedamadhye paṭhitā| evaṃ prarocanādāv api mantavyam| yad āha—"tatra *kadā cit* (conj. : *kā cit* eds.) *kāvyābhimukhaṃ nīyate pūrvaraṅgavidhiḥ tadabhimukhaṃ vā kāvyārambhas, tad bhavati sā dvividhā" *ityādi* (GOS : *ityādiḥ* Parimal)|
>
> The prologue is of two kinds: that which is part of the preliminaries, and [that which is part] of something else. Of these two, the poet is not involved in that

[6] Cf. ELAM 1997, pp. 109f.

[7] *Abhinavabhāratī* (Parimal), vol. I, p. 279; *Abhinavabhāratī* (GOS), vol. I, p. 274; GNOLI 1968, pp. 15f., cf. also *Abhinavabhāratī* (Parimal), vol. I, p. 251; *Abhinavabhāratī* (GOS), vol. I, pp. 244f.

[8] *Abhinavabhāratī* (GOS), vol. I, pp. 247f., *Abhinavabhāratī* (Parimal), vol. I, p. 254.

> one which is part of the preliminaries. The *sthāpaka* may be its independent composer, or another poet, as well as in the case of the *dhruvā*-songs. (...) The second kind [of prologue] is that which is mentioned among the varieties of dramatic style. The same should be held about the exciting of the spectators' interest, etc. As [someone] said: "There [in the prologue] sometimes the performance of the preliminaries is directed towards the play [i.e. the drama written by the playwright], or the beginning of the play [is directed] towards that [i.e. the preliminaries]. Therefore it [the *prastāvanā*] is of two kinds.", and so forth.

Commenting on the second occurrence of the prologue in the *Nāṭyaśāstra*, Abhinava says:[9]

> *evaṃ ca yadā sthāpako 'pi sūtradhāratulyaguṇākāro rāmādivad eva prayujyate tad *eva* (conj. : *evaṃ* eds.) *kavikṛtam āmukhaṃ bhavati|*
>
> And thus, when the *sthāpaka*, having similar qualities and bearing as the *sūtradhāra*, is also presented on the stage like Rāma and other [characters], that alone is the prologue written by the poet.

What we have in practice is essentially the latter kind of prologue. All the existing Sanskrit (and Prakrit) plays begin with a *prastāvanā, āmukha,* or *sthāpanā*, and it is unlikely that any of these prologues preserve the impromptu (or precomposed) introduction by a director. But precisely because the actors appear *as actors* in the prologue, the audience perceives their performance *as if* it were part of the actual world. This enables the poet to address the audience through the Director: he can introduce (or even praise) himself and the merits of his play, or he can defend his work against its critics. Since the prologue has metadramatic

[9] *Abhinavabhāratī* (GOS), vol. III, p. 93, *Abhinavabhāratī* (Parimal), vol. III, p. 89; cf. *Nāṭyadarpaṇa*, p. 136: *kadā cit tu sanāndīkaṃ raṅgam anuṣṭhāya viśrānte sūtradhāre tattulyaguṇākṛtiḥ sthāpaka āmukham anutiṣṭhati| tathā cānaṅgavatyāṃ nāṭikāyām dṛśyate—pūrvaraṅgānte sthāpakaḥ| atra ca pakṣe āmukhānuṣṭhāne 'pi kaver vyāpāraḥ, sthāpakasya sūtradhārānukāriṇo rāmānukāriṇo naṭasyeva kavinaiva praveśāt|*

functions, that is, it focuses the attention of the audience on the theatrical and dramatic realities, it also provides an excellent opportunity for the playwright to 'talk shop': he can define his position on dramaturgical questions, on the justification of dramatic art, or on the relation between the actual world and the drama-world. The *prastāvanā* of the *Āgamaḍambara*, however unusual it may seem at first sight, fulfills these functions of the prologue of a classical Indian play.

2.

But at first sight it *is* a very strange prologue. At the beginning of an ordinary Sanskrit play, the Director usually enters the stage in high spirits. He feels happy and honoured to put on the most excellent play of the most excellent poet to the most excellent audience, not to mention the most distinguished sponsor. Certainly there are individual differences among the playwrights: Rājaśekhara has a particular weakness for self-admiration (*yad vā kiṃ vinayoktibhiḥ?*),[10] while Kālidāsa vindicates a place for himself with proper pride by the side of his glorious predecessors. The criticisms against his art seem to cut Bhavabhūti to the quick, but he is confident that the merits of his plays are conceded by some people, or at least will be acknowledged in the future. The Director in Śyāmilaka's *bhāṇa* summons the wet blankets and hypocrites to leave, because the wags want to enjoy the performance. A typical example of the *sūtradhāra*'s efforts to kindle the interest of the spectators in the poet and his work is found in the plays of king Harṣa:[11]

> *śrīharṣo nipuṇaḥ kaviḥ pariṣad apy eṣā guṇagrāhiṇī*
> *loke hāri ca vatsarājacaritaṃ nāṭye ca dakṣā vayam|*
> *vastv ekaikam apīha vāñcitaphalaprāpteḥ padaṃ kiṃ punar*
> *madbhāgyopacayād ayaṃ samuditaḥ sarvo guṇānāṃ gaṇaḥ||*

---

[10] *Bālabhārata*, verse 5.

[11] *Ratnāvalī*, p. 327, also found in *Priyadarśikā* and *Nāgānanda*.

> The illustrious Harṣa is a clever poet, and this audience can appreciate the merits [of one's art]. The story of King Vatsa has a grip on people, and we are experts in theatrical art. Each one [of the above] facts could be the cause of obtaining the desired result on the present occasion, how much more this whole group of merits which has arisen due to the accumulation of my good fortune?

In glaring contrast with the confidence of an average *prastāvanā*, Jayanta's play promises to be a dead frost right in the beginning. The Director does not beam on the audience as usual, on the contrary, he is utterly fed up with his profession and tired of life in general. Moreover, he is supposed to stage a trashy play of a dilettante poet (Jayanta), and it is insufficient solace for him that the audience is equally dilettante (students of philosophy).

However if we examine the prologue of the *Āgamaḍambara* closely we shall discover that Jayanta achieved his highly unconventional *prastāvanā* by utilising entirely conventional techniques. The *Nāṭyadarpaṇa* mentions several established methods of transition from the (pseudo-real) world of the prologue to that of the drama. One of these methods is the *avalagita*, which is defined by some theoreticians as follows: 'doing something else having entrusted one's own occupation to another character'.[12] The example which is cited to illustrate this dramatic device is strikingly similar to what happens in the prologue of Jayanta's play:

> *yathā kṛtyārāvaṇasyāmukhe—*
> *sūtradhāraḥ (niḥśvasya)—ārye, nanu bravīmi,*
> *vākprapañcaikasāreṇa nirviśeṣālpavṛttinā|*
> *svāmineva naṭatvena nirviṇṇāḥ sarvathā vayam||*
> *tad gacchatu bhavatī putram mitraṃ vā kamapi puras-*
> *kṛtya kramāgatām imāṃ kujīvikām anuvartayitum|*
> *tataḥ kramād āha—*
> *parigrahorugrāhaughād gṛhasaṃsārasāgarāt|*
> *bandhusnehamahāvartād idam uttīrya gamyate||*

[12] *Nāṭyadarpaṇa*, p. 132: *ke cit tu pātrāntare svavyāpāram nikṣipya yat kāryāntarakaraṇaṃ tad avalagitam ity āhuḥ|*

atra svajīvikāṃ dāreṣu nikṣipya paralokahetukāryakaraṇaṃ svayam āśritam|

As in the prologue of the *Kṛtyārāvaṇa*:
'DIRECTOR (*sighing*). Why, I'll tell you, my lady.
I have become completely disillusioned with [my profession of] being an actor, which only consists of verbosity and the moods of which are wishy-washy and trivial, as if with a boss *whose tongue is always wagging and who gives a small salary without any discrimination [among his employees].*
So, my lady, please carry on with this wretched profession I inherited, and put at the head [of the troupe] anyone, [either] a son or a friend.'
Later on he says:
'Here I go ashore from the ocean of secular life in the household, which abounds in large crocodiles: the members of my family, and has great whirlpools: the affections for one's relatives.'
Here [in this prologue the director] entrusts his own profession on his wife and becomes himself engaged in an activity which is a means of [attaining a better] afterlife.

Judging from its fragments surviving in quotations, the *Kṛtyārāvaṇa* must have been a remarkable play. It was well-known in Kashmir, and Śaṅkuka quoted from its sixth act, which means that Jayanta might also have been familiar with it.[13] But already the prologue of king Harṣa's play, the *Nāgānanda*, contains a very similar scene. The director's wife tells her husband that his parents have renounced this world and left for the forest. The Director is deeply moved by this news and is ready to give up his inherited wealth (*tyaktvaiśvaryaṃ kramāgatam*) and follow his parents, just as Jīmūtavāhana, the hero of the play, relinquishes his kingdom to serve his parents in the forest. We can trace this motif back as far as the *Lokānanda*, a Buddhist play by Candragomin sur-

[13] *Abhinavabhāratī* ad *Nāṭyaśāstra* 19.88 (ed. Parimal, vol. III, p. 52), pointed out by Raghavan (Some lost Rāma plays, p.30). On Śaṅkuka's date see p. 107.

viving only in Tibetan translation.[14] The *Nāgānanda* is a play in which quietude (*śānta*) is the leading aesthetic relish, which is well suggested by the resigned, disillusioned attitude of the Director. The *Lokānanda*, apart from being also a *śāntarasa*-play, is called '*nāṭaka-śāstra*' (*zlos gar gyi bstan bcos*) in its colophon,[15] that is a play in which a doctrinal subject (the Buddha's teaching in this case) is introduced. The *Āgamaḍambara* was perhaps the first classical Indian play which had *śānta* as its dominant *rasa* and which presented the teachings of various religions, but definitely not from the Buddhist perspective.

Apart from such introductory devices as the *avalagita*, the entire behaviour of the actors conversing in the Prologue foretells in many ways the story of the actual play. Sometimes the actors tell us explicitly which role they are going to take, and the Director often becomes the protagonist, as for instance in the *Priyadarśikā*,[16] or one of the first characters who enter the stage.[17] Therefore it is very tempting to imagine that in the *Āgamaḍambara* the Director re-enters after the Prologue as the Vedic graduate and the Assistant as the Boy, his sidekick. The Director gives up his profession with the resolution to 'strive to reach the highest goal of man' and to 'acquaint himself with holy places', starting with a Buddhist monastery. And this is more or less the agenda of the Graduate, with the exception that he already knows how worthless most teachings are and he is 'testing' them for the sake of demolishing their false doctrines. We might say that the Graduate is as uncompromising in doctrinal truths as the Director is in questions of dramaturgy. On the other hand, both the Assistant and the Boy represent a more conformist attitude: they also observe the rule of falsity in the world, but they do not consider it as their duty to lead a crusade against *māyā*, Universal Delusion. Everyone has to

---

[14]According to Hahn he is probably identical with the grammarian Candragomin, and can be dated to the fifth century A.D. (*Candragomins Lokānandanāṭaka. Nach dem tibetischen Tanjur herausgegeben und übersetzt von Michael Hahn*. Wiesbaden, 1974.) See also STEINER, pp. 23ff.

[15]Hahn's edition, pp. 196f; he translates it as 'lehrreiche Schauspiel'.

[16]In the *Karpūramañjarī*, the Director and his wife are said to have taken the roles of the king and the queen.

[17]E.g. in the *Mālatīmādhava* and the *Viddhaśālabhañjikā*. In the *Uttararāmacarita*, the Director turns into a resident of Ayodhya already in the Prologue.

make a living somehow, either as an actor, or as a Jain monk. Are we entitled to ruin their existence in the name of some Ultimate Reality? The Graduate permits the Buddhists to go on with their hypocritical conduct as a way of livelihood, but he asserts roundly that Buddhism is actually harmful for someone who hopes for a better afterlife. But what about the Jains, Śaivas and Vaiṣṇavas? Does one have the right to upset their beliefs? And what of the depraved practices of the *nīlāmbaras*? Should we persecute them, or should we just wave our hand in resignation and refer to general tendencies in the Age of Decadence? And what happens if our sponsor, may he be a king or the producer of a play, requires us to act against our principles?

We shall return to these questions, but first let us see what is exactly that makes this play so despicable for an actor who has turned grey in the honourable service of dramatic art.

3.

According to Indian authorities on aesthetics, certain types of man are simply incapable of appreciating the beauties of poetry. It is pointless to test the veracity of poems, says Ānandavardhana, and if somebody had the impudence to employ for instance the methods of logic to prove that a piece of art is true or false, he would only make himself ridiculous.[18] Such a person, as Abhinavagupta remarks in his commentary, is certainly not a connoisseur, but only 'a fellow who is hard-hearted because of the application of dry logic, and who is therefore unable to feel [aesthetic] delight'.[19] Ritualists were considered perhaps the most hopeless cases in this respect. Uttuṅgodaya at least, who wrote a commentary on Abhinavagupta's *Dhvanyālokalocana*, has a poor opinion of them: he mentions the *mīmāṃsakas* and the *śrotriyas* as the typical rep-

[18] *Dhvanyāloka* 3.33+ (KRISHNAMOORTHY, p. 222; MASSON-PATWARDHAN 1970, vol. II, p. 179): *kāvyaviṣaye ca vyaṅgyapratītīnāṃ satyāsatyanirūpaṇasyāprayojakatvam eveti tatra pramāṇāntaravyāpāraparīkṣopahāsāyaiva sampadyate|*

[19] *Locana ad Dhvanyāloka* 3.33 (quoted in MASSON-PATWARDHAN 1970, vol. II, p. 143): *nāyaṃ sahṛdayaḥ kevalaṃ śuṣkatarkopakramakarkaśahṛdayaḥ pratītiṃ parāmarṣṭuṃ nālam ity eṣa upahāsaḥ|*

resentatives of those who are quite incapable of art and honeyed phrases.[20]

The cobbler should stick to his last, and one should not apply *mīmāṃsaka* exegesis in the interpretation of poetry.[21] And what's more, one should not write a poem in the style of a scientific treatise. *Kāvya*, poetry, and *śāstra*, doctrinal or scientific literature,[22] have always been regarded in Indian aesthetics as two distinct worlds. Bhāmaha, the ancient Kashmirian *ālaṅkārika*, holds a much higher opinion of a poet's work than pure scientific knowledge:[23]

> *adhanasyeva dātṛtvaṃ klībasyevāstrakauśalam|*
> *ajñasyeva pragalbhatvam akaveḥ śāstravedanam||*
> *vinayena vinā kā śrīḥ kā niśā śaśinā vinā|*
> *rahitā satkavitvena kīdṛśī vāgvidagdhatā||*
> *gurūpadeśād adhyetuṃ śāstraṃ jaḍadhiyo 'py alam|*
> *kāvyaṃ tu jāyate jātu kasyacit pratibhāvataḥ||*
>
> If someone who is not a poet knows the *śāstras*, it is just as the munificence of a pauper, the dexterity of an effeminate in handling weapons, or the pretentiousness of a fool. What is wealth without self-control? What is night without the moon? What skill in speech can there be if one is not a true poet? Even a thick-headed person can learn *śāstra* following the teaching of his master, but poetry is born rarely and only for a few people who have inspiration.

Rājaśekhara also distinguishes these two genres, but he thinks that there are some channels of contact:

---

[20]Uttuṅgodaya's *Kaumudī ad Locana* (quoted in MASSON-PATWARDHAN 1970, vol. II, note 144): *adhikārī ca kāṣṭhāprāptasahṛdayabhāvaḥ kaś cid eva na sarvaḥ, mīmāṃsakaśrotriyādes tatprakārādarśanāt|; anye tu iti| mīmāṃsakaśrotriyādīnām īdṛśī cāṭūktiḥ durlabheti sahṛdayānām ity uktam|*

[21]This is why Abhinavagupta criticizes Bhaṭṭa Nāyaka's way of analysing a poem (*Locana ad Dhvanyāloka* 2.1, ed. *Kāvyamālā*, p. 77): *jaiminīyasūtre hy evaṃ yojyate na kāvye 'pi|*

[22]This category includes technical literature, law-books, and any kind of specialist book, but also manuals on ritual and philosophy, and even the Vedas themselves. We may say that *śāstra* is a treatise which contains teaching about the real nature of things.

[23]*Kāvyālaṅkāra* 1.3–5.

iha hi vāṅmayam ubhayathā śāstraṃ kāvyaṃ ca| śāstrapūrvakatvāt kāvyānāṃ pūrvaṃ śāstreṣv abhiniviśet| na hy apravartitapradīpās tamasi tattvārthasārtham adhyakṣayanti| (...)

bhavati prathayann arthaṃ līnaṃ samabhiplutaṃ sphuṭīkurvan|
alpam analpaṃ racayann analpam alpaṃ ca śāstrakaviḥ||[24]

For here [in our system] literature is of two kinds: *śāstra* and *kāvya*. Because [the study of] *śāstra* must precede [the writing of] poetry, first one should delve into scientific works, for those who do not use a lamp cannot observe the multitude of real things. (...) The *śāstrakavi* is someone who exposes hidden things, makes obscure things clear, composes an extensive [treatise] out of a small [subject], and a concise one out of a vast [subject].

pratibhāvyutpattimāṃś ca kaviḥ kavir ity ucyate| sa hi tridhā| śāstrakaviḥ, kāvyakavir, ubhayakaviś ca| 'teṣām uttarottarīyo garīyān' iti śyāmadevaḥ| 'na' iti yāyāvarīyaḥ| yathāsvaviṣaye sarvo garīyān| na hi rājahaṃsaś candrikāpānāya prabhavati, nāpi cakoro 'dbhyaḥ kṣīroddharaṇāya| yac chāstrakaviḥ kāvye rasasampadaṃ vicchinatti, yat kāvyakaviḥ śāstre tarkakarkaśam apy artham uktivaicitryeṇa ślathayati| ubhayakavis tūbhayor api varīyān yady ubhayatra paraṃ pravīṇaḥ syāt| tasmāt tulyaprabhāvāv eva śāstrakāvyakavī| upakāryopakārakabhāvaṃ tu mithaḥ śāstrakāvyakavayor anumanyāmahe| yac chāstrasaṃskāraḥ kāvyam anugṛhṇāti śāstraikapravaṇatā tu nigṛhṇāti| kāvyasaṃskāro 'pi śāstravākyapākam anuruṇaddhi kāvyaikapravaṇatā tu viruṇaddhi| tatra tridhā śāstrakaviḥ| yaḥ śāstraṃ vidhatte, yaś ca śāstre kāvyaṃ saṃvidhatte, yo 'pi kāvye śāstrārtham nidhatte|[25]

---

[24] *Kāvyamīmāṃsā*, Second Adhyāya, pp. 2f., 5.
[25] Ibid. Fifth Adhyāya, p. 17.

> That poet is called [real] poet who has imagination and learning. And he is of three kinds: the poet who writes *śāstra*, the poet who writes *kāvya*, and the poet who writes both. According to Śyāmadeva, the above order is also the order of their excellence. Rājaśekhara disagrees. Each of them exceeds [the other two] in his own field. For the swan is not able to drink moonlight, nor the Cakora bird to separate milk from water. As for the poet who writes *śāstra*, he ruins the harmony of aesthetic flavours in a poem; as for the poet who writes *kāvya*, he makes flaccid with the variety of diction in a technical work even a subject which is tough because of logical arguments. But the poet who can write both [*śāstra* and *kāvya*] is better than either of the other two if he is skillful in both fields in the highest degree. Therefore the poet who writes *śāstra* and the one who writes *kāvya* are of equal rank. We admit, however, that the poet who writes *śāstra* and the one who writes *kāvya* can mutually benefit each other. For education in *śāstra* benefits poetry, but exclusive proficiency in *śāstra* suppresses it. Education in *kāvya*, too, aids the perfection of sentences in a scientific work, but exclusive proficiency in *kāvya* suppresses it.
> Of these two, the poet who writes *śāstra* is of three kinds: the one who composes a doctrinal or scientific treatise, the one who introduces poetry in a *śāstra*, and the one who puts a doctrinal or scientific subject into poetry.

This passage makes it clear that the word *kavi* could also be applied to writers of doctrinal and scientific works.[26] There also seems to have been a view, represented here by Śyāmadeva, which

[26]When Bhāmaha classifies poetry according to its subject matter, he does mention *śāstra* as a possible subject (*Kāvyālaṅkāra* 1.17):

> *vṛttadevādicaritaśaṃsi cotpādyavastu ca|*
> *kalāśāstrāśrayaṃ ceti caturdha bhidyate punaḥ||*

> Then [*kāvya*] is [also] divided into the following four categories: that which relates the past feats of gods and other [heroes],

placed the writers of *kāvya* before the authors of *śāstra*, and preferred those who could stand the test in both fields. If we have a look at the history of Sanskrit literature, we do find examples of such 'crossbreeds' of a swan and a *cakora*-bird. Ānandavardhana is just one of these geniuses, who is not far removed from Jayanta's time and who was also his compatriot. Today he is best known for his highly influential work on aesthetics, but he composed several poems as well. Of these only a *citrakāvya*, the *Devīśataka* survives, but he also refers to his *mahākāvya*, the *Arjunacarita* (*Dhvanyāloka*, 3.10–14+) and a Prakrit poem called *Viṣamabāṇalīlā* (*Dhvanyāloka*, 3.15+). He must have had great confidence in his erudition in philosophy, which is proved by the fact that he ventured to interpret Dharmakīrtian ideas in a commentary on Dharmottara's *Pramāṇaviniścayaṭīkā* (mentioned in *Locana ad Dhvanyāloka* 3.47).

Being such a versatile writer, it is natural that Ānandavardhana also took interest in the nature of relation between *śāstra* and *kāvya*. His work on this topic, the *Tattvāloka*, is unfortunately lost for us, but the following passage from the *Dhvanyāloka* and Abhinavagupta's commentary thereon throws some light on it:[27]

> Ānandavardhana: *tad evam anukramaṇīnirdiṣṭena vākyena bhagavadvyatirekiṇaḥ sarvasyānyasyānityatāṃ prakāśayatā mokṣalakṣaṇa evaikaḥ paraḥ puruṣārthaḥ śāstranaye, kāvyanaye ca tṛṣṇākṣayaparipoṣalakṣaṇaḥ śānto raso mahābhāratasyāṅgitvena vivakṣita iti supratipāditam|*
>
> So thus it has been well established that the sentence announced in the chapter of contents, which reveals that nothing is permanent except for the Lord, wishes to express that with regard to the *śāstra* aspect it is the single supreme goal of man, namely *mokṣa*, which is predominant in the *Mahābhārata*, and with regard to the *kāvya* aspect it is the aesthetic relish of quietude,

that which has a fictitious story, that which is about art and that which is about doctrine or science

[27] *Dhvanyāloka ad* 4.5 (ed. Krishnamoorthy, p. 278); *Locana ad loc.*, Kashi ed. p. 533.

> which is characterised by the full development of the dying away of desires.
>
> Abhinavagupta: *śāstranaya iti| tatrāsvādayogābhāve puruṣeṇārthyata ity ayam eva vyapadeśaḥ sādaraḥ, camatkārayoge tu rasavyapadeśa iti bhāvaḥ| etac ca granthakāreṇa tattvāloke vitatyoktam iha tv asya na mukhyo 'vasara iti nāsmābhir darśitam|*
>
> 'With regard to the *śāstra* aspect.' Since it [i.e. the *śāstra* aspect] has no connection with aesthetic relishing, it is this term alone [i.e. "goal of man"] which is appropriate, inasmuch as "man strives to obtain it"; but when [in the *kāvya* aspect] there is a connection with aesthetic wonder, then the designation of *rasa* [is appropriate]: this is what he means. And the author has set this forth in detail in the *Tattvāloka*, but the present context is not the best occasion for [discussing] it, so I have not expounded it.

Some works could be regarded both as *śāstra* and as *kāvya*, depending on the way of approach. This was especially true in the case of literary pieces that also had a religious importance, such as, for instance, the *Mahābhārata*. Bhoja lists both *kāvyaśāstra* and *śāstrakāvya* among the varieties of *śravyakāvya*.[28] He mentions the *Bhaṭṭikāvya* and (extending the category to *dṛśyakāvya*) the *Mudrārākṣasa* as examples of *kāvyaśāstra*, that is a poetic composition in which a scientific or doctrinal subject is introduced (*yatrārthaḥ śāstrāṇāṃ kāvye niveśyate*). *Śāstrakāvya*, on the other hand, is apparently a scientific composition written in the manner of poetry, e.g. the *Kāmandakīya-nītisāra*, and the *Ratavilāsa*.[29] Put differently, *kāvyaśāstra* is essentially a piece of poetry which also teaches us some *śāstraic* subject, while *śāstrakāvya* is essentially a *śāstra*-treatise 'dressed up' as a poem. As Raghavan observed, among Rājaśekhara's *śāstrakavis*, the second type writes *śāstrakāvya*, and the third type writes *kāvyaśāstra*.[30]

---

[28] RAGHAVAN 1978, p. 593.

[29] Ibid. pp. 607f.

[30] Ibid.: *yaś ca śāstre kāvyaṃ saṃvidhatte, yo 'pi kāvye śāstrārthaṃ nidhatte*, cf. above.

Nevertheless there are clear differences between poetic and scientific dictions, and if a Fachidiot *śāstrakavi* ventures to write pure poetry, the consequences, as Rājaśekhara pointed out, can be disastrous.[31] We have already met the view that the source of poetry is the poet's imagination or inspiration (*pratibhā*) rather than his erudition. In the opinion of Udbhaṭa, the eight-century Kashmirian rhetorician, poetry and science also differ in their domains:[32]

> *astu nāma niḥsīmārthasārthaḥ| kiṃtu dvirūpa evāsau, vicāritasusthaḥ, avicāritaramaṇīyaś ca| tayoḥ pūrvam āśritāni śāstrāṇi, tad uttaraṃ kāvyāni|*
>
> Let there be a limitless multitude of subjects, but this [multitude] is only twofold: [either] well-established [even] after they have been analysed, or pleasing [only] as long as they are not analysed.[33] Of these two, scientific works are concerned with the former, poems with the latter.

According to a certain Āparājiti, who is probably the same as Bhaṭṭa Lollaṭa, another Kashmirian living perhaps in the ninth

---

[31]Bhāmaha put it clearly (*Kāvyālaṅkāra* 1.12):

> *nākavitvam adharmāya vyādhaye daṇḍanāya ca|*
> *kukavitvaṃ punaḥ sākṣānmṛtim āhur manīṣiṇaḥ||*
>
> If someone is not a poet, this fact is not a sin, it does not result in disease or punishment. The wise say, however, that being a bad poet equals incarnate death.

[32]Quoted in *Kāvyamīmāṃsā*, p. 44.

[33]The concept of *avicāritaramaṇīyatā* appears in Cārvāka context as well, e.g. in the conclusion of Jayarāśi's *Tattvopaplavasiṃha* (TUS (GOS), p. 125): *upapluteṣv eva tattveṣv avicāritaramaṇīyās sarve vyavahārā ghaṭanta iti.* Jayanta also quotes this Cārvāka view both in his *magnum opus*, and in his play: *Nyāyamañjarī*, vol. I, p. 317: *avicāritaramaṇīyataiva tattvaṃ na tu lakṣaṇaniyamaḥ śakyakriyas tasyeti*; *Āgamaḍambara*, Act Three, ll. 324f.: *tad ayaṃ avicārita eva ramaṇīyo vyavahāraḥ, etad eva ca tattvam iti tattvavidaḥ.* Cakradhara, the commentator of the *Nyāyamañjarī* identifies the 'well-trained *Cārvākas* (*suṣikṣitacārvākāh*)' with Udbhata and co. (*udbhaṭādayaḥ*), and the 'cunning Cārvāka (*cārvākadhūrtaḥ*)' with Udbhaṭa himself (see *Granthibhaṅga* pp. 19, 43, 197, 198).

century, only those things are worth including in a poetic composition which are 'tasty' in an aesthetic sense.[34]

Rājaśekhara, however, considers the expressions of the poet more important in this respect than the chosen subject:[35]

> *ām iti yāyāvarīyaḥ| asti cānubhūyamāno rasasyānuguṇo viguṇaś cārthaḥ, kāvye tu kavivacanāni rasayanti virasayanti ca nārthāḥ, anvayavyatirekābhyāṃ cedam upalabhyate|*
>
> 'Amen', says Rājaśekhara. Certain things that we perceive are congenial to aesthetic relish, others are uncongenial. In poetry, however, it is the expressions of the poet which do or do not possess aesthetic relish, and not the subject, and we ascertain this fact through positive and negative concomitance.

Perhaps the most important difference between *śāstra* and *kāvya* lies in their function. While we study the *śāstra*s in order to receive instruction about the true nature of things, this does not seem to be enough reason to read poetry. Bhāmaha named proficiency (*vaicakṣaṇya*) in the four goals of man and the arts, pleasure (*prīti*), and fame (*kīrti*), as the threefold gift of poetry.[36] Later aestheticians, however, disagreed. Dhanañjaya and Dhanika felt strongly on this point:[37]

> *ānandaniṣyandiṣu rūpakeṣu*
> *vyutpattimātraṃ phalam alpabuddhiḥ|*
> *yo 'pītihāsādivad āha sādhus*
> *tasmai namaḥ svāduparāṅmukhāya||*
>
> Homage to that holy fool, who has turned his back on charm, and who says that the only fruit in plays that drip bliss is learning, similarly to legends and the like.

[34]Quoted in *Kāvyamīmāṃsā* (Ninth Adhyāya, p. 45): *astu nāma niḥsīmārthasārthaḥ, kiṃ tu rasavata eva nibandho yukto na nīrasasya iti āparājitiḥ|* Āparājiti is probably another name of Lollaṭa, since the second one of the two verses following this sentence, also written by Āparājiti according to Rājaśekhara, is attributed to Lollaṭa by Hemacandra in the *Kāvyānuśāsana*, p. 307.

[35]*Kāvyamīmāṃsā*, ibid.

[36]*Kāvyālaṅkāra* 1.2.

[37]*Daśarūpaka* 1.6.

> *Avaloka ad loc.*:
> *tatra ke cit—dharmārthakāmamokṣeṣu vaicakṣaṇyaṃ kalāsu ca| karoti kīrtiṃ prītiṃ ca sādhukāvyaniṣevaṇam|| ityādinā trivargādivyutpattiṃ kāvyaphalatvenecchanti tannirāsena svasaṃvedyaḥ paramānandarūpo rasāsvādo daśarūpāṇāṃ phalaṃ na punar itihāsādivat trivargādi-vyutpattimātram iti darśitam| nama iti solluṇṭham|*
>
> In this context some people assert with verses such as the following that the fruit of poetry is learning the three goals of man, etc.: 'Adherence to [i.e. reading and composing] good poetry bestows proficiency in *dharma*, *artha*, *kāma*, *mokṣa*, and the arts, and it also gives fame and pleasure.' In order to refute this it has been shown that the fruit of the ten kinds of plays is the tasting of aesthetic relish, which everyone experiences in himself, and which is of the nature of the highest bliss, and [this fruit is] not just education in the three goals of man, etc., like in the case of legends, etc. The word "homage" is used ironically.

Bhaṭṭa Nāyaka expressed a similar opinion on this subject. He held that the major effect of poetry is the enjoyment (*bhoga*) of aesthetic relish, which enjoyment is similar to the Brahman-experience (*brahmāsvāda*). Any instruction a poem may give us is secondary (*vyutpattir nāma apradhānam eva*).[38]

Abhinavagupta also quotes Bhāmaha's verse to show that the audience can derive both instruction and pleasure from poetry, but then he remarks that of these two pleasure is the predominant result.[39] Then he relates one of his favourite allegories to illustrate that different literary genres teach us in different ways: the Veda (= *śāstra*) instructs in the manner of a master, we learn from the legends in the way we learn from our friends, and poetry teaches us after the fashion of a loving wife.[40] Abhinavagupta

---

[38] Quoted by Abhinavagupta in *Locana ad Dhvanyāloka* 2.4.

[39] The poet's happiness is provided by his fame (*Locana ad Dhvanyāloka* 1.1.)

[40] *Locana* ibid. (ed. Krishnamoorthy, p. 17): *tathāpi tatra prītir eva pradhānam| anyathā prabhusammitebhyo vedādibhyo mitrasammitebhyaś cetihāsādibhyo vyutpattihetubhyaḥ ko 'sya kāvyarūpasya vyutpattihetor jāyāsammita-*

takes the view (following his teacher) that it is pointless to separate pleasure and instruction in poetry, since without delight coming from the tasting of *rasa* no lesson can enter the hearts of the connoisseur audience.[41] Accordingly drama, too, does not instruct us as a rigorous professor, but rather it 'increases our understanding.'[42] Certainly the conduct of the hero is set as a good example to the spectators, but still before that their imagination is expanded through the savoring of *rasa*, which is an (at least) equally important side of instruction.[43]

Poetic diction can facilitate the mastering of any kind of teaching. Princes, for instance, must be educated to become righteous kings. But, given their natural inclinations, they would be bored to tears while listening to the *śāstras*. Poetry, however, is an excellent way to engage their interest: 'entering into the hearts [of the princes, etc.]', says Abhinavagupta, 'is accomplished by the tasting of aesthetic relish alone.'[44] Reading a scientific treatise can be a painful experience for a *sahṛdaya*. It is like swallowing a bitter medicine, to use this ancient allegory, while reading poetry is almost equivalent to drinking ambrosia, which is sweet *and* healthy at the same time.[45] It is an ancient wisdom that if you don't want to frighten people away from your *śāstra*, the trick is

---

tvalakṣaṇo viśeṣa iti pradhānyenānanda evoktaḥ| Cf. also *Locana ad Dhvanyāloka* 3.10–14.

[41] *Locana ad Dhvanyāloka* 3.10–14.

[42] *Nāṭyaśāstra* 1.115. (ed. GOS, vol. I, p. 41): : *dharmyaṃ yaśasyam āyuṣyaṃ hitaṃ buddhivivardhanam| lokopadeśajananaṃ nāṭyam etad bhaviṣyati||* Abhinavagupta *ad loc.*: *nanu kiṃ guruvad upadeśaṃ karoti? nety āha| kintu buddhiṃ vivardhayati|*

[43] *Locana ad Dhvanyāloka* 2.4.

[44] *Locana ad Dhvanyāloka* 3.10–14 (ed. *Kāvyamālā*, p.183): *hṛdayānupraveśaś ca rasāsvādamaya eva.* Cf. *Vakroktijīvita*, prose after 1.3 (ed. p. 10): *abhijātāḥ khalu rājaputrādayo dharmādyupeyārthino vijigīṣavaḥ kleśabhīravaś ca, sukumārāśayatvāt teṣām| tathā saty api tadāhlādakatve kāvyabandhasya krīḍanakadiprakhyatā prāpnotīty abhidhatte—dharmādisādhanopāyaḥ|*

[45] Cf. *Vakroktijīvita*, prose after 1.5 (ed. p. 15): *duḥśravadurbhaṇadur-adhigamatvādidoṣaduṣṭo 'dhyayanāvasara eva duḥsahaduḥkhadāyī śāstra-sandarbhas tatkālakalpitakamanīyacamatkṛteḥ kāvyasya na kathañ cid api spardhām adhirohatīty etad apy arthato 'bhihitaṃ bhavati| kaṭukauṣadhavac chāstram avidyāvyādhināśanam| āhlādy amṛtavat kāvyam avivekagadāpaham||1*

to drip some poetic honey into bitter science.[46] 'How great is the weight put on the poet's shoulders!', sighs Bhāmaha. No wonder: all words and meanings, all arguments and arts, if they deserve their name, become the components of poetry.[47]

4.

We can ascertain from the foregoing that, according to the standards of classical Indian aesthetics, it was not completely impossible to write a play introducing philosophical subjects, but it was apparently a daring enterprise, and the poet must have reckoned with the scathing criticism of the *sahṛdaya*s.

When Jayanta composed his unique play, probably at the very end of the ninth century, studies in poetics and poetry itself had achieved a high standard in the kingdom of Kashmir. We have already met the name of Bhāmaha, the ancient *ālaṅkārika* (eight century or earlier). Udbhaṭa, who wrote a commentary on Bhāmaha's work, may be identical with the *sabhāpati* of king Jayāpīḍa (779–813) mentioned in the *Rājataraṅgiṇī*. This king sponsored a remarkable circle of intellectuals: Kalhaṇa mentions the poet Dāmodaragupta and Vāmana (possibly the author of the *Kāvyālaṅkārasūtra*), who were also his ministers, and several other poets; the grammarian Kṣīra was the king's teacher, and the Buddhist philosopher Dharmottara also entered his kingdom.[48] About half a century later king Avantivarman (855–883) was a similar patron of literature. Kalhaṇa names four illustrious members of his *sabhā*: Ānandavardhana, Muktākaṇa, Śivasvāmin (the author of the *Kapphiṇābhyudaya*), and Ratnākara (who wrote the *Haravijaya*).[49] Avantivarman's successor and the king appearing in Jayanta's play, Śaṅkaravarman (883–902), was more interested in military conquests than in literature: Bhallaṭa and other poets led a miserable existence during his reign, and *horribile dictu*

[46]Cf. *Kāvyālaṅkāra* 5.3: *svādukāvyarasonmiśraṃ śāstram apy upayuñjate| prathamālīḍhamadhavaḥ pibanti kaṭu bheṣajam||*

[47]Ibid. 5.4: *na sa śabdo na tad vācyaṃ na sa nyāyo na sā kalā| jāyate yan na kāvyāṅgam aho bhāro mahān kaveḥ||*

[48]*Rājataraṅgiṇī* 4.495 seqq.

[49]*Rājataraṅgiṇī* 5.34.

the king himself spoke *apabhraṃśa* instead of Sanskrit.[50] According to Kalhaṇa, Śaṅkaravarman put a certain Nāyaka in charge of two new Śiva-temples.[51] It is very tempting to identify this Nāyaka with Bhaṭṭa Nāyaka, the famous aesthetician, who wrote his *Hṛdayadarpaṇa* in order to demolish the *dhvani*-theory.[52] Another important source of aesthetic theory was certainly the *Nāṭyaśāstra*. Its most famous commentary was written by Abhinavagupta, but his work was not unprecedented. He quotes among others three Kashmirian commentators: Udbhaṭa, Bhaṭṭa Lollaṭa, and Śaṅkuka. We know from Abhinavagupta that Śaṅkuka contested the views of Lollaṭa.[53] Kalhaṇa mentions a poet called Śaṅkuka, who composed a *kāvya* about the battle between the mighty Mamma and Utpalaka, which took place around 851.[54] On the other hand, we know about a Lollaṭa who commented on the *Spandakārikā* of Vasugupta,[55] who was the teacher of Kallaṭa, who lived under Avantivarman (855/6–883).[56] Now certainly everything depends on the identity of the above Śaṅkukas and Lollaṭas, but it is at least not impossible that both were roughly of the same age and lived under the reign of Avantivarman. In that case Jayanta might have known their works.

That Jayanta was familiar with the *dhvani*-theory becomes clear from the *Nyāyamañjarī*:[57]

> *etena śabdasāmarthyamahimnā so 'pi vāritaḥ|*
> *yam anyaḥ paṇḍitammanyaḥ prapede kaṃcana dhvanim||*
> *vidher niṣedhāvagatir vidhibuddhir niṣedhataḥ|*

---

[50] *Rājataraṅgiṇī* 5.204 seqq.

[51] *Rājataraṅgiṇī* 5.159.

[52] On Bhaṭṭa Nāyaka see KANE, pp. 221ff. Abhinavagupta refers to him as one who uses *mīmāṃsaka* ideas in literary criticism (*Locana ad Dhvanyāloka* 2.1, ed. *Kavyamālā*, p. 77: *jaiminīyasūtre hy evaṃ yojyate na kāvye 'pi|*); and judging from a verse of invocation also quoted by Abhinavagupta he seems to have been a devotee of Śiva (*namas trailokyanirmāṇakavaye śambhave yataḥ| pratikṣaṇaṃ jagannāṭyaprayogarasiko janaḥ||*, *Abhinavabhāratī* (GOS), vol. I, p. 6). Now the Nāyaka who was placed in charge of the two Śiva-temples is called both *caturvidyaḥ* and *vāgdevīkulamandiram* in the *Rājataraṅgiṇī*.

[53] *Abhinavabhāratī* (GOS), vol. I, p. 266.

[54] *Rājataraṅgiṇī* 4.703 seqq.

[55] GNOLI 1908, p. xvii, note 2.

[56] Cf. *Rājataraṅgiṇī* 5.66.

[57] *Nyāyamañjarī*, vol. I, p. 129f.

yathā
'bhama[58] *dhammiya vīsattho', 'mā sma pāntha gṛhaṃ viśa'||*
mānāntaraparicchedyavasturūpopadeśinām|
śabdānām eva sāmarthyaṃ tatra tatra tathā tathā||
athavā nedṛśī carcā kavibhiḥ saha śobhate|
vidvāṃso 'pi vimuhyanti vākyārthagahane 'dhvani||
tad alam anayā goṣṭhyā vidvajjanocitayā ciraṃ
paramagahanas tarkajñānām abhūmir ayaṃ nayaḥ|
prakṛtam adhunā tasmād brūmo na bhāty anumānataḥ
tanur api satām arthāpatter viśeṣa iti sthitam||

By this greatness of the word's signifying power that so-called '*dhvani*' is also refuted to which another self-appointed scholar resorted. [When there is] the understanding of a prohibition from [hearing] an injunction, [and] the comprehension of an injunction from [hearing] a prohibition, as for example [in the verses beginning with the following words]: 'Walk confidently, pious man...', [and] 'Don't enter the house, traveler...', it is nothing but the signifying power of words [which operates] in all such cases in various [appropriate] ways—words that refer to the real nature [of things] which can be precisely determined with the help of other means of valid knowledge. Or rather it is not right [to open] such a discussion with poets. Even the wise go astray on the path which is hardly passable due to [the difficulties in explaining] the sentence-meanings. So let's finish at last this discourse which is suitable [only] for the wise. This highly impenetrable issue is beyond the reach of logicians. Therefore now I shall speak about the subject in hand: it is proved that sensible people do not see the slightest difference between inference and presumption.

It appears that Jayanta was not only acquainted with the *dhvani*-theory, but he probably knew the *Dhvanyāloka* as well, since

[58] *bhama*] em. following *Dhvanyāloka* 1.4+ (ed. Krishnamoorthy, p. 8.) : *bhava* ed.

the two verses he refers to are the first two examples of *dhvani* cited by Ānandavardhana.[59] In this case the 'self-appointed scholar' may well have been Ānandavardhana himself,[60] and this attribute also betrays that Jayanta did not have a high opinion of him. On the other hand Jayanta probably knew that the refined aesthetes shuddered at the views of the 'dry logicians', so while he modestly (?) declines to deal with the impervious subject of words and their meanings, he also suggests that poets or literary critics are even less competent to handle the problem.

This does not mean, however, that Jayanta did not speak about poets with the greatest respect, provided that they stick to their last. 'Kālidāsa's beautiful expressions', he says, 'are, so to say, sprinkled with ambrosia, smeared with sandal, [and] washed by moon-beams. Bāṇa's words bedazzle crowds of poets with the formidable / spacious arrangement of their letters, which is congenial to the aesthetic relish manifested [in the text].'[61] He was probably familiar with the poetry of his native land as well, and he does mention one famous Kashmirian *kāvya*: the *Kuṭṭanīmata* (cf. *Nyāyamañjarī*, vol. I, p. 649).

But Jayanta was not just an appreciative reader of poetry. We find ample evidence in the *Nyāyamañjarī* of his poetic vein and gift for satire. He took care to mix the right quantity of honey into his *śāstra*, although in his opinion the *sūtras* of Gautama are already 'the most excellent juice (*rasa*) extracted from the

---

[59] *Dhvanyāloka* 1.4+ (ed. Krishnamoorthy, p. 8). The second verse quoted by Ānandavardhana is actually a Prakrit poem which seems to be slightly different from the verse Jayanta refers to, but both illustrate the phenomenon of '*vidhibuddhir niṣedhataḥ*'. Perhaps Jayanta relied on his memory and recalled a verse very similar to the one in the *Dhvanyāloka*. It is interesting to note that Bhaṭṭa Nāyaka also commented on these two verses. According to him it is not the *arthasāmarthya*, that is the suggesting power of the content expressed by the words, which brings about the apprehension of the hidden intention, but the words themselves, when applied in a skillful way (*Locana ad Dhvanyāloka* 1.4, ed. Krishnamoorthy, pp. 29, 31).

[60] Cf. *Granthibhaṅga*, p. 32: *etena paṇḍitaṃmanya ity ānandavardhanācāryaṃ dhvanikāraṃ parāmṛśati|*

[61] *Nyāyamañjarī*, vol. I, p. 582: *amṛteneva saṃsiktāḥ candaneneva carcitāḥ| candrāṃśubhir ivonmṛṣṭaḥ kalidāsasya sūktayaḥ|| prakaṭarasānuguṇavikaṭākṣararacanācamatkāritasakalakavikulāḥ bāṇasya vācaḥ|* The invocatory verses of the *Nyayamañjarī* and the *Harṣacarita* resemble each other in many respects.

cluster of the medical plants of *nyāya*'.[62] If we did not know the *Āgamaḍambara* and were to speculate which Indian philosopher might have endeavoured to write a play, Jayanta would be perhaps the most likely guess.

5.

'My friend,' complains the Director to his Assistant in the Prologue of the *Āgamaḍambara*, 'as is well known, I have exerted myself in the staging of the ten dramatic styles as taught by Bharatamuni. But today the circle of pupils of this honourable Bhaṭṭa Jayanta, who is also well known as the Writer of the Commentary because he wrote an exegetical work on grammar when he was just a child, has ordered me to put on the work of their teacher, a new, extraordinary play called Much Ado About Religion. So how shall I stage it, since it is not worldly, does not follow the dramatic rules, and has never been performed before? Therefore it is better just to give up this wretched livelihood.'

His last objection against the play, namely that there is no tradition of its performance the director could rely upon, is a well-known complaint since the time of Kālidāsa, although in the *Mālavikāgnimitra* the Director shows more solidarity with the author and actually defends the play against this charge. The first two objections deserve closer attention.

To begin with, why is it a problem if a play is 'not worldly'? Well, a refined connoisseur might say that if a play is riddled with disputes on utterly abstract topics such as, 'Can this pot be destroyed by a hammer, or are there only pot-phases perishing in every moment?', it might prove to be a trifle boring for the average audience (not to speak about the spoiled princes). After all the main purpose of drama is entertainment. Already the gods

---

[62] *Nyāyamañjarī*, vol. I, p. 3: *nyāyauṣadhivanebhyo 'yam āhṛtaḥ paramo rasaḥ*. Jayanta placed a high value on correct and clear usage, and he could not refrain from mocking the wise Dharmakīrti who 'could not put together correctly even a pair of words when he wanted to formulate a definition' (*Nyāyamañjarī*, vol. I, p. 259: *iti sunipuṇabuddhir lakṣaṇaṃ vaktukāmaḥ padayugalam apīdaṃ nirmame nānavadyam*|). Both Cakradhara, the commentator of the *Nyāyamañjarī*, and Abhinanda, Jayanta's son, praised the poetic qualities of Jayanta's writings.

addressed Brahmā with the following words: 'we want something to play with, which has to be pleasing both to our eyes and our ears.'[63] This 'plaything', says Abhinavagupta, 'is similar to a bitter medicine coated in sugar', a familiar concept, but 'the sole effect of which is the distraction of the mind'.[64] One should find pleasure in watching a play and in listening to it: it is not a means to generate religious merit (*na dharmasādhanam*, *Abhinavabhāratī ad Nāṭyaśāstra* 1.11). The diction of a play should be straightforward and agreeable (*śakyam*), and not for the most part ugly and harsh (*durbhagaparuṣaprāyam*, *Abhinavabhāratī* ibid.).[65] As Dhanañjaya observed with a sharp eye: 'The spectators amusing themselves with characters such as Arjuna are just like children playing with clay elephants: they relish their own zeal.'[66] A good performance holds the audience, diverts their mind from everyday miseries:[67]

> *duḥkhārtānāṃ śramārtānāṃ śokārtānāṃ tapasvinām|*
> *viśrāntijananaṃ kāle nāṭyam etad bhaviṣyati||*
>
> This [thing called] drama will be the production of repose in the appropriate time for those who are tormented by suffering, fatigue, or grief, [and also] for ascetics.

So even ascetics, who might be inclined to contemplate the ultimate questions of existence, would prefer to be entertained while watching a play and to forget about their self-afflicted tortures[68]

---

[63] *Nāṭyaśāstra* 1.11 (GOS, vol. I, p. 10): *krīḍanīyakam icchāmo dṛśyaṃ śravyaṃ ca yad bhavet|*

[64] *Abhinavabhāratī* on *loc. cit.* (GOS ibid.): *guḍapracchannakaṭukauṣadhakalpaṃ cittavikṣepamātraphalam.*

[65] Another interpretation of *dṛśyaṃ śravyaṃ ca* given by Abhinavagupta (GOS p. 11): *dṛśyam iti hṛdyaṃ śravyam iti vyutpattipradam iti prītivyutpattidam ity arthaḥ.*

[66] *Daśarūpaka* 4.41b–42a: *krīḍatāṃ mṛnmayair yadvad bālānāṃ dviradādibhiḥ| svotsāhaḥ svadate tadvac chrotṝṇām arjunadibhiḥ||*; cf. *Nāṭyaśāstra* verses between 1.119 and 120 (GOS vol. I, p. 44, Abhinavagupta does not comment on them): *vinodakaraṇaṃ loke nāṭyam etad bhaviṣyati|*

[67] *Nāṭyaśāstra* 1.114 (GOS vol. I, p. 40).

[68] Cf. *Abhinavabhāratī ad Nāṭyaśāstra* 1.114 (GOS vol. I, p.39): *tapasvinām anavaratakṛcchracāndrāyaṇādyācaraṇakalitadaurbalyātiśayaparikhinna hṛdayāṇāṃ viśrāntijananaṃ duḥkhaprasaraṇavighātakam|*

(including the mental tortures of thinking about hammers approaching pots from various angles, our man of taste might add). As for those fortunate ones who are not familiar with suffering, for instance the spoiled princes, drama gives them useful instructions about the way of the world (*lokavṛtte*).[69]

The objection that they do not please the general audience was brought up against *śāntarasa*-plays in general (and, as we are going to see, the *Āgamaḍambara* is such a play, if we can label it in any way at all). 'Even if it is not within everyone's range of experience,' says Ānandavardhana in defence of *śāntarasa* occurring in plays such as the *Nāgānanda*, 'just because of that it cannot be rejected as a special state of mind of illustrious persons who are different from the plebs.'[70] So even a philosophical play can be a hit, one just has to find the right audience. And that's the conclusive argument of the Assistant in reply to the hesitation of the Director: what could be a better audience than the devoted philosophy-students of professor Bhaṭṭa Jayanta? They'll just love the play.

But there are other problems, too, with the *Āgamaḍambara*. Some critics would say that actually it is too *laukika* in the sense that it is very closely linked with the time and place of the author. Abhinavagupta was an eminent promoter of the thesis that aesthetic experience is essentially supramundane, *alaukika*.[71] In his view, 'the heart [of the spectator] becomes similar to a spotless mirror because he forgets about his everyday life in the world due to the relishing of the appropriate songs and music'.[72] 'Due to listening to the recitation [of the actors] and [watching] the entering of other characters', says Abhinavagupta, 'an apprehension

---

[69] Abhinavagupta commenting on *Nāṭyaśāstra* 1.115 (*lokopadeśajananaṃ nāṭyam*) (*Abhinavabhāratī* (GOS), vol. I, pp. 40f): *ye na duḥkhitāḥ sukhabhūyiṣṭhavṛttaya eva rājaputrādyās teṣāṃ lokavṛtte dharmādyupāyavarge upadeśakāry etan nāṭyam| lokaśabdena lokavṛttam| nanu kiṃ guruvad upadeśaṃ karoti? nety āha| kintu buddhiṃ vivardhayati|*

[70] *Dhvanyāloka* 3.26+ (ed. Krishnamoorthy, p. 182): *yadi nāma sarvajanānubhavagocaratā tasya nāsti naitāvatāsāv alokasāmānyamahānubhāvacittavṛttiviśeṣaḥ pratikṣeptuṃ śakyaḥ|*

[71] Most of Abhinavagupta's predecessors did not consider *rasāsvāda* as something essentially different from our everyday experiences.

[72] *Abhinavabhāratī ad Nāṭyaśāstra* 1.107 (GOS vol. I, p. 36): *ucitagītātodyacarvaṇāvismṛtasāṃsārikabhāvatayā vimalamukurakalpībhūtanijahṛdayaḥ.*

arises [in the mind of the spectator]. [This apprehension] has as its object such [characters] as Rāma and Rāvaṇa, it is not embraced by the influence of any particular place or time, [and] it is not the domain of [any] reflection on whether it is to be regarded as a cognition which is correct, or false, or which is a doubt, or a supposition.'[73]

Already Bhaṭṭa Nāyaka had pointed out that when we watch a Rāma-play, we do not regard Sītā as our own beloved, so the erotic *rasa* we relish cannot be awakened by the actual Sītā. To say that each spectator remembers his own beloved during the performance might be correct (especially if the performance is boring), but it does not explain how the *play* contributes to our aesthetic experience. As for Rāma, we cannot actually recall his heroism since we have never witnessed his heroic deeds. If we learn them from some written testimony, this knowledge still does not guarantee that we can relish *vīrarasa*.[74] One of the key concepts of Bhaṭṭa Nāyaka's aesthetic theory is 'generalisation', *sādhāraṇīkaraṇa*.[75] Words in poetry have a special function called *bhāvakatva* ("bringing into being") by Nāyaka, which gives rise to the aesthetic experience of *rasa* in the audience. This special operation must necessarily comprise the generalisation (or universalisation, depersonalisation) of the various factors which contribute to the arising of *rasa*, that is to say the *vibhāvas*, *anubhāvas*, and *vyabhicārībhāvas* (eliciting factors, indicatory symptoms, and ancillary mental states).[76] Now if we see king Udayana and Ratnāvalī on the stage, we can easily be convinced that they are not our personal acquaintances, the lovely garden in which they sit is not one particular garden in our city, and the heroin's oblique glances or blushing do not have any personal relationship with us, since they are more than the amorous gestures of just one particular girl. But what happens if

[73] *Abhinavabhāratī* ibid.: *pāṭhyākarṇanapātrāntarapraveśavaśāt samutpanne deśakālaviśeṣāveśānāliṅgite samyaṅmithyāsaṃśayasambhāvanādijñāna-vijñeyatvaparāmarśānāspade rāmarāvaṇādiviṣayādhyavasāye...*

[74] See *Locana ad Dhvanyāloka* 2.4.

[75] It was accepted by Abhinavagupta, and probably already by Tauta (Abhinavagupta follows his teacher when he writes: *nartakāntare 'pi ca rāmo 'yam iti pratipattir asti| tataś ca rāmatvaṃ sāmānyarūpam ity āyātam|*, *Abhinavabhāratī ad rasasūtra*, GOS, vol. I, p. 269; GNOLI 1968, p. 7).

[76] *Locana ad Dhvanyāloka* 2.4. See also *Kāvyaprakāśa*, vol. I, p. 216ff; GEROW AKLUJKAR, p. 80.

the scene of the plot is the city we live in, the time is the reign of our king, and the events happening on the stage give us the strange feeling of *dejà vu*?

The factors that produce the *rasa* are also capable of shielding our aesthetic relish from various obstacles,[77] so if the *vibhāvas*, *anubhāvas*, and *vyabhicārins* do not function properly, we might expect that the "wonder" *camatkāra* of our aesthetic perception will be blocked. One of the major obstacles occurs when the spectators regard these factors as real, actual, and personal. The right way to counteract this obstacle is to employ the theatrical conventions (*nāṭyadharmins*), which include various dances, makeups, the stage, costumes, and other *alaukika* accessories. These conventions hide the identity of the actor (which was, however, revealed in the preliminaries of the play), and distance the performance from all actualities.[78] To sum up, they contribute to the aesthetic experience through the accomplishment of the state of generality, *sādhāraṇībhāva*.[79]

Ānandavardhna held that Vālmīki's grief (*śoka*) felt upon the lamentation of the *krauñca*-bird was transformed into verse (*śloka*).[80] But Abhinavagupta hastens to remark that it was rather *karuṇarasa* that was felt by the first poet and not actual grief, since in the latter case the poet would merely suffer, and he could in no way experience aesthetic pleasure which is indispensable for composing a poem.[81] The same observation holds good with regard to the audience of *kāvya*. According to Bhaṭṭa Nāyaka, if a performance produced sorrow in the spectators, they would never return to the theatre to watch a play in which *karuṇa* is the dominant *rasa*.[82]

---

[77] *Abhinavabhāratī ad rasasūtra* (GOS, vol. I, p. 274): *tatra vighnāpasārakā vibhāvaprabhṛtayaḥ|*

[78] *Abhinavabhāratī* (GOS) ibid. The spectator's cognition cannot rest either in the actuality of the actor, or in the reality of the character.

[79] *Abhinavabhāratī* (GOS), vol. I, p. 275.: *eṣa sarvo muninā sādhāraṇībhāvasiddhyā rasacarvaṇopayogitvena parikarabandhaḥ samāśritaḥ|*

[80] *Dhvanyāloka* 1.5+ (ed. Krishnamoorthy, p. 12): *tathā cādikaver vālmīkes sannihitasahacarīvirahakātarakrauñcākrandajanitaḥ śoka eva ślokatayā pariṇataḥ|*

[81] *Locana ad loc.* (ed. Krishnamoorthy, p. 39): *na tu muneḥ śoka iti mantavyam| evaṃ hi sati tadduḥkhena so 'pi duḥkhita iti kṛtvā rasasyātmateti niravakāśaṃ bhavet| na ca duḥkhasantaptasyaiṣā daśeti|*

[82] Quoted in *Locana ad Dhvanyāloka* 2.4. We might add that while Abhi-

It is easy to see that if, for instance, the Rāma-story had been presented to an average Indian audience, no spectator would have had any difficulty in distancing what was happening on the stage from the realities of his own life. But what would have happened if Rāvaṇa himself had been among the audience? This is precisely what occurs in the third act of Rājaśekhara's play, the *Bālarāmāyaṇa*, when the king of the *rākṣasas*, who is pining for Sītā, sends for the troupe of Kohala to perform Bharata's brand-new play, called *Sītāsvayaṃvara*, in order to distract his mind. He could not have opted for a worse kind of entertainment. First he seems to enjoy the show, gloating over the princes' fiasco as they try to bend Śiva's bow in vain. He becomes a bit annoyed with the playwright when one of the characters remarks that even Rāvaṇa's arms would fail to accomplish this great deed. When king Śatruñjaya is introduced as a great hero who wishes to defeat Indrajit, Rāvaṇa draws his sword to protect his dearest son, and Prahasta, his general, has to remind him that they are just watching a play. But Rāvaṇa has entered too far into the dramatic world. When one of the contestants tries to carry away Sītā forcefully, his anger makes him spring up, just to realise within seconds that he has made a fool of himself again.

When all the other kings have failed to bend Śiva's bow, and the door-keeper is still musing if he should announce finally the young prince of the *sūryavaṃśa*, Rāvaṇa suddenly decides to act and rises to enter into the contest. 'My lord', says Prahasta, 'this is not Janaka's daughter, and this is not the bow of the moon-crested god.' 'What is it then?' asks Rāvaṇa at a loss. And Prahasta benignly informs him: 'It is a play.'[83] Then Rāma enters and vows that either he will string the bow or the bow will break. 'This is indeed the thunder of an actor',[84] laughs Rāvaṇa, and when Rāma does start bending the bow he says, 'This is how an actor shows off'.[85] When the bow miraculously bursts in Rāma's

navagupta would have no objection against the arising of *karuṇarasa* in the spectators, he would definitely oppose the arising of actual *śoka* in them.

[83] *Bālarāmāyaṇa*, Act Three, verse 67+: PRAHASTAḤ: *deva! neyaṃ jānakī, na cedam ainduśekharaṃ dhanuḥ*| RĀVAṆAḤ: *tat kim idam?* PRAHASTAḤ: *prekṣaṇakam idam*|

[84] Ibid., verse 74+: *idaṃ tan naṭagarjitaṃ nāma*|

[85] Ibid.: *iyam api sā naṭavibhiṣika*|

hands, Rāvaṇa accuses the poet that he has given the reins to his imagination: 'This is the wish-granting speech-cow of poets, which gives birth [i.e. makes real] even to unreal things'.[86] But when king Janaka places Sītā's hand on Rāma's, Rāvaṇa looses his self-control, and exclaims: 'Ah, what?! This falsely and vainly sophisticated bug of a *kṣatriya*-boy is clutching Sītā's hand, although I, the lord of Laṅkā, am present! So he is as good as dead.'[87] Prahasta cannot help laughing to himself, and remarks somewhat ironically: 'Lord of the *rākṣasa*s! The performance is almost over. So please, Sire, consider the actors' talent in clever acting and the way they intensify the aesthetic relish.' Rāvaṇa pulls himself together and feels like an idiot: 'Why, this is a play. I've become enraged for no reason.'[88] Needless to say, his aesthetic pleasure is completely ruined, and the only thing he feels is fury.[89]

The third act of the *Bālarāmāyaṇa* is an excellent study of the complete failure of a dramatic performance.[90] Rāvaṇa's is a typical example of a gross error in theatrical framing. 'The theatrical frame', writes Elam, 'is in effect the product of a set of transactional [actor-spectator] conventions governing the participants' expectations and their understanding of the kinds of reality involved in the performance. The theatregoer will accept that, at least in dramatic representations, an alternative and fictional reality is to be presented by individuals designated as the performers, and that his own role with respect to that represented reality is to be that of a privileged "onlooker".'[91] But there are cases when the operation of the dramatic and theatrical conventions (*nāṭyadharmins*) fails, the spectators mistake the performance for

[86]Ibid., verse 77+: *seyaṃ kavīnāṃ vacanakāmadhenuḥ, yad asadbhūtam api sūte|*

[87]Ibid., verse 84+: *āḥ, katham ayam alīkadurvidagdhaḥ kṣatriyabaṭukīṭo mamāpi laṅkeśvarasya purataḥ sītāyāḥ pāṇiṃ pāṇinā pīḍayati! tad eṣa na bhavati|*

[88]Ibid., verse 85+: PRAHASTAḤ: *rākṣasapate! paryavasitaprāyaḥ prekṣāvidhiḥ| tad bhāvayatu caturābhinayāṃ buddhiṃ rasavṛddhiṃ ca nartakānāṃ devaḥ|* RĀVAṆAḤ (*sasmaraṇalajjam ātmagatam*): *kathaṃ prekṣaṇakam etat| mudhā saṃrabdham asmābhiḥ|*

[89]Ibid., verse 90: *yātaḥ padaṃ mama ruṣāṃ ca mṛṣaiva rāmaḥ|*

[90]Other examples from Sanskrit literature are the third act of Harṣa's *Priyadarśikā*, and the seventh act of Bhavabhūti's *Uttararāmacarita*. See also BANSAT-BOUDON 1992, p. 148ff.

[91]ELAM 1997, p. 88.

real-life activity, and they start collecting money for the liberation of a poor slave-girl they have seen in a soap-opera.[92] But apart from such gross mistakes as running up to the stage and trying to change the course of events, the collapse of boundaries between real and fictional worlds in the mind of the spectator results in the failure of any kind of aesthetic experience, since the adequate emotional answer for something we perceive as actual can only be actual itself, that is, it cannot be *rasa*, only a *sthāyibhāva*.

There was a view current among Sanskrit aestheticians that if the aim of the poet is to satisfy his king, he may present the deeds of the latter in a play.[93] Abhinavagupta, however, did not share this opinion, precisely because he reckoned the spectators should maintain a certain emotional distance from the performance.[94]

> *'prabhuparitoṣāya prabhucaritaṃ kadācin nāṭye varṇanīyam' iti 'yathā daityāḥ surair jitā'* (*Nāṭyaśāstra* 1.57) *ity etasmāl labhyata iti kecid āhuḥ| tad asat, daśarūpakalakṣaṇayuktivirodhāt| tatra hi kiñcit prasiddhacaritaṃ kiñcid utpādyacaritam iti vakṣyate| na ca vartamānacaritānukāro yuktaḥ, vineyānāṃ tatra rāgadveṣamadhyasthatādinā tanmayībhāvābhāve prīter abhāvena vyutpatter apy abhāvāt|*
>
> Some people assert that the view, according to which sometimes the deeds of a ruler may be presented in a play in order to satisfy the ruler, follows from the verse '[at the end of the *nāndī*, a representation was made of] how the gods defeated the demons'. That [assertion] is not correct, because it contradicts the definition of

[92]As it actually happened in Hungary. 'Gross errors in framing,' observes ELAM (pp. 89f.), '[...] are less common in the theatre than with popular mass-media drama [...], since the conventionalized markers are much clearer. The legend of the cowboy spectator who shoots the stage villain is fairly apocryphal (although Goffman [...] reports an actual case of a drunken Virginian spectator shooting a "devil" represented by a mere puppet).'

[93]This view is also represented in the *Nāṭakalakṣaṇaratnakośa* (p. 3). *vartamānam api nṛpater mahābhūtasya kavibuddhiprakarṣād āsāditabījabindvādikaṃ yadi bhavati, bhavaty eva nāṭakaviṣayam|*. But cf. *Nāṭyadarpaṇa*, p. 25. *vartamāne ca netari tatkālaprasiddhibādhayā rasahāniḥ syāt|*

[94]*Abhinavabhāratī* ad *Nāṭyaśāstra* 1.58 (*tato brahmādayo devāḥ prayogaparitoṣitāḥ*) (GOS, vol. I, p. 27). Cf. GNOLI 1968, p. 64, note 1; BANSAT-BOUDON 1992, p. 128, note 212.

> the ten dramatic genres. For, as it will be shown [in the following], in [these dramatic genres] sometimes the deeds of a well-known [hero], and sometimes the deeds of an invented [hero] [are presented]. But the imitation [in a dramatic representation] of the deeds of a contemporary person is not appropriate, since in this case the disciples [i.e. the spectators] could not identify themselves [with the presentation] because of their [various emotions] such as lust, hatred, or indifference; thus they would not feel pleasure, and therefore no instruction could take place either.

If an individual of the real world appears as a character in the dramatic world, their 'trans-world identity' can be the source of problems. Rolf Hochhuth's play *Soldiers* 'was banned in England because the central figure, "Churchill", was seen at once to refer to and to defame (through inventive elaboration) the W_o [real world] original. Arguments in favour of the autonomy of the dramatic world in this case were not persuasive.'[95] The main criterion in determining the 'trans-world identity' of a character in a play and a historical figure is, as Elam pointed out, 'to consider the culturally determined *essential properties* of the figure in question and to judge whether they are preserved in the world of drama'.[96] This question appears in the context of *prasiddhatva* in Sanskrit dramatic theory. Classical Indian plays can be divided into two broad categories on the basis of their plot. On the one hand there are those plays the story of which is the invention of the poet (*utpādyavastu*). Among the classical genres of Indian drama, *prakaraṇa*s are the typical representatives of this group.[97] On the other hand the story of several plays can be traced back to some well-known (*prakhyāta*) source, such as the *purāṇa*s or the epics. The *nāṭaka* belongs to this category. As Bharata teaches in the *Nāṭyaśāstra*:[98]

---

[95] ELAM 1997, p.106.

[96] ELAM 1997, ibid.

[97] *Nāṭyaśāstra* 18.45 (GOS, vol. II, p. 430): *yatra kavir ātmaśaktyā vastu śarīraṃ ca nāyakaṃ caiva| autpattikaṃ prakurute prakaraṇam iti tad budhair jñeyam||*

[98] *Nāṭyaśāstra* 18.10 (GOS, vol. II, p. 412).

prakhyātavastuviṣayaṃ prakhyātodāttanāyakaṃ caiva|
rājarṣivaṃśyacaritaṃ tathaiva divyāśrayopetam||

[That play is called a *nāṭaka*] the subject of which is a well-known plot, which also has a well-known, illustrious hero, which presents the deeds of those who belong to the families of sage-like kings, and which is endowed with [the motif of] divine assistance as well.

The above interpretation of *prakhyātavastuviṣayaṃ* is roughly the same as that of Śaṅkuka.[99] Abhinavagupta (following his teacher, Bhaṭṭa Tauta) preferred a more precise definition of *prasiddhatva* (renown, celebrity), consisting of three factors: 'A certain person acted in a certain way in a certain place' (*amuka evaṃkārī amutra deśe*).[100] For example, everybody knows that the scene of king Udayana's adventures is mainly Kauśāmbī, and if a poet continuously presented him as residing in some other place, without mentioning that he has some reason to be there, such a description would not be plausible and therefore it would ruin the aesthetic relish of the play.[101]

This does not mean, however, that a poet cannot modify a traditional story in any way, or cannot expand it with freshly invented episodes. Since the dramatic world is always conceived as a 'hypothetical variation' of the actual reality, even when the two worlds are brought into contact, the characters in a play are only the possible varieties of their real counterparts, who serve as a model or a point of departure for the poet.[102] In fact, sometimes he has to make some modifications in order to preserve the aesthetic unity of the play. Ānandavardhana put great emphasis on the autonomy of the poet in fashioning his own world of poetry.[103] He lists several means which can assist a poetic work in

[99] *Abhinavabhāratī ad loc.* (GOS, vol. II, p. 411): *prakhyāte bhāratādau yad vastu tad viṣayo 'sya ... iti śrīśaṅkukaḥ|* ' "Its subject is a story [which is found] in a well-known [source] such as the *Mahābhārata*", says Śrīśaṅkukaḥ.'

[100] *Abhinavabhāratī*, ibid.

[101] *Abhinavabhāratī*, ibid.: *cakravartino 'pi hi vatsarājasya kauśambīvyatirikte viṣaye kāryāntaropakṣepeṇa vinā yan nirantaraṃ nirvarṇanaṃ tad vairasyāya bhavati, tatra prasiddhikhaṇḍanena pratītivighātāt, kā kathā rasacarvaṇāyāḥ|*

[102] Cf. ELAM 1997, p. 109.

[103] Cf. *Dhvanyāloka* 3.42+ (ed. Krishnamoorthy, p. 250): *apāre kāvyasaṃsare kavir ekaḥ prajāpatiḥ| yathāsmai rocate viśvaṃ tathedaṃ parivartate||*

the suggestion of *rasas* and the like. One of these means is as follows:[104]

> *itivṛttavaśāyātāṃ kathañcid rasānanuguṇāṃ sthitiṃ tyaktvā punar utprekṣyāpy antarābhīṣṭarasocitakathonnayo vidheyaḥ|*
>
> Having left out a situation he met in the context of a narrative, which is in some way not in harmony with the *rasa* [of the poem or play], [the poet] should further introduce a story, even if he has invented it, which is appropriate to the *rasa* he has in mind.

But, as Abhinavagupta points out, some stories require too drastic modifications to become fit for dramatic representation. First of all, if a poet presents a deity as the main character of his *nāṭaka*, he has two options to choose from. He can invest his divine hero with human emotions, such as longing for the beloved, fear, or astonishment, but then his hero would become nothing more than a human being. On the other hand, if he stuck to the divinity of his hero, the attribution of mental anguishes to a god would contradict our knowledge about the nature of divine beings. The poet's other option would be to present his hero as a real god, free from all the painful and interesting human emotions, but then the play would lack any variety and therefore it would lose its attraction for the spectators' heart. And since the gods never suffer, how could we learn from their stories the means of obviating our painful experiences?[105]

Roughly the same train of thought can be applied to the presentation of contemporary figures in *nāṭakas*. Although Ānandavardhana encourages the poets to get rid of any motif which could hinder the aesthetic experience and to insert freely invented stories, since after all their task is to write *kāvya* and not

---

[104] *Dhvanyāloka* 3.11+ (ed. Krishnamoorthy, pp. 142f.)

[105] *Abhinavabhāratī ad Nāṭyaśāstra* 18.10 (GOS, vol. II, p. 412): *yadi tu mukhyatvenaiva devacaritaṃ varṇyate, tat tāvad vipralambhakaruṇādbhutabhayānakarasocitaṃ cen nibadhyate, tan mānuṣacaritam eva sampadyate, pratyuta devānām *ādhyādhānaṃ* (conj. : *adhiyādhānaṃ* ed.) *prasiddhivighātakam| tatra cokto doṣaḥ| vipralambhādyabhāve tu kā tatra vicitratā, rañjanāyā etat*prāṇatvāt|* (conj. RAGHAVAN : °*pramāṇatvāt* ed.) *ata eva hṛdayasaṃvādo 'pi devacarite durlabhaḥ| na ca teṣāṃ duḥkham asti, yatpratīkāropāye vyutpādanaṃ syāt|*

itihāsa,[106] still the more recent events are described in a story, the more difficult it becomes to alter any incident without running up against the incredulous indignation of the audience. And if we cling to the bare facts, what's the point in writing poetry? Says Abhinavagupta:[107]

> *ata eva pratītivighātasya vairasyadāyinaḥ sambhavo yatra, tan nāṭake nopanibaddhavyam| tena vartamānacaritaṃ cāvarṇanīyam eva, tatra viparītaprasiddhibādhayādhyāropasyākiñcitkaratvāt|*
>
> For this very reason, if with regard to [some story or other motif in a play] there is a possibility of contradicting common knowledge, which could cause the lack of aesthetic relish, that [sort of story, etc.] should not be written in a *nāṭaka*. Therefore the deeds of a contemporary character should definitely not be related, since in such a case the attribution [of invented qualities to the character] could not succeed because of the opposition of the contradictory common knowledge.

Certainly it would not be fair to accuse Jayanta of crude naturalism. His play is rather a curious mélange of the real and the fictional. One could call it a *Dokumentarspiel*[108] inasmuch as its plot is based on the events of the playwright's recent past: Śaṅkaravarman and Sugandhā were a real royal couple ruling in the last decades of the ninth century, most probably the king did ban the sect of the *nīlāmbaras*, and the concept of *sarvāgamaprāmāṇya* seems to have been an important issue of that period. But we can be sure that for instance the two Śaiva *sādhakas* in the cremation-ground, or the servant who dupes the Jaina monk, were invented by Jayanta on the basis of his experiences, or rather his prejudices. The same is true about the Buddhist monk, whose name Dharmottara echoes that of the famous Buddhist philosopher, or the

---

[106] *Dhvanyāloka* 3.11+ (ed. Krishnamoorthy p. 144): *kavinā kāvyam upanibadhnatā sarvātmanā rasaparatantreṇa bhavitavyam| tatretivṛtte yadi rasānanuguṇāṃ sthitiṃ paśyet tāṃ bhaṅktvāpi svatantratayā rasānuguṇaṃ kathāntaram utpādayet| na hi kaver itivṛttamātranirvahaṇena kiñcit prayojanam, itihāsād eva tatsiddheḥ|*

[107] *Abhinavabhāratī ad Nāṭyaśāstra* 18.10 (GOS, vol. II, p. 413).

[108] WEZLER 1976, p. 340.

hero of the play, the Mīmāṃsaka Saṅkarṣaṇa, who might represent a portion of Jayanta's own character.

The elusiveness of the *Āgamaḍambara* could be very disturbing for an expert in *nāṭyaśāstra*. Should one classify it as a *nāṭaka*, with the king as its real hero? This solution is not very plausible, since the king, apart from being *vartamāna*, does not even appear on the stage, even if his interests stand clearly behind the course of events. Is it then a *prakaraṇa*? Not quite, since its story is not entirely invented, and even if Bharata allows the poet to derive the plot and the characters of his *prakaraṇa* from a text which was 'not handed down by the ancient sages' (*anārṣa*), provided that he endows the events and characters with new qualities,[109] this only means, in Abhinavagupta's interpretation, that the playwright may borrow the plot from such collections as the *Bṛhatkathā* (e.g. the story of Mūladeva), or from the works of some earlier poet (e.g. the deeds of Samudradatta). He certainly cannot pick up a story from just anywhere he pleases (*tatra yo 'nutpādyo 'ṃśo na kutrastho grāhyaḥ*), and I doubt that Abhinavagupta would have rejoiced in a *prakaraṇa* which had a contemporary setting.[110]

On the other hand, a *prakaraṇa* is taught to be a play which presents the stories of Brahmins, merchants, ministers, priests, officials, and travelling tradesmen, and such stories should be 'of various kinds' (*naikavidham*), which in Abhinavagupta's interpretation means, 'connected with various *rasas*' (*anekarasayuktam*).[111] And Jayanta does introduce such characters: the hero of the play is a 'twice-born', who becomes later the subordinate of *amātya* Jayanta; we witness the complaints of two Vedic priests in the prelude before the last act, and even a rich merchant, who

---

[109] *Nāṭyaśāstra* 18.46 (GOS, vol. II, p. 430): *yad anārṣam athāhāryaṃ kāvyaṃ prakaroty abhūtaguṇayuktam| utpannabījavastu prakaraṇam iti tad api vijñeyam||*

[110] *Abhinavabhāratī ad loc.* (GOS, vol. II, pp. 429f): *yatra samutpādyaṃ na bhavati tatra yo 'nutpādyo 'ṃśaḥ na kutrastho grāhya iti darśayitum āha 'yad anārṣam' ityādi| 'anārṣam' iti purāṇādivyatiriktabṛhatkathādyupanibaddhaṃ mūladevacaritādi| 'āhāryam' iti pūrvakavikāvyād vāharaṇīyaṃ samudradattaceṣṭitādi|* Cf. SRINIVASAN, p. 73, which contains Schmithausen's emendations proposed for the rest of the passage.

[111] Cf. *Nāṭyaśāstra* 18.48 (GOS, vol. II, p. 431): *vipravaṇiksacivānāṃ purohitānāṃ amātyasārthavāhānām| caritaṃ yan naikavidhaṃ jñeyaṃ tat prakaraṇaṃ nāma||*, and Abhinavagupta's comm. *ad loc.*

sponsors a huge feast for the ascetics, gets an important role in the second act (although he does not actually enter the stage). But are there servants, rakes, and courtesans appearing in the play?[112] Well, one could possibly say yes. The *ceṭa* in the prelude of the second act does not require further comment. The decadent life of the Buddhist monks is pretty close to a *viṭa*'s, and both the maidservants and the Jain nun (and the *ceṭa* disguised as a Jain nun) are all for amorous entertainment. But can, for instance, the lengthy lecture of the Naiyāyika professor at the end of the play be fitted into a *prakaraṇa*, or indeed into any kind of play?

The Director simply calls the *Āgamaḍambara* 'an extraordinary / strange play' (*kim api rūpakam*), without any further specification, and I think we should reconcile ourselves to the fact that this play is truly *aśāstrīyam*. Still, no Sanskrit drama can oppose the classical tradition to such an extent as not to have a predominant aesthetic flavour, and the nature of this *rasa* is well worth examining.

6.

Already Raghavan observed that the *Āgamaḍambara* can be fitted in the tradition of 'philosophical plays' in classical Indian literature, other examples of which include the *Śārīputraprakaraṇa* of Aśvaghoṣa, and the *Prabodhacandrodaya* of Kṛṣṇamiśra.[113] He also pointed out that the dominant *rasa* of these plays is *śānta*, the aesthetic relish of quietude.[114] *Śānta* is a relatively new arrival in the system of *rasas*, and its very existence was the subject of serious debate among Indian aestheticians.[115] Nevertheless if we

---

[112] *Nāṭyaśāstra* 18.50 (GOS, ibid.): *dāsaviṭaśreṣṭhiyutaṃ veśastryupacārakāraṇopetam|*

[113] *Āgamaḍambara (ed. pr.)*, p. viii.

[114] RAGHAVAN 1975, p. 40.

[115] Cf. MASSON-PATWARDHAN 1969, *passim*. The verses dealing with *śāntarasa* are clearly interpolations in the text of the *Nāṭyaśāstra*, and already Abhinavagupta mentioned that they could not be found in all manuscripts (Abhinavahupta's comm. on these verses (*Abhinavabhāratī* (GOS), vol. I, p. 333:) *cirantanapustakeṣu 'sthāyibhāvān rasatvam upaneṣyāma' ity anantaraṃ 'śānto nāma śamathāyibhāvātmaka' ityādi śāntalakṣaṇaṃ paṭhyate|*). Cf. SRINIVASAN, pp. 51ff.

examine two early definitions of *śāntarasa*, the interpolated passage in the *Nāṭyaśāstra*[116] and the verses of Rudraṭa,[117] we find that several of its characteristics are found in Jayanta's play. True knowledge is essential to attain final liberation from the world of eternal rebirth: the Mīmāṃsaka hero of the play is convinced that he possesses this knowledge, and he is ready to defend it against deluded heretics who are completely mistaken about the real nature of things. The quest for liberation is incompatible with plunging into mundane pleasures, so no wonder that our hero is deeply shocked and disgusted when he witnesses the depraved practices of the Buddhists and the *nīlāmbaras*, but praises the asceticism of the Jains and the *śaivas*. He also betrays great compassion when he lets the Jain teacher beat a retreat. The sole obstacle for him in realising complete dispassion is his ambitious nature, but his initial zeal will much abate towards the end of the play.

But already the *nāndī* and the *prastāvanā* indicate clearly the *rasa* of the play. The opening benediction invokes Brahman 'by which beginningless ignorance is gradually destroyed', and 'at the very start of whose "descent" to the level of consciousness desires for the enjoyment of other pleasing objects cease (*śāmyanti*)'. Then in comes the Director whose disillusion with his profession and life in general does not seem to be completely out of place if we consider that *nirveda* was held by many to be the permanent

---

[116] *Nāṭyaśāstra* after 6.82 (GOS, vol. I, pp. 326ff): *atha śānto nāma śamasthāyibhāvātmako mokṣapravartakaḥ| sa tu tattvajñānavairāgyāśayaśuddhyādibhir vibhāvaiḥ samutpadyate| tasya yamaniyamādhyātmadhyānadhāraṇopāsanasarvabhūtadayāliṅgagrahaṇādibhir anubhāvair abhinayaḥ prayoktavyaḥ| vyabhicāriṇaś cāsya nirvedasmṛtidhṛtisarvāśramaśaucastambharomāñcādayaḥ| atrāryāḥ ślokāś ca bhavanti—mokṣādhyātma*samutthas* (v.l. °*nimittas*) *tattvajñānārthahetusaṃyuktaḥ| *naiḥśreyasopadiṣṭaḥ* (v.l. *niḥśreyasasaṃyuktaḥ*) *śāntaraso nāma *sambhavati* (v.l. *vijñeyaḥ*)|| *buddhīndriyakarmendriya*saṃrodhādhyātmasaṃsthitopetaḥ* (v.l. °*nirodhato 'dhyātmasaṃjñitaś caiva*|) *sarvaprāṇi*sukhahitaḥ* (v.l. °*hitaḥ khalu*) *śāntaraso nāma vijñeyaḥ|| na yatra duḥkhaṃ na sukhaṃ na dveṣo nāpi matsaraḥ| samaḥ sarveṣu bhūteṣu sa śāntaḥ prathito rasaḥ||*

[117] *Kāvyālaṅkāra* 15.15–16 (quoted in RAGHAVAN 1975, p. 48): *samyagjñānaprakṛtiḥ śānto vigatecchanāyako bhavati| samyagjñānaṃ viṣaye tamaso rāgasya cāpagamāt|| janmajarāmaraṇāditrāso vairāgyavāsanā viṣaye| sukhaduḥkhayor anicchādveṣāv iti tatra jāyante||* Rudraṭa flourished between 825 and 850 (according to KANE 1971, p. 155), and was probably Kashmirian.

mental state behind *śāntarasa*.[118] Abhinavagupta attributed this view to Ānandavardhana,[119] who actually preferred to use the expression 'bliss of the destruction of desires', *tṛṣṇākṣayasukha*.[120]

As we have already seen, Ānandavardhana believed that Vyāsa had a double objective in view with the *Mahābhārata*: on the level of *śāstra* he wanted to direct our attention towards *mokṣa*, and on the level of poetry he intended to compose an epic with quietude as its predominant *rasa*, and he achieved his goal by evoking dispassion in the reader. This becomes clear from the rather pessimistic conclusion of the *Mahābhārata*, 'which produces sadness by the cruel end of the Vṛṣṇis and the Pāṇḍavas'.[121] The great Bhīṣma's admonishing words are part of this concept:[122]

> *yathā yathā viparyeti lokatantram asāravat|*
> *tathā tathā virāgo 'tra jāyate nātra saṃśayaḥ||*
>
> As the unsubstantial course of worldly things goes gradually amiss, so does disaffection arise with it by degrees, there is no doubt about this.

But the predominance of *mokṣa* and *śāntarasa* has already been suggested in the Contents (*anukramaṇī*) of the epic, namely in the following sentence: 'And the eternal Blessed Vāsudeva is glorified here' (*bhagavān vāsudevaś ca kīrtyate 'tra sanātanaḥ*, *Mahābhārata* 1.1.193). Says Ānandavardhana:[123]

> *anena hy ayam artho vyaṅgyatvena vivakṣito, yad atra mahābhārate pāṇḍavādicaritaṃ yat kīrtyate, tat sarvam avasānavirasam avidyāprapañcarūpaṃ ca| paramārthasatyasvarūpas tu bhagavān vāsudevo 'tra kīrtyate| tasmāt tasminn eva parameśvare bhagavati bhavata bhāvitacetaso, mā bhūta vibhūtiṣu niḥsārāsu rāgiṇo, guṇeṣu vā nayavinayaparākramādiṣv amīṣu kevale-*

[118] Cf. *Abhinavabhāratī* (GOS), vol. I, p. 327: *tattvajñānotthito nirveda [śāntasya sthāyī] iti ke cit|*

[119] *Locana ad Dhvanyāloka* 3.26, 4.5.

[120] *Dhvanyāloka* 3.26+ (ed. Krishnamoorthy, p. 182): *śāntaś ca tṛṣṇākṣayasukhasya yaḥ paripoṣas tallakṣaṇo rasaḥ pratīyata eva|*

[121] *Dhvanyāloka* 4.5+ (ed. Krishnamoorthy, p. 274): *vṛṣṇipāṇḍavavirasāvasānavaimanasyadāyinīm...*

[122] *Dhvanyāloka* ibid., cf. *Mahābhārata* 12.168.4.

[123] *Dhvanyāloka* 4.5+ (ed. Krishnamoorthy, p. 276).

> *ṣu keṣu cit sarvātmanā pratiniviṣṭadhiyaḥ| tathā cāgre paśyata niḥsāratāṃ saṃsārasyeti| amum evārthātiśayaṃ dyotayan sphuṭam evāvabhāsate vyañjakaśaktyanugṛhītaś caśabdaḥ| evaṃvidham evārthaṃ garbhīkṛtaṃ sandarśayanto 'nantaraślokā lakṣyante 'sa hi satyam' ityādayaḥ|*
>
> For by this [sentence] the following meaning is intended as the suggested one: 'Here, in the *Mahābhārata*, the deeds of the Pāṇḍavas and others, which are sung, are all tragic in their conclusion and are essentially the manifold manifestation of ignorance. But [in fact] the Blessed Vāsudeva, whose true nature is the ultimate reality, is glorified here. Therefore concentrate your thoughts only on that blessed Greatest God, do not hanker after unsubstantial riches, and do not focus wholeheartedly just on these few good qualities such as righteous conduct, discipline, valour, and the like. And thus behold in what follows the insubstantiality of the world.' The word "and", which is endowed with the power of suggestion, shines forth clearly, illuminating the same superior sense. The immediately following verses, beginning with 'for he is reality', are seen to reveal the same meaning, which is hidden within them.

It is the same revelation about the shadowy nature of our reality which is the wellspring of the Director's highly unprofessional behaviour. He realised that 'being an actor is indeed an extremely wretched means of supporting one's family, in which one is continuously practicing a display of utterly false behaviour', and he is not consoled by the fact that 'all this multitude of creatures, from Brahmā down to the animals, roams about in worldly existence through Illusion alone'. His disillusion (*nirveda*), which has reached its apex when he was asked to stage an utterly worthless play, turns him towards the highest goal of man, and provides the play the keynote of *śāntarasa*.

Nevertheless there was a significant opposition against the acceptance of *śānta* as the ninth *rasa*, and even those who acquiesced in its existence had serious doubts about the possibilities of its presentation on the stage. The *Daśarūpaka* refers to 'some people' who list *śānta* among the other *rasas*, but Dhanañjaya hastens to add that 'it cannot thrive in plays'.[124] Dhanika in his commentary mentions the radical view of those who deny *in toto* the possibility of a quietistic *rasa*, 'since it is impossible to destroy desire and hatred which reached [our present age] in a beginningless continuity of time'. Others include it in the heroic, or the repulsive, or other *rasas*.[125] 'However that may be', says Dhanika, 'we do not accept at all that quietude (*śama*) could be the permanent sentiment in *nāṭakas* and other [kinds of drama] the soul of which is performance, since it is not suitable for performance because it consists of the cessation of all activities.'[126] Therefore the permanent sentiment of the *Nāgānanda* cannot be *śama*, especially because the hero is in love and becomes the king of the *vidhyādharas*, neither of which facts goes well with quietude. The permanent sentiment of this play is fortitude (*utsāha*), and its *rasa* is the compassionate kind of heroism (*dayāvīra*).[127]

This kind of criticism was already familiar to Ānandavardhana, who spoke up for the presence of *śānta* even in the dramatic genre. According to him, even if its permanent sentiment, that is the pleasure of the cessation of all desires (*tṛṣṇākṣayasukha*) 'might not be part of everyone's experience, still it cannot be rejected as the special mental operation of exalted persons who are not like the other people'.[128] It is not right to include *śānta* in *vīra*, since heroism necessarily contains some egoism, which runs counter with quietude.[129] Abhinavagupta adds that its equation

[124] *Daśarūpaka* 4.35: *śamam api ke cit prāhuḥ puṣṭir nāṭyeṣu naitasya||*

[125] *Avaloka ad loc.*, p. 202: *anye tu vastutas tasyābhāvaṃ varṇayanti, anādikālapravāhāyātarāgadveṣayor ucchettum aśakyatvāt| anye tu vīrabībhatsādāv antarbhāvaṃ varṇayanti|*

[126] *Avaloka*, ibid.. *yathā tathāstu, sarvathā nāṭakādāv abhinayātmani sthāyitvam asmābhiḥ śamasya neṣyate, tasya samastavyāpārapravilayarūpasyā bhinayāyogāt|*

[127] *Avaloka*, ibid., p. 203: *yat tu kaiścin nāgānandādau śamasya sthāyitvam upavarṇitam, tan malayavatyanurāgeṇāprabandhapravṛttena, ante vidyādharacakravartitvaprāpteś ca viruddham| (...) ato dayāvīrotsāhasya tatra sthāyitvam...*

[128] *Dhvanyāloka* 3.26+ (ed. Krishnamoorthy, p. 182). *yadi nāma sarvajanānubhavagocaratā tasya nāsti, naitāvatāsāv alokasāmānyamahānubhāvacittavṛttiviśeṣaḥ pratikṣeptuṃ śakyaḥ|*

[129] *Dhvanyāloka*, ibid.: *na ca vīre tasyāntarbhāvaḥ kartuṃ yuktaḥ, tas-*

with repulsion is equally misleading, since *jugupsā* is only the transitory ancillary sentiment of *śānta*. He also observes that even if the culmination of *śānta* cannot be presented because of the absence of indicatory symptoms (*anubhāvas*), its earlier phases can, through such signs as self-control, religious observances, and even bearing the yoke of a kingdom.[130]

But even Ānandavardhana's eloquent justification was not enough to dispel all doubts about the aesthetic relish of quietude. The author of the *Candrikā* commentary on the *Dhvanyāloka* remarked that '*śāntarasa* should not be employed as the leading [relish of a poetic work].'[131] Even Abhinavagupta admitted the following:[132]

> *śāntabībhatsarasau tu caramapumarthayogāt, tatra ca sarvasya nādhi*kāre 'pi* (conj. : °*kāro 'pi* ed.) *kasya cid apaścimajanmano 'dhikārān nāṭake yady api tatphalapradhānatayā prādhānyam avalambeyātāṃ, tathāpi nāsau pracuraprayoga iti tayoḥ puruṣārthapravarapraṇitayor api vīrādirasāntarādhyāvāpenāvasthāpanam|*
>
> But although the *rasas* of quietude and repulsion, because they are appropriate to the ultimate goal of man [i.e. liberation], and since some extraordinary people of excellent birth *are* qualified [for *mokṣa*], even if not everyone is qualified for it, could become predominant in a *nāṭaka* inasmuch as that [i.e. liberation] is the principally intended result, still this is not an extensive practice. Therefore even if these two [i.e. quietude and repulsion] are animated by the best of the human goals, still they are employed with other *rasas* such as heroism mixed into them.

---

yābhimānamayatvena vyavasthapanāt, asya cāhaṅkārapraśamaikarūpatayā sthiteḥ|

[130] *Locana ad loc.*

[131] *Locana*, ibid. (Kashi ed., p. 394): *ādhikārikatvena tu śānto raso na nibaddhavya iti candrikākāraḥ|*

[132] *Abhinavabhāratī ad Nāṭyaśāstra* 18.110 (GOS, vol. II, p. 451); cf. J.C. WRIGHT, 'Vṛtti in the *Daśarūpakavidhānādhyāya* of the *Abhinavabhāratī*' in: BSOAS 26 (1963), pp. 92ff.

Before expounding his own ideas, Abhinavagupta refers to several theories about the *sthāyibhāva* of *śāntarasa*. Among those who held the opinion that it was *nirveda*, some made reference to the *Nyāyasūtra*.[133] Others, however, adopted the belief that any of the eight permanent mental states can be the *sthāyī* of *śānta*:[134]

> *anye manyante| ratyādaya evāṣṭau cittavṛttiviśeṣā uktāḥ| tata eva kathitavibhāvaviviktaśrutādyalaukikavibhāvaviśeṣasaṃśrayāḥ vicitrā eva tāvat| tataś ca tanmadhyād evānyatamo 'tra sthāyī| tatra anāhatānandamayasvātmaviṣayā ratir eva mokṣasādhanam iti, saiva śānte sthāyinīti| yathoktaṃ, 'yaś cātmaratir eva syād ātmatṛptaś ca mānavaḥ| ātmany eva ca santuṣṭaḥ tasya kāryaṃ na vidyate||' iti| evaṃ samastaviṣayaṃ vaikṛtaṃ paśyataḥ, viśvaṃ ca śocyaṃ vilokayataḥ, sāṃsarikaṃ ca vṛttāntam apakāritvena paśyataḥ, sātiśayam asammohapradhānaṃ vīryam āśritavataḥ, sarvasmād viṣayasārthād bibhyataḥ, sarvalokaspṛhaṇīyād api pramadāder jugupsamānasya, apūrvasvātmātiśayalābhād vismayamānasya mokṣasiddhir iti, ratihāsādīnāṃ vismayāntānām anyatamasya sthāyitvaṃ nirūpaṇīyam|*
>
> 'Others embrace the following view: "It is delight etc. which are taught as the eight particular kinds of mental operations. It is they that first of all become very diverse when they are connected with special, supramundane eliciting factors (*vibhāvas*) such as the study of Scripture, which are different from the [already] mentioned eliciting factors. And therefore any one among just these [eight *vibhāvas*] [can be] its [i.e. *śāntarasa*'s] permanent [mental basis] *(sthāyī)*. Of these, delight which has as its object one's own self which is full of unimpaired bliss, is a means of attaining liberation, so it is indeed a permanent mental state of *śānta*.

[133] *Abhinavabhāratī* (GOS), vol. I, p. 329: *nanu mithyājñānamūlo viṣayagandhas tattvajñānāt praśāmyatīti duḥkhajanmasūtreṇākṣapādapādair vadadbhir mithyājñanapacayakāraṇaṃ tattvajñānaṃ vairāgyasya doṣāpāyalakṣaṇasya kāranam uktam| nanu tataḥ kim? nanu vairāgyaṃ nirvedaḥ|*

[134] *Abhinavabhāratī* (GOS), ibid. (I am following the reading of RAGHAVAN 1975, p. 109.)

> As it is taught, 'That man has nothing left to accomplish whose delight is in his Self alone, who is contented in his Self, and who finds complete satisfaction in his Self.' (*Bhagavadgītā* 3.17) Likewise, that person succeeds in attaining liberation who notices that everything is grotesque, who considers the whole world lamentable, who notices that worldly affairs are harmful, who resorts to great heroism which is based on true insight, who is afraid of all the multitude of sense-objects, who is disgusted by women and the like, even if the whole world lusts after them, and who is astonished when he obtains the unprecedented excellence of his self. Therefore any one of [the eight permanent mental states] beginning with delight, laughter, etc. and ending with wonder, can be seen as the permanent [basis of *śānta*].'

This could also explain why the *Āgamaḍambara*, an allegedly *śāntarasa* play, resembles a kaleidoscope of various sentiments. The Mīmāṃsaka hero is fully self-confident in his knowledge, which entitles him to enlighten and humiliate those who stray in darkness. He truly admires himself, but he is also capable of appreciating other people's values, such as asceticism. The *baṭu* calls him 'supremely compassionate' when he refrains from beating up the Jains with a stick. He mocks the hypocrite behaviour of the Buddhists, is utterly disgusted and shocked by the eccentric ritual of the *nīlāmbara* couples, and is even unwilling to enter into a debate with them because of the dangers of their impurity. So is Saṅkarṣaṇa a true *śāntarasa* hero? I cannot help hearing a tone of gentle irony in the way Jayanta presents the Mīmāṃsaka. Saṅkarṣaṇa is too much of an idealist, who believes that it is his sacred duty to turn back to the right track all who deviated from it, even in the service of worldly authorities that (mis)use his zeal for their own purposes. He is too self-conceited, therefore he has to fail and realise that his knowledge was not yet adequate.

If we glance over the *Dhvanyāloka*-passages about the role of *śāntarasa* in the *Mahābhārata*, it appears that although Ānandavardhana did distinguish the doctrinal and the poetic aspects of the epic, he also held that the emotions awakened by the narrative can assist the reader in attaining liberation:[135]

> *pāṇḍavādicaritavarṇanasyāpi vairāgyajananatātparyād vairāgyasya ca mokṣamūlatvān mokṣasya ca bhagavatprāptyupāyatvena mukhyatayā gītādiṣu pradarśitatvāt parabrahmaprāptyupāyatvam eva paramparayā|*
>
> Even the description of the deeds of the Pāṇḍavas and other [heroes], since its aim is to produce disillusion, since disillusion is the basis of liberation, and since liberation had been shown in the *Gītā* and other [sacred texts] to be the most important means of attaining the Lord, [therefore even this description] *is* indirectly a means of attaining the highest Brahman.

But the first theoretician who explicitly stated that there is an intimate relation between Brahman-experience and aesthetic relish in general appears to have been Bhaṭṭa Nāyaka, whose ideas are condensed by Abhinavagupta as follows:[136]

> *bhāvite ca rase tasya bhogo yo 'nubhavasmaraṇapratipattibhyo vilakṣaṇa eva drutivistaravikāsātmā rajastamovaicitryānuviddhasattvamayanijacitsvabhāvanirvṛtiviśrāntilakṣaṇaḥ parabrahmāsvādasavidhaḥ|*
>
> 'And after the *rasa* has been produced [through the operation of the words called "*bhāvakatva*, bringing into being"], its enjoyment [becomes possible], which very much differs from [ordinary] cognitions [whether] direct experience or memory, whose nature is melting, intensity, and expansion,[137] which is characterised by the repose in the beatitude of the true form of one's consciousness which is full of purity *(sattva)*

---

[135] *Dhvanyāloka* 4.5+ (ed. Krishnamoorthy, p. 278).

[136] *Locana ad Dhvanyāloka* 2.4 (ed. *Kāvyamālā*, p. 83, ed. Kashi, p. 183).

[137] Ingalls (-Masson-Patwardhan) translate *vistara* as 'expansion', and *vikāsa* as 'radiance' (*Dhvanyāloka*(HOS), p. 222), GNOLI (1968, p. 108) as 'enlargement' and 'expansion', respectively. *vikāsa* might also have the sense of 'cheerfulness'. Raghavan notes (RAGHAVAN 1978, p. 426, note 1) that in the *Daśarūpaka* the mental state of *vikāsa* corresponds to the erotic and the comic *rasas*, while *vistara* to the heroic and the marvellous.

> blended with the variety of energy *(rajas)* and darkness *(tamas)*, and which is similar to the experience of the highest Brahman.

Mammaṭa also summarises the theory of Bhaṭṭa Nāyaka:[138]

> *kāvye nāṭye cābhidhāto dvitīyena vibhāvādisādhāraṇīkaraṇātmanā bhāvakatvavyāpāreṇa bhāvyamānaḥ sthāyī sattvodrekaprakāśānandamayasaṃvidviśrāntisatattvena bhogena bhujyate—iti bhaṭṭanāyakaḥ*|
>
> 'In poems and in plays the permanent sentiment is transformed [into *rasa*] by the operation of "bringing into being" which is essentially the generalisation of the eliciting factors and [the indicatory symptoms and the temporary mental states] and which is different from [the word's operation called] denotation, [and then *rasa*] is enjoyed with enjoyment which is the same in its essence as the repose in [one's] consciousness which is full of bliss and radiance due to the abundance of purity (*sattva*)'—this is what Bhaṭṭa Nāyaka says.

If we review the opening benediction of the *Āgamaḍambara*, it might appear less puzzling now in the light of Ānandavardhana's and Bhaṭṭa Nāyaka's ideas. The invocation of the Brahman at the beginning of a *śāntarasa*-play seems natural. The Brahman's 'descent' to the path of consciousness might signify the prelude to the highest kind of mystical experience which must entail the arising of disillusion *(virāga, nirveda)* and the gradual awakening to the knowledge of reality. That this experience also involves bliss might sound perhaps unusual from the mouth of a Naiyāyika,[139] but we might say that someone who proceeds on the path leading to final liberation will rejoice as this radiant reality dawns upon him. And one station along this path may well be a play with

[138] *Kāvyaprakāśa*, vol. I, pp. 217ff.

[139] Jayanta (together with the mainstream *naiyāyikas*) held that the liberated state of the soul is not a blissful state, since it is equally without suffering *and* pleasure (cf. *Nyāyamañjarī*, vol. II, pp. 436ff). Bhāsarvajña represents another view among the *naiyāyikas*, namely that the liberated soul *does* experience beatitude (cf. *Nyāyabhūṣaṇa*, pp. 594ff).

quietude as its predominant *rasa* which distracts the spectator from the everyday world and directs his attention towards higher truths.

The fictitious world of drama offers an excellent analogy with the illusory nature of the world we live in. The world we call 'actual' 'is nevertheless a possible world in itself—that is, a construct deriving from the conceptual and textual constraints on the spectator's understanding.'[140] The poet has an almost divine autonomy in fashioning his poetic world. 'In the boundless world of poetry', says Ānandavardhana, 'the poet is the only Creator. This whole universe revolves as he pleases. If the poet is amorous, a world full of flavour arises in the poem. If the same [poet] is disenchanted, all that world is without flavour. In a poem a good poet freely makes insentient things behave as sentient and sentient beings as insentient, as he pleases.'[141] A comparable idea is expressed in the words of semiotic analysis as follows: 'It should not be thought that the "accessibility" of dramatic worlds renders them always and necessarily realistically mimetic. On the contrary, it is precisely the constant assumption that W_D [the dramatic world] is defined in relation to W_O [the actual world] as a hypothetical variation which allows any number of invented and even fantastic elements to be introduced into the drama without destroying the audience's ability to recognize what is going on.'[142]

The actor also participates in the creation of the dramatic universe: he infuses life into the characters invented by the playwright or, put differently, he dissembles his real identity. As the Director says in the Prologue of the *Āgamaḍambara*: 'Shame, for shame, being an actor is indeed an extremely wretched means of supporting one's family, in which one is continuously practicing a display of utterly false behaviour. Hara, Viṣṇu, Brahmā, a sage, a king, a brutish fool, a rake, a coward, a hero, a happy man, a sad

[140] ELAM 1997, p. 108.

[141] *Dhvanyāloka* 3.42+ (ed. Krishnamoorthy, p. 250): *apāre kāvyasaṃsāre kavir ekaḥ prajāpatiḥ| yathāsmai rocate viśvaṃ tathedaṃ parivartate|| śṛṅgārī cet kaviḥ kāvye jātaṃ rasamayaṃ jagat| sa eva vītarāgaś cen nīrasaṃ sarvam eva tat|| bhāvān acetanān api cetanavac cetanān acetanavat| vyavahārayati yatheṣṭaṃ sukaviḥ kāvye svatantratayā||* Abhinavagupta hastens to add in his commentary *ad loc.* that an 'amorous' poet is not an actual womaniser (*strīvyasanī*), but someone who is filled with the aesthetic relish of the Erotic.

[142] ELAM 1997, p. 107.

one: taking all roles the actor plays, feeling no shame before the people—in reality he is [just] resorting to craft to fill his belly.' But his Assistant reminds him that he is no exception: 'Who among gods, humans or animals has ever escaped from deceit and then reached the supreme goal? All this multitude of creatures, from Brahmā down to the animals, roams about in worldly existence through Illusion alone. Is your lot any worse?' Creative illusion rules the whole world.

Theatre and acting are excellent allegories of the world that surrounds us and the activity of the Creator who puts on the masks of worldly phenomena. In fact, Bharata says in the very first verse of the *Nāṭyaśāstra*: 'I shall teach the science of dramaturgy which was related by Brahmā as an illustration (*udāhṛtam*).'[143] Now it is certainly possible to take the word *udāhṛtam* simply to mean 'announced', but Bhaṭṭa Nāyaka understood this sentence as an allusion to the allegorical nature of drama. This is how Abhinavagupta presents Nāyaka's ideas:[144]

> *bhaṭṭanāyakas tu 'brahmaṇā paramātmanā yad udāhṛtam, avidyāviracitanissārabhedagrahe yad udāharaṇīkṛtaṃ nāṭyaṃ tad vakṣyāmi| yathā hi kalpanāmātrasāraṃ tata eva anavasthitaikarūpaṃ, kṣaṇena kalpanāśatasahasrasahaṃ, svapnādivilakṣaṇam api suṣṭhutarāṃ hṛdayagrahanidānam, atyaktasvālambanabrahmakalpanaṭoparacitaṃ rāmarāvaṇādiceṣṭitam asatyaṃ kuto 'py adbhutavṛttyā bhāti, tathā bhāsamānam api *caramapumarthopāyatām* (conj. ISAACSON : *ca pumarthopāyatām* ed.) *eti, tathā tādṛg eva viśvam idam asatyanāmarūpaprapañcātmakam atha ca śravaṇamananādivaśena paramapumarthaprāpakam, iti lokottaraparamapuruṣārthasūcanena śāntarasopakṣepo 'yaṃ bhaviṣyati, 'svaṃ svaṃ nimittam ādāya śāntād utpadyate rasaḥ' iti| tad anena pāramārthikaṃ prayojanam*

[143] *Nāṭyaśāstra* 1.1 (ed. GOS, vol. I, p. 1): *nāṭyaśāstraṃ pravakṣyāmi brahmaṇā yad udāhṛtam* (v.l. *udīritam*)|

[144] *Abhinavabhāratī ad loc.* (ed. GOS, vol. I, pp. 5f). It seems likely (as already T. R. Chintamani observed in 'Fragments of Bhaṭṭanāyaka', *Journal of Oriental Research*, Madras, vol. I, p. 268.) that Abhinavagupta does not actually quote Bhaṭṭa Nāyaka, but just elaborates an interpretation of what was probably the introductory verse of the *Sahṛdayadarpaṇa*.

uktam|' iti vyākhyānaṃ sahṛdayadarpaṇe paryagrahīt|
yad āha
'namas trailokyanirmāṇakavaye śambhave, yataḥ|
pratikṣaṇaṃ jagannāṭyaprayogarasiko janaḥ||' iti|

Bhaṭṭa Nāyaka, however, embraced the following interpretation [of *Nāṭyaśāstra* 1.1] in his *Sahṛdayadarpaṇa*: 'Drama, that was presented as an example by Brahmā, the Supreme Self, that is to say that was made into an example of the grasping of insubstantial multifariousness created by ignorance—that is what I shall teach. For just as the fictitious story of Rāma, Rāvaṇa, and other [characters], which is essentially just fancy and therefore does not have a single, established form, [but] is accompanied by a vast number of fancies in every moment, which [story], though different from dreams, is the cause of rapture, [when it is] performed by the actors who have not abandoned their own identity and who are similar to Brahmā, appears in an extraordinarily wonderful way; [and] even while appearing as such, it becomes a means of [attaining] the highest goal of man, in the same way this whole world is exactly like that [drama], inasmuch as it consists of the diversity of names and forms, and it also leads us to the highest goal of man through reading the scriptures, reflection, and [meditation]. Thus, through referring to the highest goal of man which transcends this world, this [verse] may be an allusion to the aesthetic relish of quietude, on the basis of the verse "resorting to its respective cause [each] *rasa* arises from *śānta* ".[145] Therefore by this [verse] the ultimate object [of the *Nāṭyaśāstra*] has been declared.' [Bhaṭṭa Nāyaka embraced this interpretation] when / for he said, 'Obeisance to Śiva, the poet who composes the

[145]One of the interpolated verses on *śānta*, *Nāṭyaśāstra* 6. (ed. GOS, vol. I, p. 329). The edition actually reads '*svaṃ svaṃ nimittam āsādya śāntād bhāvaḥ pravartate*', something which for Abhinavagupta, who was very particular about the precise differentiation of *rasa* and *bhāva*, would clearly not have suited.

> triad of the worlds, thanks to whom people relish the performance of the world-play at every instant'.

So illusion is not that harmful after all, at least if we know how to handle it. It would be a mistake to look upon the imaginary world of theatre as something real or actual, and when we watch the characters on the stage being engaged in wooing or lamenting, their identity as actors always lurks in the back of our awareness. And as the actor's emotions are not 'real' so our emotional responses are different from our everyday sentiments: we savour these sentiments in a pure form while the fictitious world of the play enraptures us. Moreover, precisely through this rapture we also learn a lot about the real, unobscured nature of our mental attitudes: our understanding is augmented.

One of the various terms used to describe aesthetic experience is *viśrānti*, reposeful awareness, that is the cognition of the fundamental emotions in their pure, universalised form, free from all obstacles.[146] This 'mental repose' entails a higher stage of concentration, and it is also a blissful state[147] akin to the beatitude of mystical experience. To regard *śānta* as the basis of all other *rasa*s seems to have been a logical step.[148] As Gerow observed,[149] 'Since all the dramatic *rasa*s aim at a state of mental repose *(viśrānti)*, the reductionist "insight" that all the *rasas* are fundamentally *śānti* is neither very daring nor very unexpected, particularly in the spiritual-devotional climate in which Abhinavagupta lived. *Śānta* was a *rasa* whose time had come—which, if it did not exist, would have had to be invented.' In Abhinavagupta's view the relishing of *śāntarasa* is a more conscious kind of aesthetic experience, since in it any emotion can be savoured in its universalised *rasa*-form as a temporary hue on the surface of the uniquely permanent Self.[150] This kind of aesthetic rapture can

[146] *Abhinavabhāratī ad rasasūtra* (ed. GOS, vol. I, p. 274): *tathā hi loke sakalavighnavinirmuktā saṃvittir eva camatkāranirveśarasanāsvādanabhogasamāpattilayaviśrāntyādiśabdair abhidhīyate|*

[147] *Abhinavabhāratī* ibid. (ed. GOS, vol. I, p. 276): *aviśrāntirūpataiva duḥkham| tata eva kāpilair duḥkhasya cāñcalyam eva prāṇatvenoktaṃ rajovṛttitāṃ vadadbhir ity ānandarūpatā sarvarasānām|*

[148] *Abhinavabhāratī* on *śāntarasa* (ed. GOS, vol. I, p. 333): *tatra sarvarasānāṃ śāntaprāya evāsvādaḥ, viṣayebhyo viparivṛttyā|*

[149] GEROW-AKLUJKAR, p. 81, note 6

[150] Cf. *Abhinavabhāratī* (GOS), vol. I, p. 330.

teach us the most about the true nature of any experience. But even if we regard *śānta* as essentially the artistic representation of disenchantment born from the realisation of the illusory nature of existence, it can still be regarded as occupying the highest rank among all *rasas* since it directs our attention towards liberation, the supreme goal of man.

The characters and their transactions we see on the stage are merely the products of the poet's and the actors' creative skills; still we are both delighted and taught by the play. According to Bhaṭṭa Nāyaka and Abhinavagupta, the same is true about the world outside the theatre. God likes to play. He disguises his real identity with a multitude of appearances, but we can cast a glance behind all these masks with the help of His scriptures and practising meditation. And when we have recognised the illusory nature of all worldly phenomena we still have the choice of being entertained by this illusion, as if watching an amusing performance.

The *Āgamaḍambara* begins with the complaints of an artist, who is fed up with deceiving people. He wants Truth instead of Delusion, and he hopes to find it among the teachings of philosophies. But what happens if the venerable masters of various doctrines turn out to be more interested in making a good living than in Truth and Reality? What if being a monk or a Vedic priest is just an occupation, a job like being an actor? Or even if we suppose that the followers of these doctrines are not just cynical opportunists but they really believe in what they teach, what guarantees that all these religions are not just roles in the gigantic play of the Lord? Says Kṣemarāja, 'The positions, i.e. the tenets of all doctrines beginning with [that of] the materialists, are the adopted roles of that Self like [those] of an actor, which it takes on at pleasure.'[151] One possible attitude is to say that God fools the followers of all the *other* religions to a higher or lesser degree, but the world-view that *I* follow allows me to understand His real nature. Or one might arrive at an extremely liberal position and say that God takes on various roles to propound various

[151] *Pratyabhijñāhṛdayam* 8+ (ed. p. 16): *sarveṣāṃ cārvākādidarśanānāṃ sthitayaḥ siddhāntāḥ tasyaivātmano naṭasyeva *svecchayā gṛhītāḥ* (em. SANDERSON : *svecchāvagṛhītāḥ* ed.) *kṛtrimā bhūmikāḥ*|

teachings, and he does so not just for fun but out of compassion towards us, miserable creatures with limited capacities. So in fact all scriptures derive from God, each of them being adjusted to our particular needs and talents.

This latter view seems to be triumphant at the end of the *Āgamaḍambara*, but not with the active participation of the Mīmāṃsaka protagonist. He could not resolve the tension between his religion as a devotee of Viṣṇu and his duty to protect the Veda as a Mīmāṃsaka.[152] Or rather, there was one solution for him: devotion to God and asking for his illuminating favour.[153] He visits the nearby Raṇasvāmī-temple where he sings praises to the Lord who 'shows the right path to liberation' *(vyañjate mokṣasanmārgam).* Unfortunately the manuscripts of the play are fragmentary at this place, but from the auspicious omen of the sound of a conch-shell we may safely infer that Viṣṇu dispelled the doubts of his devotee, as a result of which he was able to rejoice in the ultraliberal lecture delivered by the great Naiyāyika scholar.

At the beginning of the play we saw that art could not make the Director, a determined and uncompromising seeker after Truth, entirely happy. Learned scrutiny of the true nature of things may have given satisfaction to the *snātaka*, especially when he defeated his opponents, but ultimately it could not give him serenity and peace of mind. That direct experience of the Lord's grace is superior to both aesthetic rapture and philosophical investigation was expressed by Ānandavardhana in the following beautiful verse:[154]

> *yā vyāpāravatī rasān rasayituṃ kācit kavīnāṃ navā*
> *dṛṣṭir yā pariniṣṭhitārthaviṣayonmeṣā ca vaipaścitī|*
> *te dve apy avalambya viśvam aniśaṃ nirvarṇayanto vayaṃ*

[152] *Āgamaḍambara*, Act Four, verse 5: *ye viśvasthitisargasaṃhṛtidaśāparyāyasampādanakrīḍāsaktamater mataṃ bhagavato nārāyaṇasyāśritāḥ| taddṛṣṭeḥ katham anyathātvam anayā brūmo vayaṃ jihvayā śakṣyāmaḥ kṛtināṃ trayīmayadhiyāṃ sthātuṃ kathaṃ vāgrataḥ||*

[153] *Āgamaḍambara*, Act Four, verse 7: *pathi vedavirodhadāruṇe nipuṇenāpi na śakyanirṇaye| kim ahaṃ karavāṇi hanta me śaraṇaṃ śārṅgarathāṅgaśaṅkhabhṛt||*

[154] *Dhvanyāloka* 3.43+ (ed. Krishnamoorthy, p. 256.)

śrāntā naiva ca labdham abdhiśayana tvadbhaktitulyaṃ sukham||

That which is the extraordinary, fresh vision of poets, active in making the *rasas* tasteful, and that which is the [vision] of the wise, opening upon thoroughly ascertained things as its object: resorting to both, while I was ceaselessly observing the world, I became tired and I could not find bliss equal to devotion to you, O God resting on the sea.

Appendix: The Prologue of Bhaṭṭa Jayanta's *Āgamaḍambara*

tad brahma vaḥ kramavinaśyadanādyavidyam
uddyotatāṃ sphuradamandanavābhinandam |
saṃvitpade 'vataraṇonmukha eva yatra
śāmyanti kāntaviṣayāntarabhogavāñchāḥ ||1||

nāndyante SŪTRADHĀRAḤ:
aho aho naṭatvaṃ nāma jaghanyaḥ ko 'pi satatābhyastasūtkaṭakapaṭavyāpāraḍambaraḥ kuṭumbabharaṇopāyaḥ!

Haro Viṣṇur Brahmā Munir Avanipaḥ Pāmarapaśur
viṭo bhīruḥ śūraḥ pramuditamatir duḥkhita iti |
spṛśan sarvākārān viharati jane nistrapatayā
naṭo vastusthityā jaṭharabharaṇe śilpaśaraṇaḥ ||2||

tad varam imaṃ kuśilpam alpaphalam alaghukleśam atitrapākaram upasaṃhṛtya kva cid āśrame kim api gurukulam upāsīnaḥ sakaladuḥkhoparamaṃ paramaṃ puruṣārtham abhigantuṃ yatiṣye. *(vimṛśya)* tat kvemaṃ kṛpaṇakaṃ kṛpāpātraprāyaṃ kuṭumbabharam arpayitvā gamyatām? *(agrato 'valokya)* bhavatu, amuṣya tāvad āśayaṃ vijñāsye.

praviśya PĀRIPĀRŚVAKAḤ SŪTRADHĀRAM avalokya:
kim ayam adya nirvedaparimlānavadana iva dṛśyate? pṛcchamy enam. *(upasṛtya)* bhāva, kim idaṃ viṣaṇṇavadanam āsyate? nanu kva cana viniyukto 'si Vṛttikāraśiṣyaiḥ?

SŪTRA° *(pūrvoktaṃ yatiṣya ityantaṃ paṭhati.)*

PĀRI° alam asthāne nirvedena. ko nu khalu deveṣu manuṣyeṣu tiryakṣu vā kapaṭacaryām uttīrya paramārthe paryavasitaḥ? sarva evāyaṃ Brahmādis tiryakparyanto jantugrāmaḥ saṃsāre māyayaiva parivartate. bhavataḥ kim adhikaṃ jātam?

> māyāviḍambyamānasya viśvasya jagato yathā |
> vyavahāro na satyārthas tathāsmākaṃ bhaviṣyati ||3||

SŪTRA° māriṣa, yathāha bhavān. kiṃ tv ayam īdṛśo 'py aśakyanirvāha āsmākīno vyavahāraḥ.

PĀRI° bhāva, katham iva?

SŪTRA° māriṣa, Bharatamuninopadiṣṭe daśarūpakaprayoge kila kṛtaśramā vayam. adya cātrabhavataḥ śaiśava eva vyākaraṇavivaraṇakaraṇād Vṛttikāra iti prathitāparanāmno Bhaṭṭajayantasya śiṣyapariṣadāham ājñapto yathāsmadguroḥ kṛtir abhinavam Āgamaḍambaraṃ nāma kim api rūpakaṃ prayoktavyam iti. tad idam alaukikam aśāstrīyam aprayuktapūrvaṃ kathaṃ prayuñjmahe? tad asyāḥ kujīvikāyā upekṣaṇam eva śreyaḥ.

PĀRI° bhāva, maivam. anatikramaṇīyaśāsanāḥ khalv atrabhavanto Vṛttikārasya śiṣyāḥ. yat punar aśāstrīyam iti śaṅkase, tatra kaḥ prayoktur aparādhaḥ?

> kāvyaṃ karoti sa kavir Bharatopadeśam
> ullaṅghya, tasya ca tathā prathayanti śiṣyāḥ |
> sāmājikās tava ta eva, bhavān prayuṅktāṃ.
> pārśvasthitaḥ parivadiṣyati kiṃ jano 'nyaḥ? ||4||

SŪTRA° kṛtaṃ janāpavādena.

PĀRI° tat kiṃ rājabhayam āśaṅkase?

SŪTRA° *(sasmitam)* tad api nāsti.

PĀRI° tat kiṃ vilambase? nanu niyujyantāṃ tāsu tāsu Saugatārhatādibhūmikāsu kuśīlavāḥ.

SŪTRA° māriṣa, na śaknomy eva durvaham idam udvoḍhum indrajālamāyāprāyaṃ naṭavṛttam.

aśāstrakaṃ vāstu tadanvitaṃ vā
kāvyaṃ, janaḥ kupyatu rajyatāṃ vā |
ahaṃ tu nirviṇṇamanāḥ svavṛttim
utsṛjya tīrthāni cinomi tāvat. ||5||

bhavān punaḥ kṛpaṇakam asmatkuṭumbakaṃ vā saṃvāhayatu, mām eva vānugacchatu. mayā tv idānīm evāsmin mahati vihāre vītarāgabhikṣuśataparigṛhīte nātidūranirvāṇamārgadeśini tattvabubhutsunā praveṣṭavyam.

iti niṣkrāntau.

prastāvanā

Works Consulted

Primary Sources

[*Abhinavabhāratī* (GOS)] *Nāṭyaśāstra of Bharatamuni with the commentary Abhinavabhāratī of Abhinavaguptācārya*, vol. I, Chapters 1–7 illustrated, 4th ed., revised and critically edited by K. Krishnamoorthy, Gaekwad's Oriental Series, no. 36, Oriental Institute, Vadodara, 1992; vol. II, Chapters 8–18, edited with an Introduction and Index by M. R. Kavi, 2nd ed., revised and critically edited by V. M. Kulkarni and T. Nandi, Gaekwad's Oriental Series, no. 68, Oriental Institute, Vadodara, 2001.

[*Abhinavabhāratī* (Parimal)] *Nāṭyaśāstra of Bharatamuni with the commentary Abhinavabhāratī of Ācārya Abhinavagupta*, ed. R. S. Nagar, vols. 1–4, Parimal Sanskrit Series No. 4, Delhi, 1998.

[*Āgamaḍambara*] see DEZSŐ 2004.

[*Āgamaḍambara (ed. pr.)*] *Āgamaḍambara, otherwise called Ṣaṇmatanāṭaka of Jayanta Bhaṭṭa*, edited by Dr. V. Raghavan and Prof. Anantalal Thakur, Mithila Research Institute, Darbhanga, 1964.

[*Kāvyaprakāśa*] *Kavyaprakasha of Mammata, with Sanketa of Acharya Manikyachandra, Madhumati of Ravi Bhattacharya and Bhavukapriya tippani*, 2 vols., ed. N. S. Venkatanathacharya, Oriental Research Institute Series 120, 122, Mysore, 1974–1977.

[*Kāvyānuśāsana*] *Kāvyānuṣāsana with Alaṃkārachūḍāmani and Viveka by Achārya Hemachandra, with an anonymous Ṭippaṇa*, ed. Rasiklal C. Parikh, vol. I, Bombay, 1938.

[*Kāvyamīmāṃsā*] *Kāvyamīmāṃsā of Rājaśekhara*, ed. C.D. Dalal and R.A. Sastry; revised and enlarged by K.A. Ramaswami Sastri, Gaekwad's Oriental Series No. 1, 3rd. ed., Oriental Institute, Baroda 1934.

[*Kāvyālaṅkāra*] *Kāvyālaṅkāra of Bhāmaha*, edited with English translation and notes by P. V. Naganatha Sastry, 2nd ed., Motilal Banarsidass, Delhi, 1970.

[*Granthibhaṅga*] *Cakradhara's Nyāyamañjarīgranthibhaṅga*, edited by Nagin J. Shah, L. D. Series 35, Ahmedabad, 1972.

[*Daśarūpaka*] *Śrīdhanañjayaviracitaṃ Daśarūpakam, Dhanikakṛtāvalokasaṃskṛtavyākhyopetam Ālokahindīvyākhyopetañca*, ed. Baijanāth Pāṇḍey, Delhi, 1999 (reprint of 1979 edition).

[*Dhvanyāloka* (ed. Krishnamoorthy)] *Dhvanyāloka of Ānandavardhana*, critically edited with introduction, translation & notes by K. Krishnamoorthy, 2nd ed., Motilal Banarsidass, Delhi, 1982.

[*Dhvanyāloka* (HOS)] *The Dhvanyāloka of Ānandavardhana with the Locana of Abhinavagupta*, translated by Daniel H.H. Ingalls, Jeffrey Moussaieff Masson, and M.V. Patwardhan; edited with an introduction by Daniel H.H. Ingalls, Harvard Oriental Series, vol. 49, Harvard University Press, Cambridge, Mass, 1990.

[*Nāṭyadarpaṇa*] *Nāṭyadarpaṇa of Rāmacandra and Guṇacandra with their own commentary*, edited with a Preface in English and Indices by G. K. Shrigondekar and L. B. Gandhi, revised second edition with a Sanskrit Introduction by L. B.

Gandhi, Gaekwad's Oriental Series No. 48, Oriental Institute, Vadodara, 1999.

[*Nāṭyaśāstra*] see [*Abhinavabhāratī* (GOS)]

[NM I,II, *Nyāyamañjarī*, vol. I, II] *Nyāyamañjarī of Jayantabhaṭṭa, with Ṭippaṇi—Nyāyasaurabha by the editor*, critically edited by K. S. Varadacharya, vol. I, Oriental Research Institute Series No. 116, Mysore, 1969; vol. II, Oriental Research Institute Series No. 139, Mysore, 1983.

[*Bālabhārata*] *Rājaśekharapraṇītaṃ Bālabhāratam, "Gaṅgā"-Saṃskṛta-Hindīvyākhyopetam*, ed. Gaṅgāsāgararāyaḥ, Vidyābhavana Saṃskṛta Granthamālā 167, 2nd ed., Varanasi, 1989.

[*Bālarāmāyaṇa*] *Bālarāmāyaṇam. Rājaśekhara-viracitaṃ mahānāṭakam*, sampādaka-samīkṣaka Bhāskarācārya Tripāṭhī, Nag Publishers, Delhi, 1995.

[*Ratnāvalī*] of Śrī Harṣa: Capeller's edition in *Otto Böhtlingk's Sanskrit-Chrestomatie.* Dritte verbesserte und vermehrte Auflage, herausgegeben von Richard Garbe, Leipzig, 1909, pp. 326–369.

[*Rājataraṅgiṇī*] *Rājataraṅgiṇī of Kalhaṇa*, ed. by Vishva Bandhu, in collaboration with Bhīma Dev, K. S. Rāmaswāmi Sāstrī and S. Bhāskaran Nair. Part I, Taraṅgas I–VII, Hoshiarpur, 1963.

[RT(S)] *Kalhaṇa's Rājataraṅgiṇī*, vol. I–II: translated with an introduction, commentary, and appendices by M. A. Stein, Motilal Banarsidass, Delhi, 1989 (reprinted from the edition of 1900); vol. III: Sanskrit text with critical notes, edited by M. A. Stein, Motilal Banarsidass, Delhi, 1988 (reprinted from the Bombay edition of 1892).

[*Locana* (ed. Kashi)] *Dhvanyālokaḥ Śrīmadānandavardhanācāryaviracitaḥ, Śrīrāmasāraka Mahādevaśāstriviracitābhyāṃ Bālapriyādivyañjanābhyāṃ samupetena Śrīmadabhinavaguptapādaviracitena Locanena sahitaḥ, Paṭṭābhirāmaśāstriṇā bhumikāvivecanādibhis saṃyojya saṃśodhitaḥ*, Kashi Sanskrit Series 135, Banaras, 1940.

[*Locana* (ed. *Kāvyamālā*)] *Śīmadānandavardhanācāryapraṇīto Dhvanyālokaḥ Śrīmadācaryābhinavaguptaviracitayā vyākhyayālaṅkṛtaḥ*, ed. Pt. Durgāprasād and Kāśīnāth Pāṇḍurang Parab, revised by Laxmaṇ Śāstrī Paṇśīkar, Kāvyamālā 25, Bombay, 1935.

[*Locana* (ed. Krishnamoorthy)] *Abhinavagupta's Dhvanyālokalocana, with an anonymous Sanskrit commentary*, critically edited with a complete English translation by K. Krishnamoorthy, Meharchand Lachhmandas Publications, New Delhi, 1988.

[*Vakroktijīvitam*] *Śrīmad-Rājānakakuntakaviracitaṃ Vakroktijīvitam, saṭippana-Prakāśa-hindīvyākhyopetam*, vyākhyākāraḥ Rādheśyāma Miśra, Kaśī Saṃskṛta Granthamālā 180, 4th ed., Varanasi, 1998.

Secondary Sources

BANSAT-BOUDON, Lyne. *Poétique du théâtre indien. Lectures du Nāṭyaśāstra*. Publications de l'École française d'Extrême-Orient, volume 169, Paris, 1992.

DEZSŐ, Csaba. *'Much Ado About Religion': A Critical Edition and Annotated Translation of the Āgamaḍambara, a Satirical Play by the Ninth Century Kashmirian Philosopher Bhaṭṭa Jayanta*. D.Phil. thesis submitted to Balliol College, Oxford, 2004. (The critical edition is downloadable from www.claysanskritlibrary.org/extras.php)

DEZSŐ, Csaba (ed. and transl.). *Much Ado About Religion by Bhatta Jayánta*. Clay Sanskrit Library, New York University Press – JJC Foundation, 2005.

ELAM, Keir. *The Semiotics of Theatre and Drama*. Routledge, London and New York, 1997. (reprint of 1980 ed.)

GEROW, E. – AKLUJKAR, A. 'On *śānta rasa* in Sanskrit Poetics' in *Journal of the American Oriental Society* 92, 1972, pp. 80–87.

GNOLI, Raniero. *The aesthetic experience according to Abhinavagupta.* Chowkhamba Sanskrit studies, vol. 62, 2nd ed., Varanasi 1968.

KANE, Pandurang Vaman. *History of Indian Poetics.* Delhi, 1971[4].

MASSON, J. L. and PATWARDHAN M. V. *Śāntarasa and Abhinavagupta's philosophy of aesthetics*, Bhandarkar Oriental Research Institute, Poona, 1969.

MASSON, J. L. and PATWARDHAN M. V. *Aesthetic rapture. The rasādhyāya of the Nāṭyaśāstra*, 2 vols., Deccan College, Postgraduate and Research Institute, Poona, 1970.

RAGHAVAN, V. *The Number of Rasa-s.* Third revised edition, The Adyar Library and Research Centre, Madras, 1975.

RAGHAVAN, V. *Bhoja's Śṛṅgāra Prakāśa.* Third Revised Enlarged Edition, Punarvasu, Madras, 1978.

SRINIVASAN, S. A. *On the composition of the Nāṭyaśāstra*, Studien zur Indologie und Iranistik 1, Reinbek, 1980.

STEINER, Roland. *Untersuchungen zu Harṣadevas Nāgānanda und zum indischen Schauspiel*, Indica et Tibetica 31, Swisttal-Odendorf, 1997.

WEZLER, Albrecht. 'Zur Proklamation religiös-weltanschaulicher Toleranz bei dem indischen Philosophen Jayantabhaṭṭa' in *Saeculum* 27, 1976, pp. 329–347.

Five

Notes on the *Matsyendrasaṃhitā*

Csaba Kiss*

A. Manuscripts of the *Matsyendrasaṃhitā*

There is some confusion (e.g. in WHITE 1996 and SENSHARMA 1994) concerning Sanskrit manuscripts entitled *Matsyendrasaṃ-*

*It is with a feeling of great gratitude that I dedicate this article to my first *guru*, Prof. Csaba Töttössy. I would also like to thank the following people for all their help. First of all, I express my heart-felt thanks to my present supervisor, Professor Alexis Sanderson (Oxford) for sharing his vast knowledge, his manuscripts and other sources with me and giving invaluable help in every aspect of my research. I am extremely grateful to Dr James Mallinson (Oxford) for lending me his copy of the MS of the *Matsyendrasaṃhitā* and other MSS and giving help whenever needed. I owe also many thanks to Dr Harunaga Isaacson (Hamburg), Dr Somadeva Vasudeva (Oxford), Dr Dominic Goodall (Pondicherry), Dr Csaba Dezső (Budapest), Dr Judit Törzsök (Lille), Gergely Hidas (Oxford), Ralf Kramer (Oxford), Dr Diwakar Acharya (NAK), Dr Ferenc Ruzsa (Budapest), Dr Alex Watson (Oxford), Mr Kr. Mahendra Singh Tanwar (Jodhpur), Shaman Hatley (UPenn), Dr Nikolaj Serikoff (Wellcome Library, London), Ms Zita Gábor (Budapest) and my family. My research would be impossible without the generous support of the Clarendon Fund (Oxford), the Max Müller Memorial Fund (Oxford). The article was written within the framework of the project no. T 038047 of the Hungarian Research Fund (OTKA).

hitā or *Matsyendranāthasaṃhitā*.[1] This title appears in the colophons of several different texts. I am aware of the following *Matsyendrasaṃhitā* (hereinafter MaSaṃ) manuscripts:

1. MaSaṃ. MS Sanskrit β 1115 in the collection of the Wellcome Library for the History and Understanding of Medicine (hereinafter MS 'W').[2] The label[3] on the title page says:

> 64657 00 Bhajan Lal Mss Dealer & Bookseller/ Gali Tokrian, Katra Safaid, Amritsar/ Title of the Mss Matsyendra Samhita/ Subject/ Character Devanagari/ Author Matsya Natha/ Commentator/ Size 12 x 6 / Folios 120/ Lines 22/ Recension Kasmir/ Where from obtained/ When written Near 1900 V.S.[4] / C. C. Page

Paper. *Devanāgarī*.[5] In very good condition.[6] Complete (all 55 *paṭala*s). Date of MS: probably the middle of the 19th century. Numbered at top left and bottom right of verso.[7] Size: 30 x 14 cm (12 x 6 inches). 11 lines to a side. Approximately 40 *akṣara*s per line.[8] Marginal colophons (top left of verso): *Ma° Sa° Tā°* standing probably for *Ma° Nā° Saṃ°*. Colophons marked with red powder / pencil (not visible in photocopy). Corrections in yellow substance (not visible in photocopy). *Paṭala*s 1–20 have been published by SENSHARMA 1994, but his edition is totally unreliable.[9]

MALLINSON collated 14.1 to 17.1 (= first 3 *paṭala*s of the *haṭha*-yogic text *Khecarīvidyā* included in the MaSaṃ) as well

---

[1] On the title see below.

[2] MS No. is given as No. 2/9/9 [sic] in SENSHARMA 1994:1. MS 'A' in MALLINSON 2001.

[3] Actually there are two labels, one on top of the other, the original seemingly reading the same information.

[4] I.e. Vikrama Saṃvat, appr. 1843–44 AD

[5] "bold Kashmirian *Devanāgarī*" in VASUDEVA 2000:358.

[6] Not "full of lacunæ" as in SENSHARMA 1994:vi.

[7] MALLINSON (2001:49) says "at top right and bottom left of verso".

[8] "10 letters per line" in SENSHARMA 1994:1, which is wrong.

[9] There is a review of this edition by Enrica GARZILLI in the JAOS (1998 vol. 118 number 4 pp. 543–545), but she had evidently not consulted the MS, thus has nothing critical to say about SENSHARMA's work. There are hundreds of editorial blunders in SENSHARMA's edition, which make the text appear much more corrupt than the MS really is. In fact, it is easy to see that he worked from a very bad transcript of the MS, and was unable to improve on it.

as *paṭala* 28 (= *paṭala* 4 of the *Khecarīvidyā*) of this MS in his critical edition of the *Khecarīvidyā* (= MALLINSON 2001). He also edited *paṭalas* 17, 18 and 27 (2001:284–293) as an appendix to this edition.[10]

2. There are four more MSS, all unpublished, of the same MaSaṃ in the Maharaja Man Singh Library, Jodhpur (MMSL).[11]

2a. MaSaṃ. MS No.1784.[12] Hereinafter MS 'J_a'. ('J_6' in MALLINSON 2001):

Paper. *Devanāgarī*. Complete and in good condition, c. 19th century. 83 folios, numbered at top left and bottom right of verso. 26 x 10.5 cm with 11 lines to a side and appr. 60 *akṣaras* per line. Marginal colophons (top left of verso): *Ma*° *Nā*°, once *Ma*°*Nāthī* (f.4), up to f.11 (beginning of *paṭala* 7) and *śrī*° from f.38 to f.41 (*paṭalas* 17–23). This is evidently the best one of all MaSaṃ MSS. It is unique also in that in the margin it gives most of the coded mantras of the text in their 'decoded' form.

2b. MaSaṃ. MS No.1783.[13] Hereinafter MS 'J_b':

Paper. *Devanāgarī*. Complete and in good condition, c. 19th century. 172 folios. 13.3 x 28.5 cm with 11 lines per page and appr. 30 *akṣaras* per line. Numbered at bottom right of verso. Marginal colophons (top left of verso): *Ma*° *Nā*° *Saṃ*° .

---

[10] Beginning of the MS (f.1^v) (N.B.: when describing MSS, I use diplomatic transcription, i.e. do not emend or correct anything, but report the text as it is): *oṃ śrīgaṇeśāya namaḥ śrīnāthāya namaḥ oṃ vaṃde saṃbhujagannāthaṃ sarvavighnānadhīmayaṃ*. End (f.120^r): *iti śrīmatsyeṃdrasaṃhitāyāṃ paṃcapaṃcāśaḥt paṭalaḥ samāptasaṃpūrṇam// oṃ yādṛśaṃ pustakaṃ dṛṣṭā tādṛśaṃ liṣitaṃ mayā yadi śuddhaḥm aśuddhaṃ vā/ mama doṣo na dīyate*//1//⊕//⊕//⊕//⊗//⊗//⊗//⊕//⊕//⊕//⊕//

[11] MALLINSON collated the relevant *paṭalas* of two of them (2a and 2c) for his critical edition of the *Khecarīvidyā* (2001). All four MSS are described in VYAS & KSHIRSAGAR 1986:184. On the sizes of the MSS I rely on this catalogue.

[12] Beginning (f.1^{v1}): *śrīgaṇeśaśaradagurubhyo namaḥ// vaṃde śaṃbhuṃ jagannāthaṃ sarvavijñānadhīmayaṃ*/ End (f.83^{v11}): *kulajo bhairavatanuḥ//46// iti śrīmatsyeṃdra(saṃhitāyāṃ paṃca paṃcasaḥ* ⋆ ⋆ ⋆ *samāptaṃ pañcāśaḥ paṭala //55// samāptaṃ(*

[13] Beginning (f.1^{v1}): *śrīnāthāya namaḥ/ śrıgurubhyo namaḥ/ vaṃde śaṃbhuṃ jagannāthaṃ sarvavijñānadhīmayaṃ*. End (f.172^{v3}): *kulajo bhairavatanuṃḥ//46// iti śrīmatsyeṃdrasaṃhitāyāṃ paṃcapaṃcaśa paṭalaḥ saṃpūrṇaṃ// iti matsyeṃdrasaṃhitā saṃpūrṇaṃ//*

2c. MaSaṃ. MS No.1782.[14] Hereinafter MS 'J_c'. ('J_7' in MALLINSON 2001):

Paper. *Devanāgarī.* Complete and in good condition, c. 19th century. 179 folios. 27.5 x 12.5 cm with 10 lines to a side and c. 30 *akṣaras* per line. Numbered at top left and bottom right of verso. No marginal colophons.

2d. MaSaṃ. MS No.1785.[15] Hereinafter MS 'J_d'.

Paper. *Devanāgarī.* Incomplete but in good condition, c. 19th century. 52 folios. 12 x 27.8 cm with 10 lines to a side and c. 30 *akṣaras* per line. Numbered at bottom right of verso. No marginal colophons.

It would be very difficult to draw a proper stemma for these five MaSaṃ MSS mentioned above, but J_a is evidently the best one of them. In fact, all MSS from Jodhpur are much more reliable than W. J_a and J_b are close to each other, and usually give better readings than J_c and J_d, which are again closer to each other than to J_a or J_b.[16]

3. There are two unpublished MaSaṃ MSS in the Nepal National Archives, Kathmandu, Nepal (NAK):

3a. MaSaṃ. Access No.: 2/102. Reel No.: B 39/11 (hereinafter NepMaSaṃ_1). 38 folios. Paper. Size: 23 x 11 cm. Language: Sanskrit. *Maithilī* script. This MS contains actually two texts in the same hand: ($3a_1$) *Matsyendraśataka* (hereinafter MaŚat_1), an unpublished *haṭha*-yogic text.[17] ($3a_2$) MaSaṃ (hereinafter Nep-

---

[14]Beginning (f.1^{v1}): *śrīnāthāya namaḥ/ vaṃde śaṃbhuṃ jagannāthaṃ sarvavijñānadhīmayaṃ.* End (f.179^{v9}): *kulajo bhairavatanuḥ//46// iti śrīmatsyeṃdrasaṃhitāyāṃ paṃcapaṃcāśaḥ paṭalaḥ samāptaḥ*//55

[15]Beginning (f.1^{v1}): *śrīnāthāya namaḥ/ vaṃde śaṃbhuṃ jagannāthaṃ sarvavijñānadhīmayaṃ* End (f.52^{v10}): *iti madhye bhūyaḥ pravinyaset/ ramalavarayūṃ etatkūṭaṃ raktavarṇaṃ anāhatapadme smaret* (Last word in different hand and the MS breaks off in the middle of *paṭala* 13.)

[16]One of the most telling phenomena is 7.20b (*barbarordhvaśiroruhām*), which is damaged but perhaps right in J_a, and is filled in with gaps by all the other scribes, thus J_a may be the source of all the other MSS. See also 4.63d where J_a has *manuṣyāḥ* first, misreading probably an original *mukhyāḥ* (*conj.* SANDERSON) written as *muṣyāḥ*, then, to fit the metre, corrects it to its synonymous *narāḥ*. All the other MSS have the same wrong *narāḥ*: it seems that J_a had the most reliable source(s) at hand.

[17]Beginning (f.1^{v1}): *oṃ gurave namaḥ/ namo 'stu gurave nityaṃ brahmaṇe 'vyaktarūpiṇe/ matsyendraśatakaṃ vakti yogināṃ hitakāmyayā// kartavyataiva saṃsāro na tāṃ paśyanti sūrayaḥ/ śūnyākārā nir-*

MaSaṃDiff$_1$), which is a completely different text from the MaSaṃ MSS mentioned above, and is an incomplete *haṭha*-yogic text containing some passages from the *Haṭhayogapradīpikā*.[18]

3b. MaSaṃ. Access No.: 5/2717. Reel No.: B 39/23 (hereinafter NepMaSaṃ$_2$). Size: 20.5 x 16.5 cm. 23 folios. Paper (an exercise-book from the year 1923). Language: Sanskrit. Modern *Devanāgarī* script. This MS contains two texts in the same hand, and is a *Devanāgarī* transcription of the NepMaSaṃ$_1$ MS mentioned above: (3b$_1$) *Matsyendraśataka* (hereinafter MaŚat$_2$).[19] (3b$_2$) MaSaṃ (hereinafter NepMaSaṃDiff$_2$).[20]

ākārā nirvikārā nirāmay⌊āḥ⌋// akurvann api saṃkṣobhād vyagraḥ sarvatra mūḍhadhīḥ/ kurvann api tu kṛtyāṇi kurvāno hi nirākulaḥ// End (f.9^{v2}): *saṃsārā⌊vdi⌋nimagnānāṃ yogināṃ hitakāmyayā/ jñānasūryyopamaṃ hy etat matsyendrena prakathitaṃ//⊕// iti matsyendraśatakaṃ samāptam//⊕//*

[18]Beginning (f.10^{v1}): *oṃ namaḥ paramātmane/ namo 'stu parameśāya brahmaṇe yogarūpiṇe/ yenopadiṣṭā vividhā haṭhavidyā ⌊jagattr⌋aye// śāradānandacaurāṅgīmīnagorakṣabhairavāḥ/ machindraṃ paripapracchur jñānaṃ ⌊tattva⌋sya yat param// sa tac chrutvā hṛṣṭamanā praṇamya manasā guruṃ/ machindrasaṃhitāṃ vakti yogināṃ hitakāmyayā// ye jānanti haṭhajñānaṃ jyotirūpaṃ nirañjanam/ khaṇḍaṃ kṛtvā kāladaṇḍaṃ brahmāṇḍe vistarasthitaṃ//* End (f.38^{v5}): *sarve layahaṭhābhyāsā rājayogasya siddhaye/ rājayoge samārūḍhaḥ puruṣaḥ kālavañcakaḥ/ ⌊sa nyedyo⌋ sarvasārāṇāṃ kathayanti vinā japam/ te sarve*...[breaks off]

[19]Beginning (f.1): *oṃ gurave namaḥ/ namo 'stu gurave nityaṃ brahmaṇe 'vyaktarūpiṇe/ matsyendraśatakaṃ vakti yogināṃ hitakāmyayā// kartavyataiva saṃsāro na tāṃ paśyanti sūrayaḥ/ śūnyākārā nirākārā nirvikārā nirāmayāḥ// akurvann api saṃkṣobhād vyagraḥ sarvatra mūḍhadhīḥ/ kurvann api tu kṛtyāṇi kurvāno hi nirākulaḥ//* End (f.8): *saṃsārāvdi nimagnānāṃ yogināṃ hitakāmyayā/ jñānasūryopamaṃ hy etat matsyendrena prakathitam// iti matsyendraśatakaṃ samāptam/*

[20]Beginning (f.10): *oṃ namaḥ paramātmane/ namo stu parameśāya brahmaṇe yogarūpiṇe/ yenopadiṣṭā vividhā haṭhavidyā jagattraye// śāradānandacaurangīmīnagorakṣabhairavāḥ/ machindraṃ paripapracchur jñānaṃ tattvasya yat param// sa tac chrutvā hṛṣṭamanā praṇamya manasā guruṃ/ machindrasaṃhitāṃ vakti yogināṃ hitakāmyayā// ye jānanti haṭhajñānaṃ jyotirūpaṃ nirañjanam/ khaṇḍaṃ kṛtvā kāladaṇḍaṃ brahmāṇḍe vistarasthitaṃ//* End (f.23): *sarve layahaṭhābhyāsā rājayogasya siddhaye/ rājayogasamārūḍhaḥ puruṣaḥ kālavañcakaḥ/ ⌊sa nyedyo⌋ sarvasārāṇāṃ kathayanti vinā japam/ te sarve* [this is where 3a$_2$ above breaks off] *muktiṃ āyānti nirañjanavido varāḥ/ etad yo vetti vidhivat sarvabhāvena mānavaḥ/ nirañjanapadaṃ tasya jāyate nātra saṃśayaḥ/ na mṛtyur na jarā tasya na śoko na bhayaṃ bhavet/ yo jānāti haṭhajñānaṃ brahmarūpaṃ nirañjanam/ nirvāṇapadavīrūpaṃ jñānaṃ etat sanātanam/ muktānanda* (^{pc}; *aktānanda* ^{ac}) *pradaṃ hy etan matsyendreṇeha bhāṣitam//* Marginalia: *maithilākṣarapulakā ⋆ ⋆ ⋆ likhiteyaṃ saṃhitā*[/] *haṭhayogapradīpikāsthitānu-*

To sum it up: there is one MS of the MaSaṃ in the Wellcome Library, London, four in the Maharaja Man Singh Library, Jodhpur, while the MaSaṃ MSS in the NAK are completely different from these.

I am in possession of copies of all the above mentioned MSS,[21] thus it is clear to me that WHITE's remark (1996:421) on the MaSaṃ is somewhat misleading. He says:

> A very late haṭhayogic source, entitled the *Matsyendra Saṃhitā* is found in manuscript form in the MSL [= MMSL] and the NNA [= NAK]. Cf. Pandeya [= PĀṆḌEYA 1976], introduction to *Gorakṣa Saṃhitā*, vol. 1, p. gha.[22]

Here WHITE wrongly equates the MaSaṃ MSS to be found in the MMSL and those in the NAK, while he does not mention the better-known MaSaṃ MS in the Wellcome Library (W), which has been partly published by SENSHARMA in 1994. Also, his opinion of the MaSaṃ as a "very late haṭhayogic source" is highly debatable since most of the text of the MaSaṃ is Tantric in nature. It

pūrvūrī militāḥ ślokā madhye madhye tyaktās tata eva pūraṇīyāḥ viśeṣayātra muldvultam/ mudritahaṭhayogapradīpikāyām atra ca vidyamānānāṃ ślokānām api prāyaḥ kramo visaṃvādīti dhyeyam.

[21] I am deeply indebted to Dr James Mallinson for all his help that made it possible for me to get access to the five MSS (W, Ja, Jb, Jc, Jd) that constitute the source of the critical edition of the MaSaṃ under preparation as part of my D.Phil. thesis. I owe many thanks also to Ms Zita Gábor, the Max Müller Memorial Fund (Oxford) and all the staff at the MMSL.

[22] Janārdana PĀṆḌEYA actually writes in the passage referred to by WHITE: *Matsyendranāthaviraciteṣu grantheṣv ete prasiddhāḥ—1. Matsyendrasaṃhitā* [etc.] *Itaḥ param api bahavo granthā etatpraṇītā Nepāladaravāragranthasaṃgrahe Jodhapurarājasaṃgrahe ca santīti śrūyate. Anyā ca ekā Matsyendrasaṃhitā bṛhadākārā Muktāpuramaṅgalūrataḥ prakāśitā vartate. Sā ca yady api Matsyendrapraṇītasaṃhitāto bhinnā tathāpi Matsyendrasambandhinī pracurā sāmagrī tatra dṛśyate.* In translation: "The most well-known texts composed by Matsyendranātha are the following ones—1. *Matsyendrasaṃhitā* [etc.] Moreover, there are said to be (*śrūyate*) a great number of texts composed by him in the Darbar Library, Nepal and in the [Maha]raja [Man Singh] Library, Jodhpur. A certain other long *Matsyendrasaṃhitā* is published by/in Muktāpura[?], Mangalore. This [text], though different from the *Saṃhitā* composed by Matsyendra, seems there [(*tatra*), i.e. judging from that edition] to be related to Matsyendra, rich [in material (*pracurā*) and] complete (*sāmagrī*)." Thus PĀṆḌEYA does not state at all that the MSS in Nepal and in Jodhpur are identical.

has all the characteristics that make up a Tantra.[23] It contains long descriptions of mantras, *dīkṣā*, *yoginīs*, *siddhis*, *tīrthas* and *nyāsa*, and relatively little of complicated *āsanas* and *bandhas*, the hallmarks of *haṭha*-yoga. The tendency of *haṭha*-yogic texts to exaggerate the importance of *āsanas*, *bandhas*, *prāṇāyāma*, *kuṇḍalinīyoga* and bodily cleansing exercises at the expense of e.g. visualization of deities, rituals and mantras is very far from being a characteristic of the MaSaṃ, which in fact devotes most of its *paṭalas* to external and internal Tantric ritual.

B. The title

The title *Matsyendrasaṃhitā* is actually slightly doubtful. It is confirmed in all the colophons of the MaSaṃ MSS (*iti śrīmatsyendrasaṃhitāyāṃ prathamaḥ* [etc.] *paṭalaḥ*) except in those of the best and probably oldest one (J_a). The colophons of J_a show signs of rather indelicate corrections in different hand. There are several patterns:

A: *Paṭala* 1 shows extensive corrections with a long gap. It is probably the same pattern as *paṭala* 55, which said before the correction: *iti śrīmatsyendranāthaviracitāyāṃ* ⋆ ⋆ ⋆ ⋆ ⋆ ⋆ ⋆ ⋆, and then was corrected to: *iti śrīmatsyendrasaṃhitāyāṃ pañcapañcāśaḥ paṭalaḥ*...

B: *Paṭalas* 2–8 seems to have originally read *iti śrīm* ⋆ *drasaṃ* ⋆ *tāyāḥ*..., then corrected to *iti śrīmatsyendrasaṃhitāyāṃ*...[24]

---

[23]Cf. for example GOUDRIAAN 1981:1 and 10 for typical topics in a Tantra: mantras, construction of *maṇḍalas*, *nyāsa*, *dhyāna*, *pūjā*, *dīkṣā*, *yoga*, fearsome and erotic practices, results (*phala*) of rites, supernatural powers (*siddhis*), rules of conduct (e.g. *kulācāra*), praise of deities, the legendary history of the school. In fact, all of these can be found in the MaSaṃ.

[24]The illegible *akṣaras* might be remains of a title other than *Matsyendrasaṃhitā*. There are countless possibilities to reconstruct these colophons, but none of them yield any satisfactory meaning. My guesses so far are: *śrīmacchanda*, *śrīmacchendra*, *śrīmaccolendra*, *śrīmata* (= the Paścimāmnāya), *śrīmadbhadra*, *śrīnarendra*, *śrīnāthendra*, *śrīmadrudra*, *śrīmahendra*, *śrīmadānanda*, *śrīyogendra* ... *saṃkrānta*, *sāmyatā*, *samatā*, *sāmatā*, *saṃjñitā*.

C: *Paṭalas* 9–10 read *iti śrīmatsyendra* ⋆⋆ *[nātha?] saṃhitāyāṃ*

D: *Paṭalas* 16–25 read an original *iti śrīmatsye saṃhitāyāṃ*, here and there corrected to *iti śrīmatsyendrasaṃhitāyāṃ* in different hand, elsewhere left thus.

The marginal colophons in J_a up to the beginning of *paṭala* 7 and in *paṭala* 26, as well as those in J_b up to 1.47 give *Ma° Nā° Saṃ*, evidently referring to an original *Matsyendranāthasaṃhitā*. (J_a actually gives *Ma° Sa° Tā°* , standing probably for the same.)

One wonders why any evident association with the Nātha tradition would be something to be concealed by any scribe. After *paṭala* 10, there was less need for corrections in J_a since most of the colophons read *śrīmatsyendarsaṃhitāyāṃ*..., though some of them read *śrīmatsye saṃhitāyāṃ*... (corrected from an original ...*matsyasaṃhitāyāṃ*...?), while others seem to have been corrected to *matsyendra-* from *yogendrasaṃhitā*. From all these data, it seems possible that *paṭalas* 2–8, and 1 and 55 formed distinct units once, or perhaps separate texts, in the early phases of the redaction of the MaSaṃ.

C. Character, dating and context of the MaSaṃ

The MaSaṃ[25] is a Śaiva text, a Śaiva tantra of 55 *paṭalas*, approximately 3000 verses, mainly *ślokas* with some verses in other stanza forms and also some prose passages. Its Śaiva nature is clear from the following basic facts:

a. most of the text (*paṭalas* 2–54) is presented in the traditional form of a (rather one sided) dialogue between Śiva (Bhairava, Īśvara) and Pārvatī (Devī);

b. the first and last (55th) *paṭalas* constitute a narrative framework relating an interesting version of the

[25] Hereinafter, the text I refer to and quote as MaSaṃ is that of my critical edition based on five MaSaṃ MSS. This means that some quotations from the text may involve emendations/conjectures made by others, mostly Prof. Alexis Sanderson and Dr. James Mallinson, which are duly acknowledged in my edition. Nevertheless, I will reproduce the apparatus here only at crucial textual problems.

legend of the great yogin Matsyendra and his disciple Gorakṣa (mostly mentioned as 'the Cola king'), whose connection with the Śaiva Kaula tradition is very well-established;[26]

c. the main topic of the text is 'Śāmbhava/Śaiva yoga practice' (*śāmbhavaṃ yogasādhanam* 2.2d and 44.88b).

The MaSaṃ is a significant text, or collection of texts, of a relatively late phase of the Śaiva tradition, particularly of its yogic teachings. It is long, detailed and mostly not very badly preserved. It is unique in its concentrating mainly on yoga, a topic treated in many cases rather briefly and peripherally in Śaiva Tantras. It provides some clues for, among other things, the understanding of the transition from the early Indian yoga traditions (Pātañjala and Śaiva) to the late and fully developed *haṭha* yogic teachings as well as of the transition from the early Kula traditions to the later Kaula teachings associated with the figure of Matsyendra.[27] It can also throw some light on the connection between the Kaula traditions of the Paścimāmnāya and Dakṣiṇāmnāya, and the Nātha tradition of *haṭha*-yogins.[28] The MaSaṃ is an encyclopædic compilation of yogic and ritualistic techniques: from *āsanas* and *prāṇāyāma* to visualisation and *mudrās*, from mantra techniques to *maṇḍalas*, the text describes a whole world of religious/psychological practices and rites. MALLINSON 2001:7 describes the MaSaṃ as a text "on Kaula ritual and yoga", which is true for the collection as we now have it, though its Kaula layer might not be the central one. It might contain some material from other, e.g. Saiddhāntika, sources. No doubt, the MaSaṃ incorporates also later *haṭha*-yogic material. This technique of compilation

[26]Cf. e.g. SANDERSON 1988:156 and 1985:214 n.110, GOUDRIAAN 1981:50 and HEILIJGERS 1994:9.

[27]Here I follow SANDERSON 1985:214 n.110 concerning the Kula/Kaula distinction: "The distinction between Kula and Kaula traditions [...] is best taken to refer to the clan-structured tradition of cremation-grounds seen in the BY-PM [Brahmayāmala-Picumata], JY [Jayadrathayāmala], TS [Tantrasadbhāva], SYMT [Siddhayogeśvarīmatatantra], etc. (with its Kāpālika *kaulikā vidhayaḥ*) on the one hand and on the other its reformation and domestication through the banning of mortuary and all sect-identifying signs (*vyaktaliṅgatā*), generally associated with Macchanda /Matsyendra."

[28]Cf. HEILIJGERS 1994:1, 7, 9

of texts from several different traditions is a common feature of Sanskrit textual transmission. One of the most interesting tasks of any editor of the text would be to isolate its layers and identify some of its sources and thus try to draft the history of its textual development.

Of course, to contextualise MaSaṃ within the Śaiva tradition (or to determine its relation to the Śaiva tradition) is a challenging task. The text consists of several layers, which, lacking in references to dates, and having only a few references to traditions and geographical locations, are difficult to distinguish between. Nevertheless, the following facts may help us place the text in its historical context.

There are three instances in the MaSaṃ of referring to itself as 'tantra' or 'great tantra': *asmin tantre vare divye* (14.16c); *tanre 'smin* (43.34b); *asmin mahātantre* (55.39a). These references are thus distributed among the frame story (*paṭala* 55), the *Khecarīvidyā*-section and the remaining text of the MaSaṃ.

The MaSaṃ contains some specific references to other Tantric works. This fact faciliates us with very important tools to date it and to place it within the Śaiva tradition. There is a list of Tantras in *paṭala* 14:

> *tantrāś ca bahavo devi mayā proktāḥ surārcite* //13//
> *na teṣu khecarī siddhir ākhyātā mṛtyunāśinī* /
> *mahākālaṃ ca mārtaṇḍaṃ vivekādyaṃ ca*
> *śābaram*[29] //14//
> *viśuddheśvarasaṃjñaṃ ca tathā vai jālaśaṃvaram*/
> *eteṣu tantravaryeṣu tadabhyāsaṃ prakāśitam* //15//

Thus the text mentions five works: *Mahākāla*,[30] *Vivekamārtaṇḍa*,[31] *Śābara*, *Viśuddheśvara* and *Jālaśaṃvara*.[32] Since *paṭala* 14 is part of the *Khecarīvidyā*, MALLINSON has tried to identify these references (2001:2 n.4 and p.125–126 n.184–187), but any *terminus*

[29]Em. MALLINSON for *śābharaṃ* and *śāṃvaraṃ*

[30]It is probably the *Mahākālasaṃhitā*. See Bibliography.

[31]The *Vivekamārtaṇḍa* is probably the *haṭha*yogic text well-known by the title *Gorakṣaśataka* (cf. BOUY 1994:18 and MALLINSON 2001:2–3 n.5).

[32]Compare this list of tantras with that of the *Vāmakeśvarīmata* 1.13ff, which includes a *Śambara*-, a *Jālaśaṃvara*-, a *Tattvaśambaraka*-, a *Kālasāra*- and a *Viśuddheśvaratantra*.

post quem reached thus is valid only for the *Khecarīvidyā* section of the MaSaṃ (*paṭala*s 14–16 and 28), which is very likely an addition to the core of the text (cf. MALLINSON 2001:9).

What is more important is that there are some references in the MaSaṃ to the Southern Kaula Tradition (Dakṣiṇāmnāya, i.e. the cult of Tripurā or Tripurasundarī; the goddess is worshipped in/as the Śrīcakra, and her mantra, the 15-syllable Śrīvidyā),[33] as well as parallal passages with the basic scriptures of that tradition.[34] MaSaṃ 25.27ff are similar to *Yoginīhṛdaya* 1.82ff. But note that there is no trace of the Dakṣiṇāmnāya in *paṭala*s 2–7, the main yoga-section.

---

[33]On the Dakṣiṇāmnāya in general, see SANDERSON 1988:156–158.

[34]The basic scriptures of the Dakṣiṇāmnāya/Śrīvidyā cult are the *Nityāṣoḍaśikārṇava* (alias *Vāmakeśvarīmata*, sometimes *Vāmakeśvaratantra*, NṢA) and the later *Yoginīhṛdaya*. Their dating is as difficult as of most Tantric scriptures. All we might assume is that "...the cult was introduced into Kashmir at some time between 900 and 1100 CE" (SANDERSON 1988:157). References to the NṢA in the MaSaṃ: 25.50ab: *tasyā saṃsādhanaṃ sarvaṃ proktaṃ śrīvāmakeśvare*; 25.61: *etāsāṃ †tiṣṭhi† nityānāṃ pūjāmantrakriyādikam/ purā tava mayā proktaṃ nityāṣoḍaśikārṇave//* 34.19cd–20ab: *asyāḥ pūjāvidhir nyāsaḥ phalaṃ ca parameśvari/ śrīvāmakeśvare tantre mayā pūrvaṃ prakāśitam.* MaSaṃ 1.72d mentions 'Śrīvidyā' (*śrīvidyāyogacāriṇe*). MaSaṃ 1.72a mentions Tripurā's Kādikūṭa mantra. Parallel passages in the MaSaṃ with the NṢA: MaSaṃ 1.75 *kālahallāhalollolakalanāśayakāriṇe* ≈ NṢA 1.2cd (an important techincal term there, cf. Jayaratha's commentary *ad loc*; I am grateful to Professor Sanderson for pointing out this parallel); MaSaṃ 11.2cd–3ab *tarjanībhyāṃ samākrānte sarvorddhvam api madhyame/ aṅguṣṭhau tu maheśāni kārayet saralāv api* = NṢA 3.16cd-17ab; MaSaṃ 11.4ab *puṭākārau karau kṛtvā tarjanyaṅguṣṭhakau samau* ≈ NṢA 3.9ab; MaSaṃ 12.5ab *pūrvavat prāsam āsthāya mudrāsaṃnaddhavigrahaḥ* ≈ NṢA 5.7; MaSaṃ 12.5cd *pūrvoktadhyānayogena saṃcintya japam ārabhet* = NṢA 5.6cd; MaSaṃ 22.9cd *śaktyā vinā śive sūkṣme nāma dhāma na vidyate* = NṢA 4.7ab; MaSaṃ 22.10ab *śuklaḥ prasādhitaṃ sarvaṃ śaktyā yukto yadā bhavet* ≈ NṢA 4.6cd; Other references to the Śrīvidyā tradition: MaSaṃ 24.12 mentions the Vāgbhava, which is the name of the first third of the Śrīvidyā (KA E Ī LA HRĪṂ in the *kādi* variety); MaSaṃ *paṭala* 25 is on the Śrīcakra; MaSaṃ *paṭala* 34 gives the Kādividyā (cf. Jayaratha's commentary *ad* NṢA 1.93). Tripurā's name is mentioned in MaSaṃ 25.21b, 26d, 32–35, 47. Her typical visualization (4-armed, with a bow and arrows, in a Jewel-island etc.) appears e.g. in *paṭala*s 8, 24, 25 and 34.

There are several significant references to the Western Kaula Tradition (Paścimāmnāya).[35] MaSaṃ 44.27cd hints at this tradition: *etat te paramāmnāyam auttaraṃ*[36] *paścimānvayam.* 18.67–68ab refers perhaps to the goddess Kubjikā, the central deity of the basic scriptutre of the *Paścimāmnāya*, the *Kubjikāmatatantra* (KMT) or, if no emendation is applied, it refers to Kubjeśavara, Kubjikā's partner (= Śiva alias Navātman): *yoginyas tatra yā devi siddhāś ca varavarṇini/ icchārūpadharāḥ sarve sarve cāmoghaśaktayaḥ/ svatantrāś ca svarūpāś ca sarve kubjeśvaraprabhāḥ.* There are some parallel passages in the MaSaṃ with the KMT.[37] The mantra referred to in 54.36b (*namo bhagavatīti*) might be that of Kubjikā.[38] Moreover, as I will show below, the iconography of the goddess Caṇḍikā in the central teaching of *dhyāna* (*paṭala* 7) has some marked similarity with that of Kubjikā in the *Nityāhnikatilaka*.

In MaSaṃ *paṭala* 4, there are extensive parallels with the *Prapañcasāra* (PrS; attributed to Śaṅkarācārya).[39]

A number of verses in MaSaṃ *paṭala* 4 describing the system of *nāḍīs* can be found in the *Haṭhayogapradīpikā*, the *Prapañcasāra*, the *Svacchandatantra*, the *Gorakṣaśataka* etc.

There are references to the Kula Tradition in general.[40] The text clearly refers to the Kulāmnāya ('Kula Tradition') in 55.42bc: *śatakoṭipravistaraṃ kulāmnāyam.* In 18.66ab, there is a reference

---

[35]On the *Paścimāmnāya* in general, see SANDERSON 1988:154–156, DYCZKOWSKI 1988 and 2001.

[36]On '*auttara*[*tattva*]' see the *Mahārthamañjarīparimala*'s *Maṅgalaśloka* 2. (I am grateful to Professor Sanderson for this piece of information.)

[37]E.g. MaSaṃ 7.43cd–44ab: *nirālambe pade śūnye yat teja upajāyate/ tad †gehaṃ† abhyasen nityaṃ yogī yogaprasiddhaye* ≈ KMT 6.23 ; MaSaṃ 54.10: *lakṣamātrakṣate jāpye vācāmātreṇa sādhayet* ≈ KMT 7.111 ; MaSaṃ 54.13: *paṭhanād eva saṃsiddhi japahomavivarjitā* ≈ KMT 7.94

[38]Cf. GOUDRIAAN 1981:53 n.86., where the whole mantra is given as NAMO BHAGAVATI ŚRĪKUBJIKĀYAI HRĀṂ HRĪṂ HROṂ ṄAÑAṆANAME AGHORAMUKHI CHĀṂ CHĪṂ KIṆIKIṆI VICCE; cf. KMT 7.20.

[39]MaSaṃ 4.44–47ab ≈ PrS 1.48-86 ; MaSaṃ 4.57–60ab ≈ PrS 1.90–93 ; The *prāṇapratiṣṭhā* ritual described in MaSaṃ *paṭala* 13 is very similar to the one described in Padmapādācārya's commentary (*Vivaraṇa*) *ad* PrS chapter 35.

[40]On the Kula tradition in general see e.g.: SANDERSON 1988:139–40 and 147–158; DYCZKOWSKI 1988:57ff.

to the Goddess of the Kula: *akṣayaṃ candradvīpaṃ*[41] *tu yatra devī kulāmbikā*. In fact, much of the MaSaṃ can be described as Kaula as it is clear from the frequent occurence of the word *kula/kaula/kaulika*.[42] Moreover, there is a whole *paṭala* (*paṭala* 40) describing *kulācāra* (Kula Conduct), which includes some sexual practices. In spite of all these, the words *kula/kaula* are not to be found in the technical sense in *paṭala*s 2–7, the main yogic section.

The text mentions some names, probably of Siddhas, or rather, Kaula initiates: Haṃsānanda (10.47, 12.33), Nityānanda (10.51),[43] Ṣaṣṭhānanda (10.53, 12.36), Bhogānanda (10. 56, 12.39),[44] Colānanda (10.58 Lolānanda in W) and Bhūṣānanda (10.59), Mūṣānanda (12.44; = probably Bhūṣānanda); Haṃsānandanātha, Nityānandanātha, [Ic]chānandanātha(?), Bhogānandanātha, Vīrānan-

[41]Candradvīpa is a location often referred to in Kaula texts. For the role of Candradvīpa in the Kaula tradition see e.g. BAGCHI 1934:34–35, KMT 1.81, and the *Kaulajñānanirṇaya* (NGMPP MS A 48/13) *paṭala* 16 (f.26a ff). (The *Kaulajñānanirṇaya* MS mentioned above is the one BAGCHI 1934 used for his edition, but as Mr Shaman Hatley demonstrated to me in 2004, this edition is totally unreliable; a transcript of *paṭala* 16 has been kindly sent to me by Mr Hatley.)

[42]E.g. MaSaṃ 14.22cd: *granthiṃ nodgranthayed asya vinā kaulikatarpaṇāt* ; 14.25: *tatra sarvārthadāyinyo vasanti kuladevatāḥ* ; 17.27a: *kulāmṛtaiś ca māṃsaiś ca* ; 18.10c: *kulāmṛtaṃ divyaṃ* ; 20.14: *śītalāmṛtakalloladhārāvṛṣṭikulāmṛtam* ; 40.1: *atha devi pravakṣyāmi kulācāravidhikramam* ; 54.15: *tasmāt parīkṣya dātavyā vidyeṣā kulaśāsane* ; 55.42: *kulāmnāyam aśeṣaṃ tu tasmād uddhṛtya sārayet.*

[43]Nityānanda(nātha) might be the author of the *Prapañcasāragūḍhārthadīpikā* (a commentary on the *Prapañcasāra*), the *Kāmaratna* (WHITE 1996:418), the *Rasaratnākara* (ibid. 1996:160) and a certain *Siddhasiddhāntapaddhati* (which is different from the one that is attributed to Gorakṣa). The name appears in the list of Siddhas in the *Haṭhayogapradīpikā* (1.7), and, according to WHITE 1996:129, he is the author of the *Śābaracintāmaṇi*, though the colophon of the edition I have consulted (*Śābaracintāmaṇiḥ. Śābar mantroṃ kā siddhi dāyak vidhi sahit.* Vārāṇasī: Yogapracāriṇī Sabhā, 1992/93. p.48) states that it was composed by Matsyendra: *iti śrīpārvatīputranityanāthasiddhamatsyendraviracite śāvaracintāmaṇāv ekādaśaḥ paṭalaḥ samāptaḥ.* This is what PĀNDEYA also confirms (1976:gha).

[44]Cf. BAGCHI 1934:2–24, who quotes the commentary by Bhāskararāya on the *Lalitāsahasranāma*: ... *bhogānandanāthādyaś catvāro 'paragurava iti...*

danātha in *paṭala* 13;[45] Gorakṣeśa, Kharparīśa and Vyālīndra in *paṭala* 55.

As regards the date of the composition of the MaSaṃ, it is important to note that there does not seem to be any known Sanskrit source that mentions or refers to it. MALLINSON (2001:7) says that a certain "*Śivamatsyendrasaṃhitā* is mentioned in the margin of f.5ʳ of the *Bṛhatkhecarīprakāśa*" (witness 'S' in MALLINSON 2001), which might be the only known reference to the MaSaṃ. The fact that we may have no references to the MaSaṃ at all might point to the late origin of this collection of texts as we have it. The pronounced familiarity of the text with the Dakṣiṇāmnāya and the Paścimāmnāya makes it clear that the MaSaṃ, or to be precise, many parts of it, definitely postdate their formation periods. The mention of *siddhimūlikā* (*cannabis*) in *paṭala*s 29 and 39 may indicate that the text "was compiled in eastern India after the advent of Islam in that region" (MALLINSON 2001:8, quoting Professor SANDERSON in n.19). MALLINSON (2001:4), after considering all data available to date the *Khecarīvidyā*, concludes that it was composed before 1400 AD. It seems very likely to me that much of the MaSaṃ is earlier than the *Khecarīvidyā* (mainly because its basic yoga teaching is closer in content to the *Bhairava-tantras* and even to the Saiddhāntika yoga-*pāda*s than the *Khecarīvidyā*),[46] thus the core of the MaSaṃ can tentatively be dated as composed before 1300 AD.

There is probably an early layer of *Śaiva-/Śāmbhava-yogaśāstra* in the text. This may be that part of the text that consists of

---

[45]On the suffix '*-ānandanātha*' added to names cf. MALLINSON 2001:2 n.3: "Members of the cults connected with the *Matsyendrasaṃhitā* and the *Mahākālasaṃhitā* [...] add the suffix *-ānandanātha* to their initiatory names [...] This suffix is rarely found in the names of Nātha yogins but is added to the names of Kaula initiates." According to GOUDRIAAN: "The names of many teachers of the Saubhāgyasampradāya [referring to the monestic order founded allegedly by Śaṅkarācārya] (as well as some other Tantric schools, for that matter) end on *-ānandanātha*, those of some other Kaula teachers on *-nātha*" (GOUDRIAAN 1981:59 fn.8). See also note 56. below on the name Tejānandanātha and also MaSaṃ 17.56: *yasmin varṇe nipatitaṃ puṣpa[ṃ] tadvarṇapūrvakam/ nāma cānandanāthāntaṃ dāpayed gurur īśvari.* "The guru should give [the initiant] a name beginning with the letter that the flower has fallen on, and ending with '*-ānandanātha*', O Goddess!"

[46]It might be significant that the word '*haṭha*' is not to be found in the MaSaṃ at all.

Śiva's answers to Pārvatī's questions in verses 2.1–10. The idea that these questions can help us define the earliest layer of the text was first raised by MALLINSON (2001:8 n.20). The topics concerning "*śāmbhavaṃ yogasādhanam*" (2.2d) that Pārvatī wants to hear about are the following ones (cf.2.5–2.10ab):

> *1. dehaśuddhi 2. āsanakrama 3. prāṇāyāma 4. pratyāhāra 5. dhāraṇā 6. dhyānayoga 7. śrīkuṇḍalīyoga 8. triliṅgārcā 9. kṣetras, 10. tīrthas 11. sarva[tīrtha]snānādhikasnāna 12. auṣadhaprayoga 13. rasāyana 14. pādukāsiddhi 15. dehasiddhi 16. vetālasiddhi 17. kapālasādhana 18. añjanasiddhi 19. yakṣiṇīsiddhi 20. aṇimādi 21. yoginīmelana*

Topics 1–6 are to be found in *paṭalas* 2–7 (*paṭala* 7 contains also a distinct section on *samādhi* from 7.75 on). Topics 7–8 are treated in *paṭalas* 22–23. Topic 9 is *paṭala* 27. Topic 10 is *paṭala* 26. Topic 11 seems to be included in *paṭala* 27. Topic 12 is *paṭalas* 28 (= *Khecarīvidyā paṭala* 4) and/or 29. Topic 13 is still to be located (end of *paṭala* 40?). Topic 14 is *paṭala* 30. Topic 15 (*dehasiddhi*) might be a corruption of *vajrasiddhi* (cf. MALLINSON 2001:8 fn.20), which is described in *paṭala* 31.[47] Topics 16–17 are *paṭalas* 32–33. Topic 18 is *paṭala* 35. Topic 19 is *paṭala* 34. Topic 20 is perhaps (MALLINSON 2001:8 fn.20) *paṭala* 36. Topic 21 is perhaps (MALLINSON ibid.) *paṭala* 37 (or rather 40).

Thus, of the 55 *paṭalas* of the MaSaṃ (or rather 53 *paṭalas*, since *paṭalas* 1 and 55 constitute a frame-story with perhaps very little direct connection to the rest of the text)[48] the following can perhaps be considered as answers to Pārvatī's questions: 2–7, 22–23, 26–37 (= 20 *paṭalas*). Of course, there may have been some additions to and/or omissions from Pārvatī's "original" questions

[47] Or see PĀṆḌEYA's introduction to his edition of the *Gorakṣasaṃhitā* (Bhūtaprakaraṇa p.Ka): "*... aṇimādyaṣṭaguṇasampannadehavattvam iti yāvat. etad eva dehasiddhir iti kāyasiddhir iti padena vā nigadyate*", i.e. the state of having your body endowed with the eight Powers (minuteness etc.) is called *dehasiddhi* or *kāyasiddhi*.

[48] There are very few traces of Matsyendra being mentioned or referred to in the main text (i.e. *paṭalas* 2–54) of the MaSaṃ, the only exception being *paṭala* 38.

(if there was indeed an original layer), and at the same time additions to and/or omissions from the main text. One important addition to Pārvatī's questions might be 2.10cd. The whole verse goes like this:

> *aṇimādi katham deva yoginīmelanaṃ katham /*
> *etāny eva tathānyāni bhavatā sūcitāni ca /*
> *tāni sarvāṇi me brūhi vistareṇa maheśvara* //2.10//

> How are [the Powers] minuteness and [the seven other ones to be described]? How is the encounter with the *yoginīs* [to be accomplished], O God?
>
> These [topics] were certainly (*eva*) hinted at by you Sir, and other things, too.
>
> Tell me all of them (*tāni sarvāṇi*) in detail (*vistareṇa*), O Śiva.

2.10cd looks suspicious: the '*ca*' at the end of 2.10d seems to be out of place, and 2.10 could perfectly work without 2.10cd. This line, if better-written, may have been a simple and elegant way of preparing the original layer of the text for expansion.

MALLINSON, concluding his own reasoning, says (2001:8 fn.20): "Thus it seems likely that MaSaṃ *paṭalas* 8–21, 24–25 and 39–54 are additions to the earliest layer of the text." Theoretically, there might be some problem with this reasonig, i.e. with the idea that Pārvatī's questions define the earliest layer of the text. Firstly, one can manipulate a 'table of contents' of this kind easily, secondly, the beginning of *paṭala* 2, including Devī's questions, seems to belong to the frame-story (*paṭalas* 1 and 55), which is possibly the latest addition to this collection of texts. Devī refers back in 2.3cd-4ab to Śiva's concern in *paṭala* 1 that his yoga teaching might be overheard if not delivered in a completely deserted place (cf.1.39cd–1.40), which might lead us to the conclusion that *paṭala* 1 and the beginning of *paṭala* 2 are connected in some way. If the frame-story is indeed a late addition to the text and Devī's questions in fact belong to it, then this list of topics cannot help us at all defining what was "original" and what is an "addition", since any redactor of the text could increase or decrease the number of questions at his own will. For example, *paṭala*s describing *dehaśuddhi* and *kuṇḍalinyutthāpana*, though both mentioned by Devī, seem to be worlds apart: the description of *dehaśuddhi* seems to be Tantric and perhaps rather early, while that of *kuṇḍalinyutthāpana* resembles late *haṭha*-yogic texts.[49]

Another attempt at locating the text in time and place, or at least at finding out in what terms the text identifies itself, to what tradition it claims to belong to, would involve the examination of the central deities on whose worship it focuses. In *paṭala* 7, we find the central and most detailed teaching of *dhyāna*, visualization of the deities.

D. *Dhyāna* in the MaSaṃ

The process of *dhyāna* in the MaSaṃ follows the typical Tantric model, i.e. the practioner visualizes a lotus throne for Śiva and places the mental image of the god and his consort onto it.[50] There are alternative ways of meditation described in the MaSaṃ, the first of which (7.1–18) is briefly the following:

Sitting in an *āsana* described before (in *paṭala* 3), the yogin should first meditate on his own body as the whole world (7.3–7).[51] Then the yogin should imagine a lotus in his own heart, with fire as its petals, the sun as its fibres, the moon as its filament,[52] glowing like ten thousand rising suns, together with the nine Śaktis. In the middle of the lotus, one should visualize Parameśāna, who is black like a black cloud, with serpents in his *jaṭā*, the crescent moon on his crest, fearful (*bhīma*), pervading all the directions with the sacred syllable HUṂ. His attributes (*āyudha*s) are: a sword (*khaḍga*), a trident (*śūla*), the gesture of fearlessness (*abhaya*), a serpent-noose (*nāgapāśa*), a skull (*kapāla*), a

[49]One may also argue that it is not that easy to manipulate a text in this way, thus it is also conceivable that the frame-story and Devī's questions belong to an early layer, and some *paṭala*s were added/eliminated without paying attention to Devī's questions. (Personal communication with Dr Vasudeva in May 2005.)

[50]On this process of 'mental creation' see BRUNNER 1994:442.

[51]This technique is somewhat similar to that of *Nādabindūpaniṣad* 1–4.

[52]The difference between the last two (fibres and filament, i.e. *kesara* and *kiñjalka*) is not clear to me.

bell (*ghaṇṭā*), the gesture of generosity (*varada*), and one more (†*viṣārṇa*†). Thus he is eight-armed. He is wearing a red garment and is ornamented with red garlands and their scent. He has also a necklace of eight snakes (*nāga*). He is roaring and laughing and has a tiger-skin as his upper-garment covered with lion-skin. His three eyes are the sun, the moon and fire. He has tusks in his big mouth. His eyes are rolling with intoxication from wine.

Then the yogin should visualize the goddess Caṇḍikā (7.19ff.), sitting on Śiva's left (or his left hip: *vāmāṅka*).[53] She looks like a black cloud. She is adorned with severed heads (*muṇḍa*), rings of serpents and red flowers. She has six heads, each having three eyes and twelve arms. She is wearing the same garments as Śiva (tiger-skin and lion-skin). She is holding a thunderbolt (*vajra*), an elephant-goad (*aṅkuśa*), a disc (*cakra*), a conch (*śaṅkha*), a shield (*kheṭa*), a trident (*triśūla*), a knife (*karttṛkā*), a staff (*daṇḍa*), a pestle (*muśala*), the gesture of fearlessness (*abhaya*) and the gesture of generosity (*varada*). (One *āyudha* seems to be missing.) She is benevolent (*bhadra*) and young. She has the moon on her crest. She is drunk on wine. She is surrounded by the *yoginī*s. She swallows/destroys time (*kālagrasanarūpiṇī*).

Although the description of Caṇḍikā is rather detailed and she seems to be at least as powerful as Śiva, this *dhyāna* section does not give the impression of being Śākta. Descriptions of Śiva's other forms are scattered through this *paṭala* from 7.28 to 7.74. He is to be visualized with the following attributes:

7.31ff.: (six-armed) *varada, abhaya, ṭaṅka, mṛgamudrā,*[54] *akṣasrak, pustaka*;

7.37ff.: (four-armed) *akṣamālā, varada,* †*viśiṣṭa*†*, abhaya*;

7.69ff.: (four-armed) *varada, pāśa, veda, akṣasūtra*;

7.71ff.: (eight-armed) *śūla, khaṭvāṅga, ghaṇṭā, kuliśa, varada, kapāla, abhīti* (= *abhaya*), *aravinda*.

The name of the goddess Caṇḍikā might evoke the figure of Mahiṣāsuramardaṇī alias Caṇḍikā, who, according to one tradi-

---

[53]See the Bhāskararāya's gloss on *kāmeśvarāṅkanilayā* in verse 37 of the *Kāmakalāvilāsa* of Puṇyānanda concerning Tripurā sitting on Navātma's left hip/thigh: *aṅkaṃ vāmorubhāgaḥ*.

[54]The iconographical feature of Śiva holding a *mṛga* might support the idea that the text is a product of South Indian thought.

tion,[55] is six-faced and twenty-armed (*vajra, aṅkuśa, cakra, śaṅkha, kheṭaka, śūla, gadā, dvaja, ghaṇṭā, dhanus, abhaya, khaḍga, śakti, ḍamaru, chattra, nāgapāśa, bāṇa, paraśu, darpaṇa, mudgara*), with a golden complexion, handsome, young, wrathful and sitting on a lion. Moreover, the description of the divine couple in the MaSaṃ can also evoke the image of Kubjikā and Navātman of the Paścimāmnāya, or its parallel and masculinised tradition, the Śāmbhava (cf. SANDERSON 1988: 155).[56] In fact, Kubjikā and Navātmā's (i.e. Śiva's) description in the *Nityāhnikatilaka* (NĀT) of Muktaka,[57] a text of the Kubjikā tradition, is not only similar to the couple in the MaSaṃ, but there are some parallel passages to be found in it. In the NĀT, Kubjikā is also six-faced and twelve-armed as in the MaSaṃ, with the following attributes: *triśūla, cakra, vajra, aṅkuśa, śara, karttṛkā, nīlotpala, muṇḍa, khaṭvāṅga, ghaṇṭā, pustaka, dhanus*. Only five of these match the description of Caṇḍikā in the MaSaṃ, but it seems very plausible that we are dealing with a variant of the Goddess Kubjikā in the MaSaṃ, with her name almost completely concealed.[58] It is also remarkable that in the margin of MS J_a (undoubtedly the best MS of the five that we have) f.21^v (bottom) the word *navāntarātmā* is to be read. In MaSaṃ *paṭala* 43, there are parallel verses with Navātman's *dhyāna* in the NĀT (f.26^{r2-4}).[59]

---

[55]See RAO 1914:346 Vol I. Part 2.

[56]I have just begun studying some MSS (all mentioned in SANDERSON 1988:155) of the Śāmbhava tradition, namely the *Śambhunirṇayatantra* (Madras Govt. Lib. R. No. 3203c), Śivānandamuni's *Śambhunirṇayadīpikā* (Madras Govt. Lib. R. No. 3203d), the *Nityāhnikatilaka* of Muktaka (NGMPP Access: 3/384) and Umākānta's *Ṣaḍanvayaśāmbhavakrama* (MS β 353 in the Wellcome Library) in search for parallel passages. I am extremely grateful for Prof. Sanderson for giving me access to his copies of the above mentioned MSS. A brief study of the *Ṣaḍanvayaśāmbhavakrama* has shown me that it has much to do with the Kubjikā-influenced sections of the MaSaṃ, although there does not seem to be any parallels. Tejānandanātha's *Ānandakalpalatā* also belongs to this tradition (on the suffix *-ānandanātha* see note 45).

[57]NGMPP Access: 3/384, Reel: A 41/11, f.27^{r2}–28^{v4}. I am grateful to Professor SANDERSON for drawing my attention to this text-passage and sending me his transcription of it.

[58]For a reference to Kubjeśvara or perhaps Kubjeśvarī, see MaSaṃ 18.67–68ab.

[59]MaSaṃ 43.7cd: *dviraṣṭavarṣasaṃpannaṃ ratnasarpāsthicarcitam* ~ NĀT. *dvirastavarṣadeśīyo ratnasarppāsthicarcitaḥ*. MaSaṃ 43.8cd: *pañcāsanānane vahninābhipadmāṅgulīyakam* cf. NAT: *vahninābhisitāmbhoje*

The image in the MaSaṃ of her sitting on Śiva's left while he is in a sitting position, but being twelve-armed seems rather unusual, since the common iconographic image of the couple of Śiva and Devī is either that of an embracing couple facing each other, or that of Devī sitting on his left but being two-armed or sitting on his lying body and having more than two arms. The concealment of Kubjikā's and Navātman's name and their unusual, or to put it in another way, forced and arbitrary juxtaposition can be seen as a tendency to de-Śāktaize the cult of Kubjikā and to conceal all its sectarian marks. It indicates that the core of the text in fact belongs to a Kaula yoga tradition originating from a masculinised version of Kubjikā's cult.

E. The yoga of the MaSaṃ

After examining the main *dhyāna* section of the MaSaṃ, let us see in what yogic context it is taught. The basic yoga teaching of the MaSaṃ, which is to be found mainly in *paṭala*s 2–7,[60] can be described, unfortunately, mainly in negative terms. This form of yoga seems to be devoid of the system of *cakra*s of the Kubjikāmata or *haṭha*-yogic texts. It does not refer to Siddhas. It does not teach complex yogic postures (*āsana*) other than intricate sitting postures. It does not speak of the *haṭha*-yogic technique of *khecarī* (the blocking of the throat with the tongue), though other parts of the MaSaṃ contain the whole *Khecarīvidyā*. It is

kṛtāṅguṣṭheti bhairavaḥ. MaSaṃ 43.10cd: *śūlacakradhvajādānaṃ dadhād vāme paraṃ śṛṇu* cf. NĀT: *bibhrat śūlacakraṃ dhvajaṃ* (*em.* SANDERSON; *dhvajā* Cod.) *dānañ ca dakṣabāhubhiḥ.* MaSaṃ 43.11ab: *pārijātajāpya(kṣa)mālāpustakaṃ cābhayaṃ priye* ≈ NĀT: *pārijātajāpyamālāputakābhayakaṅ karaiḥ.* MaSaṃ 43.11cd: *śeṣābhyāṃ caiva jānubhyāṃ brahmavarmavidāraṇam* NĀT: *anyad bāhudvayābhyāñ ca gajacarmmāvṛtavigrahaḥ* (°*gaja*° *em.* SANDERSON; °*kaca*° Cod.).

[60] In a certain sense, which might correspond very closely to what the redactor of the MaSaṃ intended, the whole text is yogic. Nevertheless, I restrict the sense of the term 'yoga' here to that physical and mental process which leads the yogin to fusion with the deity, and I exclude practices, which aim 'only' at obtaining worldly *siddhi*s/magical powers (e.g. *japa* and *nyāsa* for obtaining victory over one's enemy). The basic reason for this restriction of the yoga of the MaSaṃ to *paṭala*s 2–7 is that they teach a complete sequence of *aṅga*s from *dehaśuddhi* to *samādhi.*

not *ṣaḍaṅga* in the Tantric sense,[61] since it includes an extra purificatory rite as its seventh *aṅga* and it does not teach *tarka* or *japa* as an auxiliary, which would be typically Tantric.

In contrast with these, it does refer to *yoginīs*, it teaches *mudrās*,[62] it mentions *sādhakas*, a designation that refers to *siddhi*-seeking Tantric initiates in this context.[63] (Other, more *haṭha*-yogic parts of the text often refer to Siddhas instead of *sādhakas*, and at one point [17.37cd ff.] it distinguishes between the two groups.) The system of *aṅgas* in *paṭalas* 2–7 corresponds to Pātañjala-yoga. If we are to treat the purification section (*paṭala* 2) as a kind of *yama-niyama*, we can find all the *aṅgas* of the Pātañjala model in the traditional order: *āsana* (*paṭala* 3), *prāṇāyāma* (*paṭala* 4), *pratyāhāra* (*paṭala* 5), *dhāraṇā* (*paṭala* 6), *dhyāna* (*paṭala* 7) and *samādhi* (not mentioned by Devī and not having a separate *paṭala* in the MaSaṃ, but inserted in *paṭala* 7).

Let us examine the *aṅgas* briefly one by one:

Dehaśuddhi (*paṭala* 2; 67 verses): after he has heard Devī's questions (2.1–10), Śiva begins delivering his yogic teaching (*yoga-śāstram* 2.11b) by describing/prescribing purification to be performed before any yogic practice. The yogin should bath in water or in ashes, and, correspondingly, should perform his mantric purification with water (*jalasnāna*) or with ashes (*bhasmasnāna*). The perform (*jalasnāna*) is basically to cast one's sins on a stone (*vajraśilā*) in the form of water. Reciting the Root-mantra, the yogin should sprinkle his body with water, and sip some of it. Then he should immerse himself in the water with the Cow Ges-

[61]On *ṣaḍaṅgayoga* cf. VASUDEVA 2000:282ff. Śaiva *ṣaḍaṅgayoga* very frequently includes '*tarka*', which is absent from the MaSaṃ. VASUDEVA (2000:290) treats the MaSaṃ (with reference to MS W) first as if it had only four *aṅgas* (*prāṇāyāma*, *dhāraṇā*, *pratyāhāra* and *dhyāna*), then, on the same page, as *aṣṭāṅga* (*yama*, *niyama*, *āsana*, *prāṇāyāma*, *dhāraṇā*, *pratyāhāra*, *dhyāna* and *samādhi*). In fact, the MaSaṃ does not contain *yama* or *niyama* in the Pātañjala sense of the word, but it does have all the ancillaries of the Yogasūtra except *yama* and *niyama* for which it has a *dehaśuddhi* section (note also *niyama* mentioned in 6.31, 52.35 and 55.46).

[62]In *paṭala* 11. Strictly speaking, the chapter on *mudrās* is outside the main yoga section I am dealing with here but I think it is of the same layer as *paṭalas* 2–7. It includes a description of the *khecarīmudrā*, which has very little to do with the *khecarī*-technique in the *Khecarīvidyā* section.

[63]On the *sādhakas* as the 'target audience' of Śaiva (Saiddhāntika) yoga, see BRUNNER 1994:431–435.

ture (*dhenumudrā*). He should perform *nyāsa* of the *bhūtabījas* on his body and recite mantras. This is the *aghamarṣaṇa* (Pardoning of Sin) rite. The *bhasmasnāna* (2.23–43) is to be performed with ashes in the left hand, touching it with the right and performing *nyāsa* first with the five *tāra* (i.e. *praṇava*) syllables, then with four, three, two and one, a rite that is related to the five *kalā*s and the five (*mūrti*)s of Śiva. 2.44 starts a new section on *śoṣaṇa* (Drying Off [Of Sin]). It involves *prāṇāyāma*, mantra recitation and visualization as well as imagining that a miraculous wind dries off all sins in one's body. From 2.50cd on, *dāhana* (Burning [Of Sin]) is being described, then immersion in *amṛta*. The whole teaching is a variation on typical Tantric purification.[64]

Āsana (*paṭala* 3; 46 verses): *vīra-*, *kūrma-*, *svastika-*, *kukkuṭa-*, *mayūra-*, *vyāghra-*, *padma-*, *vijaya-*, *dṛḍha-*, *gṛdhra-*, *garuḍa-*, *yakṣa-*, *siddha-*, *vṛṣabha-āsana*s and the results of their practice. Some of these forms of *āsana*s seem to be different in nature from their late *haṭha*-yogic counterparts. The description of *siddhāsana* and *vṛṣabhāsana* (3.33–36), two rather peculiar sitting postures, has some resemblance to a painting (dated ca. 1804 AD) from the Mahāmandir Temple, Jodhpur (the city where four MaSaṃ MSS are to be found). A small detail of this painting is reproduced on the cover of WHITE's *The Alchemical Body*.

Prāṇāyāma (*paṭala* 4; 92 verses): 4.2 states that yoga is nothing but victory over *prāṇa*. 4.3–5 describe situations and locations that should prevent the yogin from performing *prāṇāyāma*, while 4.6–8 gives some details on where the yogin should practice it. 4.9–15 gives basic instruction and defines *pūraka*, *kumbhaka* and *recaka* as well as their lengths. 4.16–22 describes the auspicious signs of proper practice. 4.23–39 gives remedies for consequent health problems. 4.40–92 teaches the purification of the *nāḍī*s after enumerating the most important ones. This section contains well-known verses to be found in the *Svacchandatantra*, the *Haṭhayogapradīpikā*, the *Gorakṣaśataka*, the *Mahākālasaṃhitā* etc.

Pratyāhāra (*paṭala* 5; 18 verses): a short chapter on the withdrawal of the senses (*pratyāhāra*) and absorption in the Self (*svātmani layaḥ*). It defines yoga, *tapas* and *jñāna* as victory over the

[64] See e.g. the *Svacchandapaddhati* (MS), the *Kaulāvalīnirṇaya*, the *Somaśambhupaddhati* etc.

mind (*manaso vijayaḥ*; 5.8cd–9ab). It teaches the gradual withdrawal (*saṃhāra*) of the five senses (*indriyas*), the five elements (*bhūtas*) and the five *tanmātras*.

Dhāraṇā (*paṭala* 6; 31 verses): in contrast with Patañjali, who teaches one-pointed concentration (*dhāraṇā*) that gets transformed into *dhyāna*, the MaSaṃ echoes Tantric concentration techniques similar to those of the *Kiraṇa* (58.18c ff.), the *Raurava* (*Vidyāpāda* 7.6–10)[65] and the *Mataṅgapārameśvara* (*Yogapāda* 2.35c–65),[66] which teach *āgneyī/pāvakā, vāruṇī/saumyā, aiśānī* and *amṛtā dhāraṇās*, as well as those of the *Mālinīvijayottaratantra* (cf. VASUDEVA 2003:319 ff).[67] There are three kinds of *dhāraṇā* described in the MaSaṃ: *vāyavā, āgneyī* and *amṛtā*. (There might also be a reference to *vāruṇī dhāraṇā* in 6.4b.) While *prāṇāyāma* destroys faults/impurites (*doṣa*), *dhāraṇā* is said to destroy sins (*kilbiṣa*, 6.13ab). Terrible *guhyakas* may obstruct the success of the yogin (6.15). He should bestow offerings (*bali*) on them after he has drawn a *maṇḍala* and recited the appropriate mantras. This way he can pacify *Bhūtas*, *Yakṣas*, *Rākṣasas*, *Kṣetrapālas*, *Devas*, *Nāgas* and *Bhairavas* and their female consorts.

Dhyāna (first part of *paṭala* 7; 74 verses): see above, pp. 163ff..

Samādhi (end of *paṭala* 7; 16 verses): *samādhi* is seven times longer than *dhyāna* (7.77cd). The yogin should visualize Śiva without any sense of duality (*ātmāvibhedena* 7.79c). In *samādhi*, there is an enormous flash of lightning, which indicates *mukti*. 7.82–87 describes the auspicious signs the yogin will experience, and 7.88–89 hints on the problems that may arise, which are to be fought off with the method described earlier (probably at the end of *paṭala* 6).

As regards the yoga teaching of the whole MaSaṃ, it might be possible to find some clues to separate the layers of which it is made up. We have seen that the MaSaṃ shows parallel passages with the KMT, and has definitely some connections with

---

[65] *Rauravāgama*. Vol. I. Ed. NṚ. Bhatt. Pondicherry: Institut Français D'Indologie, 1985. p.182.

[66] *Mataṅgapārameśvara*. (*Kriyāpāda, Yogapāda, Caryāpāda*) Ed. NṚ. Bhatt. Pondicherry: Institut Français D'Indologie, 1982. p.259–64.

[67] VASUDEVA (2000:319 n.113) says: "A derivative of the four fixations is also taught in the *Matsyendrasaṃhitā*..." I agree, but clearly there are only three kinds of *dhāraṇās* in the text. (Cf. MaSaṃ 6.2a: *dhāraṇā trividhā devi*)

Kubjikā's cult. Our earliest source of the systems of five (or six or seven) *cakras* by the names *mūlādhāra, svādhiṣṭhāna, maṇipūra, anāhata, viśuddhi/viśuddha, ājñā* and *sahasrāra* or *brahmarandhra* is probably the very same KMT. It would be interesting to examine in what form the system of *cakras* of the KMT is present in the MaSaṃ. Any mentioning of the *cakras* might help us define a *terminus post quem* for those passages that contain them. This might be important since I suspect that the MaSaṃ contains some yogic teachings that are earlier than the *cakra* system of the KMT. According to SANDERSON (1988:155-156) this system of *cakras* is "quite absent in all the Tantric traditions except this [i.e. the Kaula cult of Kubjikā] and the cult of the goddess Tripurasundarī [i.e. the Dakṣiṇāmnāya]. The yoga of these two traditions sets them apart from the earlier Kaula traditions of the Trika and the Kālī cult." Thus it seems worthwhile to examine which sections of the MaSaṃ know of the system of *cakras*. It is also important that the earlier traditions tend to refer to these "power centers" as knots (*granthi*) or locations (*sthāna*), sometimes lotuses (*padma*) or by the place they are located in, e.g. heart (*hṛt*), throat (*kaṇṭha*), palate (*tālu*) etc., and not by the above mentioned names well-known from *haṭha*-yoga.[68]

For example, *paṭala* 12 contains several references to the system of *cakras*: 12.36: *maṇipūrākhye*; 12.39: *svādhiṣṭhāne ṣaḍāre*; 12.41: *svādhiṣṭhāne ca rājake*; 12.43: *ājñāyāṃ dvidale*; 12.47: *sahasrāramahāpadme*. In contrast with these, MaSaṃ 2–7, the central yoga teaching of the text, which follows the Pātañjala model, does not refer to the *cakras* by these names at all. An interesting exeption is the mentioning of *mūlādhāra* in 4.40, 4.51 and 4.59, which fits well in the notion that Tantric texts often refer to it without knowing of any system of *cakras* similar to that of the KMT. MaSaṃ 7.8cd is even more telling: *dhyāyet svahṛdaye padmaṃ śivaśaktyātmakaṃ param*, i.e. "one should imagine a lotus in his own heart containing Śiva and Śakti." Although the absence of data is no proof, one may argue that this section of the

---

[68] Cf. BRUNNER (1994:437), who deals with yoga in Śaivasiddhānta texts. She says that though Śaivasiddhānta texts "sometimes use the terms *mulādhāra* and *brahmarandhra*, [they] ignore the names *svādhiṣṭhāna, maṇipūra, anāhata* and *viśuddha*". The same seems to be true also much of the Bhairavatantras.

text does not know of the system of lotuses, since then it would call the power center by its well-known name *anāhata*, or would at least refer to it by some fixed expression stating the number of its petals. 7.41c refers to the *hṛtpadma*, which is a frequent expression in Śaiva tantra. The compound *daśaśatadalapadmaṃ* (thousand-petalled lotus) in 7.69 is doubtful. It seems to refer either to Śiva ("He, who has, i.e. is located on, a thousand-petalled lotus") or, if we are to emend it to the obvious *daśaśatadalapadme*, to the *sahasrāracakra*, as in *haṭha*-yogic texts. As regards *cakra*s, e.g. *paṭala* 13 is of a totally different world of thought. It clearly teaches visualization in the seven *cakra*s. This method of marking off sections aware of the system of *cakra*s or ignorant of them might be a powerful tool to separate the layers of the text.

It seems possible that most of the yogic teaching in the MaSaṃ is two-layered: an early yoga text has been expanded by such insertions that teach the system of *cakra*s. I suspect that the beginning of *paṭala* 8 might be one of the *loci* where this method of insertion can be observed:

ātmānaṃ bhāvayec chuddha-
tattvagocaram īśvaram /
dhyātvā ciraṃ praśāntātmā
pūrvoktadhyānayogataḥ //8.2//
pūjayed gandhapuṣpādyair
yogī bhāvamayaiḥ śubhaiḥ /
ṣaḍādhāreṣu vidhivad
dvādaśānte viśeṣataḥ //8.3//
pūjayec chambhum avyagraṃ
śaktyā sahitam avyayam /
saṃsmaran niyato devi
pīyūṣārṇavam uttamam //8.4//

[The yogin] should visualize himself as God, who dwells in the Pure Tattvas. Meditating for a long time, with a peaceful disposition, according to the meditation method described earlier,

the yogin should worship [*missing object*] with mentally imagined fine scents and flowers etc. in the six

> *ādhāras* [i.e. *cakras*] according to the rule, and especially in the *dvādaśānta* [i.e. twelve *aṅgulas* above the *Brahmarandhra*],
>
> [the yogin] should worship the imperishable Śambhu, steadily, together with [his] Śakti, visualizing, [with a] controlled [mind], O Goddess, the Supreme Flood of Nectar.

8.3 seems to be an insertion. The repetition of *pūjayet*, and also the fact that at its first occurrence it has no direct object, makes these verses sound rather unnatural, while if we eliminate 8.3, the remaining two verses make perfect sense.

The fact that the whole text of *Paṭala* 8 seems to be made up of two distinct sections supports this tentative emandation. The first section is a description of two ways of meditation on Śiva (8.1–48). The second section (8.48 ff.) is perhaps an addition that teaches visualization in the *cakras* (8.49 ff. in the *mūlādhāra* ; 8.52 ff. in the *svādhiṣṭhāna* ; 8.55 ff. in the *maṇipūra* etc.). It is plausible that, in order to integrate the second section in *paṭala* 8, a redactor inserted a reference to the *cakras* after 8.2.

To sum it up: the main yoga teaching of the MaSaṃ (*paṭalas* 2–7) is more Tantric than *haṭha*-yogic, but it seems to be a Pātañjalised[69] and non-Śākta form of Tantric yoga that has strong connections with the Kubjikā tradition. It might prove to be fruitful to compare it to the Pātañjala-like yoga of the *Netratantra* and other Tantric *yoga-pādas* as well as other yoga-teachings of the Dakṣiṇāmnāya and the Paścimāmnāya, especially of its Śāmbhava tradition. The yoga of the MaSaṃ might turn out to be a rather complex mixture of Śaiva-, Pātañjala- and *haṭha*-yoga.

F. Matsyendra: facts and legends

Another angle from which we might get some more insight for dating and contextualising the text is the figure of Matsyendra, who the text is ascribed to and who is the hero of *paṭalas* 1 and 55. To

[69] In addition to the Pātañjala *aṅga*-system of the MaSaṃ, 7.7bcd evokes *Yogasūtra* 1.2 (*yogaś cittavṛttinirodhaḥ*): *yoginaś cittavṛttayaḥ śanair niścalatāṃ yāti divyajñānavicintanāt.*

say anything definite on the date and life of Matsyendra(-nātha) is a daunting task. Many of the legends concerning his life have been collected by BRIGGS 1989, BAGCHI 1934, WHITE 1996 and SENSHARMA 1994 (who draws upon BAGCHI heavily). These legends connect him with Tibet and Nepal, as well as Bengal and many other parts of India. His possible date spans from the 5th to the 13th century.[70] It is quite plausible that WHITE (1996:466 n.26) is right saying that "Matsyendra's name [...] cannot be attached to a single historical figure." The name Matsyendra can denote persons with "often the same gurus and disciples, but living in different centuries, under different kings, and in different regions of India." (WHITE 1996:110) The name Macchanda, a vernacular form of 'Matsyendra', is mentioned in Abhinavagupta's *Tantrāloka* (1.7, 29.32, 30.102).

An interesting source of the legend of his life is Vidyāpati's *Gorakṣavijaya*.[71] The plot of the *Gorakṣavijaya* has some resemblance with the account given in *paṭala* 55 of the MaSaṃ.[72]

The works traditionally attributed to Matsyendra (other than the MaSaṃ) are:

[1.] *Kaulajñānanirṇaya* (see in BAGCHI 1934)

[2.] *Akulavīratantra* (there are two versions in BAGCHI 1934 of this text)

[3.] *Kulānandatantra* (ibid.)

[4.] *Jñānakārikā* (ibid.)

[5.] *Matsyendranāth kā pad* (in MALLIK 1954)

[6.] *Yogaviṣaya* (ibid.)

[7.] *Candrāvalocana*

[8.] *Śābaracintāmaṇi*

[9.] *Śrīkāmākhyāguhyasiddhi* (BAGCHI 1934:70).

PĀṆḌEYA (1976:gha) adds:

[10.] *Kaulāvalīnirṇaya*

[11.] *Kulārṇava*

[70] This leads SENSHARMA to the surprising conclusion: "Matsyendranātha therefore probably flourished in [the] 5th or 6th century AD. and lived for 400 years or so [...]" (1994:26)

[71] Vidyāpati was born around 1360/80. See MCGREGOR 29–33.

[72] But in Vidyāpati it is by disguising himself a dancer that Gorakṣa saves Matsyendra from worldly enjoyments, and not by killing Matsyendra's son, as in the MaSaṃ.

[12.] *Kaulārṇava*

[13.] *Mahākaulārṇava*

[14.] the *Kulakāmadhenu* in MaSaṃ 38 attributed to Matsyendra may have been once an independent text.

The contents in brief of the two *paṭala*s containing a version of Matsyendra's legend in the MaSaṃ follows below:

Paṭala 1 (134 verses): The *paṭala* begins with five verses of salutation to Śiva, Gaṇeśa and Sarasvatī, the gurus and Matsyendranātha. Matsyendra was born a fisherman. One day he meets some *brāhmaṇa*s performing a secret ritual on the banks of a river. He approaches them and learns that they are Śaivas, and when he promises that he will not pass their secret to anyone, they offer him their knowledge/mantra (*vidyā*) that is very hard to obtain. He stays there in an island performing *japa* and *tapas.* Six months pass. Incidentally, he is swallowed by a big fish and driven accidentaly to the very place where Śiva is just about to relate the science of yoga to Pārvatī. After he has listened, eavesdropping, to the teaching, he addresses Śiva, who, killing the fish, rescues him.[73] Verses 1.61–84 contain Matsyendra's praise of Śiva and Pārvatī. (This section contains in 1.72 a reference to 'Śrīvidyāyoga'.) Matsyendra wanders around the earth, and, following Śiva's instruction, tries to find a worthy disciple. He finds none, but continues his roaming. The Cola king hears about him, finds him and asks him who he is and what his secret is. Mat-

[73]This part of the story is similar to the version of Matsyendra's legend found in the *Skandapurāṇa* (*Nāgarakhaṇḍa* 6, Adhyāya 263.50–59ab [*Matsyendranāthotpattikathanam*]): *tava vākyāmṛtair ebhir jñānayogo mahān abhūt/ tena tvaṃ sakalo jñāto mayāmūrto 'tha mūrtagaḥ//50// anujñāṃ mama deveśa dehi niṣkramaṇāya ca/ yathāhaṃ pitṛpo brahman bhavānyāś cāpi lakṣyate//51// hara uvāca/ vipro 'si sutarūpo 'si pūjyo'syā'si babhāṣataḥ/ bahir niṣkrama vegena stambhito 'si mahājhaṣaḥ//52// tato 'sau śirasā jātaḥ utkleśān matsyayojitaḥ/ tato hi vikṛtaṃ vaktraṃ kṣaṇād bahir upāgataḥ//53// rūpavān pratimāyukto matsyagandhena saṃyutaḥ/ somakāntisamas tatra hy abhavad divygandhabhāk//54// umāpi praṇataṃ cāmuṃ sutaṃ svotsaṅgabhājanam/ cakāra tasya nāmāpi haraḥ paramaharṣitaḥ//55// yasmān matsyodarāj jāto yogināṃ pravaro hy ayam/ tasmāt tu matsyanātheti loke khyāto bhaviṣyati//56// acchedyaḥ syān naratanur jñānayogasya pāragaḥ/ nirmatsaro 'pi nirdvandvo nirāśo brahmasevakaḥ//57// jīvanmuktaś ca bhavitā bhuvanāni caturdaśa/ ityuktaś ca maheśānaṃ praṇamaṃś ca punaḥ punaḥ//58// maheśvareṇa sahito mandarācalam āyayau/*

syendra refuses to teach him. Disappointed, the king leaves his city and embarks upon ascetism. Finally he meets Matsyendra again, receives initiation from him, and Matsyendra starts to relate the teaching he overheard when Śiva was teaching Pārvatī. The *paṭala* ends with an *upajāti* stanza, saying that this sacred tradition (*divyāgama*) is the essence of all essences. Matsyendra's story continues in *paṭala* 55.

Paṭala 55 (46 verses): The Cola king has become immortal. Matsyendra wanders on, and learns that the king of Alūra in the south has just died. He decides to enter the corpse of the king[74] to enjoy kingly enjoyments for some time. He arrives at the castle of the king, which is situated on a hill (*giridurga*) and is called Śilādroṇī (Rocky Moat?). He leaves his own body behind and enters that of the king, and begins enjoying a royal life. The Cola king[75] learns about Matsyendra's fall, hurries to his court and starts working as his servant. Due to his new and excessive life, Matsyendra has forgotten everything about himself. One day Matsyendra orders his servant to wash his little prince, and not being satisfied with the results, sends him back to wash him over and over again. The servant (i.e. the Cola king disguised) has had enough: he cuts the child into pieces. The shock awakens Matsyendra from his stupefied state and praises his disciple. He revives his own son, initiates the Cola king, and gives him the name Gorakṣeśa(!).[76] Gorakṣa later becomes a great yogin, a Siddha. Matsyendra gives him a mantra (*vidyā*), which is the Goddess Kāmākhyā herself. Gorakṣa initiates Matsyendra's son, Kharparīśa(?), to teach. His (probably Kharparīśa's) son, Vyālīndra, becomes a heretic (? corrupt passages). Therefore, for

---

[74]Is this part of the story influenced by Punjabi versions of the Matsyendra legend (cf. BAGCHI 1934:20)? Also, it is worth mentioning that some of the legends of Śaṅkarācārya describe him entering the body of a dead king in order to learn about worldly enjoyments. Since the MaSaṃ cites the PrS attributed to Śaṅkara, one wonders if its legend of Matsyendra is in any way influenced by the Śaṅkarasampradāya.

[75]Here called Lokanātha ('lord of the world, king'), a confusing word since it is usually Matsyendra who is designated by this name when venerated as an incarnation of Avalokiteśvara (cf. e.g. BRIGGS 1989:151).

[76]55.17cd–18ab: *tataḥ svaśiṣyaṃ colendraṃ dīkṣayitvāgamoditaiḥ/ dadau vidyakaro nāma gorakṣeśeti yogirāṭ* : "Then, having ordained the Cola king as his disciple with utterances of the tradition, the wise (*vidyākara*) king of the yogins (*yogirāj*) [i.e. Matsyendra] gave [him] the name Gorakṣa-īśa."

the sake of the Siddhas (*siddhānāṃ hitakāmyayā*), Matsyendra summarises the teaching he heard directly from Śiva.[77] The section 55.25–41 teaches how to protect and worship this book. The end of the *paṭala* tells us that after Matsyendra had composed the text, summarising the teachings of the *Kulāmnāya*, he 'sang' it to the Cola king.

There are several points to examine in this unique version of the Matsyendra legend. Firstly, the name of the city where Matsyendra assumes the form of a king is said to be Alūra. There is also a reference in 55.3 that the king was a 'southerner': *alūrādhipatiṃ bhūpaṃ dākṣiṇātyaṃ purā kila/ dadarśa mṛtam ekāgraḥ...* The name Alūra might evoke the name of the well-known city Vellūra (modern Vellore) in Tamil Nāḍu, with its Fort built in the 16th century, but the Tamil ending *-ūra* (-ore) is too wide-spread to allow us to draw any conclusions. Secondly, the fact that the redactor of the text equates the Cola king with Gorakṣanātha, a surprising feature of this version, might perhaps point to the Cola era (10–13th century AD) or the Cola region (Thanjāvur and its surrounding areas) as the time and place of the origin of the text, or at least of the frame story in *patala*s 1 and 55.

G. Some conclusions

Before giving in brief the content of all the *paṭala*s of the MaSaṃ, I summarise the main points I have raised. The MaSaṃ, preserved in five MSS, is a Sanskrit Śaiva Tantric text concentrating on yogic teachings. Its core probably originates from 13th-century South India (see the mixture of Kubjikā's / Śāmbhava's and Tripurā's cult typical of South India, references to South India and the Cola era, possible Śaṅkarasampradāya influence). Its religious teachings are influenced by the Kaula worship and *cakra*-oriented yoga of the goddesses Kubjikā (with Navātmā) and Tripurā, Saiddhāntika rituals and yogic processes devoid of the teaching of *cakra*s and Pātañjala-yoga. It is a composite text, constructed in its present form probably from several different texts whose titles might per-

[77] Is the problematic '*bhadrajā*' in 55.24 a reference to the title of his or Gorakṣa's composition?

haps be reconstructed from the confused colophons of one of the MSS.

H. Contents of the MaSaṃ

In the following, I will give in brief the content of all the *paṭala*s of the MaSaṃ.

Paṭala 1 (134 verses): the first part of the frame-story about Matsyendra. See above in section F.

Paṭala 2 (67 verses): *dehaśuddhi.* See above in section E.

Paṭala 3 (46 verses): *āsanas.* See above in section E.

Paṭala 4 (92 verses): *prāṇāyāma.* See above in section E.

Paṭala 5 (18 verses): *pratyahāra.* See above in section E.

Paṭala 6 (31 verses): *dhāraṇā.* See above in section E.

Paṭala 7 (74 + 16 verses): *dhyāna* (see above in section D) + *samādhi* (see above in section E).

Paṭala 8 (82 verses): *antararcana.* The yogin should visualize himself as god with the previously described method (cf. *paṭala* 7). The first part of the *paṭala* (8.5–48) is a long description of visualization: Śiva is to be seated on a throne in a miraculous gemstone island in the form of a beautiful and richly adorned god with Ambikā, the Mātṛkas and Rudras or as blazing light. In 8.49, a new section on meditation on the *cakras* begins somewhat abruptly, which I consider a later addition, since a reference to it seems to be inserted in 8.3 in a way that confuses the syntax of the introductory stanzas. Thus perhaps neither this reference nor the section it refers to were originally part of the text.

Paṭala 9 (55 verses): the *mantroddhāra* of the *mantrarāja* (Chief Mantra). Connection is established between the letters of the alphabet, the seven *yoginīs* and the seven *ādhāras* of the body. *Nyāsa* is to be performed (9.16–34) as well as *dhyāna* of Śiva (9.35–44) and of Parameśvarī (9.45–51). There seems to be some Tripurā influence.

Paṭala 10 (83 verses): beginning of *dīkṣāvidhi*, construction of a *maṇḍala* and *pūjā* of *yoginīs*.

Paṭala 11 (57 verses): *mudrās* (*khecarīmudrā, dīpamudrā, śṛṅgamudrā, saubarīmudrā*) and *Śambhubhairavīvandana* as well as description of *yoginīs* and rules of initiation (*dīkṣā*) including the transmission of the *mantrarāja* from guru to disciple. End of *dīkṣā*. *Paṭala*s 10 and 11 seem to form a whole, a long teaching on *dīkṣā*.

Paṭala 12 (61 verses): *mantrasādhana*, *nyāsa* of *kūṭa*s on the *cakra*s.

Paṭala 13 (16 verses): *yoginīnyāsa* on the *cakra*s.

Paṭala 14 (79 verses): *vidyā khecarasaṃhitā* = *Paṭala* 1 of the *Khecarīvidyā*. Cf. MALLINSON 2001.

Paṭala 15 (83 verses): *catuṣkalāpana*, *amṛta* = *Paṭala* 2 of the *Khecarīvidyā*. Cf. MALLINSON 2001.

Paṭala 16 (114 verses): = *Paṭala* 3 of the *Khecarīvidyā*. Cf. MALLINSON 2001.

Paṭala 17 (60 verses): *khecarīmelana*. Cf. MALLINSON 2001:284–287 for the edited text of this *paṭala*.

Paṭala 18 (72 verses): *melaka*. Cf. MALLINSON 2001:288–291 for the edited text of this *paṭala*.

Paṭala 19 (26 verses): *dhyāna* on *amṛta*.

Paṭala 20 (31 verses): *dhyāna* similar in content to that of *paṭala* 19.

Paṭala 21 (29 verses): *dhyāna* on the seven *padma*s.

Paṭala 22 (32 verses): *kuṇḍalyutthāpana*.

Paṭala 23 (47 verses): *triliṅgārcā*: worship of the *bāṇaliṅga*, *tārāhvayaliṅga* and *jyotirliṅga*.

Paṭala 24 (74 verses): *vāñchāsiddhi*, description of *pītha*s with visualization of deities, Kāmeśvara.

Paṭala 25 (70 verses): *dhyāna* on the *sahasrāra*, Tripurā.

Paṭala 26 (64 verses): 50 *tīrtha*s in the body.

Paṭala 27 (30 verses): *kṣetrajñāna*. Cf. MALLINSON 2001:292–293 for the edited text of this *paṭala*.

Paṭala 28 (16 verses): *auṣadhi* = *Paṭala* 4 of the *Khecarīvidyā*. Cf. MALLINSON 2001.

Paṭala 29 (77 verses): *auṣadhi*.

Paṭala 30 (16 verses): *pādukāsiddhi*.

Paṭala 31 (11 verses): *vajrasiddhi*.

Paṭala 32 (18 verses): *vetālasiddhi*.

Paṭala 33 (14 verses): *kapālasādhana*.

Paṭala 34 (66 verses): *yakṣiṇīsādhana*. *Vāmakeśvaratantra* mentioned.

Paṭala 35 (81 verses): *añjanasiddhi*.

Paṭala 36 (35 verses): *bhairavīyamantra.*

Paṭala 37 (6 verses): a very short description of a mantra.

Paṭala 38 (46 verses): *kulakāmadhenumantra*, *-stotra*, Matsyendra mentioned.

Paṭala 39 (100 verses): for those without yoga; *kālamṛtyujayakaramantra, homa, kulāmṛta, siddhimūlikā.*

Paṭala 40 (17+54 verses): *kulācāravidhikrama, śivatīrtha, mantra, kulācāranirṇaya, yoginī māyā pāśavī ca nārī, māyayā saṃgamaḥ.*

Paṭala 41 (29 verses): *mantra, kuṇḍalinī.*

Paṭala 42 (20 verses): *kṣetrapālanirṇaya, śāmbhavamantrasādhana.*

Paṭala 43 (39 verses): *sarvasiddhimantra, śāmbhavamantrasādhana.* Kubjikā influence.

Paṭala 44 (98 verses): *kṣetra, tīrtha, avadhūta, tattvas.*

Paṭala 45 (107 verses): *mantra, yantra, mudrā, pūjā.*

Paṭala 46 (46 verses): Beginning of the *ṣaṭkarma* section, *vaśya; mudrās* (*yoni, kṣobhinī, drāviṇī*).

Paṭala 47 (48 verses): *ākarṣaṇayantra.*

Paṭala 48 (29 verses): *vidveṣanamantra.*

Paṭala 49 (68 verses): *stambhanamantra.*

Paṭala 50 (28 verses): *uccāṭanamantra* and *yantra.*

Paṭala 51 (71 verses): *vidviṣa.* End of *ṣaṭkarma* section?

Paṭala 52 (37 verses): the *nigrahamantra* for defeating one's enemies, *guruvandana.*

Paṭala 53 (35 verses): Vijayā's *vaśaṃkaramantra* (for victory in a battle), *dhyāna* (of the four-armed goddess), *māṃsamadyatarpaṇa.* Kubjikā influence.

Paṭala 54 (44 verses): *Aparājitā*'s *vidyā, dhyāna.* Parallels with the KMT.

Paṭala 55 (46 verses): the second part of the frame-story. See above in section F.

Abbreviations and Symbols

^{ac} : before correction (*ante correctionem*)

^{pc} : after correction (*post correctionem*)

† † enclose corrupted text in MSS

⊕ and ⊗ : ornamental characters in MSS

≀ ≀ enclose unclear *akṣaras*

⋆ stands for an illegible *akṣara*

Cod : codex, the reading in the MS

em. : emendation (by X)

JAOS : Journal of the American Oriental Society

J_a, J_b, J_c, J_d, W : see *Matsyendrasaṃhitā* MSS

KMT : *Kubjikāmatatantra*

MaSaṃ : *Matsyendrasaṃhitā*

$MaŚat_1$ $MaŚat_2$ and $MaŚat_3$: see *Matsyendraśataka* MSS

MMSL : Maharaja Man Singh Library, Jodhpur

NAK : National Archives Kathmandu

NĀT : *Nityāhnikatilaka*

$NepMaSaṃ_1$, $NepMaSaṃ_2$, $NepMaSaṃDiff_1$, $NepMaSaṃDiff_2$ see *Matsyendrasaṃhitā* MSS

NGMPP : Nepal-German Manuscript Preservation Project

NṢA : *Nityāṣodaśikārṇava*

PrS : *Prapañcasāra*

Bibliography

Manuscripts:

Nityāhnikatilaka of Muktaka : NGMPP MS Access: 3/384 Reel: A 41/11

Matsyendraśataka $MaŚat_1$: NGMPP MS Access: 2/102. Reel: B 39/11

Matsyendraśataka $MaŚat_2$: NGMPP MS Access: 5/2717. Reel: B 39/23

Matsyendraśataka $MaŚat_3$: NGMPP MS Access: 5/6558. Reel: A 63/18

Matsyendrasaṃhitā J_a : MS No. 1784, MMSL

Matsyendrasaṃhitā J_b : MS No. 1783, MMSL

Matsyendrasaṃhitā J_c : MS No. 1782, MMSL

Matsyendrasaṃhitā J_d : MS No. 1785, MMSL

Matsyendrasaṃhitā W : MS β 1115, Wellcome Library for the History and Understanding of Medicine, London

Matsyendrasaṃhitā $NepMaSaṃ_1$: NGMPP MS Access : 2/102. Reel: B 39/11

Matsyendrasaṃhitā $NepMaSaṃ_2$: NGMPP MS Access: 5/2717. Reel: B 39/23

Śambhunirṇayadīpikā of Śivānandamuni : MS R. No. 3203d, Madras Govt. Lib.

Śambhunirṇayatantra : MS R. No. 3203c, Madras Govt. Lib.

Ṣaḍanvayaśāmbhavakrama of Umākānta : MS β 353, Wellcome Library.

Printed sources:

Kubjikāmatatantra. The Kulālikāmnāya version. Critical edition by T. Goudriaan and J. Schoterman. Leiden: E.J. Brill, 1988.

Kāmakalāvilāsa of Puṇyānanda. Pt. Mukuṇḍa Rāma Śāstrī ed. Kashmir Series of Texts and Studies. No. XII Bombay: Tatvavivechaka, 1918.

Gorakṣaśataka. See in BRIGGS 1989:284–304.

Gorakṣavijaya [by Vidyāpati]. Dr. Harimohan Miśra ed. Paṭnā: Bihār Rāṣṭrabhāṣā Pariṣad, 1984.

Prapañcasāra. 2 Vols. Arthur Avalon's Tantrik Texts XVIII & XIX. Calcutta: The Sanskrit Press Depository, 1935.

Mahākālasaṃhitā. Guhyakālīkhaṇḍaḥ. Parts I-III. Dr. Kiśoranāth Jhā ed. Gaṅgānātha Jhā Kendrīya Saṃskṛta Vidyāpīṭha: Illāhābād, 1976.

Mahākālasaṃhitā. Kāmakalākhaṇḍaḥ. Dr. Kiśoranāth Jhā ed. Gaṅgānātha Jhā Kendrīya Saṃskṛta Vidyāpīṭha: Illāhābād, 1976.

Vāmakeśvarīmatam. Published by Acharya Krishnanand Sagar. Gujarat: Shri Madhvanand Ashram, 1985.

Śābaracintāmaṇiḥ. Śābar mantroṃ kā siddhi dāyak vidhi sahit. Vārāṇasī: Yogapracāriṇī Sabhā, 1992/93. p.48

ŚrīSkandamahāpurāṇam. Nag Sharan Singh ed. 8 Vols. Delhi: Nag Publishers, 1986-1989.

Haṭhayogapradīpikā of Svātmārāma. Madras: Adyar Library, 1972.

Secondary sources:

BAGCHI 1934: Bagchi, Prabodh Candra ed. *Kaulajñānanirṇaya and Some Minor Texts of the School of Matsyendranātha*. Calcutta Sanskrit Series, No.3. Calcutta: Metropolitan, 1934.

BRIGGS 1989: Briggs, George Weston. *Gorakhnāth and the Kānphaṭa Yogīs*. Delhi: Motilal Banarsidass, 1989. [1938.]

BRUNNER 1963: Brunner, Hélène. *Somaśambhupaddhati*. Pondichéry: Institut Français d'Indologie, 1963.

BRUNNER 1994: Brunner, Hélène. "The Place of Yoga in the Śaivāgamas." In: Paṇḍit NṚ. Bhatt Felicitation Volume. Ed. P-S. Filliozat, S.P. Narang, C.P. Bhatta, Delhi, 1994. p.425–461.

BOUY 1994: Bouy, Christian. *Les Nātha-yogin et les Upaniśads*. Paris: Diffusion de Boccad, 1994.

DYCZKOWSKI 1988: Dyczkowski, Mark S.G. *The Canon of the Śaivāgama and the Kubjikā Tantras of the Western Kaula Tradition*. Albany: State University of New York Press, 1988.

DYCZKOWSKI 2001: Dyczkowski, Mark S.G. *The Cult Of The Goddess Kubjikā. A Preliminary Comparative Textual and Anthropological Survey of a Secret Newar Goddess*. Stuttgart: Franz Steiner Verlag, 2001.

GARZILLI 1988: Garzilli, Enrica. "[Review of] Matsyendra Saṃhitā, Ascribed to Matsyendranātha, Part I. Edited by Debabrata SENSHARMA". JAOS 1998 vol.118 number 4 p.543-545.

GOUDRIAAN 1981: Goudriaan, Teun and Gupta, Sanjukta. *Hindu Tantric and Śākta Literature*. Wiesbaden: Harrasowitz, 1981. In: A history of Indian literature. Ed. by Jan Gonda. Vol.2. Epics and Sanskrit Religious literature. Fasc.2.

HEILIJGERS 1994: Heilijgers-Seelen, Dory. *The System of Five Cakras in Kubjikāmata-tantra 14-16*. Groningen Oriental Studies IX. The Netherlands: Egbert Forsten Groningen, 1994.

KHANNA, Madhu. *The Concept and Liturgy of the Śrīcakra based on Śivānanda's Trilogy*. DPhil thesis, Oxford, 1986.

MALLIK 1954: Mallik, Kalyani. *Siddha-siddhānta-paddhati and other works of the Nātha Yogīs*. Poona: Poona Oriental Book House: Poona, 1954.

MALLINSON 2001: Mallinson, James. *The Khecarīvidyā of Ādinātha. A critical Edition and Annotated Translation.* D.Phil. thesis, Balliol College, Oxford University, 2001.

MCGREGOR 1984: McGregor, Ronald Stuart. *Hindi literature from its beginnings to the nineteenth century.* Wiesbaden: Harrasowitz, 1984. In: A history of Indian literature. Ed. by Jan Gonda. Vol.8. Modern Indo-Aryan literatures. Pt.1. Fasc.6.

PĀṆḌEYA 1976: *Gorakṣasaṃhitā.* Part I. Ed. Janārdana Pāṇḍeya. Varanasi: Sampūrṇānanda Saṃskṛta Viśvavidyālaya, 1976.

RAO 1914. Gopinath Rao, T. *Elements of Hindu Iconography.* 2 Vols (4 parts). Madras: Law Printing House, 1914–16.

SANDERSON 1985: Sanderson, Alexis. "Purity and power among the Brahmans of Kashmir." In: The Category of the Person. Ed. Michael Cassithers et al. Cambridge: Cambridge University Press, 1985.

SANDERSON 1988: Sanderson, Alexis. "Śaivism and the Tantric Traditions." In: The World's Religions/Religions of Asia. Ed. Friedhelm Hardy. London: Routledge, 1988. [Reprint: 1990.]

SENSHARMA 1994: *Matsyendrasaṃhita.* [sic] *Ascribed to Matsyendranātha.* Part I. Ed. Debabrata SENSHARMA. Calcutta: The Asiatic Society, 1994.

VASUDEVA 2000: Vasudeva, Somadeva. *The Yoga of the Mālinīvijayottaratantra.* D.Phil. thesis. Wolfson College, Oxford, 2000.

VYAS & KSHIRSAGAR 1986: Vyas, Kaluram and Kshirsagar, D.B. *A Catalogue of Manuscripts in Maharaja Man Singh Pustak Prakash, Jodhpur.* Pt. 2. Jodhpur: Maharaja Man Singh Pustak Prakash, 1986.

WHITE 1996: White, David Gordon. *The Alchemical Body: Siddha traditions in medieval India.* Chicago: University of Chicago Press, 1996.

Six

Remarks on the Use of the *Dhāraṇīs* and Mantras of the *Mahāpratisarā-Mahāvidyārājñī*

Gergely Hidas*

This paper considers one of the *Pañcarakṣā* (PR) protections, the *Mahāpratisarā-Mahāvidyārājñī* (MPMVR), and attempts to reconstruct the practices related to the earliest phase of this tradition on the basis of textual passages from the Sanskrit recensions and some Central and Eastern Asian archaeological evidence.[1]

*I am indebted to Professor Alexis Sanderson, my DPhil supervisor for his help and guidance and for reading and commenting on a final draft of this paper. I also thank Gerd Mevissen for his useful remarks. Responsibility for remaining errors is only mine. An earlier version of this paper was read at the XIVth Conference of the International Association of Buddhist Studies in London in September 2005. This publication was supported by the Hungarian Research Fund (OTKA, project no. T 038047) and the János Szerb Foundation, Budapest.

[1]For a preliminary introduction to this scripture see HIDAS 2003.

Textual Sources

The earliest independent Sanskrit witnesses of the MPMVR are five fragmentary birch-bark mss. from Gilgit[2] which can be dated most probably to the first half of the seventh century.[3] About a dozen xylographic and painted amulets[4] usually with the first *dhāraṇī* and the four mantras of this scripture were excavated in Central and Eastern Asia, the earliest of which is from the tenth century.[5] Four fragmentary pieces of bricks inscribed with the two *dhāraṇīs* and four mantras of the *Mahāpratisarā* survive in Yunnan. These are dated to the period between the ninth and eleventh centuries.[6] There exists an Uigurian fragment containing a short section of the first *dhāraṇī* of the *Mahāpratisarā*.[7] The rest of the Sanskrit witnesses are to be found almost exclusively[8] in PR mss. which come partly from Eastern India from the eleventh to the thirteenth centuries and partly from Nepal from the eleventh to the twentieth centuries.[9]

---

[2]See SCHLIEKER 1984. While four of the Gilgit-fragments (GBMFE 1080–1165) most likely contain parts of the first recension of the MPMVR, the fifth one (GBMFE 3328–3335) does not seem to be the MPMVR itself. Approximating the length of this ms. on the basis of its folio numbers, one comes to the conclusion that this ms. most probably contains a shorter auxiliary scripture of the MPMVR, perhaps, a *Mahāpratisarā-dhāraṇī*.

[3]The donor of one of these mss. (GBMFE 3328-3335) appears to have been the queen of a Paṭola Ṣāhi ruler who reigned in the first half of the seventh century (VON HINÜBER 2004: 88–90). Palaeography suggests that the other four mss. are also likely to originate from this period (VON HINÜBER 2004: 6–7).

[4]One hand-painted amulet was excavated in a tomb near Xian (MEVISSEN 1999: 109 plate 8.9, DRÈGE 1999-2000: 32). A Japanese *Mahāpratisarā*-amulet kept at the Ferenc Hopp Museum of Eastern Asiatic Arts, Budapest is also hand-painted (FERENCZY 1987: 41, CSEH 1996: 54–56).

[5]A number of these amulet-prints are reproduced and dealt with in DRÈGE 1999-2000. Some Chinese sources quoted there date a few of these xylographs to the eighth century.

[6]LIEBENTHAL 1947. These bricks originate from a temple where they were placed inside the walls as spiritual relics.

[7]ZIEME 2005: 160–161. I am grateful to Dr. Alice Sárközi for drawing my attention to this paper.

[8]There exist a few later independent mss. of the MPMVR as well. See, for example, TSUKAMOTO *et al.* 1989: 82–84.

[9]The majority of these mss. are listed in TSUKAMOTO *et al.* 1989: 62–64, the NGMPP CD-ROM catalogue and MEVISSEN 1989: 366–372.

The MPMVR is available in Chinese in a shorter recension (T. 1154) translated by Ratnacinta in 693 and a longer one (T. 1153) translated by Amoghavajra in the eighth century. The text preserved in the Gilgit mss. appears to be close to T. 1154, while the text in the Eastern Indian and Nepalese mss. appears to be close to T. 1153.

The Tibetan translation of this text dates from around 800 and is included in various *Kanjurs*.[10] It seems that only the later recension of the MPMVR was translated into Tibetan.

Historical Contexts

The earliest version of the MPMVR belongs to the *dhāraṇī*-literature of the Mantranaya.[11] This first recension can probably be dated to the sixth century and it appears to have been known as *Mahāpratisara-Mahāvidyārāja* at that time. The most plausible explanation for the original masculine gender of this protection is that the roots of this tradition go back to Brahmanism, to texts as early as the *Atharva-veda*, where protective threads or amulets called *pratisara* are mentioned.[12] It is not known exactly when the Buddhists started to integrate this protective tradition into their practice, but it seems that various amulet-cults with their own scriptures existed within the Sangha by the middle of the first millennium, for example the *Asiloma-pratisara* found among

---

[10]Peking 179; Derge 561; Stog Palace 520; Phug brag 363, 622. See HARRISON 1996: 53 for further references.

[11]"Though the term *mantrayāna* is often used in preference to *mantranaya* in (academic) discussions of tantric Buddhism, it does not appear in texts until well after the appearance of the term *Vajrayāna*, upon which it is probably modelled. As a result *mantranaya* is the more appropriate term to describe the self-perception of pre-Vajrayāna tantric Buddhism." (WILLIAMS with TRIBE 2000: 271). It is important to note here that this first recension already contains some pieces of *vajra*-terminology. As for Tibetan classification, in the *Introduction to the Buddhist Tantric Systems*, the *Pratisarā* and its auxiliary scriptures are listed in the 'Mother of the Family' section of the 'Tathāgata Family' of the *Kriyā*-tantra class (LESSING and WAYMAN: 113).

[12] AV 4.40, 8.5. Further places of occurence include the *Yajur-veda* and the *Śatapatha-brāhmaṇa*. See IWAMOTO 1938: Introduction and SEN 1965: 68, 70.

the Turfan mss.[13] Finally, however, the *Mahāpratisara* appears to have become the most popular scripture incorporating this tradition and probably in the late seventh century its second recension was composed. This recension most likely served the better integration of this text into the Vajrayāna,[14] changing the historical locus of the *nidāna* to a mythical Vajrayānic setting.[15] It seems that from about the same time this protection was considered to be have a feminine nature.[16] This shift of gender may have happened simultaneously with the deification of this scripture,

---

[13]WALDSCHMIDT 1965: 38–39, 1971: 85–88, WALDSCHMIDT and SANDER 1980: 272–274.

[14]"A significant point in the history of tantric Buddhism occurs, probably sometime during the late seventh century, with the appearance of the term *Vajrayāna*, 'The Diamond Way'. (...) It is worth stressing that the term 'Vajrayāna' was not employed before this period, and that, therefore, the expressions 'Vajrayāna Buddhism' and 'tantric Buddhism' are not synonymous. (...) An earlier term used to distinguish tantric from other forms of practice was *mantranaya*, 'the path *(naya)* of mantras'. This expression was paired with *pāramitānaya*, the path of perfections (i.e. the path elaborated in the Mahāyāna Perfection of Wisdom literature). Together, the two paths were considered to constitute the Mahāyāna. (...) Indian tantric Buddhism, in its pre-Vajrayāna phase at least, saw itself as part of the Mahāyāna, a fact that can be obscured by suggestions that Buddhism is comprised of three paths—the Hīnayāna, Mahāyāna, and Vajrayāna." (WILLIAMS with TRIBE 2000: 196). A line in the MPMVR suggests that the composers of this scripture associated themselves with the Mahāyāna: *mahāyānodgrahaṇalikhanavācanapaṭhanasvādhyāyanaśravaṇadhāraṇābhiyuktānāṃ paripālikeyaṃ mahādhāraṇī* (IWAMOTO 1938: 20.26–27) "This great *dhāraṇī* is the protector for those absorbed in comprehending, writing down, reciting, reading, daily repeating, listening to and preserving the [teachings of the] Mahāyāna."

[15]The sermon of the first recension takes place on the Gṛdhrakūṭa near Rājagṛha. The place of teaching in the later recension is the Mahāvajrameru-mountain. I am grateful to Dr. Jundo Nagashima for his help with the translation of the opening parts of T. 1154 and 1153 from Chinese.

[16]In China and Japan the original masculine nature of certain deities of the Mantranaya appears to have been preserved. DE VISSER 1920: 377–378 interprets this phenomenon differently and argues that the existence of the masculine forms of these deities in Eastern Asia is is due to linguistic misunderstanding. He writes the following on the gender of Mahāmāyūrī: "Es ist jedoch eigentümlich, daß die Tantrische Schule nicht aufhörte, diese Figur trotzdem als eine männliche Gottheit darzustellen, welches hervortritt aus den hier unten zu behandelnden Gemälden. Wie alle die vorherigen Übersetzer benutzt er [i.e. Amoghavajra] das Wort wang, König, welches aber auch Königin heißen kann. Ich vermute, daß eben der Gebrauch dieses Characters schon in alten Zeiten in China und Japan das Mißverständniss verursacht

when Mahāpratisarā, a protective goddess appeared.[17] Probably in the early eighth century, the MPMVR was grouped together with other apotropaic scriptures and became a prominent member of the*Pañcarakṣā*.[18] In the second half of the first millennium the cult of the *Mahāpratisarā* gradually spread to Nepal, Tibet, Central Asia, China, Mongolia, Korea, Japan and Indonesia.[19]

The Structure of the MPMVR

The MPMVR consists of two ritual instructions[20] and contains two *dhāraṇīs*, four mantras,[21] nine narratives, the description

---

hat, als wäre dies eine männliche Gottheit." Ibid. 382: "Ein kleiner Schnur- und Kinnbart sind die Bestätigung, daß diese Figur in China und Japan als männlich betrachtet wird; die modernen japanischen Autoren nennen diese Gottheit auch meistens Mahāmayūra-Vidyārāja, als ob feststehe, daß es ein männlicher Pfauen-Vidyā-König sei."

[17]Mahāpratisarā first manifested in two- then in eight-, ten- and twelve-armed forms. On the iconography of this goddess see the various articles of MEVISSEN and CHANDRA 1999–. After the deification new auxiliary scriptures including *stotras, hṛdayas, vidhis, kriyās, kalpas, upāyas* and *sādhanas* were composed, related to this goddess. See, for example, TSUKAMOTO *et al.* 1989: 83–84.

[18]While the Chinese translated these texts separately (SKILLING 1992: 180–182), the late eighth–early ninth-century *Ldan kar ma* catalogue of two Tibetan translators lists the following texts after one another in its section XIII, titled "The Five Great *Dhāraṇīs (gzuṅs chen po lṅa la)*: *Mahāmāyūrī, Mahāsāhasrapramardana, Mahāpratisarā-vidyārājñī, Mahāśītavana* and *Mahāmantrānudhāri* (LALOU 1953). An early ninth-century manuscript folio found in Tabo also lists these texts after one another, although in a different order: *Mahāsāhasrapramardanī-sūtra, Mahāmāyūrī-vidyārājñī, Mahāśītavana-sūtra, Mahāpratisarā-vidyārājñī, Mahāmantrānudharaṇi-/Mahāmantrānudhāri-sūtra* (HARRISON 1996: 53). It is possible that these five texts constituted the earliest Sanskrit PR collection and later on two of them, the *Mahāśītavana* and the *Mahāmantrānudhāri* were replaced with the *Mahāśītavatī* and the *Mahāmantrānusāriṇī* respectively. See SKILLING 1992: 138–144 on the seven PR texts.

[19]See e.g. MEVISSEN 1999.

[20]The *Mahāpratisarā-Mahāvidyārājñī-Prathamakalpa* (First Ritual Instruction of the Great Amulet, Great Queen of Spells) and the *Mahāpratisarā-Mahāvidyārājñī- Vidyādhararakṣāvidhānakalpa* (Ritual Instruction of the Protection Performance for the Spell-master of the Great Amulet, Great Queen of Spells).

[21]*oṃ amṛtavare vara 2 pravaraviśuddhe hūṃ 2 phaṭ 2 svāhā / oṃ amṛtavilokini garbhasaṃrakṣaṇi ākarṣaṇi hūṃ 2 phaṭ 2 svāhā / oṃ vimale*

of an amulet-making and a healing ritual furthermore general sections about the various benefits of this protection. The first *dhāraṇī* is called *samanta-jvālā-mālā-viśuddhi-sphurita-cintāmaṇi-mudrā-hṛdayāparājitā-dhāraṇī*, "The *Dhāraṇī* Invincible by Reason of the Essence of the Wish-granting Jewel Seal that Glitters with the Purity of a Garland of Enveloping Flame". The second *dhāraṇī* is given without a name in this text.[22]

Regarding the various practices related to this scripture, not only the two *dhāraṇīs* and the four mantras but also the whole text of the MPMVR were employed in different ways.

The Use Of The First *Dhāraṇī*

From the general sections of the first *kalpa* one learns that the first *dhāraṇī* should be recited silently[23] or aloud.[24] According to another passage, this *dhāraṇī* should be worshipped and revered first with different fragrances, incenses and flowers then wrapped up in cloths of various kinds mounted at the top of a flagstaff over a *caitya*, and circumambulated on the right with the music of various string and wind instruments being played.[25]

---

vipule jayavare jayavāhini amṛte viraje hūṃ 2 phaṭ 2 svāhā / oṃ bhara 2 saṃbhara 2 indriyabalaviśodhani hūṃ 2 phaṭ 2 rurucale svāhā (IWAMOTO 1938: 20.2–9). Sometimes a fifth mantra is also given in various PR mss. (*oṃ maṇidhari vajriṇi mahāpratisare hūṃ 2 phaṭ 2 svāhā* (IWAMOTO 1938: 20.10–11)). It seems that this mantra was added with the appearance of the second recension. The Sanskrit passages of the MPMVR quoted in this paper are based on drafts of two separate critical editions of the Gilgit and Eastern Indian and Nepalese mss. being prepared by the author. These may differ from Iwamoto's romanized transcription at certain places. Iwamoto's page numbers are always given for comparison.

[22]In a later auxiliary scripture of the MPMVR it is called *ārya-pratisarā-kalpa-dhāraṇī* (ŚĀŚANĪ 1999).

[23]*tasmāt tarhi mahābrāhmaṇa nityam evānusmaraṇamātreṇa manasikāreṇa manasikartavyā* (IWAMOTO 1938: 22.2–3) "Therefore, Great Brahmin, it should always be recollected by concentrating on it and keeping it in mind." Translations given in this paper are by the author.

[24]*grahāḥ sarve vinaśyanti nāmagrahaṇakīrtanaiḥ* (IWAMOTO 1938: 5.16) "All Grahas are destroyed by mentioning or reciting its name."

[25]*yasmin viṣaya iyaṃ mahāvidyārājñī mahāpratisarā nāma pracariṣyati tatra taiḥ sarvasattvair jñātvā pūjāsatkāraṃ kṛtvā nānāgandhair nānādhūpair nānāpuṣpair nānāvastraiḥ pariveṣṭayitvā caityasyopari dhvajāgrāvaropitāṃ kṛtvā nānāvādyatūryasaṃgītibhir vādyamānābhiḥ pradakṣiṇīkartavyā*

The rest of the general instructions[26] about the employment of the first *dhāraṇī* refer to what is probably the most significant function, namely, that an amulet with this *dhāraṇī* should be painted[27] and be worn around the neck or arm.[28] The prepara-

---

(IWAMOTO 1938: 17.11–14) "In whichever region this Great Amulet, Great Queen of Spells is circulated, there all people, having learnt it, should perform its worship and reverence with different fragrances, incenses and flowers. Wrapped up in cloths of various kinds [and colours] it should be mounted at the top of a flagstaff over a *caitya* and it is to be circumambulated on the right with the music of various string and wind instruments being played." These instructions apparently prescribe the act of placing the wrapped up *dhāraṇī* at the pinnacle of a plag-pole, presumably in some sort of container which protects it. There is no mention in the text whether a banner should also be used simultaneously. Such a practice of placing rolled up magical formulas sometimes along with other ritual objects at the top of prayer flag standards is still extant in Tibetan Buddhist practice (I am grateful to Dr. Karma Phuntso for this information. Personal communication October 2005). The fifth narrative of the MPMVR gives an account of a similar act: "Right after this the great caravan-leader painted the Great Amulet, Great Queen of Spells, fixed it at the top of a flagstaff, and raised it." The *Sarvatathāgatoṣṇīṣasitātapatrā-dhāraṇī* should also be mounted at the top of a flag-pole and having been worshipped it should be raised at the city-gates or various other places (Dhīḥ 2002: 154.4–9, no author named). The *Sarvatathāgatādhiṣṭhāna-sattvāvalokana-buddhakṣetrasandarśana-vyūham* gives a reference to mounting the text on a flagstaff (DUTT 1939: 80.20–21: *imaṃ dharmaparyāyaṃ pūjayitvā vācayitavyaḥ dhvaje vā ucchrāpitaṃ kṛtvā pūjayitvā nānāgandhapuṣpadhūpavādyaiḥ praceṣṭavyaḥ*). The Tibetan version of the *Dhvajāgra-keyūra-nāma-dhāraṇī* gives the following instruction for use: "If you put round the neck or on the pinnacle of a victory banner, kings and heroic people shall all be protected." (Quoted from a translation by Dr. Michael Willis to whom I am grateful for sending me his work in progress). "Flowers, incense, banners, flags, music, and dance were used in the ceremonies accompanying *stūpa* worship. Even at the Buddha's funeral, the Mallas of Kuśinagara employed music, dance, flowers, and incense to honor, revere, and respect the corpse of the Buddha before it was cremated, as is described in detail in the *Mahāparinibbānasutta*." (HIRAKAWA 1990: 273)

[26]Beside the instructions in the general sections, the nine narratives describing the efficacy of this protection in the first *kalpa* of the MPMVR are also good sources of information. These stories support all types of use included in the general sections. The protagonists of these narratives recite this spell silently or aloud (first, second, eighth and ninth narratives), wear it as an amulet (third, fourth, sixth, seventh and ninth narratives) or fix it at the top of a flagstaff (fifth narrative).

[27]*kīdṛśena bhadanta vidhāneneyaṃ mahāpratisarā mahāvidyārājñī likhitavyā* (IWAMOTO 1938: 23.22–24) "Venerable One, what is the method of painting this Great Amulet, Great Queen of Spells?"

[28]*yaḥ kaścid dhārayed vidyāṃ kaṇṭhe bāhau ca nityaśaḥ / tasya sarvāṇi*

tion of such an amulet is described in detail at the end of the first *kalpa*. Firstly, one should fast at the constellation called *Puṣya*, and having generated the intent to awaken, compassion and loving kindness, one should perform the worship of the Buddha. Then one should prepare a *maṇḍala* on a purified piece of ground and he should present various offerings there. Thereafter, one should paint the amulet on birch-bark or cloth with bezoar or saffron. One should paint a boy (*dāraka*) in the middle, surrounded by the *dhāraṇī*, various symbols,[29] and deities.

Since about a dozen *Mahāpratisarā*-amulets have been excavated in various places in Central and Eastern Asia, I shall briefly compare the details of the ritual instructions with these.[30] The perhaps most important and somewhat problematic differences concern the deification and the gender of this protection.

As stated in the ritual instruction, a boy should be painted in the center of the amulet, which implies that this protection was

---

kāryāṇi sidhyante nātra saṃśayaḥ (IWAMOTO 1938: 5.27–28) "Anybody who wears this spell around the neck or the arm all the time, All his matters are accomplished, there is no doubt." *yaḥ kaścin mahābrāhmaṇa imāṃ mahāpratisarāṃ mahāvidyārājñīṃ yathāvidhinā likhitvā bāhau kaṇṭhe dhārayiṣyati sa sarvatathāgatādhiṣṭhito veditavyaḥ* (IWAMOTO 1938: 13.12–14) "Great Brahmin, whoever wears this Great Amulet, Great Queen of Spells around the arm or the neck having painted it according to the precept, he should be considered to be empowered by all the Tathāgatas." *yasyaiṣā vidyā kāyakaṇṭhagatā bhaviṣyati sa sarvatathāgatādhiṣṭhito bhaviṣyati* (IWAMOTO 1938: 19.17–18) "The one who fixes this spell on the body or around the neck becomes empowered by all Tathāgatas." *tasmād avaśyam eveyaṃ mahāvidyārājñī kāyakaṇṭhagatāṃ kṛtvā satkṛtya dhārayitavyā* (IWAMOTO 1938: 23.18–19) "Therefore one should wear this Great Queen of Spells fixed on the body or around the neck respectfully by all means." *tena hi mahābrāhmaṇa parijñātapūrvaṃ tasmād avaśyam eveyaṃ mahāpratisareti dhārayitavyā vācayitavyā likhitavyā yathāvidhinā nityaṃ śarīragatāṃ kṛtvā dhārayitavyā* (IWAMOTO 1938: 15.21–24) "Therefore, Great Brahmin, following this example from the past, this Great Amulet should, by all means, be memorised, recited and painted according to the precept and it should always be worn fixed on the body."

[29]It should be remarked here that the symbols to be painted on the sides of the amulet appear in the hands of Mahāpratisara after the deification of this scripture.

[30] For a detailed description of such an amulet see SØRENSEN 1991–92. To the best of my knowledge, no such *Mahāpratisarā*-amulets survive in South Asia. CHANDRA 1964: 306 reports about a *rakṣācakra* of Mahāpratisarā from the Mdzod-dge-sgar-gsar monastery in Amdo.

closely related to fertility and the production of male offspring. As for the actual Central and Eastern Asian amulets, on the majority of these a male deity,[31] Mahāpratisara is depicted in the middle, generally in an eight-armed form.[32] These variations relating to the central image of the amulets can probably be interpreted as reflections of a complex historical process, namely, the deification of the MPMVR. It is likely, that with the course of time, after this scripture had become personified, the originally prescribed central image of a boy was most commonly changed to various iconographical representations of the deity Mahāpratisarā.[33]

---

[31]SØRENSEN 1991–92: 295–298, MEVISSEN 1999: 110–111. In Chinese and Japanese sources he is referred to as a Bodhisattva or Vidyārāja.

[32]Three amulets have different central images. Once the Bodhisattva Tejaprabha surrounded with the nine planetary deities and the twelve divisions of the zodiac is depicted (DRÈGE 1999–2000: Fig. 6). This image is probably connected to the following couplet in the Sanskrit recensions: *candrasūryau sanakṣatrau rāhuketugrahāṣṭakam / likhec ca ṣaṇḍapaṇḍānāṃ putralābho bhaviṣyati* (IWAMOTO 1938: 26.8–9) "One should paint the sun and the moon with the constellations, Rāhu, Ketu and the eight planets, [Thus even] impotent people and eunuchs become able to produce a son." Twice a figure holding a vajra and touching the head of a kneeling person is placed in the middle of the *dhāraṇī*-diagram (DRÈGE 1999–2000: Figs. 8 and 9). These images are probably connected to the following couplet in the Sanskrit recensions: *bhikṣuṃ vajradharaṃ kuryād duṣṭatarjanatatparam* (IWAMOTO 1938: 25.14) "One should paint a monk who holds a *vajra* and threatens the wicked." It is, however, also possible that the aforementioned images reflect peculiarities related to the Chinese adaptation of this tradition. On an eighth-century illuminated Chinese ms. of the *Mahāpratisarā-dhāraṇī* there are only symbolic characters representing Mahāpratisara in the middle of the diagram. See MATSUMOTO 1937: 598–603, plates 158-160.

[33]In the MPMVR the *mahāpratisara* is never referred to as a goddess, it is an amulet and a magical formula. However, the MPMVR contains some feminine vocatives in its two *dhāraṇīs* which may be considered as proto-iconographic references. The longest and most complex of these refers to a deity holding a *vajra*, an axe *(paraśu)*, a noose *(pāśa)*, a hammer *(mudgara)*, a sword *(khaḍga)*, a conch *(śaṅkha)*, a wheel *(cakra)* and a trident *(triśūla)* in her hands. Some of these objects also appear in the eighth narrative from which one learns how the recitation of this spell makes an army of men armed with daggers, axes, nooses, hammers, swords, clubs and tridents come out of the pores of a Tathāgata so that they destroy the enemy.

As far as the masculine gender of the central image of Mahāpratisara is concerned, this phenomenon is most probably the result of a process during which the earlier, masculinc form of the Mahāpratisarā-tradition was transmitted to Central and Eastern Asia. A similar process can be seen, for example, in the case of Mahāmāyūrī who was also represented in a masculine form in China and Japan.[34]

The Use Of The Second *Dhāraṇī*

From the general sections of the second *kalpa* we learn that the second *dhāraṇī* should be recited,[35] should be taught in detail,[36]

---

[34] See e.g. CHOU 1945: 324, DE VISSER 1920 and the earlier footnote in section two of this paper.

[35] *yasyāṃ bhāṣitamātrāyāṃ munīnāṃ vajramayāsane / mārāś ca mārakāyikā grahāḥ sarvavināyakā / vighnāś ca santi ye kecit tatkṣaṇād vilayaṃ gatāḥ* (IWAMOTO 1938: 29.26–28) "The moment it is uttered in the adamantine seat of the Buddhas, The Māras and their entourage, the Grahas, all the Vināyakas, And Vighnas, all that exist, are destroyed immediately." *uccāraṇamātreṇa vā vajrāvamārjanena vā akālamaraṇān mahāvyādhibhyaś ca parimucyate / sarvarogāś cāsya praśāmyanti / dīrghaglānir avamārjanamātreṇa vā praśamaṃ gacchati / dine dine svādhyāyaṃ kuryān mahāprājño bhavati* (IWAMOTO 1938: 31.12–15) "One gets released from untimely death and from the great diseases either by uttering [the *dhāraṇī*] or by *vajra*-purification. All his illnesses disappear. Long-lasting sickness ceases just by the purification. One should recite it day by day, [thus] he becomes very wise." *rājāgnir udakaṃ caiva vidyud vā taskaro 'pi vā / yuddhasaṃgrāmakalahā daṃṣṭriṇo ye ca dāruṇāḥ / sarve te pralayaṃ yānti vidyāyā lakṣajāpataḥ / vidyām imāṃ parāṃ siddhāṃ sarvabuddhair hi deśitām / kīrtamānā na sīdanti bodhisaṃbhārapūraye / sarveṣu caiva sthāneṣu imāṃ vidyāṃ prayojayet* (IWAMOTO 1938: 33.11–16) "King, fire, water, thunderbolt or robber, Wars, battles, strifes and frightening carnivorous animals, These are all eliminated by uttering this spell a hundred thousand times, The ones reciting this most excellent, accomplished spell taught by all Buddhas, Are not hindered in accomplishing the Equipments for Enlightenment, One should employ this spell in every place.

[36] *parebhyaś ca vistareṇa saṃprakāśayiṣyati* (IWAMOTO 1938: 31.27-28) "Manifests it to others in detail."

should be written down,[37] and should be worn around the neck or the arm.[38]

As we can see, the above ways of use are rather close to those of the first *dhāraṇī* and it is historically confirmed by a Japanese painting that the second *dhāraṇī* was written on an amulet with the first.[39] However, if we look at the instructions for the healing ritual at the end of the second *kalpa*, the most important way of employment for this *dhāraṇī* appears to be recitation, since only this practice is mentioned there. To perform this healing ritual one should prepare a *maṇḍala* on a purified piece of ground and place various offerings there. After this has been done, one should bring the sick person to the middle of the *maṇḍala*. Then one should recite the second *dhāraṇī* twenty-eight times and should throw seven flowers in each direction. By this method the sick person is healed.

Such an employment of this *dhāraṇī* is reported in a textual account from eighth-century China. At the end of the Shang-yuan period (760–761) Emperor Su-tsung (756–762) was ill and it was Amoghavajra who exorcised the evil spirits by reciting the *Mahāpratisara-dhāraṇī* seven times. As a result the Emperor recovered by the next day.[40]

---

[37] *grastaś cet kālapāśena nītaś cāpi yamālayam / āyus tasya vivardheta pratisarālikhanād api / parikṣīṇāyuṣo yas tu saptāhamṛta eva ca / yāval likhitamātreṇa sa jīvati na saṃśayaḥ* (IWAMOTO 1938: 28.4–7) "If someone is seized by the noose of death and lead to Yama's abode, His duration of life increases just by painting this Amulet, The one whose life-span has terminated and even the one dead for a week, Continues to live just by painting [the Amulet]; there is no doubt." *atha pāpavināśe tu likhanād eva mucyate* (IWAMOTO 1938: 28.26) "Moreover, when there is [the danger of] death caused by misdeeds, one gets released just by painting it." *asyā likhitamātrāyāḥ sarvasaukhyaṃ samṛddhyati* (IWAMOTO 1938: 29.9) "All kinds of welfare increase just by painting it."

[38] *likhitāṃ dhārayet prājño bāhau baddhvā maharddhikām* (IWAMOTO 1938: 35.1) "Having painted it, the wise one should wear [the Amulet] of great supernatural power tied around the arm."

[39] FERENCZY 1987: 41 reports that this is a painting on paper from the fifteenth–sixteenth centuries; CSEH 1996: 54–56 lists this object as a silk amulet from the seventeenth–eighteenth centuries. It should be remarked here that in the actual ritual instruction for preparing an amulet there is no reference to the inclusion of the second *dhāraṇī*.

[40] CHOU 1945: 295. On Emperor Su-tsung see WEINSTEIN 1987: 57–59.

The Use Of The Mantras of the MPMVR

As far as instructions for the use of the four mantras of the MPMVR are concerned, we learn from the text that these mantras should be worn fixed on the body or around the neck, should always be concentrated on, and should be recited, repeated, and meditated upon.[41] They should be written down, read, memorised, daily repeated and taught to others.[42] The writing down of these mantras is proved by the Central and Eastern Asian *Mahāpratisara*-amulets, on which these four mantras can usually be seen placed after the first *dhāraṇī*.[43]

Further Types Of Use

So far we have dealt with practices prescribed in the MPMVR itself. However, there were further ways in which this protection was employed which are not mentioned in this scripture but obvious from historical evidence.

Firstly, as can be seen in all the Gilgit mss, the donor's name was inserted at certain places in both *dhāraṇīs* of this scripture.[44]

---

[41] *satatasamitaṃ likhitvā kāyakaṇṭhagatāni kṛtvā dhārayitavyāni satatasamitaṃ manasikartavyāni vācayitavyāni svādhyāyitavyāni bhāvayitavyāni cādhyāśayena* (IWAMOTO 1938: 19.27–29) "Having written them down, one should always wear them fixed on the body or around the neck. One's mind should constantly be concentrated on these. They should be recited, repeated daily, and meditated upon with strong determination."

[42] *atidurlabham apy eṣāṃ śravaṇaṃ kiṃ punar likhanapaṭhanavācanadhāraṇasvādhyāyanabhāvanaparadeśanā* (IWAMOTO 1938: 20.15–17) "It is very rare even to hear them, how much more it is to write them down, to read, recite, memorise, repeat them daily, meditate upon them and to preach them for others."

[43] In the actual ritual instruction for preparing an amulet there is no reference to the inclusion of these mantras.

[44] E.g. *rakṣa rakṣa mama Dinaśinasya; ye mama Trailokadevisya ahitaiṣiṇas teṣāṃ sarveṣāṃ śarīraṃ jvālaya; svastir bhavatu mama Maṇikeasya; ye mama Śābyakhātunenasya ahitaiṣiṇas; rakṣa rakṣa mama Vāyuphanasya.* Such practice of inserting names in *dhāraṇīs* can be found in various other scriptures as well. One of the Turfan-fragments of the *Asiloma-pratisara*, a text closely related to the MPMVR, reads: *[yo ma]ma Mokṣayaśasya pāpaṃ karoti imāya asilomaprat(i)sar(e)ṇa : ātmarakṣaṃ karomi / paritraṃ parigrahaṃ paripālanaṃ* (WALDSCHMIDT and SANDER 1980: 274). The Gilgit ms. of the *Sarvatathāgatādhiṣṭhāna-sattvāvalokana-buddhakṣetrasandarśana-*

This phenomenon indicates that it was a widespread custom to get this whole text copied for the protection and benefit of the manuscript-donor.[45] The popularity of this custom is suggested by the relatively high number of *Mahāpratisarā*-mss. which survived in Gilgit. Oddly, there is no definite instruction in the MPMVR to copy this whole scripture or to place any name in the *dhāraṇīs*. There are only instructions to copy the *dhāraṇīs*, especially the first. Nevertheless, it is likely that the cult of the book was such a powerful tradition that even without direct instructions in this scripture it was copied in its entirety without hesitation.[46]

Evidence for the rest of the practices not referred to in the MPMVR come from Eastern Asia. Two xylographic amulets of the *Mahāpratisara* were found on the third floor of the Ruiguang *stūpa* in Suzhou. These two amulets were discovered among other relics, including small statues and a copy of the *Lotus Sūtra* written in golden characters.[47] Beside *stūpas*,[48] it seems that placing *Mahāpratisara*-amulets in tombs was also a widespread practice in Eastern Asia, since several such objects were excavated at funerary sites in Central China.[49] Evidence for yet another sort of practice are bricks inscribed with the two *dhāraṇīs* and four man-

---

vyūham includes inserted names (DUTT 1939: 56, 58, 71) and so do the *Sitātapatrā-dhāraṇī* from Khotan (VON HINÜBER 1981: 169) and certain inscriptions from Central Asia (VON HINÜBER 1987-8: 246–247), for example. DOUGLAS 1978: XI. mentions that on Tibetan amulet-prints empty spaces are left for names to be added by hand.

[45]Beside the Gilgit mss, the donor's name was inserted at certain places in the MPMVR in numerous Eastern Indian and Nepalese PR mss. as well. In most of these cases the donor's name was also included in the colophone.

[46]On the cult of the book see SCHOPEN 1975.

[47]DRÈGE 1999–2000: 30–31 and Figs. 5 and 6.

[48]Although it has been shown that the practice of placing various *dhāraṇī*-scriptures in *stūpas* was a widespread custom in South Asia and beyond (SCHOPEN 1982: 106, SCHERRER-SCHAUB 1994 and BENTOR 1995), directions for placing mss. of this tradition in *stūpas* are not present in the MPMVR and, to the best of my knowledge, there is no evidence for such practice related to this scripture in South Asia. The function of the building where the five *Mahāpratisarā*-mss. were found near Gilgit was most probably different from that of a *stūpa*. VON HINÜBER 2004: 2 suggests that it may have been a monastic library, while FUSSMAN 2004 proposes that it may have been both the chapel and the lodgings of an *ācārya* with a collection of mss.

[49]DRÈGE 1999–2000: Fig. 1. Found in a tomb in Sichuan, Fig. 7. in a tomb in Luoyang, an amulet mentioned on p. 32 (reproduced in MEVISSEN 1999: 109, plate 8.9) in a tomb near Xian, Fig. 9. in a tomb in Xian.

tras of the MPMVR. These used to be placed inside the walls of a pagoda in Yunnan and they appear to have been used as spiritual relics perhaps with a protective function as well.[50]

The Users Of The MPMVR

According to the references in the MPMVR, the *dhāraṇī*s and mantras of this scripture were available for use by everyone in both the monastic and lay communities.[51]

As for historical evidence, there is plenty of information about the actual users of this scripture. These appear in the form of donors' names either in the *dhāraṇī*s or the colophones of vari-

[50]See LIEBENTHAL 1947.

[51]Those expected to employ this magical lore were supposed to be: sons and daughters of good families (*asyā mahāpratisarāyā mahāvidyārājñyāḥ sahaśravaṇamātreṇa mahābrāhmaṇa tasya kulaputrasya vā kuladuhitur vā sarvapāpavinirmuktir bhavati* (IWAMOTO 1938: 11.18–21) "Great Brahmin, merely upon hearing this Great Amulet, Great Queen of Spells, the son or daughter of a good family is freed from all misdeeds."); Brahmins, Kshatriyas, Vaishyas and Shudras (*brāhmaṇeṣv īśvaro lekhyaḥ kṣatriyeṣu maheśvaraḥ / śūdreṣu ca sadā saumyaṃ cakrasvāminam ālikhet / vaiśyeṣu ca vaiśravaṇam indraṃ caiva sureśvaram* (IWAMOTO 1938: 25.16–18) "For Brahmins one should paint Īśvara, for Kshatriyas Maheśvara, For Shudras one should always paint the benign Viṣṇu, For Vaishyas [one should paint] Vaiśravaṇa and Indra, the Lord of the Gods."); monks and nuns, male and female lay followers, kings, princes, royal ministers or anybody else (*ya imāṃ mahāpratisarāṃ mahādhāraṇīṃ śrāddhaḥ kulaputro vā kuladuhitā vā bhikṣur vā bhikṣuṇī vā upāsako vā upāsikā vā rājā vā rājaputro vā rājāmātyo vā brāhmaṇo vā kṣatriyo vā tadanyo vā yaḥ kaścit sakṛc chroṣyati śrutvā ca mahatyā śraddhayā gauraveṇādhyāśayena likhiṣyati likhāpayiṣyati dhārayiṣyati vācayiṣyati tīvreṇa manasā bhāvayiṣyati parebhyaś ca vistareṇa saṃprakāśayiṣyati (...)* (IWAMOTO 1938: 31.22–28) "The faithful son or daughter of a good family, a monk or nun, a layman or laywoman, a king, a prince or a royal minister, a Brahmin or a Kshatriya or anybody else who once hears this Great Amulet Great Dhāraṇī and having heard it writes it down, gets it written down, memorises it and recites it with great faith, respect and religious determination, [furthermore] meditates upon it with sharp mind and manifests it to others in detail . . ."). The nine narratives in the first *kalpa* of this scripture are another source of information. The users of the first *dhāraṇī* in these narratives are the following persons: Prince Rāhula, the son of Siddhārtha (first narrative); kings (third and sixth narratives); lay followers (second and fourth narratives); a wealthy merchant (fifth narrative); Śakra, the King of Gods (seventh narrative); a Tathāgata (eighth narrative); and an ordinary person (ninth narrative).

ous mss. or amulets.[52] Among the donors' names inserted in the *dhāraṇīs* of the *Mahāpratisarā*-mss. found at Gilgit, two queens, Trailokadevī and Śābyakhātu(nā) are identified,[53] the former being the wife of King Surendravikramādityanandi[54] of the Paṭola Ṣāhis.[55]

As far as Eastern Asia is concerned, the donor-inscriptions on some of the *Mahāpratisara*-amulets usually contain the names of various *śramaṇas* and *bhikṣus*.[56] Beside these people, this scripture is also reported to have been used by the great master and translator, Vajrabodhi and his disciple Amoghavajra. Vajrabodhi recited this *dhāraṇī* on his way to China in 719 to save his ship from sinking in a storm. Amoghavajra, to whom I have already referred to in relation with the healing ritual, recited this protection during his voyage from China to India in 741 to escape from a terrible sea-storm and a large whale.[57] In 758 Amoghavajra presented Emperor Su-tsung a copy of the *Mahāpratisara-dhāraṇi* and requested the Emperor to carry it with him.[58]

Conclusion

From textual and archaeological evidence it seems that the *dhāraṇīs* and mantras of this protection were primarily used for preparing an amulet. It should not be forgotten that *pratisara* means amulet and there are plenty of references in various scriptures of the

[52]In those Nepalese and Eastern Indian PR mss. which I have consulted, the donors' names include *bhikṣus*, *śākyabhikṣus*, *upāsakas*, and an *upāsikā-rājñī* called Ḍaddākā who was perhaps a queen of the Pāla King, Nayapāla in the mid-eleventh century. The great number of illuminated PR mss. suggests that it was a popular custom among well-to-do people to have such costly mss. copied for their protection and religious merit.

[53]On the queens of the Paṭola Ṣahıs see VON HINÜBER 2004: 114–117.

[54]On this king of the first half of the seventh century see VON HINÜBER 2004: 88–89.

[55]VON HINÜBER 1981: 165 and 2004: 17, 90. See JETTMAR 1993 and VON HINÜBER 2004 on a detailed treatment of the Paṭola Ṣāhis.

[56]DRÈGE 1999–2000 gives the following references to the donors: Fig. 3: a monk; Fig. 5: four *śramaṇas*, a *bhikṣu* and twenty-five male and thirty-four female lay followers; Fig: 7. a monk.

[57]CHOU 1945: 275, 290, MEVISSEN 1999: 117 and 123 (fn. 57).

[58]CHOU 1945: 322.

Mantranaya that the use of different sorts of amulets was popular in the Sangha around the middle of the first millennium.[59]

The second most important function of this protection appears to be healing. Again, various texts of the *dhāraṇī*-literature indicate that curing all sorts of illnesses was one of the main functions of these scriptures.[60]

---

[59]Evidence that Buddhists widely used amulets comes already from the first centuries CE when Gandhāran Bodhisattvas were usually depicted wearing a thread similar to an *upavīta* with small pendant boxes on it presumably containing amulets (MEVISSEN 1991-92: 356). The use of talismanic strings and threads *(sūtraka)* is mentioned in the *Amoghapāśahṛdaya-dhāraṇī* (MEISEZAHL 1962: 298): "A string must be tied for every kind of fever. (...) The evil demons are to be killed with the sword; white thread will protect against them. (...) White thread is to be tied to the ear in case of sore eyes. (...) The five-fold thread is to be used against all demons. The white thread is to be used for every fever." The same text also gives instructions for making a talisman *(maṇi)* of the [mantra-]essence *(hṛdaya)* which should be worn on the body as a protection (MEISEZAHL 1962: 299): "After having recited [the *hṛdaya*] hundred-eight times over the medicinal herbs *jayā, vijayā, nākulī, gandhanākulī, cāriṇī, abhayapāṇi, indrapāṇi, gandhapriyaṅgu, tagara, cakrā, mahācakrā, viṣṇukrānta, somarājī* and *sunandā*, a talisman *(maṇi)* is to be made [from them] which must be put on the head or on the upper arm; boys [wear it] around the neck and girls around the waist. It will be the cause of great prosperity, elimination of misfortune and bestowing with children. When the talisman is worn, every possible protection is assured. Poison and fire shall not approach. Poisoning shall not occur, and if [such a case] were possible, it will be cured quickly." There are references to protective threads *(sūtra)* in the *Mekhalā-dhāraṇī* (TRIPATHI 1981: 157), the *Hayagrīvavidyā* (Dutt 1939: 44.10), the *Mahāsāhasrapramardanī* (IWAMOTO 1937a: 41–2), the *Mahāmāyūrī* (Takubo 1972: 58) and in the *Mahāśītavatī* (IWAMOTO 1937b: 4). There are references to the use of amulets with a spell written on them in the *Vijayavati-pratyaṅgirā-dhāraṇī* (WADDELL 1914: 93), the *Sarvatathāgatādhiṣṭhāna-sattvāvalokana-buddhakṣetrasandarśana-vyūham* (DUTT 1939: 74.15), and the *Āryasarvatathāgatoṣṇīṣasitātapatrā-dhāraṇī* (*Dhīḥ* 2002: 153.16–18, no author named). DOUGLAS 1978 and SKORUPSKI 1983 discuss the use of amulets in Tibetan Buddhism. LALOU 1936 describes an amulet inscribed with the *Sitātapatrā-dhāraṇī* from Dunhuang. STRICKMANN 2002 writes at length on Buddhist talismanic seals used in China.

[60]The *Mahāmāyūrī-dhāraṇī* is included in the *Bhaiṣajyavastu* section of the *Vinayavastu* of the *Mūlasarvāstivādin Vinaya*, where it is stated that once the Buddha healed a young monk bitten by a snake using this *dhāraṇī* (PANGLUNG 1981: 61). In Bāṇa's *Harṣacarita* the *Mahāmāyūrī* is mentioned being recited for healing at the royal palace (KANE 1918: 76, 445). A verse by Rājaśekhara in Jalhaṇa's *Sūktimuktāvalī* gives a reference to the *Māyūrī-vidyā* which works efficiently against snake poison (WINTERNITZ 1933: vol.

Further uses include reciting the *dhāraṇīs* and mantras silently or aloud, keeping them in mind and meditating upon them, teaching them to others, mounting the first *dhāraṇī* at the top of a flagstaff above a *caitya*, copying the entire text and inserting the donor's name in the *dhāraṇīs*. In Eastern Asia *Mahāpratisara*-amulets were placed in a *stūpa*, the two *dhāraṇīs* and four mantras were carved in bricks and placed inside the walls of a temple, and it is likely that in this region this protection was related to funerary rites as well.

As we have seen, while the majority of the functions of this protection are prescribed by textual passages, a number of the practices can only be reconstructed from material evidence. Consequently, it is possible that there were even further ways of use related to this tradition neither described in this scripture nor surviving as historical evidence. To explore such possibilities requires further research which compares the functions of closely related texts of the *dhāraṇī*-literature with the present scripture. Nevertheless, for the time being it can be stated that the MPMVR was held in a remarkably high esteem among distinguished groups of users, and it was applied in various ways already in the middle of the first millennium.

II. 372. fn. 1). There are references to the *Mahāmāyūrī* as a means of protection against diseases and Grahas in Indian medical literature (MEULENBELD 1999: IA: 560, IIA: 10, 217). Fragments of the *Mahāmāyūrī* were found among medical treatises in the Bower Manuscript (HOERNLE 1893–1912). The *Mahāmāyūrī* was widely used for healing in China and in the eleventh-twelfth centuries it was often employed to cure the Emperor in Japan (DE VISSER 1920: 373, 387). The *Mahāsāhasrapramardanī* includes instructions for various demonifugic and healing rituals towards its end with one of these giving a long list of medicinal herbs (IWAMOTO 1937a: 30–43). The *Amoghapāśahṛdaya-dhāraṇī* includes a list of various medicinal herbs, furthermore specifies several diseases that are cured by reciting this magical formula (MEISEZAHL 1962: 291, 299). The Red-copper Beak *Dhāraṇī* (not extant in Sanskrit), the Thunderbolt-beak *Dhāraṇī (Vajra-tuṇḍa-dhāraṇī)* and the *Tathāgatoṣṇīṣa-sitātapatra-aparājita-pratyaṅgirā-dhāraṇī* all have references to their healing function (Translated from Tibetan by WADDELL 1914: 39, 41 and 49). STRICKMANN 2002 presents various examples of early Chinese Buddhist ritual manuals used for healing. ABÈ 1999: 159-164 writes that healing played an important part in eighth-century Japanese Buddhism with the extensive use of *dhāraṇīs*.

Abbreviations

GBMFE Gilgit Buddhist Manuscripts Facsimile Edition

NGMPP Nepal-German Manuscript Preservation Project

MPMVR *Mahāpratisarā-Mahāvidyārājñī*

PR *Pañcarakṣā*

T Taishō Edition of the Chinese Tripiṭaka

References

ABÈ, R. (1999) *The Weaving of Mantra: Kūkai and the Construction of Esoteric Buddhist Discourse*. New York.

Āryasarvatathāgatoṣṇīṣasitātapatrānāmāparājitā Pratyaṅgirā Mahāvidyārājñī (2002) in *Dhīḥ* 33, Sarnath: 146–154.

BENTOR, Y. (1995) 'On the Indian Origins of the Tibetan Practice of Depositing Relics and Dhāraṇīs in Stūpas and Images' in *Journal of the American Oriental Society* 115.2: 248–261.

CHANDRA, L. (1964) 'Tibetan Buddhist Texts Printed by the *Mdzod-dge-sgar-gsar* Monastery' in *Indo-Iranian Journal* Vol. 7. No. 4: 298–306.

CHANDRA, L. and VIRA, R. (1974) *Gilgit Buddhist Manuscripts (Facsimile Edition)*. Vols. 6 and 10, New Delhi.

CHANDRA, L. (1999–) *Dictionary of Buddhist Iconography*. Vols. 1–. Delhi.

CHOU, Y. (1945) 'Tantrism in China' in *Harvard Journal of Asiatic Studies*, Vol. 8. No. 3–4: 241–332.

CSEH, É. (1996) *Japanese Buddhist Art*. The Art of Buddhism, Vol. 3. Budapest.

DOUGLAS, N. (1978) *Tibetan Tantric Charms and Amulets*. New York.

DUTT, N. (ed.) (1939) *Gilgit Manuscripts.* Vol. I. Srinagar Kashmir.

DRÈGE, J-P. (1999–2000) 'Les Premières Impressions des Dhāraṇī de Mahāpratisarā' in *Cahiers d'Extrême-Asie* 11: 25–44

FERENCZY, L. (1987) 'Buddhist Works of Art in the Ferenc Hopp Museum of Eastern Asiatic Arts, Budapest' in *Orientations*, 18, 3: 30–41.

FUSSMAN, G. (2004) 'Dans Quel Type de Bâtiment Furent Trouvés les Manuscrits de Gilgit?' in *Journal Asiatique* Nos. 1–2: 101–150.

HARRISON, P. (1996) 'Preliminary Notes on a gZungs 'dus Manuscript from Tabo' in *Suhṛllekhāḥ. Festgabe für Helmut Eimer.* (Indica et Tibetica 28) Swisttal-Odendorf: 49–68.

HIDAS, G. (2003) 'Preliminary Notes on the *Mahāpratisarā Mahāvidyārājñī*, a Buddhist Protective Text from the *Pañcarakṣā*-collection' in *Berliner Indologische Studien* 15–17: 263–284.

VON HINÜBER, O. (1981) 'Namen in Schutzzaubern aus Gilgit' in *Studien zur Indologie und Iranistik* 7: 163–171.

VON HINÜBER, O. (1987–88) 'Dhāraṇīs aus Zentralasien' in *Indologica Taurinensia* 14: 231–249.

VON HINÜBER, O. (2004) 'Die Palola Ṣāhis, Ihre Steininschriften, Inschriften auf Bronze, Handschriftenkolophone und Schutzzauber. Materialen zur Geschichte von Gilgit und Chilas' in *Antiquities of Northern Pakistan* V. Heidelberg.

HOERNLE, A. F. R. (1893–1912) *The Bower Manuscript.* Calcutta.

HIRAKAWA A. (1990) *A History of Indian Buddhism. From Śākyamuni to Early Mahāyāna.* Honolulu.

IWAMOTO, Y. (1937a) *Mahāsāhasrapramardanī.* Beiträge zur Indologie, Heft 1. Kyoto.

IWAMOTO, Y. (1937b) *Kleinere Dhāraṇī Texte. Mahāśītavatī.* Beiträge zur Indologie, Heft 2. Kyoto.

IWAMOTO, Y. (1938) *Mahāpratisarā.* Beiträge zur Indologie, Heft 3. Kyoto.

JETTMAR, K. (1993) The Paolas, their Governors and their Successors. *Antiquities of Northern Pakistan* II. Heidelberg.

KANE, P. V. (1918) *The Harṣacarita of Bāṇabhaṭṭa.* Delhi.

LALOU, M. (1936) 'Notes A Propos D' Une Amulette de Touen-Houang. Les Litanies de Tārā et la Sitātapatrā-Dhāraṇī' in *Mélanges Chinois et Bouddhiques* IV: 134–149.

LALOU, M. (1953) 'Les textes bouddhiques au temps du roi Khri-sron-lde-bcan: contribution a la bibliographie du Kanjur et du Tanjur' in *Journal Asiatique*, 241 (3): 313–353.

LESSING, F. D. and WAYMAN, A. (1968) *Introduction to the Buddhist Tantric Systems, translated from mKhas grub rje's Rgyud sde spyi.hi rnam par gzag pa rgyas par brjod, with Original Text and Annotation.* The Hague.

LIEBENTHAL, W. (1947) 'Sanskrit Inscriptions from Yunnan I' in *Monumenta Serica*: 46–68.

MATSUMOTO, E. (1937) *Tonkō ga no kenkyū (A Study of the Dunhuang Paintings).* Tokyo.

MEISEZAHL, R. O. (1962) 'The Amoghapāśahṛdaya Dhāraṇī. The Early Sanskrit Manuscript of the Reiunji Critically Edited and Translated' in *Monumenta Nipponica* 17: 265–328.

MEULENBELD, J. (1999) *A History of Indian Medical Literature.* Groningen.

MEVISSEN, G. J. R. (1989) 'Studies in Pañcarakṣā Manuscript Painting' in *Berliner Indologische Studien* 4–5: 339–374.

MEVISSEN, G. J. R. (1990) 'The Indian Connection: Images of Deified Spells in the Arts of Northern Buddhism, Part I' in *Silk Road Art and Archaeology* 1: 227–248.

MEVISSEN, G. J. R. (1991–92) 'The Indian Connection: Images of Deified Spells in the Arts of Northern Buddhism, Part II' in *Silk Road Art and Archaeology* 2: 227–248.

MEVISSEN, G. J. R. (1992) 'Transmission of Iconographic Traditions: Pañcarakṣā Heading North' in: C. Jarrige (ed.) *South Asian Archaeology 1989*, Madison Wisconsin: 415–424.

MEVISSEN, G. J. R. (1998) 'Deliberate Coincidence or Accidental Purpose? Pañcarakṣā Sequences in Xylographs and Sketchbooks' in *Berliner Indologische Studien* 11–12: 307–364.

MEVISSEN, G. J. R. (1999) 'Images of Mahāpratisarā in Bengal: Their Iconographic Links with Javanese, Central Asian and East Asian Images' in *Journal of Bengal Art* 4: 99–129.

MONIER-WILLIAMS, Sir M. (1899) *A Sanskrit-English Dictionary*. Oxford.

PANGLUNG, J. (1981) *Die Erzählstoffe des Mūlasarvāstivāda-Vinaya Analysiert auf Grund der Tibetischen Übersetzung*, Studia Philologica Buddhica, Monograph Series III. Tokyo.

ŚĀŚANĪ, Ṭh. (ed.) (1999) *Āryamahāpratisarāvidyārājñīdhāraṇī. Āryapratisarākalpadhāraṇī* in *Dhīḥ* 28, Sarnath: 127–142.

SCHERRER-SCHAUB, C. A. (1994) 'Some Dhāraṇī Written on Paper Functioning as Dharmakāya Relics. A Tentative Approach to PT 350' in P. Kvaerne (ed.) *Tibetan Studies, Proceedings of the 6th Seminar of the International Association for Tibetan Studies, Fagernes 1992*, Vol. 2. Oslo: 711–727.

SCHLIEKER, C. (1984) *Mahāmāyūrī- und Mahāpratisarā-Texte in den zentralasiatischen Fragmenten*. Schriftliche Hausarbeit zum Magisterexamen, Fachbereich 14 der Freien Universität Berlin. Unpublished.

SCHOPEN, G. (1975) 'The Phrase sa pṛthivīpradeśaś caityabhūto bhavet in the Vajracchedikā: Notes on the Cult of the Book in Mahāyāna' in *Indo-Iranian Journal* 17: 147–181.

SCHOPEN, G. (1982) 'The Text on the Dhāraṇī Stones from Abhayagiriya: A Minor Contribution to the Study of Mahāyāna Literature in Ceylon' in *Journal of the International Association of Buddhist Studies* 5: 100–108.

SEN, S. (1965) 'On Dhāraṇī and Pratisarā' in *Studies of Esoteric Buddhism and Tantrism. Commemoration of the 1,150th Anniversary of the Founding of Koyasan*. Koyasan: 67–72.

SKILLING, P. (1992) 'The Rakṣā Literature of the Śrāvakayāna' in *Journal of the Pali Text Society* XVI: 109–182.

SKORUPSKI, T. (1983) *Tibetan Amulets.* Bangkok.

SØRENSEN, H. H. (1991–92) 'Typology and Iconography in the Esoteric Buddhist Art of Dunhuang' in *Silk Road Art and Archaeology* 2: 227–248.

STRICKMANN, M. (B. Faure ed.) (2002) *Chinese Magical Medicine.* Stanford.

TAKUBO, S. (ed.) (1972) *Ārya-Mahā-Māyūrī Vidyā-Rājñī.* Tokyo.

TRIPATHI, C. (1981) 'Gilgit-Blätter der Mekhalā-Dhāraṇī' in *Studien zur Indologie und Iranistik* 7: 153–161.

TSUKAMOTO, K. *et al.* (1989) *A Descriptive Bibliography of the Sanskrit Buddhist Literature. Vol. IV. The Buddhist Tantra.* Kyoto.

DE VISSER, M. W. (1919–20) 'Die Pfauenkönigin (K'ung-tsioh ming-wang, Kujaku myō-ō) in China und Japan' in *Ostasiatische Zeitschrift* 8, Berlin: 370–387.

WADDELL, L. A. (1914) 'Dhāraṇī or Indian Buddhist Protective Spells' in *Indian Antiquary* XLIII. 37–95.

WALDSCHMIDT, E. (1965–1971) *Sanskrithandschriften aus den Turfanfunden. Teil I–III.* Wiesbaden.

WALDSCHMIDT, E. und SANDER, L. (1980) *Sanskrithandschriften aus den Turfanfunden. Teil IV.* Wiesbaden.

WEINSTEIN, S. (1987) *Buddhism under the Tang*. Cambridge.

WILLIAMS, P. with TRIBE, A. (2000) *Buddhist Thought. A Complete Introduction to the Indian Tradition*. London.

WINTERNITZ, M. (1933) *A History of Indian Literature*. New York.

ZIEME, P. (2005) 'Uigurische Fragmente aus der Pañcarakṣā' in Grivelet, S. *et al.* (eds.) *The Black Master. Essays on Central Eurasia in Honor of György Kara on his 70th Birthday*. Wiesbaden: 151–164.

Seven

atra kim prayojanam? An Essay on the Reception and Naturalization of *kāvya* in Tibet: Tracing Texts, Reading Between the Lines and Other Vanities

Péter-Dániel Szántó

Introduction

Ever since the beginning of Tibetan studies by Alexander Csoma de Kőrös, we have been aware that Daṇḍin's *alaṃkāraśāstra*, the *Kāvyādarśa* (KĀ) had been translated into Tibetan, and due to the pioneering work of consequent Tibetanist (mostly contemporary with us) we are aware to some extent of the impact it had on Tibetan monastic (and to a certain extent, on secular) literature. For example, we know that the commencing or even internal verses of later indigenous *śāstras* became more elaborate, ornate and even ingenious[1], we know of secular writings employing *kāvya*-features, and we do know it rendered the poetic chronicle of the Fifth Dalai Lama practically unreadable, and so on.

In this paper I shall deal with some aspects of the actual reception and naturalization of Indian poetics in the Land of Snows, with special emphasis on some authorities claiming its uselessness and their refutation by the commentators of the KĀ.[2] The Tibetan commentators and propagators of the KĀ, who were almost exclusively fully ordained monks, harnessed the secular art of Indian *kāvya* into the service of religion. The main reason was obviously the environment it was adapted to. Whereas in India *kāvya* flourished in an urban and / or court environment and its foremost purpose was that of offering aesthetical pleasure (*prīti*) to the receiver, in Tibet it was cultivated primarily in a monastic environment where all elements of the profane world were subjected to religious purposes. Thus, besides generating aesthetical pleasure, *kāvya*, as applied in Tibetan monastic literature, invariably has the additional and chief function of generating faith in the reader. The work (KĀ) had had an impact of some extent on secular writing, but we mustn't forget that the secular cultivators of *kāvya*-style writing (mostly educated aristocrats) also received their education in a monastery or from a monastic person.

---

[1] TUCCI 1949:104

[2] KAPSTEIN 2003:783 n.103. notes: "The reception and use of Indian literary theory in different Tibetan literary subcultures pose a fascinating and difficult question, which I cannot explore here. Its complexities are perhaps seen in the writing of some of the 'Brug pa Bka' brgyud poets of the fifteenth and sixteenth centuries [...]" This paper will not shed light on these aspects either, mostly due to the scarcity of sources available to me and my narrow scale of reading. The *yogin*-type poetry of (mostly) *Bka' brgyud pa*s, the secular poetical writings of the Tibetan aristocracy, the influence of *kāvya*-features on Old Tibetan literature and so on are beyond the scope of and the textual material available for this paper. I shall focus almost exclusively on the three great Tibetan commentaries (by *Bod mkhas pa Mi pham Dge legs rnam rgyal*, the Fifth Dalai lama *Ngag dbang blo bzang rgya mtsho*, and *Khams sprul Chos kyi nyi ma* respectively) written to the KĀ. Thus I shall limit myself to the reception and use of the KĀ in monastic circles.

Sa skya paṇḍita and the ideal of pāṇḍityam

The first, partial and the later, complete translation of the KĀ was prepared in the folds of the *Sa skya pa* order. This was all too natural, for the greatest exponent of this order was *Sa skya paṇḍita Kun dga' Rgyal mtshan*, a fervent advocate and propagator of classical Indian scholarliness (*pāṇḍityam, mkhas pa nyid*). His works are the 'paradigmatic expression of the trend insisting that the study of Buddhism had to be to a large extent enframed within a core curriculum of Indian learning'[3]. In a comparable way to classical studies in the West, the Indian curriculum became a veritable model for Tibetans. In both cases, poetic excellence was regarded as a touchstone of moral and intellectual refinement.[4] Poetics and other more or less secular topics were known as the 'five great and five minor sciences (*vidyāsthāna, rig gnas*)'. The five great sciences were grammar (*vyākaraṇa, sgra*), logic (*pramāṇa, tshad ma / rtog ge*), medicine (*cikitsā, gso / 'tsho*), technical sciences (*śilpaśāstra, bzo / phyi rig*[5]) and exegesis of the *Abhidharma* (*adhyātmavidyā, nang rig*). Among the five minor sciences, four were subjected to grammar, viz. drama (*nāṭya, zlos gar*[6]), metrics (*chandas, sdeb sbyor*), synonymics (*abhidhāna, mngon brjod*) and poetics (*kāvya, snyan ngag / snyan dngags*[7]). The fifth, astrology (*jyotis, skar rtsis*) is the odd one out, and there were some controversies indeed whether this 'science' pertains here or not. Although there were other lists and classifications, with Sa skya paṇḍita, to whom the

---

[3]KAPSTEIN 2003:776

[4]*ibid.* 776-777.

[5]This is the most variegated of the five as it includes iconography, iconometry, chemical compounds, alchemy, the arts of love (represented by one single work in the canon), ethics, etc.

[6]This is not in fact dramaturgy as seen in the *Nāṭyaśāstra* of Bharata, but dramas proper.

[7]Just as in the case above, Tibetans confuse the guidebooks of an art with the works of that art. Thus, the KĀ and the *Meghadūta* and other poems are all known as '*snyan ngag*'. The only exception I have read so far is *Sa skya paṇḍita*, who maintains the correct differentiation. In India this distinction was carefully maintained, although there were overlappings. For instance, the *Meghadūta* was a *kāvya*, and the KĀ was a *kāvyaśāstra*. However, the *kāvyaśāstras* also contain verses (i.e. *kāvya* proper) that serve as examples. Futhermore, there were *śāstrakāvyas*, *śāstras* written in *kāvya* style.

very establishment of Indian learned sciences was linked[8], the five plus five model gained overall currency.

On the other hand, the conduct of Sa skya paṇḍita (an ordained Buddhist monk) was not quite *bodhisattva*-like, which later became an issue among the literati when they were trying to link Sa skya's scholar ideal to the generally accepted *bodhisattva*-ideal. His notorious 'Eight Ego [Poem]' (*Nga brgyad ma*) stirred the Tibetan world and Sa skya was forced to write an apologetic commentary:

> *sgra pa nga yin rtog ge pa nga*
> *smra ba ngan 'joms nga 'dra med |*
> *sdeb sbyor nga mkhas snyan ngag nga nyid*
> *mngon brjod 'chad la 'gran med nga |*
> *dus sbyor ngas shes phyi nang kun rig*
> *rnam dpyod blo gros mtshungs med nga |*
> *de 'dra gang yin Sa skya pa ste*
> *mkhas pa gzhan dag gzugs brnyan yin ||*[9]

> "*I* am the grammarian. *I* am the dialectician.
> Among vanquishers of sophists, peerless am *I*.
> *I* am learned in metrics. *I* stand alone in poetics.
> In explaining synonymics, unrivaled am *I*.
> *I* know celestial calculations. In exo and esoteric science
> *I* have a discerning intellect equalled by none.
> Who can this be? Sakya alone!
> Other scholars are my reflected forms."[10]

Sa skya paṇḍita was the first translator of the KĀ. Excerpts from Daṇḍin's work are to be found in the second part of the first chapter of his famous *Mkhas pa la 'jug pa'i sgo*. According to this treatise, the three basic activities of a true scholar are composition (*rtsom pa*), rhetoric (*'chad pa*) and debate (*rtsod pa*).

---

[8]By the Fifth Dalai lama at any rate (v. KAPSTEIN 2003:776). Other sources attribute this most honourable title to Shong ston and Dpang lo. (v. ROERICH 1953:786)

[9]*Nga brgyad ma'i 'grel pa* in SA SKYA BKA' 'BUM (TOYO BUNKO ED.) vol. 4. (148-3-4 – 154-4-6).

[10]Tr. by W.S. Gilbert as reproduced in KAPSTEIN 2003:777.

The study of *kāvya* is an indispensable prerequisite for composition, therefore he treats it right after grammar. The question may arise: why did he not undertake a complete translation of the KĀ, if he considered it that important? The answer probably lies in the colophon, which is worth reproducing since it contains *kāvya*-features as well:

> *snyigs ma'i dus kyi sems can bsod nams chung |*
> *de phyir mkhas pa slob pa'i skal ba med |*
> *bdag gis 'bad kyang gzhan gyis 'dzin pa nyung |*
> *des na gzhan la phan pa'i go skabs dka' ||*
>
> *da dung bdag la legs spyad yod mod kyi |*
> *snyigs ma'i dus kyi 'gro ba'i spyod yul min |*
> *mkhas pa 'dod pa'i skye bo nyung bas na |*
> *phyed pa chung phyir rgyas pa 'dir ma sgros || [...]*
>
> *deng sang Shā kya seng ge'i bstan pa 'di |*
> *'bab chu zad pa'i rdzing bzhin nyin re 'bri |*
> *blo gsal rnams kyis tshul 'di legs rtogs la |*
> *thar pa 'dod pa dag gis 'bad dgos so ||*[11]
>
> "Slight is the merit of beings in this degenerate era,
> hence they do not attain the good fortune to become scholars.
> Although I have tried, little did others understand.
> It is hard indeed to find opportunity to work for others' benefit!
>
> Although I possess now this excellent practice,
> it is not the domain of beings of the degenerate age.
> There are few persons desiring to become scholars,
> and since they are the minority, I have written no more. [...]
>
> Nowadays, the teaching of the lion of Śākyas
> decreases day by day like a pond with a waterfall.

[11] MKHAS'JUG:111-2-4 – 111-3-6

> The intelligent should understand this [work] well,
> those desireous of liberation should exert themselves."

Although Sa skya pa's complaints about the degenerate era are a common topos in Buddhistic writing, they served well the great *paṇḍita* to present the actual situation in which he was trying to work. Furthermore, the last lines of the first and the third verses contain two well placed *arthāntaranyāsas* (apodixis, tib. *don gzhan bkod pa*) and the third verse contains an apt *upamā* (simile, tib. *dpe*): the decreasing of the Buddha's teaching is compared to a lake from which water is gradually being carried away by a waterfall.

Sa skya paṇḍita's legacy continued. His nephew, 'Phags pa bla ma ordered that the complete translation of the KĀ be made along with the translation of several other relevant specimens of Indian literature. The man for the job was the greatest Sanskrit scholar of the time, Shong ston Rdo rje rgyal mtshan. As Kapstein points out, 'these works left an enormous legacy in Tibet, and from the fourteenth century onwards virtually every Tibetan author of note, whether monk or layman, tried his hand at some kāvya.'[12] Studying the 'science of words' (of which, as we have seen, poetics was a significant part) was of paramount importance. In Dpa' bo's chronicle we find the following punning statement on grammar, the cornerstone of all learning:

> *de ltar skad rigs thams cad kyi gtso bo yin zhing yul Dbus na ya rabs rnams skad rigs gzhan la ngo tshar byed pa'i phyir dang sgra mi shes na ba lang dang 'dra bar grags pa'i phyir mkhas pa'i 'jug bya gcig po yin no*||[13]

> "Thus, the science of grammar / *correct speech* is the chief of all. In the Middle country [i.e. Gangetic India] / *the province of Ü [i.e. Central Tibet]* the nobility is ashamed to speak in any other language [than Sanskrit] / *other dialect [than the established one]* and considers that he, who does not know not grammar, is

[12]KAPSTEIN 2003:782. and *ibid.* n. 102.
[13]MKHASSTON:853

> just like an ox. Therefore, it is the sole [science] which introduces someone to [scholarly] proficiency."

Even with the gradually eclipsing political influence of the *Sa skyas*, their *paṇḍita*'s ideal of scholarliness was firmly established as a Tibetan cultural ideal.

'nanu': objections

Or was it? Browsing the commentarial tradition to the KĀ and other scattered accounts, we notice that the special portion of these *śāstras*, namely, the explanation of its purpose (in the spirit of the Indic *"atra kiṃ prayojanam"*) takes a little longer than it usually does. We see lengthy justifying quotations on seemingly unrelated matters. The opposing *pūrvapakṣas* are intriguing and the matter gets even more exciting when we get the impression that these were living voices rather than the usual imaginary opponents objecting in the name of common sense. The commentaries hasten to prove the utility of poetry and the need to study it. Of course, it is not unusual to find such lines at the beginning of a *śāstra*, yet we feel that the insistence of the commentators did have a well defined aim, besides merely fulfilling formal requirements. Evidence shows that there were parties that viewed *kāvya* and its basic text with some suspicion. All these facts indicate that the naturalization of *kāvya* (which equals the naturalization of the KĀ) did not go smoothly.

Celibate monks, lustful speech and other frivolities

One of the opposing groups must have been those monks who strictly observed the *Vinaya* code. Although I have not found any clear reference to the fact that someone would have objected in the name of the Buddha himself who had forbidden monks to attend artistic performances, there are traces of Tibetans keeping this precept in mind.[14] In this context the brief account of Dpa' bo, the historian is extremely suggestive. Having proved that there

[14]Note that the Buddha's tenet was already obsolete in classical India. Thus, there were Buddhist dramas and the earliest proper *kāvya* that has survived is Aśvaghoṣa's *Buddhacarita*, the popularity of which is shown by

are canonical references for the cultivation of secular sciences (a problem we shall consider later), he cites an objection:

> *'o na mdo Dran nye*[15] *las snyan ngag gtso bor byed pa rnams lha yul gyi bya gzhan la tshigs bcad kyis bskul zhing rang bag med du sdod par skye ba dang | des na dge slong gis thos pa ngan pa snyan ngag sdeb par mi bya'o zhes gsungs pa ma yin nam zhe na | de ni 'dod pa'i gtam gyi snyan ngag mi bya bar dgongs pa ste | de ma thag du sangs rgyas dang chos dang dge 'dun la bstod pa dang bstan pa gsal bar 'gyur ba'i snyan ngag bya'o zhes gsungs so || des na Snyan ngag me long gi mjug dgos pas don sdu ba'i skabs su |*
>
> *de ltar skyon bral skal ba bzang ldan pa yi |*
> *snyan ngag bzang pos dkon mchog rnam gsum gyi |*
> *yon tan tshul bzhin rab tu bsngags byas na |*
> *grags dang 'byor dang rgyal mchog thob par 'gyur ||*
>
> *zhes mkhas pa la 'os pa'i don sdu bdag gis kha bkang pa yin no ||*[16]

"Well then [someone may object:] isn't the *Saddharma-smṛtyupasthāna* valid when it claims that those who place *kāvya* foremost, exhort others to 'divine' deeds[17] with verses and live heedlessly; [and] consequently, it is considered wrong for a monk to listen to [poetry] or to compose verses? [The answer is:] that refers to the prohibition of composing poetry of lustful speech (*'dod pa'i gtam*). Immediatly after [this passage the following] is stated: "[However,] that kind of poetry which

the fact that its manuscripts have been found even outside the Indian subcontinent.

[15] *Dam pa'i chos dran pa nye bar bzhag pa (Tōh. 287.) Bka' Mdo (4 vols.)*

[16] [illegible]

[17] *lha yul gyi bya gzhan la* is obscure to me. It might be a euphemism. 'Divine' deeds in this case would might simply refer to living in the *carpe diem* style.

praises the Buddha, the doctrine and the congregation or ellucidates the teaching, should be composed." Furthermore, the concluding verse of the *Kāvyādarśa* that shows the need of poetry says:

> 'In this way, if one praises properly
> the virtues of the three jewels by means
> of faultless, worthy, beautiful verses,
> he will attain fame, wealth and supreme royalty.'

Hence, it teaches the need [of studying and cultivating poetry] as something worthy of a wise man. And I will shut my mouth here *(sic)*."

If 'poetry of lustful speech' is not recommended, how should one treat Daṇḍin's verses illustrating his definitions? Some of them are quite plainly of an erotic nature, shameful for a monk even to read, and probably this was the reason Dpa'Bo uses the idiom *"dod pa'i gtam"* ('lustful speech'). Tibetan commentators of the KĀ carefully avoided imitating Daṇḍin's 'frivolous' themes. Let us see a few examples:

> *valgitabhru galadgharmajalam ālohitekṣaṇam* |
> *vivṛṇoti madāvasthām idaṃ vadanapaṅkajam* || KĀ II:73 ||[18]

> *gdong pa'i 'dam skyes smin 'khyog cing* |
> *rngul gyi chu ni zags pa dang* |
> *mig dag kun tu dmar ba 'dis* |
> *myos pa'i gnas skabs gsal bar byed* ||[19]

> "The lotus of her face betrays intoxication with its fluttering brows, dripping beads of sweat, and inviting glances"[20]

---

[18]Example for *avayavirūpaka* (tib. *cha shas can gyi gzugs can*) cf. GEROW 1971:244.

[19]RNAMBSHAD:169

[20]Tr. GEROW 1971:244. 'inviting glances' goes a bit beyond the literal meaning of 'slightly reddened eyes [from intoxication]'.

The lustful intoxication of the lovely woman will be quickly transformed into the praise of Mañjuśrī, the patron of the arts, when the Fifth Dalai lama illustrates the same figure with the following verse:

'Jam dbyangs bzhin ras li khri'i thig le'i ngos |
shes bya thams cad gzigs pa'i spyan dkyus dang |
ji snyed legs bshad sgrog pa'i zhal gyi sgo |
'dzum pas skal bzang skye rgu'i ngal bso ster ||[21]

"The face of Mañjughoṣa—a drop of vermillion,
his oblong eyes see everything there is to be known.
All that issues from his mouth are elegant sayings,
he brings refreshment to the fortunate with his smile."

Or, into a veritable exhortation for the disciple ready to meditate. Mi pham's illustrating verse:

khyod thugs zag pa med pa'i me long la |
sgrib pa'i tshogs kun gzhar yang mi gnas pa'i |
rnam rtog med las skyes pa'i ting 'dzin gyi |
rnam par dpag tu med la ldang zhing 'jug ||[22]

"In the spotless mirror of your heart,
manifest and enter that meditation which is
born from non discursive thought,
forever free of defilements and utterly unfathomable."

In Daṇḍin's verse illustrating the *bhaviṣyadākṣepa* (*'byung 'gyur 'gog pa*, 'objection about the future')[23], we find an insulted damsel vehemently denying any future *rendezvous*, since his lover's eyes bear traces of lac from some other woman's lips:

---

[21] DGYESGLU:93; DPERBRJOD:91. There are slight differences between the two editions: *pada b* - dang] shing; *pada d* - skye rgu] skye dgu, ngal bso] ngal gso.

[22] DPERBRJOD:91

[23] Cf. GEROW 1971:126

satyaṃ bravīmi na tvaṃ māṃ draṣṭuṃ vallabha lapsyase |
anyacumbanasaṃkrāntalākṣāraktena cakṣuṣā ||KĀ II:125||

jo bo bden par smra'o bdag |
gzhan dang tsum ba nas 'phos pa'i |
rgya skyegs kyis dmar mig gis ni |
nam yang mthong bar 'gyur ma lags ||[24]

"I'm telling you the truth! My 'lord'! you will not see me anymore
with your eyes red with lac, smeared on by by another woman's kisses."

Note that the word 'kissing' *(cumbana)* is timidly left in the original (*tsum ba na*, in all editions I have seen), although there is a word in Tibetan for kissing (*kha sprad cing 'o bya ba*[25]). The Fifth Dalai lama in his illustration of the same *alaṃkāra* just won't miss the opportunity to flog his 'favourite' hermit-meditators (see below) once again. Obviously, there was no love lost in his case:

tshul 'chos sgom chen rgan po'i rdzu bag gis |
tha snyad gtsug lag sbyor bar mi byed pas |
mi shes blun po tshogs pa'i gral khrod du |
mgo skyes dkar po'i thor cog 'ching bar nges ||[26]

"Those not applying[27] the sciences of conventional terms
will surely tie their grizzled hair in a top-knot
and join the crowd of ignorant fools, [deluded]
by the 'miracles' of old charlatan meditators."

Finally, let us see some verses that illustrate the blaming aspect of the *tulyayogitālaṃkāra*.[28] Daṇḍin's example runs as follows:

[24] RNAMBSHAD:200
[25] DBYANGSROL:305, although *'o bya ba* alone would have sufficed.
[26] DGYESGLU:110.; DPERBRJOD:166. *pada a* - om. rgan; *pada b* - sbyor bar] sbyong bar
[27] Or: "Those not trained in..." acc. to DPERBRJOD:loc.cit.
[28] cf. GEROW 1971:192

saṅgatāni mṛgākṣīṇāṃ taḍidvilasitāni ca |
kṣaṇadvayaṃ na tiṣṭhanti ghanārabdhāny api svayam
|| KĀ II:332 ||

ri dwags mig dang 'grogs pa dang |
glog gi rtse dga' dag dang ni |
sprin gyi rtsom pa'ang rang bzhin gyis |
skad cig gnyis par mi gnas so ||[29]

"Neither affairs with young ladies, nor the fleeting bolts of lightning
last for more than two seconds—though they started in the clouds / *in a deep felt way*."[30]

Although Daṇḍin's verse is not entirely devoid of the idea that life is transitory, a favoured topic in Buddhist writings, no ladies are mentioned in the verses of the Tibetan *ālaṃkārika*s. Thus, Mi pham writes:

skye bo'i mig sngar 'khyer legs tshul 'chos khrims |
las 'bras mi bsam kha bshad skam po'i chos |
stong pa'i tshon gyis legs bris dbang po'i gzhu |
mdzes kyang nam zhig snying po'i rang mtshang ston||[31]

"Hypocrite customs brought to the presence of men,
meager empty talk with no respect to deed and consequence,
the bow of Indra [i.e. the rainbow] painted with a thousand colours:
however pleasing these may be, in time their essential fault will show."

The above verses were chosen more or less randomly. One might quote further examples to show that the verses follow Daṇḍin's technique but not his themes. The Tibetan verses are purged

[29]RNAMBSHAD:324, completely missing out on the double meaning of *ghana*.

[30]TR. GEROW 1971:192.

[31]DPERBRJOD:386. The verse is not entirely devoid of double entendre, as *'chos khrims* sound exactly like *chos khrims* 'religious law' in pronounciation.

of all erotic content and other secular themes will always be replaced with religious or ethical ones. Most frequently, they are hymns, praises to different deities, the Buddha, sages of the past, etc. Therefore, celibate monks may have rested assured that no indecent poetry would stir up their emotions. But let us look again at the *Kāvyādarśa*-passage in Dpa' bo's great historical work.

"In this way, if one praises properly
the virtues of the three jewels by means
of faultless, worthy, beautiful verses,
he will attain fame, wealth and supreme royalty."

If we try to trace this verse, to our greatest surprise we'll find a very different original. This is the last sentence from Daṇḍin's work, summarizing his view on the use of *kāvya*:

vyutpannabudhir amunā vidhidarśitena
mārgeṇa doṣaguṇayor vaśavartinībhiḥ |
vāgbhiḥ kṛtābhisaraṇo madirekṣaṇībhir
dhanyo yuveva ramate labhate ca kīrtim ||KĀ III:187||[32]

sgrub byed bstan pa'i lam 'dis skyon dang yon tan dag|
rab tu rtogs pa'i blo can skal bzang dbang gyur pa'i |
tshig dang mngon par 'grogs byas chang mig ma dag dang|
lang tsho can bzhin dga' dang grags pa thob par 'gyur||[33]

"Someone who has acquired knowledge in the excellences and the shortcomings with the help of this path taught appropriately and is approached by words that are in his control, is delighted and obtains fame, just as a fortunate youth *who is approached* by wine eyed ladies *enchanted by him.*"

One might have two kinds of assumptions at this point. Either we are reading an aging Dpa' bo (he wrote his monumental chronicle for 20 years) just at the end of his work, tired to bother about quoting precisely on a side issue, or, he is deliberately altering

[32] cf. RATNAŚRĪ:276-277
[33] RNAMBSHAD:527-8

the verse, hoping he'll get away with it on account of his authority and readers being equally tired to trace the original. Knowing Dpa' bo to be an otherwise extraordinarily precise and therefore very reliable historian, most probably the verse was meant to be a paraphrase of the concluding part of the KĀ. Note that the idiom *dkon mchog rnam gsum* ['the three jewels', i.e. the Buddha, the Teaching and the congregation] is especially dubious. Daṇḍin was known to have been non-Buddhist, therefore it is really strange that the old historian would fill out some of the words already shrouded in the mists of forgetfulness with such commonplace Buddhist expressions. If we consider it a paraphrase, and it was meant to be Dpa' bo's own verse, than we have a genuine Tibetan monastic *ars poetica* in front of us.

Making sure that the 'wine-eyed ladies' of this last verse will not give birth to further improper thinking, having explained KĀ III:187, the commentator *Khams sprul* quickly cites well-known Buddhist legends on the usage of *kāvya* even around the person of the Buddha:

> *gzhan yang 'Dul ba'i gzhir*[34] | *bram ze zhig gis sangs rgyas bcom ldan 'das la* | *gser gyi mdog can mig tu sdug pa dang* || *sogs tshigs su bcad pa'i snyan ngag gis bstod pas* | *dge ba'i rtsa ba 'dis bskal pa nyi shur log par ltung bar 'gro bar mi 'gyur te* | *'on kyang lha dang mi rnams su nying mtshams sbyar zhing 'khor nas srid pa phyi ma* | *skye gnas phyi ma dang* | *lus phyi ma dang* | *bdag gi ngo bo thob pa phyi ma la rang sangs rgyas Bstod 'os zhes bya bar 'gyur ro* | *zhes lung bstan pas dge slong rnams the tshom skyes nas slar yang de'i rgyu zhus pas* | *da ltar 'ba' zhig tu ma zad kyi ji ltar 'das pa'i dus na yang* | *Bā rā ṇa sī'i rgyal po Tshangs sbyin zhes bya ba snyan ngag la lhag par dga' ba zhig gi bzhon pa glang po cher nga nyid gyur pa'i tshe na'ang* | *'di bram ze snyan ngag mkhan zhig tu gyur pas* | *Sa srung bu yi lus kyi sha tshugs ltar* || *sogs tshigs su bcad pas bzhon pa glang po'i dam pa la mngon par bstod par gyur to* | *de'i tshe de'i dus kyi*

[34] 'Dul ba gzhi (Tōh. 1.) Bka' 'Dul

glang po che dam pa gang yin pa de ni nga nyid yin no | bram ze gang yin pa de ni bram ze 'di nyid yin te | rgyal pos grong khyer gyi mchog lnga yang de'i tshe de la byin par gyur to | zhes 'byung ba [...] |[35]

Furthermore, in the *Vinayavastu* [we read]: "One *brāhmaṇa* praised the glorious Buddha with verse-*kāvya*: 'Of golden complexion, pleasing to the eye' etc. By virtue of this merit he will not fall into damnation[36] for twenty eons *(kalpa)*. Moreover, he will be born as a god or a human, and it was prophecized that in his last existence, his last womb, last incarnation, last identity, he will be the *pratyekabuddha*[37] called 'Worthy of Praise'. The monks had nurtured some doubt and asked for the reason again. [The Buddha then answered:] 'It was not for the first time [that he had praised me with verses]. Long ago, in Benares, there was a king called Brahma's Boon (Brahmadatta) who found great pleasure in [listening to] poetry and I was born as his riding elephant. There was this *brāhmaṇa*, skilled in poetry, and he praised the holy elephant with the verses: "Thy shape is like that of Sārvabhauma[38]" etc. Who was that holy elephant? It was I. Who was the *brāhmaṇa*? It was this very *brāhmaṇa*. The king at that time presented him with five excellent towns [as a reward].' "

'Great meditators' and the futility of sciences dealing with worldly conventions

There were several ways to accomodate *kāvya* into Tibetan Buddhist doctrine. Usually its utility and the need to study it was treated together with grammar, logic and the other major or

[35]DGYESROL.701-702

[36]I.e. he will not be reborn in the hells, the realms of the hungry ghosts or as an animal.

[37]A 'solitary buddha' who, although he had reached buddha-hood, will not teach.

[38]One of the eight mythical elephants that guard the quarters.

minor sciences. These sciences, as they dealt with more or less secular topics, were termed *tha snyad rig pa*, i.e. sciences of the conventional terms. As most Tibetan buddhists were followers of the *madhyamaka*, we will present the problem from this viewpoint. This philosophical system differentiates between 'conventional' and 'supreme' truth, 'conventional' and 'transcendental' existence and so forth. While the true purport of human existence is to penetrate and recognize the 'supreme' mode of being, it cannot ignore the truths of the everyday world, causality of phenomena, universal suffering, etc. To navigate somehow in this mess of delusion, beings are forced to fabricate conventions (e.g. discursive thought), which are useful in a sense, but they also have a binding factor. Deluded as we are, the 'conventional truth' is pretty much all we have and recognize, therefore it must be harnessed and used intelligently to show the way towards transcendence. For instance, in *Dge lugs pa* and *Sa skya pa* circles, the complete mastery of logic is believed to have the result that the rational, discursive mind will eventually become aware of its own boundaries, will 'quiet down' and let the unspeakable penetrate the heart of the meditator. There are some however, who prefer to shorten this path and jump to meditation immediatly. Eager to shut out the conventional mode of being, they consider everything that has to do with it, futile. It is their objection that is voiced as a *prima facie* view throughout all three major commentaries I have consulted. The most interesting is the Fifth Dalai lama's peculiar manner of doing away with this objection, hence, he will be cited first.

> *phyag rgya pa sogs gangs khrod kyi sgom chen rnams kyis | tha snyad rig pa 'di rnams phyi rol pas kyang thos bsam du bya bas na snying po med do snyam na | khyod rang rnams kyis nyams su len pa'i phyag rgya chen po de'i lhag mthong gi rten gzhir gyur pa'i zhi gnas de la goms pa'i phyi rol pa ji snyed cig 'byung bas | khyod rang rnams kyi zhi gnas de yang spang byar mi 'gyur ram | nged kyi zhi gnas la skyabs 'gro dang sems bskyed sogs kyi khyad par yod do zhes smra na | nged cag tha snyad mkhan po rnams kyi tha snyad rig pa la'ang theg pa chen po'i sems bskyed kyi rtsis zin*

pa'i bla na med pa'i byang chub kyi rgyur 'gro'o zhes smra na ci skad zer |

*'jam mgon chos kyi rgyal po Tsong kha pa chen pos | Tshad ma rnam 'grel gyis thar pa dang thams cad mkhyen pa'i lam bstan par bzhed pa la | Stag tshang lo tsā bas | Rig gnas kun shes kyi rtsa 'grel du dgag pa mdzad pa ni | lo tsā ba mkhas pa chen po yin pas *dgongs*[39] *pa can gyi gsung yin mchi | de ltar min na | Sa paṇ gyis | Chos kyi grags pa'i gsung rab dri ma med |*[40] *ces 'gyur byang du mdzad pas | gsung rab yin phyin sde snod dang | de'i dgongs 'grel gang rung las ma 'das shing | de gang rung yin phyin thar pa dang thams cad mkhyen pa'i lam brjod byar mi byed pa mi srid pas don med kyi dgag pa mi mdzad pa zhu | gzhan yang Dpang los | mngon pa la lung gi mngon pa dang | rigs pa'i mngon pa gnyis su bzhed pas kyang | Rje bla ma'i dgongs pa'i rgyab skyor du 'gro'o ||*

Dwags rgyud pa ci rigs kyis Stag tshang pa'i gsung de dag la brten nas | Rje bla ma la zur za bar 'dod pa'i tshig gi sbyor ba byed pa ni | Sa Dge'i mkhas pa lung rigs kyi lus stobs rdzogs pa'i Stag seng kha 'thab pa'i bar du Bka' brgyud pa'i sgom chen wa skyes lta bu dag rgyu ba ni shin tu 'tshang che bas bag yod par byos shig ||[41]

"Now, if someone were to think that [it is true what] the practitioners of *mahāmudrā* and other great meditators of cave-hermitages say, viz.: 'Even non-Buddhists[42] study and reflect upon these sciences dealing with conventional terms, therefore they have no [genuine] essence', [we would reply: 'Well then,] if some non-Buddhist were to meditate upon calming the mind (*zhi*

[39] *em.* : *dgos ed.*

[40] The actual words were not found in the edition of the Tibetan translation of the *Pramāṇavarttika* I have consulted

[41] DGYESGLU:10-13

[42] Lit. "outsiders" (*phyi pa*) as opposed to "insiders" (*nang pa*), the Buddhists.

gnas, śamathā) which forms the basis of the discernment (*lhag mthong, vipaśyanā*) of your *mahāmudrā* practice, wouldn't your *śamathā* become something useless as well?' [Then] they would say: 'Our *śamathā* practice is distinguished by the generation of the thought of enlightenment (*sems bskyed, bodhicittotpāda*) and seeking refuge (*skyabs 'gro, śaraṇagamana*).' [We would reply again:] 'Our sciences dealing with the conventional terms are [viewed] as causes to attain unsurpassable enlightenment, which [of course] contain generating the thought of enlightenment.' What will they say then?

His eminence, the lord of the faith, the great *Tsong kha pa* maintained the view that the *Pramāṇavārttika* teaches the way to liberation and omniscience.[43] The translator Stag tshang, in his *Rig gnas kun shes kyi rtsa 'grel*, [seemingly] refuted this. [Now,] the translator is a great scholar, therefore he must have said that using his words in an intentional way[44]. If it weren't so [i.e. the work would not teach the path for complete liberation and omniscience, how can it be that] Sa skya paṇḍita in the addenda to the translation said: 'The scripture of Dharmakīrti is spotless.' It is a 'scripture', thus it naturally follows that it does not deviate from any scripture of the *[Tri-]piṭaka* [i.e. the *Bka' 'gyur*] or of the commentarial works [i.e. the *Bstan 'gyur*]. It is acceptable, therefore it follows that it cannot possibly teach [another] path [than that of] liberation and omniscience. Therefore, we beg that there be no more meaningless refutations. Dpang's [statement] that there are two *abhidharmas*, one of authority [of scripture] and one of reason, futher strengthens the idea of the Lord, the master [Tsong kha pa].

[43]It must be noted however, that this viewpoint was not quite in tune with the general opinion even in India. Mi pham cites Diṅnāga claiming that logic is for refutation of erroneous views, heretical opponents, but the ultimate teaching of the Buddha may not be grasped solely by it, for that is beyond conceptions. DGONGSRGYAN:7b.

[44]*abhiprāya*: tr. *ex em.*

> Some of the *Dwags* order used this statement to criticize the Lord, the master. [We say unto them:] up to the time that the scholars of *Sa skya* and the *Dge lugs* order will fight *Stag seng* who bears the perfect 'bodily' strength of scripture and reasoning, the 'great meditators' of the *Bka' brgyud pa*, sneaking as young foxes, should be ashamed of themselves for they are completely mistaken!

We have already seen that the 'Great Fifth' never misses an opportunity to wage war on the *Bka' brgyud pa* and their practices. Apart from this, however, he touches on sensitive issues: scriptural authority, adaptation of worldly and 'heretic' sciences into the Buddhist curriculum, and so on. We shall deal with these later. Other commentators strike a more charitable tone with the 'transcendentalists'. Thus, Mi pham promotes a balanced spiritual program with equal emphasis on meditation leading to transcendental wisdom on one hand and lexical knowledge on the other.

> *deng sang thos sgom gnyis 'gal ba ltag sprod du bzung nas | thos pa med pa'i bsgom pa ni | lag sdum brag la 'dzeg pa 'dra | zhes (8a)sogs kyi lung drangs nas sgom chen la 'dzer | la las kha bshad stong pa'i 'phyor mgron des | rkyen nyon mongs thul bar dka' mor gda' | zhes sogs lung 'dren dang bcas thos bsam pa la kha zer mod kyi | phyogs gnyis kas kyang Mdo sde rgyan gyi |*
>
> *de ltar bde bar gshegs pa'i bstan pa gang yin*
> *de yang don med min |*
> *de ltar rnal 'byor can gyi sgom pa gang yin*
> *de yang don med min |*
> *gal te thos pa tsam gyis don mthong 'gyur*
> *na sgom pa don med 'gyur |*
> *gal te ma thos par yang sgom 'jug 'gyur na*
> *bstan pa don med 'gyur ||*[45]

[45]MAHĀYĀNASŪTRĀLAṂKĀRA 12.3: *tasmān naiva nirārthikā bhavati sā yā bhāvanā yogināṃ tasmān naiva nirārthikā bhavati ya sa deśana saugatī | dṛṣṭo 'rthaḥ śrutamātrakād yadi bhavet syād bhāvanāpārthikā aśrutvāt yadi bhāvanām anuviśet syād deśanāpārthikā ||*

zhes gsungs pa'i don la ji mi snyam pa'i blo gros 'chal bar song 'dug | de bas na | sangs rgyas Dbyig gnyen zhabs kyis Mngon pa mdzod du |

> *tshul gnas thos dang bsam ldan pas |*
> *sgom pa la ni rab tu sbyor ||*[46]

zhes gsungs pa'i tshig don 'di nyid snying gi thig ler bzung nas thos bsam sgom gsum 'gal med du nyams su len pa ni mkhas pa yin te ||[47]

"Nowadays, there [are] some great meditators [who] claim that listening [i.e. study] and meditation are each other's opposite. In accordance with the authoritative statement: 'Meditation without study is like [someone] climbing a rock with his hands folded together', we say [the following] unto them. Some have said, even citing 'authoritative quotations' that 'riding on glamorous, idle chit-chat, it is indeed hard to subdue the obscurations (*nyon mongs, kleśa*), the very reasons [of the transmigratory world]', and thus made false accusations towards [those] studying and pondering [upon what they heard].[48] How is it that [these accusers] have entirely lost their mind and do not ponder on the meaning of the passage in the *Sūtrālaṅkāra* that [teaches] both?

> 'Nothing is futile what the Sugata has taught
>
> and none of the *yogins*' meditations are futile either.
> If the ultimate meaning could be realized merely by listening, meditation would become useless.

[46]ABHIDHARMAKOŚAKĀRIKĀ 6.5ab: *vṛttasthaḥ śruticintāvān bhāvanāyāṃ prayujyate |*

[47]DGONGSRGYAN:7b-8a

[48]This is a reference to the three basic modes of integrating the Buddhist doctrine: listening / studying (*śruti, thos*), pondering upon that which has been heard (*cintā, bsam*) and meditating on that (*bhāvanā, sgom*).

> If meditation could be entered without listening [first], the teaching would become useless.'

Consequently, the very words of the buddha[49] Vasubandhu from his *Abhidharmakośakārikā*:

> 'One who dwells [in the] right [ethical norms], has listened to and pondered upon [the teaching], enters meditation',

should be held as the very essence of one's mind. He, who [has done accordingly and] understands that listening, pondering and meditation do not present any contradiction, is considered wise."[50]

Khams sprul strikes an ever milder tone, as the allegations of the Fifth Dalai lama touched his own order, the *Bka' brgyud pa*. He, however (along the lines of Mi pham, even quoting him verbatim for entire passages), also rejects the assertion that lexical, conventional knowledge is useless. Here he is already touching on the '*bodhisattva*-argument' which will be discussed in the last chapter of this paper. First, he will defend his point by means of a quote from the *Bodhicaryāvatāra* of the Indian master Śāntideva, universally acknowledged as one of the basic Buddhist texts. Then, he reproduces a quote already found in Mi pham's commentary, from a work written by the founder of his own order, who was also famed to be a *Bka' brgyud pa* great meditator. I believe this passage was—for political reasons not openly—meant to silence the criticism of the Fifth Dalai lama.

> *'di la kha cig 'di snyam du sems te | zab mo'i don la rtse gcig tu mnyam par bzhag nas bsgom pa 'thad kyi shes bya'i mtha' rgya gcod dka' | chod kyang dgos pa med do zhe na | [...] Spyod 'jug las |*

---

[49] This is an interesting epithet for Vasubandhu.

[50] Mi pham's extreme care in choosing his authoritative citations should be appreciated. First he cites a basic scripture of the *yogācāra* school, then *Vasubandhu* of the *"śrāvaka"* school, and a few lines further he will also cite Nāgārjuna, the foremost exponent of the *madhyamaka*.

rgyal sras rnams kyis mi slob pa |
de ni gang yang yod min te |
de ltar gnas pa'i mkhas pa la |
bsod nams mi 'gyur gang yang med ||[51]

[...] 'gro ba'i mgon po Gtsang pa Rgya ras pa'i zhal snga nas Rten 'brel gyi chos skor du[52] |

thos pa rgya cher bya long med pa'i sgom chen pas kyang shes bya dang shes par byed mkhan kun la mos par bya | rjes su yi rangs par byed | tha na mgar ba yan chad la kho'i tho ba sogs lag par bzung | 'di lta bu la'ang[53] *mkhas par gyur cig ces smon lam 'debs | des rten 'brel 'grig pa yin gsungs | gzhan yang |*

rgyu 'bras bslu ba med pa 'di |
thams cad mkhyen pa'i khyad chos yin |
ma bslab pa las kun mkhyen du |
'gro na rgyu 'bras ga la bden ||

"Now, some might think: 'It is better if one sits in equiposed meditation, fixed on the profound meaning alone. It is hard to reach the end of all that is to be known, and even if one does, it is useless.' [...] The *Bodhicaryāvatāra* says:

'There is nothing that should not be learned
by the Sons of Conquerors [i.e. *bodhisattvas*].
For one with mastery therein,
there is nothing destitute of merit.'

The defender of men, Gtsang pa Rgya ras pa in his Cycle of Teachings Concerning Interdependent Causation (*pratītyasamutpāda*) had said:

[51] BODHICARYĀVATĀRA 5.100: *na hi tad vidyate kiñcid yan na śikṣyaṃ jinātmajaiḥ | na tad asti na yat puṇyam evaṃ viharataḥ sataḥ ||*

[52] This following passage is taken from Mi pham's commentary, DGONGSRGYAN:7a-7b.

[53] 'ang] om. DGONGSRGYAN

'Listening should be done extensively, even by the great meditators [who are] "in a hurry".[54] They should also cherish and be delighted in the disciplines [of study] and anything that acts as cause to attain mastery over them. Even a blacksmith when he takes hold of his hammer or any other [instrument], utters the prayer: "may I become accomplished by this." This is said to be in tune with [the law of] interdependent causation. Furthermore:

This infallible [law] of cause and effect
is the distinctive sign of omniscience.

If omniscience would arise from not studying,
how could [the law] of cause and effect be true?" '

Fear of infidels, opportunists and 'buddhicising' the *Kāvyādarśa*

A further, rather sensible objection that the commentators of the KĀ had to face was that they were defending the *śāstra* of an outsider (*phyi pa*), i.e. the non-Buddhist Daṇḍin. We have already seen that it was one of the worries the Fifth Dalai lama's 'great meditators' had.

Before we can present Khams sprul's account of this problem, a short digression has to be made. In the introduction to

[54] I.e. "not having any free time for wordly leisures but meditate incessantly". Khams sprul records a further objection from the *sgom chen* type of practitioners, namely that there simply isn't enough time to aqcuire the vastness of conventional teachings: *de lta na shes bya'i mtha' la thug pa med pa'i phyir de kun bslab nas ma lus par shes pa'i dus mi srid pa dang | rgyu mtshan des na 'bras bu rnam pa thams cad mkhyen pa thob pa'ang mi srid par 'gyur ro* (DBYANGSROL:9) "[Objection:] Even so, things that are to be known are limitless, it is impossible to learn and acquire them in their entirety. By this reason, the omniscience [you are talking about] is also impossible to attain."

his commentary[55], Khams sprul claims that he used two commentaries in the original Sanskrit to the KĀ. The manuscripts were presented to him by his master, Si tu Ka rma Bstan pa'i nyin byed. One of these is a work by a Sinhalese Buddhist called Ratnaśrī, which is easily identifiable. It survives in Sanskrit (almost complete), it has been edited, and other manuscripts are beginning to surface (at least one up to this day). The work, although never translated, circulated in Tibet as early as the late XIII. – early XIV.c., when Dpang lo made his revision on the basis of this text. The second commentary was written by (allegedly) another Buddhist, called Ngag gi Dbang phyug Grags pa. It was tempting to identify this with another, well known Indian commentator, *Taruṇavācaspati*, as the first four syllables of the Indian name translated into Tibetan may be reconstructed as * *Vācaspati*. The—seemingly minor—problems are that *Grags pa* has to be reconstructed as **kīrti*, which does not figure in the Indian name, nor does *Taruṇa* in the Tibetan. Prof. Yogeśvaradattaśarmā, a recent editor of the KĀ and four of its major commentaries edits Taruṇavācaspati's commentary *(vivṛtti)* and identifies the author as the father of one Keśavabhaṭṭāraka, the royal preceptor *(rājaguru)* of king Nareśarāmanātha of the Hoysala dynasty, whose rule began in 1255 A.D.[56] Furthermore, he records another commentary by one Vācaspati (or Dharmavācaspati) and identifies it with that of Taruṇavācaspati.[57] It is not plausible (yet not impossible) that the father of a royal preceptor at a Hindu court might have been a Buddhist, whereas the alternate name of the second Vācaspati *(Dharmavācaspati)* does sound more Buddhist. Even if the two authors are identical, then there must be two very different recensions of the same text, as Khams sprul quotes *his* *Vācaspati extensively (see below). These quotations cannot be identified with passages in the *Vivṛtti* published by Prof. Yogeśvaradattaśarmā. I think that we may safely postulate a *Vācaspati II or a third person with a similar name (perhaps *Vāgīśvarakīrti?) and a different, Buddhist commentary which Khams sprul read and reproduced in his own translation. Unfor-

[55] DBYANGSROL:17

[56] KĀ (D) I:xxiii

[57] KĀ (D) I:xxiv

tunately, Khams sprul was not so sure himself who the nebulous Ngag dbang Grags pa was, and cautiously notes that it should be investigated whether he is identical with the Vāgīśvarakīrti of the 'Six Gates' (*sgo drug*), a well-known Tantric commentator of the eleventh-century Nālandā college-monastery.

The problem under scrutiny here is that *his* Ngag dbang Grags pa demonstrated with an exegetical *tour de force* that the benedictory verse of the KĀ[58], praising Sarasvatī, may also refer to the Buddha.[59] Needless to say, this is quite untenable and there were some sensible—probably only imaginary—objections, which, however do indicate the fact that there were people who viewed Daṇḍin as a heretic (see below) and as such, to be treated with suspicion.

> *de la kha cig 'di snyam du | gzhung mdzad pa po'i slob dpon yang nang pa ma yin zhing 'chad bya'i bstan bcos kyang thun mong ba'i rig gnas yin pas sangs rgyas la mchod par brjod pa'i 'grel tshul 'di ni gzhung gi dgongs pa ma yin zhing skabs dang mi 'brel lo zhe na | de'i phyir slob dpon Ngag dbang Dbang phyug Grags pa nyid kyis sangs rgyas bcom ldan 'das ni lha dang mi'i bla mar rab tu grags pa'i phyir sogs dang | gzhung mdzad pa po slob dpon Daṇḍi 'di yang med pa ba ste chad par lta bas sangs rgyas la mi gus pa ma yin pa'i phyir | 'di ltar bkral ba gzhung gi dgongs pa ma yin pa'i skyon du mi 'gyur bar dgongs pa'o | de'i phyir 'dir sangs rgyas dran par byed par sbyar te de ni dge legs thams cad 'byung bar byed pa yin pas so ||*[60]

> "Now, concerning this [i.e. the interpretation of the *maṅgala*-verse as referring to the Buddha also], some have thought: 'The author of this text is not an insider [i.e. Buddhist] and the *śāstra* about to be explained pertains to common science, hence, commenting the

[58]KĀ I.1. *caturmukhamukhāmbhojavanahaṃsavadhūr mama | mānase ramatāṃ nityaṃ sarvaśuklā Sarasvatī ||*

[59]For the sake of no further digressions, the reader should consult DbyangsRol:35ff.

[60]DbyangsRol:37-38

> verse in this way, viz. that it praises the Buddha, was not the [original] intention of the text, and is therefore irrelevant.' For the reason that [1.] the master Ngag dbang Dbang phyug Grags pa himself said that 'since the Buddha is famous for being the master of gods and men' etc.[61] and for the reason that [2.] it is [therefore] not the case that Daṇḍin, as a nihilist, i.e. a believer of annihilation, does not respect the Buddha, [the commentator] thought that it is not erroneous to expound that the text has such an intention [as well]. Furthermore, since it calls to mind the Buddha, it is the generator of all merits."

It is quite striking that we are here—indirectly—observing an Indian Buddhist commentator 'forcing' the *maṅgala*-verse so that it becomes Buddhistic, when Sarasvatī was well established in the Buddhist pantheon as well. What was the need for such an interpretation? Was *Vācaspati II merely parading his exegetical skills and knowledge of synonimics or did he have the intention of demonstrating that Daṇḍin was a Buddhist?

We have already seen with Dpa' bo that there were authorities in Tibet trying to make a Buddhist out of Daṇḍin. Whether Dpa' bo has done it on purpose or by forgetfullness is irrelevant. In either case, it seems that the mindframe to integrate the KĀ in the doctrine by buddhicizing it, was present. Khams sprul does not claim that Daṇḍin was an all-out Buddhist, but tacitly asserts that (just like his verse) he had hidden inclinations towards the doctrine. In fact, in two paragraphs he convincingly refutes all claims considering Daṇḍin as an 'insider'. Of the two passages we will here present the latter, as it raises further interesting issues.[62]

> *gzhan yang 'di dang 'chad tshul cung mi mthun pa ni | Dmangs Do ha las |*

[61]These are the first words of the alternative interpretation of the benedictory verse referred to above.

[62]The first is a lengthy presentation of the *āśramas* a *brāhmaṇa* passes through during his lifetime and proves that the later phase of their life may be designated as 'one walking with a stick' i.e. *daṇḍin*.

> *dbyu gu dbyug gsum legs ldan gzugs |*
> *'chang zhing dus su mchod pa dang |*

zhes 'byung ba ltar ro | 'dir slob dpon Dbyug pa can grub mtha' nang par 'dod pa dang | slob dpon Dpa' bo dang gcig par 'dod pa sogs kyi 'khrul gzhi | slob dpon Dpa' bo yang dang po'i grub mtha' phyi rol pa yin pa dang | rgyal ba nyid kyis kyang bstod pa byed par lung bstan pa ltar 'dis mdzad pa'i snyan ngag gi bstod pa shin tu mang ba sogs la brten nas byung 'dug kyang | de gnyis gcig pa'i skabs med de | slob dpon Dpa' bo'i mtshan gyi rnam grangs Rta dbyangs dang | Ma khol dang | Pha khol dang | Thub dka' Nag po dang | Chos ldan Rab 'byor dang | Ma ti tsi tra | Dpa' bo zhes pa rnams kho na 'byung gi | Dbyug pa can zhes pa'i mtshan gang nas kyang ma bshad | bstan bcos 'di'i mdzad pa po slob dpon Daṇḍi ni phyis nang pa'i grub mtha' la zhugs pa'i lo rgyus kyang med do || 'di'i mtshan Dbyig pa can zer ba ma dag Dbyug pa can yin zhes phyis kyi mkhas pa kha cig gsungs pa ni de gnyis brda gsar rnying gi khyad par ma gtogs don gcig pa ma dgongs par zad do ||[63]

"Furthermore, there is another, slightly different mode of explanation, according to the *Dohā of the Commoners*, that says:

> "They take a trident-staff, bear the form of the
> Beneficial One, they sacrifice in the proper time..."[64]

Accordingly, Daṇḍin is thought to be an 'insider', and this served as a base for many errors, such as identify-

---

[63] DBYANGSROL:20-27

[64] The matter of the *dohā*-quote is confusing for two reasons. The first is that these two lines do not appear together in the edition I have consulted (the Peking Tripitaka, Bstan 'gyur), and the second is that where the first line appears (the 4th verse of the song), the author, the *mahāsiddha Saraha* seems to be referring to (and mocking) *śaiva* ascetics (the motif of the trident and the imitation of '*Legs ldan*' which is an epithet for *Dbang phyug*, *Īśvara*, i.e. Śiva.)

> ing him with the master [Ārya]Śūra. The master Śūra was also—initially—an 'outsider' and [later] wrote many hymns in verse, as it had been prophecized by the Buddha. For this and other reasons, he is [the same—or so they thought.] There is no ground whatsoever to take those two [i.e. Daṇḍin and Śūra] as one. Among the variant names of master Śūra we find: Aśvaghoṣa, *Mātṛceṭa, *Pitṛceṭa, *Durjayakṛṣṇa, *Dharmasubhūti, *Maticitra [probably Mātṛceṭa again], Śūra and only these. The name 'Daṇḍin' is nowhere to be found. Furthermore, there are no accounts that the author of this work, master Daṇḍin, later became a follower of some Buddhist school. The claim that the [form] '*Dbyig pa can*' was corrupt and '*Dbyug pa can*' is correct was made by some later authorities who did not recognize the archaic and new variants of the same word."

It is evident that some tried to force Daṇḍin into being Buddhist by identifying him with authors known for their *kāvya*s with Buddhist subjects: Aśvaghoṣa (author of the *Buddhacarita*), Mātṛceṭa (author of the *Adhyardhaśataka*) and Āryaśūra (author of the *Jātakamālā*).[65] No doubt that the identification and thus the incorporation of the KĀ into Buddhist scripture was well intended, nevertheless, it lacked the ground as the commentators point out. It is worth noting here that Khams sprul is extremely sensible in treating his subject matter. He recognises that the KĀ, as it is a text of the 'outsiders', should be treated accordingly, as to interpretation of verses, terminology, etc.[66]

Mi pham has interesting remarks on how the 'outsiders' and the real buddhists treat their conventional sciences. He condemns once more the 'great meditators' and those who use the sciences merely for their own, selfish purposes. They, he claims, aren't any better then the heretics themselves.

---

[65]It is irrelevant from our viewpoint, yet to be noted that Tibetans considered these three as the same person.

[66]*skabs 'di dag tu phyi rol pa rnams rang gi 'dod pa dang mthun par 'chad dgos [...]* (DBYANGSROL:40) "In such instances, the explanation should be done according to the very tenets of the 'outsiders'".

de las nang rig sde snod gsum dang rgyud sde bzhi dgongs 'grel dang bcas pa ni bstan pa la zhugs pa kho na'i khyad (6b)par gyi chos yin pas thun mong ma yin pa dang | gzhan bzhi phyi nang kun gyi thun mong du bslab bya yin pas thun mong pa'i rig gnas su yang bzhag || de dag kyang phyi rol pa rnams ni rnyed grags bkur sti sogs 'phral bde don gnyer gyi bsam pas 'jug pa | nang pa'i yang rigs can gsum gyi gang zag mtha' dag nang rig la theg pa gsum gyi byang chub don gnyer gyi bsam pas 'jug par mthun la | lhag ma bzhi la nyan rang rnams phas kyi rgol ba tshar bcad pa dang | rang gi grags pa bsgrags pa sogs gnas skabs kyi dgos pa 'ga' zhig gi phyir 'jug gi | gzhan don du rdzogs byang gi bsam pas 'jug pa ni med do || theg chen la zhugs pa'i byang chub sems dpa' rnams ni | rang gzhan gyi don rgya chen po sgrub pa'i slad du shes bya'i gnas kun la 'jug cing bslab par bya ba yin te | Byang chub sems dpa'i spyod pa la 'jug pa las |

> *rgyal sras rnams kyis mi bslab pa'i |*
> *dngos de gang yang yod ma yin |*
> *de ltar gnas pa'i mkhas pa la |*
> *bsod nams mi 'gyur gang yang med ||*

ces 'byung ba lags kyang | deng sang ci rigs kyi bsam blo la | spyir gyi rig gnas la slob pa ni grags 'dod langs pa'am mi tshe phyid thabs tsam yin la | bye brag mu stegs dang thun mong du gyur cing khyim pas bslab par bya rgyu'i rig gnas bzhi po de 'drar sbyang ba ni dal ba don med 'ba' zhig go snyam sems pa (7a) dang | de bas kyang blo chung ba kha cig | gzhung lugs chen po la slob pa'i gtam thos na dug sbrul gyis gla rtsi'i dri tshor ba ltar 'jigs sems dang sdang sems mnyam du 'char zhing cha bsdus lad pa'i rig pa thar thor dpe bral gyi yon tan du bsgom pa'i rigs gcig dang | yang 'ga' zhig thos pa rgya chen po la skyon du 'dzin | [...][67]

[67] DGONGSRGYAN:6a-7a

"Among the five [sciences], the inner science[68] has the characteristic that it introduces someone only to the teaching [embodied] in the three collections[69], the four tantric classes[70] and their commentaries, hence it is considered uncommon. The four other [sciences] present the object of study for both 'outsiders' and 'insiders', hence, they are placed among the common sciences. Considering these [four], 'outsiders' study them with the aim of earning wealth, fame, respect and other transitory enjoyments. On the other hand, all individuals of the three classes of 'insiders'[71] pursue the inner science with the aim of attaining the enlightenment [described] in the three vehicles[72] [respectively]—in this there is no difference. Concerning the other four, however, the *śrāvaka*s and *pratyekabuddha*s pursue them in order to refute their opponents, to make their own fame spread, and for other reasons, according to the circumstances; they do not pursue them with the intent of [attaining] perfect enlightenment. The *bodhisattva*s of the *mahāyāna*-path pursue and study every topic of anything to be known in order to act for the great benefit of themselves and others. Just as the *Bodhicaryāvatāra* says:

> 'There is nothing that should not be learned
> by the Sons of Conquerors [i.e. *bodhisattva*s].
> For one with mastery therein,
> there is nothing destitute of merit.'

However, nowadays some people's minds are intent on [using the common sciences] for winning fame or

[68]*nang rig* (*adhyātmavidyā*) in this context usually refers to the exegesis of the *Abhidharma*. Mi pham (as others do frequently) broadens the meaning of the word to denote the entire collection of teachings that refer to the Self.

[69]The *Tripiṭaka*, denoting the *Vinaya*, the *Sūtra* and the *Abhidharma*.

[70]The Tantric canon is usually divided into these four classes: *kriyā*, *caryā*, *yoga* and *anuttarayoga*.

[71]I.e. *śrāvakas*, *pratyekabuddhas*, and followers of the *mahāyāna*, i.e. would-be *bodhisattvas*.

[72]In this context: *śrāvakayāna*, *pratyekabuddhayāna* and the *mahāyāna*.

> merely as means to attain their livelihood. Hence, they are not different from the heretics[73] and accordingly, study the four sciences as something for householders, their fortune[74] thus becoming nothing but meaningless. There are some, even more stupid than them, in whom, upon hearing an account of [someone's] learning in a great treatise, fear and hostility arise in the same time, much the same way as in a venomous snake when smelling the scent of musk. Furthermore, some[75] meditate considering [their own] makeshift, scattered and faint knowledge as something having merits beyond comparison. Again, some consider vast learning a vice!"

The bodhisattva-argument

We have already made passing references to the fact that the commentators make use of what might be styled as the '*bodhisattva*-argument' in their refutations. Here, the word '*bodhisattva*' is used in two of its meanings, viz. the Buddha in his earlier life (or indeed, lives), before becoming enlightened and the desired behavioural pattern of any mahāyānist (or any follower of the *vajrayāna*[76]). A *bodhisattva*, who seeks enlightenment for the sake of other beings must acquire the skill in means (*upāyakauśalya, thabs la mkhas pa*) in order to convert and lead his or her fellow-beings out of the transmigratory world (*saṃsāra, 'jig rten*) and towards buddha-hood. Since the very cause of the saṃsāric mode of being is ignorance (*avidyā, ma rig pa*), omniscience (*sarvajñānatva, thams cad mkhyen pa nyid*) is the only antidote against it. Omniscience, again, refers to both conventional and transcend-

[73] *mu stegs pa* (*tīrthika*) is another, nonetheless a bit harsher name for the 'outsiders'.

[74] *dal ba* means to have the opportunity to practise Buddhism and not to be born in one of the eight states without that opportunity

[75] These are again the *sgom chen*.

[76] Many, if not all Tibetan and Indian *vajrayāna* followers stress the idea that ideologically there is no difference between these two levels of the doctrine. Both seek higher spiritual levels and ultimately enlightenment for the sake of other beings as well.

ental wisdom, where the first is the indispensible prerequisite of the second.

It is worth noting that Sa skya paṇḍita's ideal of *pāṇḍityam* is incorporated into the *bodhisattva*-argument. Although the paṇḍita himself would have suscribed to this idea, it seems that in his time the *pāṇḍityam* argument might have been sufficient. The shortest presentation of the '*bodhisattva*-argument' is, not surprisingly, that of the Fifth Dalai lama, a great admirer of Sa skya pa's works and personality.

In the following I am going to show how the ideas of the first paragraph are presented in Mi pham's commentary. Although this passage constitutes the beginning of the commentary, I reproduce it in this last chapter, as the aim was to reconstruct an argument with the conclusion *(siddhānta)* at the end. Khams sprul's presentation is a somewhat more elaborate version of Mi pham's text. While citing Mi pham verbatim, he presents a few additional authoritative quotations and defends the initial translation of the passage by Maitreya (see note below).

de ltar yang | Zhi ba lhas |

> *sngon chad ma byung ba ni 'dir brjod min |*
> *sdeb sbyor mkhas pa'ang bdag la yod min (3b)te |*
> *de phyir gzhan don bsam pa bdag la med |*
> *rang gi yid la bsgom phyir ngas 'di brtsams||*[77]

zhes gsungs pa bzhin | sngon du byung ba'i Rgya Bod kyi mkhas mchog rnams kyi gsung rgyun las brtsams te cung zhig gleng na | bdag cag gi ston pa mchog gi bstan pa 'di la | thar pa dang thams cad mkhyen pa'i grong khyer chen por 'jug pa'i sgo 'phar bla na med pa ni shes bya rig pa'i gnas lnga ste | Mdo las[78] *|*

> *byang chub sems dpa' rig pa'i dngos po lnga*
> *ma bslab na ni nam du yang bla na med*

[77]BODHICARYĀVATĀRA 1.2: *na hi kiñcid apūrvam atra vācyaṃ na ca saṃgrathanakauśalaṃ mamāsti | ata eva na me parārthacintā svamano vāsayituṃ kṛtaṃ mayedam ||*

[78]According to DBYANGSROL:4-5, this from the **Anukampāpratikaraṇa-sūtra* (Drin lan bsab pa'i mdo, Tōh. 353.; translated from Chinese)

> *pa yang dag par rdzogs pa'i byang chub tu thams cad mkhyen pa'i ye shes thob par mi nus so || de bas na bla na med pa'i byang chub thob par bya ba'i phyir rig pa'i dngos po lnga bslab par bya'o*

zhes dang | Rgyal tshab chen po Mi pham pas |

> *rig pa'i gnas lnga dag la brtson par ma byas na |*
> *'phags mchog gis kyang thams cad mkhyen nyid thob mi 'gyur |*
> *de bas gzhan dag tshar gcad rjes su gzung phyir dang |*
> *bdag nyid shes bya phyir de la de brtson bya||*[79]

zhes dang | Sa paṇḍi tas |

> *rang blo shes bya'i gnas lnga la ma sbyangs na |*
> *thams cad mkhyen pa nam mkha'i mtha' ltar rings |*
> *de ltar dgongs nas rgyal dang rgyal sras kyis|*
> *shes bya'i gnas kun sbyangs zhes legs par gsungs ||*[80]

zhes gsungs pa 'di dag ni rnam pa thams cad mkhyen pa'i rgyu'i gtso bo | rang gzhan gyi don gnyis 'byung ba'i gzhi | 'phral yun gyi legs pa thams cad kyi 'byung

---

[79]The other two commentaries also reproduce this verse, cf. DGYESGLU:8-9. & DBYANGSROL:5 7. There was an interesting controversy as to the correct translation of *pādas* a and b. The Fifth Dalai lama reproduces the initial translated form and then an emended version made by [Stag tshang lo tsā ba] 'Gyur-med Bde-chen. While the Dalai lama claims that the emendation is correct, Khams sprul, by virtue of his superior knowledge of Sanskrit, refutes this view (without mentioning names), dwells on the explanation of Maitreya's verse for a few paragraphs and arrives to the conclusion that the translation should be left in its original state. I think that the Dalai lama's admiration for Stag tshang voiced here as well, justifies my emendation above (*dgongs pa'i skad* for *dgos pa'i skad*).

[80]ROLBSTAN:colophon.

khungs ston pa'i (4a) gsung yin te | 'khor ba'i rgya mtsho chen po 'dir sems can rnams sdug bsngal gyi tshor ba la long su spyod pa'i rgyu ni | 'jig lta dang mtshungs par ldan pa'i ma rig pa kho na yin | de spong byed kyi gnyen po rig pa'i ye shes | rig pa de 'phel bar bya ba'i thabs su phyi nang gi rig pa'i gnas ji snyed cig 'byung ba kun kyang | de bzhin gshegs pa rnams thabs la mkhas shing thugs rje che bas | ci rigs par dngos dang brgyud pa'i sgo nas ma rig pa 'joms byed kyi thabs su bstan pa yin |[81]

"Just as Śāntideva had said[82]:

> 'Nothing will be said here which is unprecented
> and I have no talent in composing [verses].
> Therefore I am not concerned whether this might be beneficial to others.
> I wrote it only to refine my own understanding',

my brief discussion begins [with some quotations] from the exegetical tradition of earlier Indian and Tibetan great masters. Concerning the doctrine of our teacher, the best of all [i.e. the Buddha], the unsurpassable threshold of the great realm of liberation and omniscience are the five sciences. The *sūtra* says:

> 'Oh, *bodhisattva*! If you do not become learned in the five sciences you will never be able to attain the wisdom of omniscience for the sake of unsurpassable, utterly perfect enlightenment. Therefore, learn the five sciences in order to attain unsurpassable enlightenment!'

[81] DGONGSRGYAN:3a-4a

[82] Here Mi pham is merely imitating Śāntideva's 'excuse'.

Furthermore, the great regent, Ajita[83], said:

> 'Without manifesting diligence in [learning] the five sciences, even the most exalted one would not have attained omniscience. Therefore, in order to refute [opponents], to safeguard [believers] and to know the essential nature [of all there is], diligence must be applied.'

And Sa [skya] paṇḍita said:

> 'If you don't refine your intelligence in the five sciences,
> omniscience will be far away, like the boundaries of the sky.
> Thus have thought the Conquerors and their sons[84],
> and properly said that all sciences should be learned.'

Hence, all these [authoritative] quotations teach the main cause of omniscience of all aspects, the basis for the welfare of both oneself and others, the origins of all good, both ephemere and lasting. The reason why beings partake of suffering in this ocean of *saṃsāra* is ignorance which is dreaful even to be looked upon / *transitory*. Its antidote is insight wisdom. The means for broadening that wisdom are the outer and inner / *Buddhist and non-Buddhist* sciences, as many as they are. Even the Beatified Ones, since they are skillfull in means and supremely benevolent, they have taught it, by direct or derived teaching, as a means to defeat ignorance."

[83]This is Maitreya, the buddha of the coming age. He is called 'regent' since he took the Buddha's place in the *Tuṣita*-heaven when the Buddha departed to the human realm. He, Maitreya, is also thought to have appeared in a vision to Asaṅga, an early Indian *mahāyāna* master, and delivered five scriptures, commonly known in Tibet as the *Byams chos sde lnga*.

[84]I.e. the *buddhas* and *bodhisattvas*.

We have already seen the vehemence with which the Fifth Dalai lama defended logic as a conventional science capable of being a method for reaching buddha-hood. Nevertheless, he claims that poetry (or rather poetic expression) should be learned first and foremost. I interpret this passage as another covert attack against the *Bka' brgyud pa*, for it was their tradition in which the expression of esoteric teachings in 'folk songs' was in vogue.[85]

> *de yang tha snyad rig pa lnga'i nang nas thog mar gang la slob ce na | Zur mkhar Blo gros Rgyal pos |*
>
> *rgyal po lang tshos dregs gyur kyang | rgyan med pa na skye bos gleng | de bzhin snyan ngag mi ldan pa'i | bstan bcos mkhas la rtsis su med ||*
>
> *ces pa ltar | tshig sbyor phun sum tshogs pa'i snyan ngag dang mi ldan pa'i grong tshig tsam la brten nas don bzang po yod par rlom pa ni | lus kyi lang tsho rgyas pa'i skyes bu zhig rgyan gos dang 'brel te gcer bur rgyu ba na 'jig rten na 'phya smod byed pa ltar | tshig rnam par *mi nyams pa'i [em. : nyams pa'i] bstan bstan bcos la mkhas pa rnams kyis brnyas par mdzad pas na |* [...][86]

> "Then, which of the sciences dealing with conventional terms should be learnt first? Zur mkhar Blo gros Rgyal po[87] had said:
>
> 'If a king, even if boasting of youth, is unadorned,
> people will speak badly of him.
> In the same way, one, who does not know poetry,[88]

[85]Their tradition imitates the *dohās* of the Indian *mahāsiddhas*. The greatest cultivator of the genre was thought to have been Milarepa (Mi la ras pa).

[86]DGYESGLU:13.

[87]An earlier commentator of the KĀ.

[88]I.e. *alaṅkāraśāstra*, the 'ornamentation of words'

> will not be counted among those versed in *śāstra*."
>
> Therefore, someone who assumes that colloquial expressions, lacking any poetical [quality], i.e. the perfect application of composition, are agreeable—[is like someone] strolling around without jewelry and clothes, i.e. naked, whom people will invariably ridicule and denigrate. He will be likewise be condemned by the scholars versed in undeteriorated *śāstra*."

The mastery of poetical expression is not an exigence only in the later career of the *bodhisattva* scholar, when he is required to teach and compose works. The historian Dpa' bo claims that even in understanding some passages from the scripture, poetics is a must.

> *mdo'i tshigs bcad rnams la snyan ngag gi rgyan shin tu legs pa dpag dka' ba dang sgrig pa la ma ltos pa'i sdeb sbyor sbyor yod pa dang | re re'ang ming gi mngon brjod du mas brjod par mdzad pa [...]*[89]

> "Even among verses in the *sūtras* there are verses with beautiful poetic ornamentations which are difficult to fathom, which do not pay attention to common [linguistic] arrangements, and whose expression is filled with different synonyms."

Another aspect of the *bodhisattva*-argument lies in citing scripture, biographical passages about the last and previous lives of the Buddha where poetry played some role or another. In *mahāyāna* thinking, the spiritual path of a buddhist is essentially an imitation of the Buddha himself. Therefore, everything he has done is to be viewed as a veritable model. The biographical parts of the scripture (the *Vinaya* being quoted most often) present young Siddhārtha's education that consisted in mastering the 64 arts (*kalā, sgyu rtsal*) or the 18 sciences (*vidyāsthāna, rig gnas*). Metrical science and / or poetry are present in these lists, which were condensed into the five-plus-five model mentioned above.

[89] MKHASSTON:854

There are also several legends involving poetry. One has already been reproduced above, where the Buddha was an elephant in a previous life and a *brāhmaṇa* praised him, thus accumulating great merit. In another legend it is said that the Buddha himself praised an earlier buddha (by the name of Tiṣya, Skar rgyal) with a hymn for seven entire days while ritually circumambulating him. In this way he achieved the full accomplishment of the 'perfection of endurance' (*vīryapāramitā*), a prerequisite for the path towards enlightenment.[90] Of course, these poems have nothing in common with *kāvya* as such, yet it is interesting that Tibetans found it as a justification for the accomodation of poetry in their own country, to the buddhist dogma, and for themselves.

[90]Cf. the *Chos 'byung* of *Bu ston Rin chen grub*, p. 62. (Derge ed.) probably reffering to ABHIDHARMAKOŚAKĀRIKĀ IV:112 and BHĀṢYA *ad loc.cit.* where the verse is reproduced and the Buddha is said to have recited the verse for seven days standing on one foot.

Glossary

alaṃkāraśāstra — ('treatise on ornaments') Poetic treatises dealing with all the rules that make a work achieve a belletristic level. Usually two schools are distinguished, the earlier '*alaṃkāra*-school' and the later '*dhvani*-school'. Daṇḍin was a chief exponent of the former. A classical *alaṃkāraśāstra* usually defines different styles of poetry (*mārga, rīti*), the shortcomings (*doṣa*) and excellencies (*guṇa*) of different aspects of poetical expression, figures of speech (*alaṃkāra*), etc. The definitions are followed by illustrating verses (which are usually the writer's own).

ālaṃkārika — one who composes an *alaṃkāraśāstra*.

Bka' brgyud pa — 'The Oral-precept Lineage' founded by Mar pa Chos kyi blo gros (1012–1097), which later forked into numerous sister orders founded by the disciples of Sgam po pa (1079 – 1153): *Dwags po Bka' brgyud*, *Shangs pa Bka' brgyud*, *Karma Bka' brgyud*, *'Brug pa Bka' brgyud*, etc. The main focus of this order was mystical meditation on topics revealed both orally and written by Indian siddha type yogins (Tilopa, Nāropa, Saraha, etc.). The crux of *Bka' brgyud* practice is the *mahāmudrā* (tib. *phyag rgya chen po*), a mystical state of buddha-hood, beyond the grasp of discursive thought and descriptions by 'conventional terms' (*vyavahāra, tha snyad*). They gained considerable political influence in the 14–15th centuries and thus presented a problem for the rising *Dge lugs pa* order.

bodhisattva — (tib. *byang chub sems dpa'*). The ideal person of *mahāyāna* Buddhism, who relentlessly works for the welfare of sentient beings and is a candidate to complete buddha-hood. It is also a designation for the historical Buddha, during his life before enlightenment.

'Brug pa — v. *Bka' brgyud pa*.

Daṇḍin — the author of the KĀ. He may be tentatively placed in 7–8th-century Kāñcipuram, Southern India. He was a Hindu, probably a śaivite. His work draws on earlier *alaṃkāraśāstras* (in both Sanskrit and Pāli).

Dbyangs can dgyes pa'i glu dbyangs — v. *Fifth Dalai lama.*

Dbyangs can ngag gi rol mtsho — v. *Khams sprul Bstan 'dzin chos kyi nyi ma.*

Dbyangs can mgur rgyan — v. *Dpang lo.*

Dge lugs pa — 'The Order of Virtuous Conduct'. Up to this day the most influential order in Tibetan Buddhism. Founded by Tsong kha pa (at the turn of the 14–15th c.), it later produced the Dalai lamas and from the middle of the 17th century it exerted complete religious and secular supremacy over Tibet. Its doctrines stress the celibacy and perfect discipline of monks, the thorough study of logic as a prerequisite for actual fruitful practice, and the gradual path to enlightenment.

Dharmakīrti – v. *Pramāṇavārttika.*

Dpa' bo [Gtsug lag 'Phreng ba] — *Bka' brgyud pa* historian (16th c.). His most famous work is the *Mkhas pa'i dga' ston* ('The Feast of the Wise'), a monumental, multi-volume, comprehensive chronicle of the Buddhist doctrine, its spread in Tibet and further related topics. Portions of the work had been banned by the Fifth Dalai lama one century after it had been written.

Dpang lo [Blo gros Brtan pa] — (13–14th c.) An eminent translator, scholar of Sanskrit. He revised the *Shong ston* translation of the KĀ and wrote a commentary to it with the title *Dbyangs can mgur rgyan* ('An Ornament to Sarasvatī's Songs').

Dwags po — v. *Bka' brgyud pa.*

Fifth Dalai lama [Ngag dbang Blo bzang Rgya mstho] — (1617 – 1682) Also known as 'the Great Fifth', the most prominent of the Dalai lamas. During his time, spiritual and political power over Tibet merged in one hand. Also a prolific writer on a variety of subjects. He wrote his commentary to the KĀ, the *Dbyangs can dgyes pa'i glu dbyangs* in 1656.

Gtsang pa Rgya ras pa — (1161–1211). Early master in the *Bka' brgyud pa* lineage, also known as Ye shes Rdo rje, founder of *'Brug* ('Dragon') monastery after which *'Brug pa Bka' brgyud* got its name.

kāvya — **1.** poetry itself, i.e. all those works that conform to artistic and literary norms; **2.** an individual poem. It is written entirely in verse, entirely in prose, or alternates between prose and verse. In the West *kāvya* was rendered as 'ornate poetry', 'Kunstdichtung', or 'classical poetry', where classical does not refer to any definite period but to that poetry which corresponds closely to the poetic canon and the norms and ideals of *alaṃkāraśāstra.*

Kāvyādarśa — (KĀ) 'The Mirror of Poetry', (original title: *Kāvyalakṣaṇa*, 'The Definitions of Poetry') the work of Daṇḍin, one of the earliest Sanskrit *alaṃkāraśāstras* that survived up to this day. The work exerted a remarkable influence in India and in later times it was used as a basic textbook for students of poetry. It was the only work of *alaṃkāraśāstra* that was translated into Tibetan in the second half of the 13th c. by Shong ston Rdo rje rgyal mtshan and the Indian *paṇḍita*, Lakṣmīkara. Excerpts from the work had already been translated in the first half of the 13th c. by Sa skya paṇḍita. The complete translation was later revised twice (first by Dpang lo Blo gros brtan pa on the basis of an original ms. and Ratnaśrī's commentary; then by Zha lu lo tsā ba Chos skyong bzang po (1444–1529)).

Khams sprul [Bstan 'dzin chos kyi nyi ma] — also known as Sgra dbyangs zla ba bdud rtsi'i lang tsho, was born in 1730 A.D. At the age of four (1733 A.D.) he was recognized as the incarnation of the *'Brug pa Bka' brgyud* abbot of the *Kha stag dkar mo* monastery in *Khams* (South-eastern Tibet). Having studied the KĀ, the grammar of Candragomin, metrics and other common sciences, from the age of twenty five (1754 A.D.) he composed the greatest Tibetan commentary on the KĀ with the title *Dbyangs can ngag gi rol mtsho* ('The Ocean of Sarasvatī's songs'). He passed away in 1779.

Mañjuśrī — (tib. *'Jam dpal*) the Buddhist deity of both conventional and transcendental wisdom, patron of the arts. Other names: Mañjughoṣa (tib. 'Jam dbyangs), etc.

Mkhas pa la 'jug pa'i sgo — v. *Sa skya paṇḍita.*

Pramāṇavārttika — (tib. *Tshad ma rnam 'grel*) 'The Commentary on the Basic Verses of Epistemology', the work of *Dharmakīrti* (7th c.). Arguably the greatest work of Buddhist epistemology and logic, it is certainly the most influential, most widely known and commentated by Tibetan literati. Translated in the 13th c. by Sa skya paṇḍita and later revised.

Ratnaśrī[jñāna] — (9–10th c.) author of the earliest surviving Sanskrit commentary on the KĀ. He was a Buddhist (of Śrī Lankā), yet the spirit of his work reflects a general Indian learning rather than a specifically Buddhist one. The work circulated and was used in Tibet in a palm leaf ms. form, but has never been completely translated. Two manuscripts of the work survive: 1) the basis of the Darbhanga ed. (v. Bibliography) and 2) an incomplete ms. in Kathmandu.

Sa skya pa — 'The Order of the Gray-land' founded in 1073 by Dkon mchog rgyal po of the powerful *'Khon* family. The most influential order both politically and spiritually in the period of the Mongol supremacy (1241–1348). Besides its mystical doctrines (the cult of Hevajra; the *Lam 'bras* 'The path and the fruit', etc.), the order was a great propagator of classical Indian learning, much in the spirit of the great Indian Buddhist college monasteries of Nālandā, Vikramaśīla, etc. The translation and study of *kāvya* began in the folds of this order from the 13th c. onwards.

Sa skya paṇḍita [Kun dga' rgyal mtshan] — (1182–1251). The greatest figure of the *Sa skya pa* order: translator, scholar, politician and a prolific author on both religious and secular themes.

The most important works of the latter cathegory are: 1) *Mkhas pa la 'jug pa'i sgo* ('The Gateway of Scholars'), which contains the earliest translated excerpts of the KĀ; 2) *Legs bshad rin po che'i gter mdzod* ('A Jewel-mine of Eloquent Sayings'), a collection of adapted verses written in the *kāvya* style; 3) *Tshad ma rigs gter* ('A Treasury of Logic'), a most influential work in the footsteps of *Dharmakīrti*; 4) *Rol mo'i bstan bcos* ('A Treatise on Music'); 5) *Sdeb sbyor sna tshogs me tog gi chun po* ('A Bouquet of a Variety of Meters'), a treatise on prosody; 6) *Tshig gi gter* ('A Treasury of Words') a book of synonyms modelled on the *Amarakośa*, etc.

Sarasvatī — (tib. *Dbyangs can[ma]*) the Hindu and Buddhist goddess of eloquence of speech, patroness of the arts.

Shong ston [Rdo rje rgyal mtshan] — An eminent translator of the 13th c. and one of the greatest Tibetan scholars of Sanskrit. His translations include the KĀ, the *Amarakośa*[91], Jñānaśrīmitra's metrical *tour de force*, the *Vṛttamālāstuti*, the *Avadānakalpalatā* of Kṣemendra, the *Nāgānandanāṭaka* of king Harṣa, the *Kālacakra-tantra*, etc. He is also the author of the earliest Tibetan commentary on the KĀ. (cf. KAPSTEIN 2003:782; ROERICH 1953:784-785)

Tsong kha pa — (1357–1419) many a times styled as the 'Tibetan Luther'. The reformer of the *Bka' gdams pa* order (founded by Atiśa and 'Brom ston, 11th c.), which after him became known as the *Dge lugs pa.* An extremely prolific and most influential author. One of his disciples was later acknowledged as the first Dalai lama. The order gained exlusive religious and political power over Tibet during the Fifth Dalai lama and maintained it up to 1959.

Vinaya — (tib. *'Dul ba*) 'Discipline'. One of the three parts of the Buddhist Canon (*Tripiṭaka*). The Buddha's teachings showing ethics, the discipline and moral conduct that is the foundation for all Buddhist practice, both for lay and ordained people. There were many recensions of this collection of texts, the Tibetan

[91]Kapstein's assertion. The edition I have consulted (the Peking Bstan 'gyur) has Kīrticandra and Grags pa rgyal mtshan as the translators.

Vinaya is a translation of the *mūlasarvāstivādin* order's scripture. Among the teachings about moral conduct, there are many historical and legendary accounts of the Buddha's life.

Bibliography

Primary sources cited and consulted

ABHIDHARMAKOŚAKĀRIKĀ – P. PRADHAN (ED.), *Abhidharm[a] Koshabhāṣya of Vasubandhu*, Tibetan Sanskrit Works Series vol. VIII., K.P. Jayaswal Research Institute, Patna, 1967.

BODHICARYĀVATĀRA – P. L. VAIDYA & SRIDHAR TRIPATHI (EDS.), *Bodhicaryāvatāra of Śāntideva with the Commentary Pañjikā of Prajñākaramati*, Buddhist Sanskrit Texts 12, The Mithila Institute of Post graduate Studies and Research in Sanskrit Learning, Darbhanga, 1988.

BSHADSGRUB – BSHAD SGRUB, *Snyan ngag Mngon brjod Brda gsar rnying gi rnam bzhag mdor bsdus Blo gsal yid 'phrog*, Mongolian block-print ff.12., private collection.[92]

DBYANGSROL – KHAMS SPRUL BSTAN 'DZIN CHOS KYI NYI MA, *Rgyan gyi bstan bcos Dbyangs can ngag gi rol mtsho*, Bod ljongs mi dmangs dpe skrun khang, Shin hwa, 1986.[93]

DGONGSRGYAN – BOD MKHAS PA MI PHAM DGE LEGS RNAM RGYAL, *Snyan ngag gi bstan bcos chen po Me long la 'jug pa'i bshad sbyar Daṇḍi'i dgongs rgyan*, Mongolian block-print ff. 193 kept in MTA Keleti Gyűjtemény [Hungarian Academy of Sciences, Oriental Collection] prov. Tib. 143.[94]

DPERBRJOD – *Snyan ngag le'u gnyis pa'i dper brjod phyogs bsgrigs*, Delhi, 1996.

[92] I thank Prof. József Terjék for presenting me with this text.
[93] I thank *rabjampa* Karmadorje for placing his copy at my disposal.
[94] I thank Gergely Orosz for placing this text at my disposal.

KĀ (B) – OTTO BÖHTLINGK, *Daṇḍin's Poetik (Kāvyādarça) - Sanskrit und Deutsch*, Verlag von H. Haessel, Leipzig, 1890.

KĀ (D) – PROF. YOGEŚVARADATTAŚARMĀ (ED.), *Ācāry Daṇḍī Kāvyādarś (anek ṭīkāoṃ sahit)*, 4 vols., Delhi, 1999.

KĀ (M) – *Kavyadarsa by Shrimadacarya Dandi Mahakavi and Commentary by Jeevananda Vidyasagara Bhattacarya with Introduction and Notes in English by Narayana Ayer*, V. Ramaswamy Sastrulu & Sons, Madras, 1964.

KĀ (P) – S. K. BELVALKAR, *Kāvyādarśa of Daṇḍin – Sanskrit Text and English Translation*, Oriental Book Agency, Poona, 1924.

KĀ (TPT) – DBYUG PA CAN, *Snyan dngags kyi me long* in D. SUZUKI (ED.), *Tibetan Tripitaka [Peking Bstan 'gyur]* no. 4301, vol. Śe 127b-158a (pp. 183-195.)

KĀ (V) – ACARYA RANCHANDRA MISHRA (ED.), *Kāvyādarśa of Mahākavi Daṇḍī edited with 'Prakasha' Sanskrit & Hindi Commentaries*, Chowkhamba Vidyabhawan, Varanasi, 1996.

MKHAS'JUG – SA SKYA PAṆḌITA KUN DGA' RGYAL MTSHAN, *Mkhas pa rnams la 'jug pa'i sgo*, in *Sa skya bka' 'bum*, Toyo Bunko, Tokyo, 1968. vol.4. pp. 81-94.

MKHASSTON – DPA' BO GTSUG LAG 'PHRENG BA, *Mkhas pa'i dga' ston aka Lho brag chos 'byung*, vol. Tsa [11] in LOKESH CANDRA (ED.), *Śatapiṭaka Series* 4 vols., Delhi, 1962.

RATNAŚRĪ – A. THAKUR & U. JHA (ED.), *Kavyalakṣaṇa of Daṇḍin (Also known as Kāvyādarśa) with Commentary called Ratnaśrī of Ratnaśrījñāna*, Darbhanga, 1957.[95]

RNAMBSHAD – RDO RJE RGYAL PO, *Snyan ngag gi rnam*

[95] I thank Dr. Csaba Dezső and Gergely Hidas for procuring a copy of this edition.

bshad Gsal sgron, Mi rigs dpe skrun khang, Pe cin, 1983.

ROLBSTAN – SA SKYA PAṆḌITA KUN DGA' RGYAL MTSHAN, *Rol mo'i bstan bcos*, in *Sa skya bka' 'bum*, Toyo Bunko, Tokyo, 1968. vol.4. pp. 77-80.

DGYESGLU – KHENPO THUPTEN TSHONDU (ED.), *Dbyan[g]s can dgyes glu, The Commentary of Kāvyādarsha by the Fifth Dalai Lama*, Varanasi, 1966.[96]

Secondary sources cited and consulted

DIMITROV 2002 – DRAGOMIR DIMITROV, *Mārgavibhāga, Die Unterscheidung der Stilarten – Kritische Ausgabe des ersten Kapitels von Daṇḍins Poetik Kāvyādarśa und der tibetischen Übertragung Sñan ṅag me loṅ nebst einer deutschen Übersetzung des Sanskrittextes*, Indica et Tibetica 40, Marburg 2002.

KAPSTEIN 2003 – MATTHEW T. KAPSTEIN "The Indian Literary Identity in Tibet" in: SHELDON POLLOCK (ED.), *Literary Cultures in History - Reconstructions from South Asia*, University of California Press, 2003.

LIENHARD 1984 – SIEGFRIED LIENHARD, *A History of Classical Poetry Sanskrit - Pali - Prakrit*, Otto Harrasowitz, Wiesbaden, 1984. as vol. III. in JAN GONDA (ED.), *A History of Indian Literature*, idem.

GEROW 1971 – EDWIN GEROW, *A Glossary of Indian Figures of Speech*, Mouton & Co., the Hague, 1971.

GUPTA 1970 – DHARMENDRA KUMAR GUPTA, *A Critical study of Daṇḍin and His Works*, Meharchand Lachhmandas, Delhi, 1970.

ROERICH 1953 – G. N. ROERICH, *The Blue Annals*, Part Two, Royal Asiatic Society of Bengal. Monograph Series. Vol. VII., Cal-

[96] I thank Prof. Géza Bethlenfalvy for placing his copy at my disposal.

cutta, 1953.

SHASTRI 1993 – LOSANG NORBU SHASTRI "Salient Features of Sanskrit Texts Written in Tibet", in K.N. MISHRA (ED.), *Aspects of Buddhist Sanskrit: The Proceedings of the International Symposium on the Language of the Sanskrit Buddhist Texts (Oct. 1-5, 1991)*, CIHTS, Sarnath, 1993.

TUCCI 1947 - GIUSEPPE TUCCI, *Tibetan Painted Scrolls*, vol. I., Rome, 1949.

Eight

Exploring the Transmission of the *Kavitāvalī* of Tulsīdās: A Statistical Analysis of Manuscript Relationships

Dániel Balogh*

The *Kavitāvalī* and its recensions

Tulsīdās and his *Kavitāvalī*

Tulsīdās is known and renowned throughout India and scholarly circles as the author of the *Rāmcaritmānas*, a transcreation of the *Rāmāyaṇa* in the vernacular *Avadhī* language. He was probably born in 1532 CE, and died in 1623 (McGregor 1984). Ten further works beside the *Mānas* may be ascribed to him with certainty, including the *Kavitāvalī* ('String of Poems'), the subject of

*This publication was supported by the Hungarian Research Fund (OTKA, project no. T 038047).

this paper. Also called the *Kabitt Rāmāyaṇ* ('Rāmāyaṇa in Quatrains'), this work is a compilation of verses in *Brajbhāṣā*, written in literary quatrains or *kabitts*. The *kabitt* was a prevalent form of court poetry and was more frequently committed to writing than passed on orally like popular songs or *padas*.

Over half of the poems collected in the *Kavitāvalī* are vignettes with topics chosen seemingly at random from the *Rāmāyaṇa* story. Possibly the episodes depicted here were ones that Tulsīdās was particularly fond of, or ones that his personal experience gained since the composition of the *Rāmcaritmānas* allowed to write with more intense inspiration. He may also have given more space to themes that could be rendered more effectively in the metres used in the *Kavitāvalī*.

Apart from poems painting pictures of the Rāma theme, the *Kavitāvalī* includes a large number of miscellaneous quatrains bundled in the *Uttarakāṇḍa* after the final Rāma poems. These additions are responsible for the disproportionate bulk of the last chapter, which accounts for more than half of the entire opus. There is also a collection of verses called the *Hanumān-bāhuk*, appended at the end of the *Uttarakāṇḍa* in a number of manuscripts. Most of this is addressed to Hanumān in hopes that he will aid the poet in his old age and sickness.

The *Kavitāvalī* Critical Edition project

Despite (or perhaps partly due to) the fact that the *Kavitāvalī* has been immensely popular for a long time, there have been very few attempts to deal critically with the text. Dr. Imre BANGHA (2003) has gathered references from various catalogues to about 60 extant manuscripts (which must be but a small portion of the total number written) and about 120 printed editions, the first one published in 1815 CE. Presently, the most accepted edition is the *Tulsī Granthāvalī* (ŚUKLA, et al, 1923), while the most widely used is the 'penny paperback' Gita Press edition (INDRADEVNĀRĀYAṆ 1937) based on the former. However, the *Granthāvalī* is not a critical edition: the publishers chose variant readings arbitrarily and did not indicate the sources for the text they adopted.

A small group of Indologists in Budapest has started to work on a critical edition of the *Kavitāvalī*. The project is headed and coordinated by Dr. Imre Bangha, who, after an intensive search of various catalogues, visited all the sites where manuscripts of the *Kavitāvalī* are purportedly preserved. Using the copied manuscripts, we have started preparing a critical apparatus. Although MSS older than two hundred years were hardly found, the collection has resulted in a profusion of more recent manuscripts. Most of these included a large amount of scribal errors and orthographical peculiarities, but few substantial variations of the text itself. We have agreed that the number of recent manuscripts used for the critical edition should be reduced, while doing our best to preserve MSS that do indeed differ essentially from one another.

Clustering the manuscripts on the basis of structure

Analysing the structural differences of the MSS, such as verse order and the inclusion or omission of specific quatrains, Dr. Bangha was able to separate two core recensions of the *Kavitāvalī* very clearly, with several sub-groups that are less obviously delineated (probably due to the fact that many copiers of the work had collated more than one manuscript or used originals that had marginalia based on a different MS). Here follows a brief summary of his results relevant to this paper.

On the basis of structural indicators, the available manuscripts group clearly into either of two recensions, called the *short recension* (**S**) with 288 to 290 quatrains, and the *long recension* (**L**) with 380 or 382 verses. Manuscripts belonging to the latter include the *Hanumān-bāhuk*, have numerous more quatrains appended to the end of the *Uttarakāṇḍa*, and insert a few more verses in other locations.

The basic recensions, which have probably led largely separate existences for a significant length of time, may be divided into further, smaller groups, with the short recension consisting of two parts (labelled S1 and S2), one of these parts splitting into two again (S21 and S22), and one of these yet again (S221 and S222). Likewise, the long recension may be divided into L1 and L2, the latter into L21 and L22, and the latter again into L221 and L222. (As a matter of fact, a few more sub-groups have been distinguished by Dr. Bangha; however, as these include only printed editions of the *Kavitāvalī* or MSS not used in the present study, they are not detailed herein.)

The 24 MSS involved in this study are listed below with indication of their cluster membership. Note that due to the ambiguity of the categorisation on the basis of structure, several manuscripts are included in more than one (non-nested) categories. When a MS is present in more than one category, its name is italicised when listed in a category of several different lineages, but not marked as far as its allocation is unambiguous (e.g. Sitapur1 is italicised in categories L21 and L22, as it may belong to either; but it is not in italics under the general list of L2 manuscripts, where it definitely belongs).

L : Bharatpur1, Bharatpur3, Bikaner, Jaipur4, Jaipur6, Jaipur7, Jodhpur1, Prayag1, Sitapur1, Udaipur1, Udaipur2, Uniyara, Vrindaban2

- **L1** : Bharatpur1, Bikaner, Jaipur4, Jaipur7, *Jodhpur1*, *Udaipur1*, Udaipur2, Uniyara, Vrindaban2
- **L2** : Bharatpur3, Jaipur6, *Jodhpur1*, Prayag1, Sitapur1, *Udaipur1*
  - **L21** : *Jodhpur1*, *Sitapur1*
  - **L22** : Bharatpur3, Jaipur6, *Jodhpur1*, Prayag1, *Sitapur1*, *Udaipur1*
    - **L221** : Bharatpur3, Jaipur6, *Sitapur1*
    - **L222** : *Jodhpur1*, Prayag1, *Udaipur1*

S : Alvar, Bharatpur2, Dhaka, Harvard, Jaipur5, Patna1, Patna2, Patna3, Prayag2, Sitapur2, Tijara

- **S1** : Bharatpur2, Patna1, *Patna2*, Patna3
- **S2** : Alvar, Dhaka, Harvard, Jaipur5, *Patna2*, Prayag2, Sitapur2, Tijara
  - **S21** : Dhaka, Jaipur5, *Patna2*
  - **S22** : Alvar, Harvard, Prayag2, Sitapur2, Tijara
    - **S221** : Harvard, Prayag2, Sitapur2
    - **S222** : Alvar, Tijara

The figure (Figure 8.1) below shows the same information set up similar to a dendrogram, the main output of the statistical procedure used in the study.[1]

A possible origin of the recensions

The question arises: why do the manuscripts split so clearly into two groups, namely the short and the long recension? The L recension has 22 further poems attached after the point where the S recension ends, followed by yet more verses of the *Hanumān-bāhuk*. The authenticity of these additional quatrains cannot be questioned. Looking at their contents, we find a large number of powerful references to the poet's disease, which suggests that these might well be his very last works. It can therefore be assumed that the short recension is an earlier redaction of the *Kavitāvalī*, prepared before the old-age illness of Tulsīdās, while the long recension was in all likelihood edited very near to or after the end of his life.

However, apart from the additional poems attached to the end, the L recension also has some twenty further quatrains inserted at various parts of the opus, more than half of which are not included in the published editions. BANGHA (2003) postulates that two opposing tendencies in the preservation and transmission of the text have been at work here, each dominating over the other in one of the recensions.

One, labelled the 'collector tendency' is to enrich the corpus with all verses that can be ascribed to the author. Mainly a feature of oral transmission, the collector tendency can be seen to work in the copying of manuscripts as well, resulting in the inclusion of more and more verses, some of which are not authentic. The other trend, termed the 'purist tendency' strives to purge the text

[1]Note that this graph is *not* a dendrogram in the sense the term is used below in the statistical section. It is merely a plot of the structural grouping of the MSS described above, drawn to resemble a dendrogram to facilitate comparison. However, this graph does not illustrate the relative proximity of any MS or cluster to another MS or cluster joins higher up the tree; it only shows which MSS *do* join. Nor is this graph a historical stemma of the manuscripts, though it might be quite similar to the actual genealogy. Dates are given in the Common Era. Italicised MS names are those that occur in more than one category.

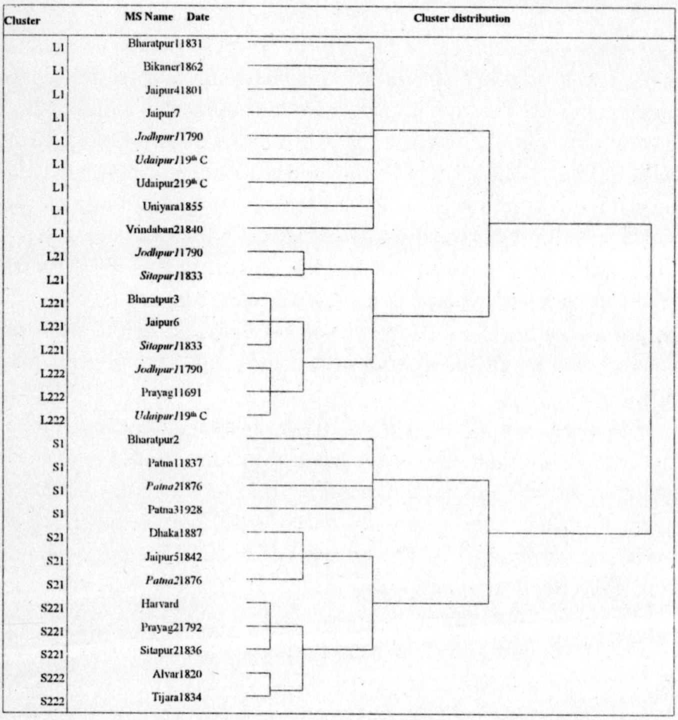

Figure 8.1: Tree graph of MSS classified on the basis of structure

of all verses that are suspected of having been written by someone else, are metrically or aesthetically weak, or ideologically not quite appropriate to the image of the poet as a saint. The poems that are included in the long recension but omitted from the short are quite diverse, but most of them satisfy one or another of the above examples of imperfection that a purist redactor would want to eliminate.

Of course, the collector tendency will have continued to work after the edition of the shorter recension, and the two versions of the text were not isolated from one another, as several transcribers seem to have used an original MS from both recensions. This resulted in occasional purging of the long recension on one hand, and the re-entry of excised verses in the short recension on the other. However, the basic structure and the number of poems in each of the recensions was probably established rather early in the transmission process.

Methodology

Basic statistical concepts

The following outlines are definitely not intended to comprise an introductory course to statistics. Rather, they have been written with the aim of giving lay readers—without encumbering them with mathematical details—just enough knowledge of statistical concepts to be able to size up the workings and advantages of the procedure used here, and simultaneously, to be aware of its limitations.

Hearing the word 'statistics', the student of humanities tends to think of huge tables of numbers, bar or pie charts, averages, and counts of the occurrence of some phenomenon. Such summaries of data serve to describe whatever is being investigated in a readily comprehensible form, bringing to the reader's notice various proportions, frequencies and typical measurements. However, the discipline of mathematical statistics goes far beyond what professionals call *descriptive statistics*.

In statistical terminology, the pool of potential subjects is referred to as a *population*. In some cases, a population to be scrutinised may be small enough to examine all its members; however, most of the time one faces dauntingly large or potentially infinite populations. Therefore the scientist needs to select some entities from that population to measure or test, and extrapolate from the results thus obtained to the population at large. *Inferential statistics* are the tool that allows us to do so. The collection of specimens that we actually measure are referred to as a *sample.* Provided that a sample is chosen in a random manner from a population, it can be regarded as *representative* of that population, i.e. a suitable basis for making inferences.

When measuring a sample for a certain characteristic, it is highly unlikely that the variable representing that characteristic have the same value for all the individuals measured. Rather, a *frequency distribution* of some form will be found, i.e. there will be a certain number of individuals with one value of the variable, and a more or less different number of individuals with many other values. The frequency distribution of most real-life variables—when measured on a large enough sample—tends to follow a bell-shaped curve, i.e. the highest number of individuals will be found with values near the average for that characteristic, and fewer and fewer individuals will have more extreme values in either direction. Many statistical procedures presuppose such a *normal distribution* of the variables.

Once it has been established that the distribution of a variable is reasonably close to the normal distribution, the next thing we want to know is how spread-out that curve is. That is to say, once we know the mean value expected as most likely in the population the sample was taken from, we would also like to know the likelihood of finding that value, or of finding any specific other value or interval of values. This is expressed in the related mathematical indicators named *variance* and *standard deviation* is more often used. A higher variance means that the different values are more dispersed along the continuum of the variable, and only the far extremes are truly rare; a low variance means that values congregate strongly around the expected value. Provided that a variable is normally distributed, there is an exactly calculable probability associated with any value, on the basis of its distance from the mean in units of standard deviation. An important statistical testing procedure called *analysis of variance* (ANOVA) is based on a comparison of the mean and standard deviation to determine whether there is a significant difference between two samples, i.e. whether the two samples were drawn from identical populations with respect to the variable examined.

Multivariate statistical analysis is an extension of descriptive and inferential statistical methods to data arrays consisting of multiple elementary responses across several observational units (MONGE & CAPPELLA 1980, Introduction). Much of the battery of multivariate statistics consists of the extension of univariate hypothesis testing procedures to allow a scientist to analyse the action of one or more factors on one or more sets of subjects.

The sheer number of variables used in some fields of research is so large, that prior to setting up any hypotheses and testing these, one often needs to explore the data at hand and look for any patterns in them. The various methods of *exploratory statistics* are computationally very intensive and were little in vogue in the not-so-distant past. However, the boom of computer development has resulted in desktop and laptop machines capable of performing in a matter of split-seconds calculations that would have taken a mathematician months or years without their aid.

Therefore, complex techniques such *cluster analysis*, the method used in this paper, are now at the fingertips of practically anyone who cares to use them. These procedures can now be used without understanding the profound mathematical concepts that underlie them. On the one hand, this is a definite advantage, since a scholar of the humanities usually would not dedicate the amount of time needed to grasp these thoroughly and may nevertheless want to make use of statistical procedures. On the other hand though, a general understanding of mathematics and some command of statistical terminology is necessary in order to be aware of the potentials and the limitations of such methods. Caution must be exercised especially before drawing conclusions of a generalised nature from the statistical study, and consultation with a professional statistician is important.

Generally, the data used for multivariate analyses are arranged in a two-dimensional table called a *case-by-variable matrix*. The rows of such a table represent individual observations or cases (in our case, manuscripts), while the columns are each a variable studied in the analysis (in our case, similarity to a specific variant reading at a specific locus of text).

Cluster analysis

It is a natural tendency of the human mind to categorise the entities it perceives. An important aspect of categorisation is the nesting and interlinking of categories—biological taxonomy is a good example of a sophisticated artificial system following this intuitive scheme. Many things and phenomena of nature plainly lend themselves to this sort of nested, or hierarchical categorisation. Therefore, common sense dictates that it might also be a useful tool in dealing with entities whose characteristics are far less easy to perceive than those of animals. When facing a large sheet of data however, we cannot fit the abstract entities represented by the data into categories at a glance. We need some sort of mathematical apparatus to assess all the aspects of these entities, and decide which ones resemble one another most closely when considering all the aspects.

Cluster analysis, or simply clustering, seeks to group or to lump together objects or variables that share some observed qualities or, alternatively, to partition or to divide a set of objects and variables into mutually exclusive classes whose boundaries reflect differences in the observed qualities of their members. Clustering thus extracts typologies from data which in turn represent a reduction of data complexity and may lead to conceptual simplifications (KRIPPENDORF 1980). Most of the traditional cluster analytical procedures fall into one of two major groups called *hierarchical* and *non-hierarchical cluster analysis.*

Non-hierarchical cluster analysis comprises methods to distribute a set (X) of entities into a fixed number (usually denoted by k) of clusters. The objective of the method is to find a partition of X into k classes, i.e. clusters, in such a way that objects lying within the same clusters are more mutually similar and compact than those lying in different clusters (KŘIVÁNEK 1991).

However, in many cases – such as in the problem of the present paper – one does not have a preconception of how many clusters the entities should be divided into. One might also be specifically interested in the way the various clusters are nested within other clusters resulting from a division into fewer groups. These are the times when **hierarchical cluster analysis** comes in useful. The objective of hierarchical clustering is to find a sequence of non-hierarchical clusterings that is nested with respect to the partition refinements and includes both extreme partitions (X, and partition of X into singletons) (*Křivánek* 1991). The intermediate levels of the sequence, i.e. divisions into all numbers of clusters from 2 to k, are obtained either by *divisive* or an *agglomerative* algorithm (KRIPPENDORF 1980).

The divisive or partitioning method starts out with the totality of the entities, and through a series of n steps, progressively divides this totality so that each division results in clusters as homogeneous as possible within themselves and as different from the others as possible, until each entity forms a cluster in itself. The agglomerative or merging method progresses the opposite way, starting out with each entity as a singleton, and reaching through successive joining the stage where all of them are combined in one cluster. Again, there are various mathematical methods to achieve the aim of the clustering procedure, namely to produce clusters that are internally as consistent as possible according to a certain criterion, while one cluster is as different from another as possible.

Usually, a geometrical approach is used in optimising this balance of differences. Each entity is conceived of as a point in a virtual space with as many dimensions as the number of variables in the analysis. At the first step, the two closest points are joined. However, at the subsequent stages of agglomeration a new problem arises: what to consider as the distance between two clusters, each of which may consist of several points. The various methods for dealing with this problem allow the researcher to choose one best suited to the shape and distribution of clusters expected from the studied phenomena.

Most of these are geometrical methods involving a measure of multidimensional distance. There are also a number of arithmetic rather than geometric methods, the most common of which is called *Ward's method*, a technique based on analysis of variance that combines clusters on the basis of minimal variance within the resulting cluster. This method is generally regarded to be very effective in isolating clusters of varied shapes and compactness, though according to some sources (e.g. FOSSE 1997) it tends to produce clusters of small and relatively equal size.

The result of hierarchical cluster analysis is most frequently plotted in the form of a *dendrogram*, a tree-like structure whose branches terminate at the objects being clustered. This tree represents at one end (the tips of the branches) every single entity on its own, and at the other (the root) all the entities bundled into one group.

Basically, a dendrogram conveys three important pieces of information. The simplest of these is obtained by viewing the dendrogram as a sequence of non-hierarchical clusters. By drawing a cross-section of the dendrogram at any point between its leaves and its root, we find a certain number of clusters (the horizontal lines cut by the cross-section) and are able to identify the entities belonging to each of those clusters.

The second item of import seen from a dendrogram is the tree structure itself, i.e. the structure and sequence in which the various individuals and smaller clusters unite to form larger clusters.

The third type of information is the relative distance of clusters from each other. Dendrograms produced by various statistical programs indicate this in different manners. The dendrograms published in this paper[2] are scaled to a standard size (width in the horizontal plot), which is the distance between its most dissimilar members. (Thus, the last joining takes place at the right extreme of the graph, and no 'root' is shown.) Each of the individual horizontal lines before a certain joining indicate the distance between the subordinate and superordinate cluster joined at that point, relative to the largest distance in the entire plot.

Variables featured in the analysis

Data were collected for the analysis from a total of 15 verses, i.e. roughly 5% of the 324 verses in the standard *Kavitāvalī* sans *Hanumān-bāhuk*. These text sections have given us 931 variables. Having selected the verses to process into numerical data, we needed to find a way to convert the variant readings of each manuscript into numbers that express the proximity of each reading in any given manuscript to the corresponding reading in the others.

---

[2] All the analyses presented in this paper have been prepared using SPSS Version 10.0.1, access to which was made possible by the courtesy of the Department of Psychology at ELTE University. SPSS stands for *Statistical Package for Social Sciences.* The software is a commercial product of SPSS Inc.

A simple solution to this task would have been to allot one variable to each *locus* that has variant readings in the available MSS, and assign respective numbers to each of the different readings found there. However, the statistical method requires one-dimensional measures of proximity to use as input, and loci with more than two dissimilar variants could not be scored on such a variable (placing the core reading at one end of the scale, and one grossly different from it at the other, there would be no score left to allot to a third reading grossly different from either, the middle section of the scale being reserved to readings intermediate between the first two).

Thus, we had to revise our idea of a variable. Rather than using one variable for each locus with variant readings, we used one variable for each variant reading. That is to say, for each locus we introduced as many variables, as there were variants. Each of these variables would describe whether the reading of the manuscript is identical to or different from the specific reading the variable pertains to.

This method allows for any number of distinct variants per locus, although it does increase the size of data tables substantially. Furthermore, by introducing a middle step to the binary scale (identical vs. distinct) described above, similarity of the variants becomes possible to note without introducing excessive subjectivity to the method.

Notice in the above description that we do not define a locus in terms of length. Although each locus must be at least one whole word, a variation extending over several words can be treated as a single locus at the discretion of the scorer.

Transforming readings into numbers

The input data for the analysis needed to be arranged in a case-by-variable matrix. The columns of this table are the variables, each of which represents a distinct variant for a certain locus of the text. The rows are the 'subjects' of the study—in this case, the manuscripts. Each cell of the table gives the result of the testing of a given manuscript for a given reading: whether the manuscript in question has that reading, one similar to that reading, or one distinct from it.

In reality, though, the boundaries between 'identical', 'similar' and 'distinct' are somewhat fuzzy, owing to the lack of a standard orthography for *brajbhāṣā*. Therefore, I needed to devise guidelines by which to assign a level of similarity to possible variant readings, minimising the bias of the subjectivity of scorers.

While working on the critical edition, we had already developed such a set of rules in order to be able to create a critical apparatus of manageable size: one that does not indicate every single insignificant orthographic variation, yet keeps all those readings that can potentially be interpreted in a different sense. When devising this system, we used stricter rules for older MSS,[3] but allowed more variation to pass unnoticed by the apparatus in case of the more recent MSS. These rules had to be altered to some extent to suit the purposes of statistical analysis.

I deemed that the interrelations of the manuscripts could best be explored on the basis of those variants which are almost *certainly not* due to a certain orthography. Therefore, to cut down the number of data in the analysis and to concentrate on the variants likely to have more weight in differentiating the MSS, I decided to exclude all potentially orthographic variants, including those that might (but not necessarily do) call for a different grammatical or lexical interpretation. Thus, the only readings featured in the analysis as separate variables for a given locus were non-orthographic variants (including all scribal errors and corruptions) that appear in the stem of a word or, though appearing in the word ending, result in an alteration of the number of syllables (including dittography and omission of syllables).

Along each of these variables pertaining to a certain locus, the readings of all MSS were scored as follows:

- **score 0 (radically distinct):** for all readings that certainly differ from the reading concerned on a non-orthographic level, i.e. that have a variable of their own

- **score 1 (similar):** all readings that do not differ enough from the reading concerned to appear in a separate variable, but are not similar enough to class as identical

[3]The boundary between 'old' and 'recent' MSS was drawn at 1800 CE.

- **score 2 (identical):** all readings whose differences from the reading concerned might be due to orthography, even if the different spelling might also indicate a grammatical or lexical difference

The analysis

First exploration

A number of preliminary analyses were carried out, including a statistical procedure called *Multidimensional Scaling* (MDS) to verify that our data do actually distribute into clusters, and several clustering runs to test various cluster agglomeration methods. These show that the manuscripts, when studied with respect to their variant readings, are distributed in relatively well-defined large clusters, which on the one hand are rather loose in arrangement, but on the other, do not overlap. Among various cluster agglomeration methods, Ward's method seems to produce the clearest and most believable results, while others generally identify the principal clusters but fail to reveal structure within these.

An exploratory clustering of all the available data yields a tree structure that corresponds to the structural grouping of the manuscripts at the basic levels, but deviates more and more from it as the details are scrutinised. This may be a result of the unreliability of the analysis, but is more likely to suggest that the actual MSS have been subjected to editing with respect to content more frequently than to editing of form, i.e. that readings have repeatedly been changed on the basis of MSS from other subgroups, but structure was less often changed by the copiers of the manuscripts.

Fine-tuning the method

A number of variations on the method were tested that might potentially increase the accuracy or interpretability of our analysis. The following details were chosen on the basis of these explorations.

The final analysis uses data scored in the manner described under Method from 15 verses, as a comparison with a more sensitive scoring procedure (using 5 verses only) indicates that the larger number of variants deemed different in the more sensitive form of analysis results in no substantial improvement of the clustering, whereas a larger text sample (easier to process at the less sensitive level) seems to ensure that idiosyncratic variation in specific verses is cancelled out.

The transformation of the three-grade scale used in the original quantification of the variants to a binary scale did not make the results clearer at a detailed level, though it did show the basic separation into primary clusters more markedly. Therefore, we shall use the original three-level scale in the final analysis.

I also investigated the possibilities of excluding from the analysis data that are not available in certain MSS and therefore needed to be complemented intuitively. Where specific small parts of individual manuscripts are damaged, it seems better to disregard altogether the loci involved, though the resulting improvement in the clarity of the cluster structure is slight.

As regards technical details, the final analysis used the Ward method of agglomeration, based on squared Euclidean distances. In order to obtain more detail at the lower levels of the dendrogram, two separate analyses have been performed: one on the MSS of the S recension (including Patna2), and another on those of the L recension. The resulting dendrograms were placed side by side, scaled to the proportions found in a single analysis of all 24 MSS, and connected, again with lines proportional to those in the comprehensive analysis.

Results

The result is presented in the figure below; in a vertical layout with the 'root' of the tree at the top and the 'leaves' at the bottom. The groups to which the individual MSS are assigned by the structural analysis are shown at the bottom of the graph below the MS names. Cluster identifying labels have been added to the various branches of the dendrogram, to facilitate reference in the following discussion. Not all these labels are actually shown among the smaller twigs of the tree, as they would interfere too heavily with readability. The table below shows cluster membership in various sections of this dendrogram, in comparison with membership in the structural groups. The proximity matrix for the final analysis is given in Appendix B.

Cluster membership in the final analysis

MS Name	Struct. cls.	2 cls.	4 cls.	9 cls.
Alvar	S222	1	1a	1aaa
Bharatpur1	L1	2	2a	2aa
Bharatpur2	S1	1	1a	1aaa
Bharatpur3	L221	2	2b	2baa
Bikaner	L1	2	2a	2aa
Dhaka	S21	1	1a	1ab
Harvard	S221	1	1a	1aaa
Jaipur4	L1	2	2a	2aa
Jaipur5	S21	1	1a	1aaa
Jaipur6	L221	2	2b	2bb
Jaipur7	L1	2	2a	2aa
Jodhpur1	L1/L222(L21)	2	2a	2aa
Patna1	S1	1	1a	1aab
Patna2	S1/S21	1	1b	1b
Patna3	S1	1	1a	1aab
Prayag1	L222	2	2b	2baa
Prayag2	S221	1	1a	1ab
Sitapur1	L21/L221	2	2b	2bab
Sitapur2	S221	1	1a	1aaa
Tijara	S222	1	1a	1aaa
Udaipur1	L1/L222	2	2a	2ab
Udaipur2	L1	2	2a	2aa
Uniyara	L1	2	2a	2aa
Vrindaban2	L1	2	2a	2aa

Final dendrogram of the studied manuscripts: see Figure 8.2.

The cluster labels at the bottom of the table are those assigned to the respective MSS by the structural analysis. The labels placed inside the dendrogram identify the clusters in this tree for easy reference in the text.

Discussion

Cluster 1 of the graph, corresponding to the **short recension**, bifurcates into 1b, which is comprised of the eccentric Patna2 alone,

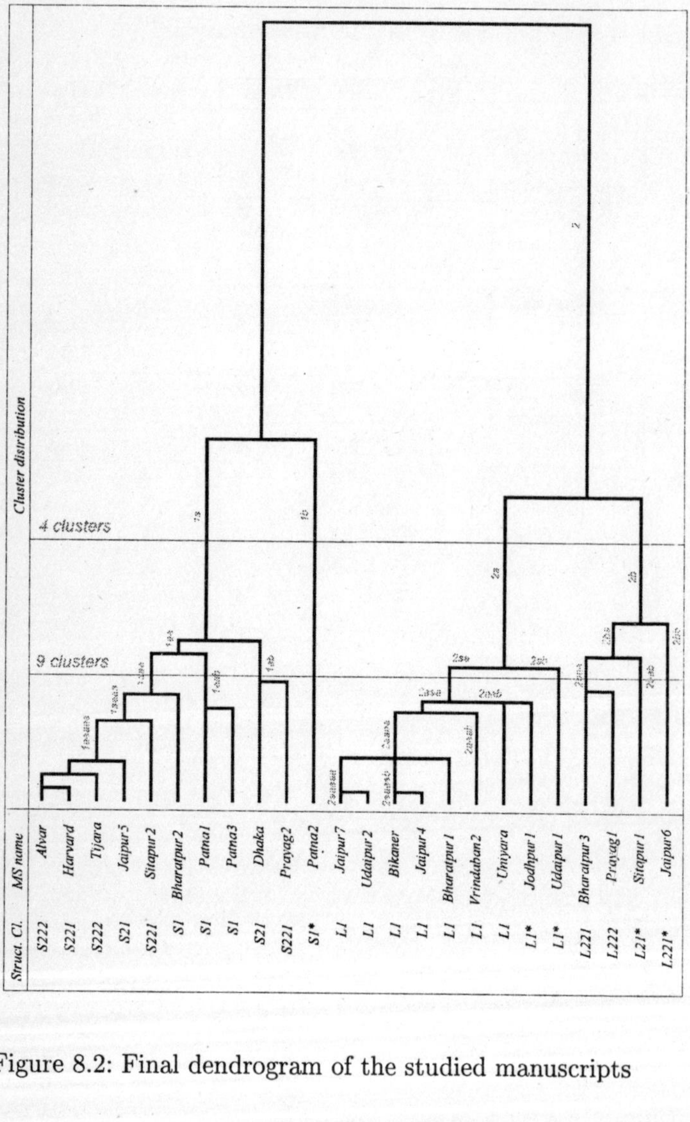

Figure 8.2: Final dendrogram of the studied manuscripts

and 1a, containing the S recension proper. The separate standing of Patna2 has been evident in all the analyses. The structural investigation of the MSS ranks it in the short recension, as do most of the various cluster analyses herein. However, its various features may be used to allocate it either to the group S1 or to S21 (actually forming the subgroups S11 and S211 alone of the MS involved in this study). Furthermore, some of the variations in the data have produced a dendrogram with Patna2 closer to the L-recension manuscripts. It is thus possible that this manuscript had been written using several originals of varied lineage. Apart from having a large number of unique and in all likelihood corrupted readings, its orthography indicates that it goes back to an original written in the *kaithī* script of Bihar *kāyastha*s, and may thus preserve a state of the text from a time before the two recensions had taken on a clearly delineated form (BANGHA, 2003).

Cluster 1a contains all the short-recension manuscripts but Patna2. It divides into a larger cluster, 1aa, and a smaller one, 1ab. The latter consists of Dhaka and Prayag2, connected rather loosely. Structurally, Dhaka goes to the S21 group with Jaipur5 and possibly Patna2, while Prayag2 is in S221 with Harvard and Sitapur2. When analysing the data of 5 verses only, Prayag2 joined with Sitapur2 and Patna1, the former of which is indeed in the S221 group. However, otherwise the proximity of Dhaka to Prayag2 is quite consistent across the different analyses, though always quite loose.

Cluster 1aa again separates into a larger 1aaa branch, and a smaller 1aab that consists of Patna1 and Patna3. This cluster is corroborated by the structural analysis, where the three Patna MSS form the cluster S1 with Bharatpur2 (wherein actually Patna1 and Patna3 are in the subgroup S12 with Bharatpur2 [and a number of editions], and Patna2 is the only manuscript in S11 [again, with several editions]). In our dendrogram, Bharatpur2 is located quite close to the Patna MSS, but linked loosely with the core of the S recension rather than with these. It seems that although the pattern of variants in these manuscripts is not grossly different, the unique features shared by all the Patna manuscripts are momentous enough to create a cluster of Patna1 and Patna3. Patna2, as described above, is of course rather different from all the other MSS.

The remainder of the S recension, cluster 1aaa follows a chained rather than clustered structure. First to separate out of it is Bharatpur2, which structurally belongs with the Patna manuscripts, as discussed above. Its clustering with the S22 group may be an indication of geographically characteristic variation in the text. Bharatpur2 might go back to an original similar in structure to the Bihar MSS, but its transcriber may have corrected the contents partially to read what he was familiar with: a western version. Sitapur2 separates out next in the chain. Preserved in Prayāg, it might have been written in the middle or eastern region on the basis of a western original. In some analyses of varied data, it has clustered with Prayag2 and Patna1, indicating that even though its form is closer to redactions known to us from the west, its contents have much in common with eastern forms of the *Kavitāvalī*.

Cluster 1aaaaa is the compact hard core of the S recension, again with a chained internal structure. Alvar and Harvard form its ultra-compact centre, and these two manuscripts have appeared very close together in all the analyses performed. Although the structural investigation allocates both of them to the L22 group, they are members of different quaternary groups. Both these MSS omit verse 7.113, and Harvard has 114 and 115 in this order, while Alvar has 115 before 114—hence their allocation to S221 and S222 respectively. Both insert the apocryphal 3.x1 and 4.x1 between the standard 3.1 and 4.1, as do most of the MSS in the S2 recension. At the typical endpoint of the S recension (after 7.161), both these MSS insert verse 1 of the *Dohāvalī*, (as do Tijara and Patna1), while Sitapur2 has verse 162 at that point like the S1 manuscripts, and Prayag2 ends after 7.148 followed by several apocrypha. Thus, the group S221 is internally not quite consistent, and Harvard shares at least some structural features with the S222 group.

Tijara is the next MS to join the pair at the core, completing the S222 structural cluster with Alvar (and a potential Harvard). The next manuscript to join this group, Jaipur5, is still much closer to the core than Sitapur2, yet it seems out of place here, as it belongs in the S21 structural group with Dhaka (and possibly Patna2) rather than in one of the S22 subgroups. It does indeed retain verse 7.113, like the S1 and L recensions. It ends after the standard verse 7.161, followed by the apocryphal 7.x12 and then

Dohāvalī 1 (also inserted here by the three members deeper inside the core, though those do not have 7.x12). Since the variant readings seem to be very close to the S222 (plus Harvard) group, it is likely that these MSS are indeed closely related, and the inclusion of *Dohāvalī* 1 at the end may be a valuable indication (though it is also present in Patna1, a MS rather removed from these four in the dendrogram).

Cluster 2, corresponding to the **L recension**, is more compact than cluster 1 including Patna2, but less so than cluster 1a, the S recension without Patna2. However, it divides clearly into two branches, clusters 2a and 2b, which are about as tight as 1a.

Cluster 2b is the rough equivalent of the L2 structural group. It does not include the MSS Jodhpur1 and Udaipur1, both of which may, on the basis of some of their structural features, be assigned to the L222 group with Prayag1 (though they may also be in L1). Cluster 2b exhibits a chained structure, starting with a rather loose core (cluster 2baa) of Bh3 and Prayag1. Structurally, Bh3 is in group L221, while Prayag1 is in L222, i.e. they are closely related, but are not in the same quaternary category. Most of the features that distinguish (rather vaguely) between L221 and L222 are in the *Ayodhyākāṇḍa*, which is missing from the Prayag1 MS (of which only the end has survived). Nevertheless, Prayag1 is the only MS allocated to no other category than L222; the others in this subgroup being Jodhpur1 (also L1 and possibly L21) and Udaipur1 (also L1). It is therefore quite possible that Prayag1 is indeed quite closely related to Bh3, though it must be kept in mind that on the one hand, the small surviving portion of this MS does not allow a very confident statistical evaluation (as most of the variables pertaining to it have been guessed), and on the other, that as the oldest by far of all the MSS available to us, it is quite eccentric in many of its readings (with the eccentricity damped down here by the large number of complemented variables) and may, like the hypothetical original of Patna2 (see above), preserve a state of the opus from before the crystallisation of the two recensions.

This duo is joined first by Sitapur1, to form the cluster 2ba. Sitapur1 is ambiguously allocated to either L21 (with Jodhpur1) or to L221 (with Bh3 and Jaipur6). Unlike the L22 group, Sitapur1 omits verse 2.4; however, unlike the L21 group, it does not insert the apocryphal 2.x2 after 2.21, and neither do the MSS in the L22 group. In the varied analyses, Sitapur1 was never far from Prayag1 and Jaipur6, and sometimes one or more of the Patna MSS also appeared in its vicinity. Preserved in Prayāg, it was likely written in the eastern or middle region, and may well have content similar to the Prayag and Bihar MSS. Cluster 2b is completed by the joining of Jaipur6, a manuscript assigned to the L221 structural group.

Studying the structure revealed by the cluster analysis and investigating the structural details on the basis of which the subcategories of the L2 group had been created, it seems that—at least as far as the 24 MSS involved in this study are concerned—distinctions within the L2 group are of little import.

Quite the opposite is the case with the L1 group, which presented no structural basis for subdivision, yet seems to exhibit some nested structure rather consistently in the statistical analyses presented herein.

The L1 group is represented in the dendrogram by cluster 2a. This is comprised of cluster 2aa and the lone Udaipur1. This may belong to the L1 group, or it may be in L222 with Prayag1 (and possibly Jodhpur1). Given its ambiguous place, it is probably no accident that it has ended up at the edge of the cluster. It is likely to be a manuscript produced by collating texts from the L1 and the L2 recensions; or possibly, it might go back to an old form of the L recension from before the separation of L1 from L2.

Cluster 2aa is again divided into two. Its smaller part, cluster 2aab, consists of Uniyara and Jodhpur1. Uniyara is a definite member of the L1 recension, though in the varied analyses it has repeatedly appeared as a loner. Jodhpur1, one of the oldest MSS in the study, may be in L1, or in L222 with Prayag1, the oldest MS, and possibly also Udaipur1, discussed above. Although it is tempting to say that, since the cluster analysis has ranked both Jodhpur1 and Udaipur1 with the L1 group, these MSS are just slightly odd members of this nondescript company, the structural details indicating that they share some features with Prayag1 and the fact that two of them are the two oldest MSS in the study (while the third is undated, but written sometime in the 19th century) hint that here we may be dealing with something close to the historical prototype of the L recension in general.

The remaining MSS, forming cluster 2aaa, are all definite members of the L1 group. However, they still show a definitely nested structure, which is also quite consistent in the varied analyses described earlier. Vrindaban2, a manuscript characterised by a very large number of scribal errors and eccentric variations, separates out early from this group.

The other 5 MSS (cluster 2aaaa) form a core as compact as that of the S recension. This core itself consists of Bharatpur1 and two extremely tight duos: Jaipur7 with Udaipur2 and Bikaner with Jaipur4. In the analysis of the more sensitively scored data (of 5 verses only), the former also included Bharatpur1 and was more closely related to Vrindaban2 than to the other core; while the latter also included Udaipur1. Bharatpur1 also appeared here, though in the latter cluster, in the analysis of the rigorous binary scale. The compactness of this core suggests that these manuscripts might belong to a rather standard, and probably relatively late, western redaction of the text, different from both the (probably oldest) L2 group and the hypothetical early L recension.

General conclusions

The suitability of cluster analysis

The application of cluster analysis in philological research is far from novel. Various clustering methods have for quite a long time been used successfully in linguistic analyses of texts (HARTIGAN 1975). Applications in Indology have also appeared over the recent years. Cluster analysis is suggested by FOSSE (1997) for grouping texts together according to certain criteria (in his own studies, according to style defined as the frequency of utilisation of various grammatical forms and word types). ROSENSTEIN (1977) has performed what she calls *cladistic analysis*, apparently a form of clustering, on manuscripts of the padas of Svāmī Haridās to help construct a genealogy of these manuscripts.

I have tested several variations in the method of analysis applied to the problem of grouping manuscripts according to their level of relatedness on the basis of variant readings. My aim with this, apart from obtaining some insight into the problem at hand, namely the clustering of the MSS of the *Kavitāvalī*, was to contribute somewhat to the methodology of such analyses. Developing a sound and reliable strategy will naturally need significantly more time and effort, and the contribution of other, more qualified scholars; however, I feel that my results are promising.

First of all, it is not a vain idea to apply cluster analysis to study the interrelations of various manuscripts of a given work. Intuitively we feel that the MSS would fit a certain cluster structure, having been created in a genealogical process of transcription. The structural analysis of the available MSS by Dr. Bangha shows that they do indeed form more or less separable categories.

The fact that cluster analysis does produce interpretable and nested categories seems to indicate that the procedure is suitable for our ends. Care must be exercised though in accepting the clustering results as decisive, for the quantity of variables involved was extremely large, while the items to be clustered were few in number.

Since the partial analyses performed in the preparatory stage of the work before all the numerical data were available resulted in trees that largely correspond to those discussed herein, and the results based on slightly modified forms of the basic data were also relatively consistent, we have reason to believe that the structure found is a genuine property of the MSS themselves, rather than an artefact emerging spontaneously from the vast and murky sea of data. This is corroborated by the fact that definite correspondence is found between the results of the structural analysis and those of the clustering procedures.

Nevertheless, the actual fine details of the dendrograms varied from analysis to analysis. Particularly important in this respect are the analyses based on data from 5 verses only. The evident differences of the results of these analyses from those using 15 verses as a basis were attributed to the individual characteristics of the verses concerned, and the analyses using a larger number of verses were suggested as more authoritative on the grounds that the idiosyncrasies of verses would cancel out in a larger sample.

However, even 15 verses is not a large number. To be more certain of the specific results, we would need to support the findings using other procedures. The simplest of these would be to divide the available data randomly into two or more sets of equal size (rather than dividing them up on the basis of which verse they pertain to), and test the consistency of the clustering of these subsets. For future studies, it might be a better idea to sample a much larger number of verses without increasing the mass of data, i.e. by taking just the first locus with variant readings from each verse; or taking every n^{th} locus with variants from the entire corpus of a text.

The quantification procedure

Apart from the original three-grade scale used by the scorers collaborating in this work, I have tested two ways of transforming the data into a binary scale. As the results presented above show, the binary data did not yield markedly clearer or more realistically structured results. Nevertheless, using a three-grade (or more detailed) scale is probably not the best solution for this problem. First, the more levels there are to a scale, the more subjective bias will be inevitably incorporated in the data. And second, the use of Euclidean metrics in cluster analysis is based on the assumption that the data are on an interval scale. It seems from the results that this does not lead to serious distortion of the clustering, yet by using a binary scale, one reduces the difference between the ordinal and the interval scales. It is also possible that using non-Euclidean metrics especially suited for lower-level and binary scale types might produce better results.

The problem with the binary scale is that it neglects the finer differences between individual variant readings. To eliminate this, it would be desirable to start out by choosing loci from the text where the finer differences are less likely to be decisive. A general way to implement this would be to continue the distinction of variant intensity and use a level of sensitivity beyond the level employed here. Another, more complicated but potentially more rewarding, way to go about the selection of loci to include would be to deploy further statistical procedures such as factor analysis and/or analyses based on multivariate correlation and regression. By finding out which of the variables used in this paper have contributed more to the final cluster structure, and studying the characteristics of these variables as distinct from those that have not been useful in deriving the clusters, we might gain insight into the general nature of data to look for in other, similar studies.

Clustering of variant readings versus structural examination

One might ask the question: why bother with the tedious task of scoring and with complex mathematical routines requiring sophisticated software, if the results are at best uncertain, and the simpler and more traditional analysis is the touchstone used to verify the findings? The frank answer to this is that I cannot guarantee it is worth the bother.

However, there are many reasons why it *might* be worth trying. Applying yet another method to tackle a problem can never hurt. In the case of the *Kavitāvalī*, the main lines of the cluster structure unveiled by the statistical analysis seem to overlap that identified by the structural examination. Many smaller details do indeed differ, and it is precisely these differences that might provide further information about the manuscripts. In the case of other works, there might not be so much structural variance, yet variant readings would in all likelihood be present, and might be used on their own to trace manuscript relationships.

Although the dendrogram created by a cluster analysis is of course not the stemma of the manuscripts, interpreting a dendrogram in the light of manuscript colophons and any other chronological and spatial information might be very helpful in learning more about actual historical lineage. Furthermore, the allocation of manuscripts to clusters can facilitate text editing in several ways. The existence of fairly clearly delineated clusters is a sign of several, historically separate recensions of the text, which an editor should be aware of. When attempting to decide on an original reading, such cluster-based information can indeed be useful. Also, if a specific manuscript, generally judged to be authoritative, is partially damaged at a certain spot, the readings found in closely related other manuscripts at the same spot may provide hints for deciphering an illegible word, as opposed to readings from manuscripts of different clusters, which are less likely to have the same reading and may thus be misleading.

Of course the statistical method is not recommended as a replacement of more traditional approaches, but rather as a supplement. The procedure described herein requires substantial time and effort, and its results, though based on theoretically unfailing numbers, are not more decisive than those of any other method of text analysis. Nevertheless, after some refinement of method and further testing, a cluster analysis of variant readings can certainly be a useful addition to the arsenal of Indological research.

References

Note: Years of publication are given according to the Common Era even for books that refer to years in *Vikram saṁvat.*

BANGHA, I. (2003): *The Kavitāvalī of Tulsīdās: Dynamics of transmission in a Hindi text.* Unpublished paper read at the conference Dynamics of Textual Transmission in Pre-Colonial India held within the seminar series Knowledge Systems on the Eve of Colonialism organised at the Department of South Asian Studies of the University of Chicago.

FOSSE, L. M. (1997): *The crux of chronology in Sanskrit literature—Statistics and Indology. A study of method.* Scandinavian University Press, Oslo.

HARTIGAN, J. A. (1975): *Clustering algorithms.* Wiley Series in Applied Mathematics, New York.

INDRADEVNĀRĀYAṆ (transl.) (1937 1st ed.): *Gosvāmī Śrītulsīdāsjī-viracit Kavitāvalī.* Gita Press, Gorakhpur (numerous editions since).

KRIPPENDORF, K. (1980): 'Clustering' in MONGE & CAPPELLA, 1980.

KŘIVÁNEK, M. (1991): *Algorithmic and geometric aspects of cluster analysis.* Academia Nakladatelství Československé Akademie Věd, Prague.

MCGREGOR, R. S. (1984): *Hindi literature from its beginnings to the nineteenth century.* A History of Indian Literature, Vol. VIII (series ed. by Jan Gonda). Publ. by Otto Harrassowitz, Wiesbaden.

MONGE, P. R. & CAPPELLA, J. N. (eds) (1980): *Multivariate techniques in human communication research.* Academic Press, New York.

ROSENSTEIN, L. L. (1997): *The devotional poetry of Svāmī Haridās.* Groningen. ŚUKLA, R & BHAGAVĀNDĪN & BRAJRATNADĀS (1923 1st ed.): *Tulsī Granthāvalī II: Mānasetar ekādaś granth.* Nāgarī Pracāriṇī Sabhā, Varanasi (2nd edition: 1974).

Nine

Apocrypha in the Eastern Manuscripts of Tulsīdās's *Kavitāvalī*

Mária Négyesi and Imre Bangha

Poetry by Tulsīdās is today an inseparable part of the religious life of a high number of North Indian Hindus. The *Rāmcaritmānas* and Tulsī's other books are readily available on railway stations or in the bookshops of the remotest towns, and they are present in almost every traditional household. The Gītāpress *Kavitāvalī* for example in 2001 was running its 41st edition.

It may not surprise any scholar of medieval Hindi literature that apart from the *Rāmcaritmānas* and the *Barvai Rāmāyan* no critical edition exists of the works of Tulsīdās. To fill this gap a research team has been formed in 2001 with the aim of preparing a critical edition of one of the most popular compositions of the Hindi author, the *Kavitāvalī*.[1]

[1]The project received support from the Max Müller Fund, Oxford, from the Hungarian Scientific Research Fund, Budapest (OTKA project no. T 038047), and the team has been made one of the research Groups of the Society for South Asian Studies (British Academy, London).

The *Kavitāvalī* is a collection of quatrains (*kabitts*) written not in the Avadhi but in the Braj dialect. Most of the poems are related to the Rāma-story, and the work is divided into seven cantos (*kāṇḍas*) imitating the *Rāmāyaṇa*; moreover in several handwritten books the name of the work is *Kabitt Rāmāyaṇa*. The *Kavitāvalī*, however, is not an epic with a continuous story line: some scenes, such as the boatman episode or the burning of Lanka, are elaborated in several quatrains while certain matters (e.g. most part of the *Araṇyakāṇḍa* and *Kiṣkindhākāṇḍa*) are omitted. There are also some poems containing various themes not related to Rāma at all such as poems on Krishna and the cowherd girls or the praise of Shiva.

The special significance of the *Kavitāvalī* lies not only in its often personal tone, but also in the fact that it contains poems from which references to Tulsī's life and time can be traced. In many places this collection is not inferior in beauty to the *Rāmcaritmānas*. Since the *kāṇḍa* structure of the the *Kavitāvalī* is far from being balanced the question arises whether it can be regarded as one literary work, composed by Tulsī himself, or a later compilation of his kabitts and savaiyās. From its uneven structure one can infer that this is a collection of Tulsī's quatrains written probably at different times. Since the order of the poems is very similar in all manuscripts, one can assume that the authority of Tulsīdās stands behind the original compilation. The possibility of later interpolations cannot, however, be excluded as it is probably the case with some 'apocryphal' poems.

As the first step of the *Kavitāvalī* project we have undertaken the task of obtaining copies of the all existing manuscripts. At present 32 manuscripts found in the Hindi belt, Panjab, the USA and the UK are accessible for our research. The earliest of them is from VS 1749 (1692 AD) and three others are dated from before 1800.[2]

The readings and the structure of the manuscripts differ in several places from the text of the 20th century published editions, which can be called the vulgate (as published by the Nāgarīpracāriṇī Sabhā[3] and the Geeta Press). Some manuscripts tend to omit

[2] For full details of all documented manuscripts see the forthcoming *Kavitāvalī* edition.

[3] *Tulsī granthāvalī*, vol. II. Ed. Rāmcandra Śukla - Bhagavānadīn -

poems and all manuscripts contain 'apocryphal' quatrains omitted from the vulgate. All this shows that the transmission of the *Kavitāvalī* was a more complex procedure than one would think on the basis of modern editions and that the reader must exercise some caution when referring to the readings of the vulgate *Kavitāvalī* as a definite text written by Tulsī.

In this article we are going to present the apocrypha as found in the easternmost recension of the *Kavitāvalī*, namely in three manuscripts from Patna and a closely related lithographed edition from Calcutta, which is also the oldest published version of the *Kavitāvalī* dating from A.D. 1815. It will be the first attempt to bring into light some forgotten poems attributed to Tulsī that were part of the textual tradition till the 19th century.

The examination of the apocrypha can also shed some light on some attitudes of pre-modern readers: what were the poems that the readers felt inauthentic or in which places did they feel that the collection required the addition of some extra poems.

Our apocrypha will be taken from the following manuscripts and edition:

- The Patna1 manuscript is preserved in the Chaitanya Library, Patna, catalogued as nr. 1774. It contains 96 folios and dates from 1894 VS (A.D. 1837).
- The Patna2 manuscript is in the Bihār Rāṣṭrabhāṣā Pariṣad, Patna, catalogued as nr. 101kha. It is found in a book containing several different works. The *Kavitāvalī* is written on folios 162-283. It dates from 1291 Hijrī (A.D. 1876/77).
- The Patna3 manuscript is in the Bihār Rāṣṭrabhāṣā Pariṣad, Patna, nr. 2895. It is an incomplete book with only folios 28-47 and 68-76 preserved.
- The lithographed edition is Sārasvat, Bāburām (ed.): *Kavitta Rāmāyaṇa*. Sanskrit Press, Khidirpur (Calcutta) 1815 (90 pp). The only copy known to us is in the British Museum catalogued as nr. 14158.d.4(1).

Brajratnadāsa. Nāgarīpracāriṇī Sabhā, Kāśī. Samvat 2039. pp. 131–218, Tulsīdās, *Kavitāvalī*, translated by Indradevnārāyan. Gorakhpur: Gita Press, 2001.

The first part of this article will give a brief description of the eastern manuscripts and some remarks on the individual apocrypha. The second part will provide a critical edition with an English translation.

The manuscripts and the edition

Patna1

The manuscript normally has 13 lines per page, and 14 syllables per line. The colophon dates it to VS 1894 (AD 1837):

> इति श्री गोसाई तुलशीदास विरंचित श्री कवित्त रामायणं संपूर्णम्। संवत् १८९४ शाके १७५९। अग्रहण क्रिष्ण द्वादश्यां तदुप[र] त्रयोदश्यां शनिवारम् इदं पुस्तकम् लिखित्वा जिवनाथ पाडे सर्मा पोथि नथन बाबु का लिखा
>
> The Kavitta Rāmāyaṇa composed by Gosvāṃī Tulsīdās is completed here. This book was written (in) the Vikrama year of 1894, (or) the Śaka year of 1759 on the 12th and on the following 13th, Saturday of the dark fortnight of the month of Agrahāyaṇa.[4] Jivanātha Pāṇḍe Śarmā wrote Nathan Bābu's book.

The order of the quatrains differs in several places from the vulgate. Using the numbering of the vulgate the following table shows the places where the order is different, and where poems are added or omitted. (The first number refers to the canto, the second to the poem within it. Poems not present in the vulgate are marked by #. Numbers in brackets refer to sequences of poems that are in the same order as in the vulgate.)

[1] *Bālakāṇḍa*: 1.1, 1.2, 1.6, 1.3, 1.4, 1.5, (1.7 ... 1.15), 1.17, 1.16, (1.18... 1.22)

[2] *Ayodhyākāṇḍa*: 2.1, 2.2, (2.5... 2.11), # 2.1, (2.12... 2.21), #2.2, (2.22... 2.25), 7.141

[4] Agrahāyaṇa is the ninth lunar month, also called Mārgaśīrṣa starting from mid November.

[3] *Araṇyakāṇḍa*: 2.26, 2.27, 2.28, 3.1, #3.1. (first two lines)

[4] *Kiṣkindhākāṇḍa*: #3.1 (last two lines), #4.1

[5] *Sundarakāṇḍa*: 4.1, (5.1...5.32), (6.1...6.7)

[6] *Laṅkākāṇḍa*: (6.8...6.58)

[7] *Uttarakāṇḍa*: (7.1...7.43), (7.45...7.90), (7.97...7.113), 7.115, 7.114, 7.116, 7.117 (the lines are put up haphazardly), (7.118...7.136), 7.137, 7.137 (written twice by mistake), (7.138...7.140), (7.142...7.148), #7.7, #7.8, (7.149...7.161), colophon

On the basis of this list one can observe that poems 2.3, 2.4, 7.44 and (7.91...7.96) are omitted, and 7.141 is placed in the *Ayodhyākāṇḍa*.

The numbering in the manuscript is occasionally inconsistent. Sometimes the scribe misnumbers the poems, e.g. at 5.29 the numbering starts with 1 again even without a *kāṇḍa* border. At the beginning of the *Laṅkākāṇḍa*, however, the numbering continues that of the *Sundarakāṇḍa*. The same phenomenon can be observed at the border of the *Laṅkākāṇḍa* and the *Uttarakāṇḍa*. A new numbering starts, however, at 7.61 and once more at 7.127.

Orthography

In Sanskrit words Sanskritic orthography is preserved, e.g. *doṣa, sukha, gaṇeśa, yakṣeśa rakṣa,* rather than the Braj *dosa, suṣa, ganesa, jacchesa raccha*. The rare exceptions include *Laṣaṇa* and *Lakṣaṇa* for *Lakṣmaṇa*. Moreover, sometimes hypersanskritisation can be observed e.g. *tirikṣi* (for *tirichī*), *śuṭhi* (for *suṭhi*) and the usual spelling of the author's name is *Tulaśī(dāśa)*.

The manuscript differentiates between the retroflex *ṇ* and the dental *na* (e.g. *pāṇi* 'hand' and *pānī* 'water') as well as between the dental *sa* and palatal *śa*, (e. g. *śyāma śarīra pasaiu lasai*).

It also differentiates between *kha* and *ṣu* (e. g. *mukha paṅkaja, dekhiya jāī, khelata; beṣa, barṣe, biṣāda*). The rare exceptions include *prabhuruṣa, liṣyule* on the *kāṇḍa* borders and *śīṣai* (for *sīkhai*) in an apocryphal quatrain.

The difference between the short and long *i* and *u* is normally given back correctly, in some cases, however, short *i* is used instead of a long one, e. g. *aisi, tirikṣi si, anaṅga ki.*

Towards the beginning of the manuscript *va* with a dot is sometimes used for *va* (e.g. *rāvare*), while without a dot the same character stands for *ba*. This usage is, however, rare and normally the same character stands for *ba* and *va*, (e. g. *rābare, nāba, pāba*). Sometimes *va* is substituted with *u* (e.g. *prabhāu*).

The beginning of the manuscript also has the tendency of putting a dot under the character *ya* probably to differentiate it from *pa*. (This rule is not followed in ligatures e.g. in the word *śyām* the dot is omitted.)

The sign *candrabindu* is not used. Nasalisation is expressed with an *anusvāra*. Hyper-nasalisation is absent.

Patna2

The manuscript usually has 17–18 lines per page, and 17 syllables per line.

It has no colophon. The catalogue, however, dates it to 1291 Hijri (A. D. 1876/77), and the old catalogue suggests that it originates from Muzaffarpur.

The book among several other works contains the quatrains from the beginning of the *Kavitāvalī* up to 7.159 on folios 162–283. Poems 7.76. . . 7.78, however, on folios 253–254 are missing.

The order of poems is as follows

[1] *Bālakāṇḍa*: (1.1. . . 1.22)

[2] *Ayodhyākāṇḍa*: (2.1. . . 2.11), #2.1, (2.12. . . 2.21), #2.2, (2.22 . . . 2.25)

[3] *Araṇyakāṇḍa*: (2.26. . . 2.29), #3.1

[4] *Kiṣkindhākāṇḍa*: #4.1, 4.1

[5] *Sundarakāṇḍa*: (5.1. . . 5.16), 5.18, 5.17, (5.19 . . . 5.32)

[6] *Laṅkākāṇḍa*: (6.1. . . 6.52), 6.53, 6.55, 6.54, (6.56. . . 6.58)

[7] *Uttarakāṇḍa*: (7.1. . . 7.75), (7.79. . . 7.90), #7.1, (7.97. . . 7.135), (7.138. . . 7.148), #7.7, #7.8, (7.149. . . 7.159)

Poems 7.91...7.96 are omitted.

The numbering of the poems is continuous from the beginning throughout the manuscript. Poems 7.136 and 7.137 have been left out. The manuscript, however, gives two numbers in their place. In this way the continuity of the numbering follows that of the vulgate text.

Orthography

In Sanskrit words Sanskritic orthography is only occasionally preserved (e.g. *jñāna*, rather than the Braj *gyāna*). The overall tendency, however, is to give Braj forms, e.g. *jogīndra munībrīnda, prāna, lachana.*

The manuscript does not differentiate between the retroflex *ṇa* and the dental *na* (e.g. *prāna, purāna*).

The two most characteristic features of the manuscript are its exaggerated use of palatal *śa* and that of the long *ī*. Although the scribe differentiates between the dental *sa* and palatal *śa*, in the overwhelming majority of the cases he uses the palatal *śa*, e. g. *Tulaśī(dāśa), śucī śundara śālī śakelī, kiśāna*. The use of *sa* and *śa* is not consistent, e.g. *śyāmaśarīra paśeu lase.*

The manuscript uses only short *u* even when long ones are required, eg. *nupura, laṃgur, bhumipāla.*

The sign for *kha (ṣa)* looks like a double *ppa* (which is actually marked with a dot, e.g. *uppama*). It is used both for *kha* (e.g. *śukhī, dekhī*) and for *ṣa* (e.g. *nikhaṅga, bīkhama, bhukhana*). Later the sign *ṣa (kha)* also appears (e.g. *liṣyate, ṣetī, baṣāna, deṣāya*). The phrase *beṣa dekhi* suggests that the scribe may have thought of differentiating between the two sounds by the two characters.

The sign for *ṛh* looks like *cha* (e.g. *ṭhāṛhe*, etc. in 2.12), while *ca* is marked by a triangular mark like in the *Kaithī* script.

The *ya* between vowels is usually avoided. Normally it is changed into *e*, e.g. *gae* (for *gaye*), *raghunaeka* (for *raghunāyaka*). In past participles it is sometimes substituted with *va*.

A dot under *va* (which often looks like *pa*) marks *va* in contrast with *ba* (without dot), e.g. *bāvare, śāṃvare* (looks like *śāmpare*), *dīvākara* (looks like *dīpākara)*, *arabīṃnda, bīlocana, banabāśu dīvo.*

Anusvāra marks both nasalisation and nasal consonants. Many times it occurs superfluously before nasals (hyper-nasalisation), e.g. *śaṃmpati, kuṃnda.*

Patna3

The manuscript contains the passages with poems (6.11...7.149). The quatrains (7.35...117) are on missing folios. The order of poems is as follows:

[7] *Laṅkākāṇḍa*: (6.11...6.58)

[8] *Uttarakāṇḍa*: (7.1...7.34), 7.35 first two lines, (7.118... 7.140), (7.142...7.148), #7.7, #7.8, 7.149 beginning words

Poem 7.141 is omitted. The scribe did not number the quatrains.

Orthography

Sanskritic orthography is only occasionally preserved, e.g. *jñāna, ghanākṣarī* (between the poems). Hyper-sanskritisation can be observed in the case of *Tulaśī* which is used along with *Tulasī*.

A characteristic feature of this manuscript is also its exaggerated use of the long *ī* (e.g. *karī kai, bhumī, nīhārī* but *birāga)*, while the manuscript uses only short *u* even when long ones are required, e.g. *annapurnā*.

Another characteristic feature is the omitting of intervocalic *-y-*, e.g. *bhāi, gae, sīa* (for *sīya*), *hia*, but the character *-y-* can be kept in ligatures, e.g. *pyāse*. A notable exception is *bhayo*.

The scribe also uses *Kaithī* characters for *kha, ca, ra* and *la*. He differentiates between *kha* (marked with the *Kaithī* character resembling *ppa*, e. g. *dekhīya, sukhamā, rukha bekha*) and *ṣa* (e.g. *seṣa, rīṣī, parīṣo, bhūṣana*). This differentiation is not kept consistently, as can be seen from the above examples.

For the signs *ca* and *la* only the *Kaithī* characters are used. For the character *ra* both the *Devanāgarī* and the *Kaithī* signs can be found, sometimes combined even in one word e.g. *murārī* (7.147.a).

The manuscript differentiates neither between the retroflex *ṇa* and the dental *na* nor between the dental *sa* and palatal *śa*, but uses only *na* (e.g. *prānana, parna, guna*) and *sa* (e. g. *mahesa, desa, lava-kusa*).

The character *va* with a dot stands for *va*, while without it for *ba* (e.g. *pāva bārī*). Intervocalic *va* is sometimes avoided in conjugation (e.g. *chuata*), but is kept in Sanskritic words, e.g. *deva, sevata.*

Anusvāra marks both nasalisation and nasal consonants. It does not occur superfluously before nasals.

The Khidirpur edition

The edition usually has 18 lines per page, and 23 syllables per line.

The colophon dates it to 27 April 1815.

> इति श्री गोसांई तुलसीदास विरंचित श्री कवित्त रामायणं संपूर्णम॥
> सारस्वत कुलोद्भूत बाबुराम द्विजन्मना॥
> शोधितं पुस्तकम दिव्यं चरित्रं रामपावनम॥
> दोहा॥
> जुग्म सप्त वसु चन्द्र सुभ सम्वत माधव मास ॥
> कृष्णपक्ष की पंचमी भृगु पूरन भो [आ]स (1872)॥
> सन 1222 साल॥ तारिख 17 वैसाख॥ सन 1815 इशवी ता॰ 27 अपरएल॥ संस्कृत श्री मदन पाल ने छापा किआ॥
>
> Here the Kavitta Rāmāyaṇa composed by Gosvāmī Tulsīdās is completed. The twice born Bāburām of the Sārasvata lineage has edited this divine book of the deeds of the holy Rāma. (Couplet:) This book has been completed on a Monday the fifth of the dark fortnight of the month of Mādhava in the auspicious year of Twin (2), Seven (7), Vasu (8), Moon (1) (1872); dated on the seventh of Vaiṣakha of the Bengali year 1222; 27 April 1815 AD. In the Sanskrit Press in Khidirpur Shri Madan Pal printed it.

The order of the quatrains in this edition differs in several places from the vulgate and is similar to Patna1.

[1] *Bālakāṇḍa*: 1.1, 1.2, 1.6, 1.3, 1.4, 1.5, (1.7...1.15), 1.17, 1.16, (1.18...1.22)

[2] *Ayodhyākāṇḍa*: 2.1, 2.2, (2.5...2.11), # 2.1, (2.12...2.21), #2.2, (2.22...2.25), 7.141

[3] *Araṇyakāṇḍa*: 2.26, 2.27, 2.28, 3.1, #3.1 (first two lines)

[4] *Kiṣkindhākāṇḍa*: #3.1(last two lines), #4.1

[5] *Sundarakāṇḍa*: 4.1, (5.1...5.32), (6.1...6.32)

[6] *Laṅkākāṇḍa*: (6.1...6.58)

[7] *Uttarakāṇḍa*: (7.1...7.43), (7.45...7.90), #7.1, (7.97...7.113), 7.115, 7.114, 7.116, 7.117, (7.118...7.140), (7.142...7.148), #7.7, #7.8, (7.149...7.161), *Dohāvalī* 1, colophon

Poems 2.3, 2.4, 7.44, (7.91...96) and 7.141 are omitted.

Orthography

In Sanskrit words Sanskritic orthography is normally preserved (e.g. *avadheśa, daśakaṇṭha, purāṇa, pūrṇa, tāraṇa, vāraṇa*) and sometimes hypersanskritisation can be observed (e.g. *Tulaśī*), even on the expense of the meter (e. g. *nayana* for *naina*). The edition uses *kha* for *kha* (e. g. *khetī, bhikhāri*) not for *ṣa*, altough in #7.7.b *bhūṣa* stands for *bhūkha* and *bhīṣa* for *bhīkha*. It does not, however, differentiate between *kha* and *ṣa* systematically, it seems that the editor tried to make the orthography consistently Sanskritising but sometimes follows his master copy.

The edition differentiates between the retroflex *ṇa* and dental *na*. The difference between the short and long *i* and *u* is normally given back correctly.

The signs for *ba* and *va* are used inconsistently (e. g. *abaloki, vanī, nabanīla, vaiṭi bilaṃva, bāri vilocana bāḍhe*). The edition does not have the tendency of putting a dot under the character *ya* or *va*.

Ligatures are widely used even instead of *anusvāra* (e.g. *bhṛṅga*) but forms like *chāra* instead of *kṣāra, ākhara* instead of *akṣara* can also be found.

The sign *candrabindu* is not used even when the meter would require it (e. g. *saṃga* for *sãga*).

Nasalisation is expressed with *anusvāra*. Hyper-nasalisation is not present, but in the colophon *viraṃcita* is found.

Jha is printed with an older form absent from modern typography, similar to a mirrored *ta*.

Just like in the manuscripts the words are not separated from each other.

The Seven apocrypha

In the examined texts seven poems were found which are not available in the vulgate edition. The main text of the apocrypha is based on the lithographed Khidirpur edition and the variants are given from the manuscripts.

Examining only three manuscripts and one printed edition, in this apparatus all minor variations are given. Unfortunately medieval Braj texts do not have a consistent orthography while modern text editions restore the text to a standardized one.

2.1 सूखि गये...

सूखि गये रतनाधर मंजुल कंज से लोचन चारु चितै।
करुणानिधि कंत तुरंत कह्यौ कित दूरि महीबन है इतवै।
सरसीरुह लोचन नीर हि देखि चितै रघुनायक सीय शीषै।
अबहीं वन भामिनि बूझति हौ तजि कोशलराज पुरी दिन
द्वै॥

1 सूखि] (hypometrical) $Kh_{ed}Pa_1$, शुखी Pa_2 • गये] $Kh_{ed}Pa_1$, गए Pa_2 • रतनाधर] $Kh_{ed}Pa_1$, रतनाशर Pa_2 • कंज] $Kh_{ed}Pa_3$, क $Pa_1{}^{ac}$, कंज $Pa_1{}^{pc}$ • से] $Kh_{ed}Pa_1$, शे xमंजुलx Pa_2 • चितै] $Kh_{ed}Pa_1$, चुबौ Pa_2

2 करुणानिधि] $Kh_{ed}Pa_1$, करुनानीधी Pa_2 • कंत] $Kh_{ed}Pa_1$, कंन्त Pa_2 • कित] $Kh_{ed}Pa_1$, कीत Pa_2 • दूरि] $Kh_{ed}Pa_1$, दुरी Pa_2 • महीबन] Kh_{ed}, महीवन Pa_1, माहाबन Pa_2 • है इतवै] Kh_{ed}; है इत तै Pa_1, भुरी जे[यौ/यै] Pa_2

3 सरसीरुह] $Kh_{ed}Pa_1$, शरशीरुह Pa_2 • हि] $Kh_{ed}Pa_1$, ही Pa_2 •

देखि] $Kh_{ed}Pa_1$, देखी Pa_2 • चितै] $Kh_{ed}Pa_1$, चीतै Pa_2 • रघुनायक] $Kh_{ed}Pa_1$, रघुनाएक Pa_2 • सीय] $Kh_{ed}Pa_1$, शीया Pa_2 • शीषै] $Kh_{ed}Pa_1$, शीषौ Pa_2
4 अबहीं] $Kh_{ed}Pa_1$, अबही Pa_2 • वन] Kh_{ed}, बन Pa_1Pa_2 • भामिनि] $Kh_{ed}Pa_1$, भामीनी Pa_2 • बूझति] $Kh_{ed}Pa_1$, बुहति Pa_2 • हौ] $Kh_{ed}Pa_1$, हो Pa_2 • तजि] $Kh_{ed}Pa_1$, तेजि Pa_2 • दिन] $Kh_{ed}Pa_1$, दीन Pa_2 • द्वै] $Kh_{ed}Pa_1$, द्यौ Pa_2

The jewels of her lips dried up and with her lovely
eyes, which are like charming lotuses, she looked up.
Suddenly she said to her beloved, the Treasury of Compassion: "How far is the Forest-land[5] from here?"
Having observed tears in her lotus-eyes, the Lord of
the Raghus instructs Sītā:
"Having left the abode of Kośala's king two days ago,
o sensitive lady, you already ask of the forest?"

This *savaiyā* is about Sītā's languor and Rāma's reaction to it. It comes after poem nr. 9 in the *Ayodhyākāṇḍa* but it is nr. 32 in the Khidirpur edition, 2.10 in Pa_1 and 34 in Pa_2. It is missing from Pa_3. It is also published in a footnote of the *Granthāvalī* (p. 138), where it is claimed to be of spurious origin because the name of Tulsī is missing from the poem.

This poem was considered as inauthentic because it gives an unfavourable picture of Rāma and Sītā. She willingly follows her husband to the exile and refuses to return to Ayodhyā or to her father's palace as it is depicted in the *Ayodhyākāṇḍa* of the *Mānas*. This dialogue does not fit in the idealized picture of Sītā and Rāma which is characteristic of Tulsī's approach. (It is very unlikely that she asks a question full of complaints and Rāma's answer also seems to be very impolite.) However it has parallels in *Gītāvalī* 2.13-14[6].

---

[5]The variant reading *mahāvana* in Pa_2 'the great forest' does not seem to be the name of a particular place.

[6]I. Bangha: *The Kavitāvalī of Tulsīdās: Dynamics of Textual Transmission in Premodern India.* Comparative Studies of South Asia, Africa and the Middle East. Vol. 24. No. 2. (2004) pp. 33–44.

2.2 दीन के दानि...

दीन के दानि दयानिधि सागर शील सुधा वसुधा उजियारे।
संत के संपति भूपन के पति मातु पिता गृह प्राण अधारे।
लिखी न मिटै विधि की तुलशी पितु आयसु ते वन को पगु
धारे।
गोरे सो गात लला मम देवर सावर सो सखि प्रीतम प्यारे॥

1 दानि] Kh$_{ed}$Pa$_1$, दानी Pa$_2$ • दयानिधि] Kh$_{ed}$Pa$_1$, दीवांकर Pa$_2$ • सागर] Kh$_{ed}$Pa$_1$, बारिध Pa$_2$ • सुधा] Kh$_{ed}$Pa$_1$, शुधा Pa$_2$ • वसुधा] Kh$_{ed}$Pa$_1$, बशुधा Pa$_2$ • उजियारे] Kh$_{ed}$Pa$_1$, उजीआरे Pa$_2$
2 संत] Kh$_{ed}$Pa$_1$, शंत Pa$_2$ • के] Kh$_{ed}$, कि Pa$_1$, ko Pa$_2$ • संपति] Kh$_{ed}$Pa$_1$, शंम्पति Pa$_2$ • भूपन] Kh$_{ed}$Pa$_1$, भुपनि Pa$_2$ • पति] Kh$_{ed}$, मणि Pa$_1$, मति Pa$_2$ • पिता] Kh$_{ed}$Pa$_1$, पीता Pa$_2$ • गृह] Kh$_{ed}$Pa$_1$, ग्रीह Pa$_2$ • प्राण] Kh$_{ed}$Pa$_1$, प्रान Pa$_2$ • अधारे] Kh$_{ed}$Pa$_1$, पीयारे Pa$_2$
3 लिखी ... धारे] Σ (hypermetrical), *om.* Pa$_2$ • लिखी] Kh$_{ed}$Pa$_1$
4 गोरे ... प्यारे] Kh$_{ed}$Pa$_1$, *om.* Pa$_2$ • सावर] Kh$_{ed}$, सांवर Pa$_1$

He who is manifest as a bestower to the needy, treasury
of mercy, ocean of virtues, nectar on the earth,
wealth of the true ones, lord of the sovereigns, parental
home,[7] support (foundation)[8] of life;
—(the fate) written by the Creator cannot be erased,
Tulsī (says),—entered the forest on his father's order.
The boy with a fair (complexioned) body is my young
brother-in-law, the dark one, my friend, is my dearest
beloved.

This *savaiyā* is nr. 43 in Khidirpur edition and nr. 21 in the *Ayodhyākāṇḍa* of Pa$_1$, nr. 45 in Pa$_2$, missing in Pa$_3$. It belongs to a group of verses describing the scene when the village women meeting the charming two young princes ask Sītā who they are. Since Sītā as the ideal woman must be too modest and shy to

[7]It probably could be also interpreted as 'my mother and father, my home'. The two genitive structures preceding this expression suggest a parallel as 'the house of mother and father'.

[8]*Adhāre* (in the text with short vowel in the beginning of the word because of metrical reason) can mean foundation, basis, support, fig. supporter, patron.

refer directly to her husband, she keeps silent.[9] After introducing her brother-in-law Sītā's straightforward reference to her husband may be the reason why several manuscripts omit these lines.

3.1 मारि कुरंग...

मारि कुरंग स्वधाम दियो तव रावन स्यंदन लै सिय धाये।
युद्धि जटायु निहार परे प्रभु तात कि भांति सरूप हिं पाये।
वाली वधे कपि राज दिये हनूमंत हि जानि सुदास पठाये।
जानकि खोज सरोजमुखी जहं भेठ ह्वै वीर सुवात सुनाये॥

1 मारि] $Kh_{ed}Pa_1$, मारी Pa_2 • स्वधाम] $Kh_{ed}Pa_1$, शुधांम Pa_2 • दियो] $Kh_{ed}Pa_1$, दीऐ Pa_2 • स्यंदन] $Kh_{ed}Pa_1$, शींदन Pa_2 • सिय] $Kh_{ed}Pa_1$, शीयं Pa_2 • धाये] $Kh_{ed}Pa_1$, धाऐ Pa_2
2 युद्धि] $Kh_{ed}Pa_1$, जुध[व/य] Pa_2 • जटायु] $Kh_{ed}Pa_1$, जटा जब Pa_2 • निहार] $Kh_{ed}Pa_1$, हारी Pa_2 • प्रभु] Pa_1, प्रमु Kh_{ed}, तब Pa_2 • कि भांति] $Kh_{ed}Pa_1$, शमेंत Pa_2 • सरूप] $Kh_{ed}Pa_1$, शरुप Pa_2 • पाये] Kh_{ed}, आए Pa_2
3 वाली] Kh_{ed}, बाली Pa_2, बालि Pa_1 • वधे] Kh_{ed}, बधे Pa_1, बध्यौ Pa_2 • दिये] $Kh_{ed}Pa_1$, दीयो Pa_2 • हनूमंत] $Kh_{ed}Pa_1$, हनुमंन्त Pa_2 • हि] $Kh_{ed}Pa_1$, हिं Pa_2 • जानि] $Kh_{ed}Pa_1$, जानी Pa_2 • सुदास] $Kh_{ed}Pa_1$, श्वदाश Pa_2 • पठाये] $Kh_{ed}Pa_1$, पठाए Pa_2
4 जानकि] $Kh_{ed}Pa_1$, जानकी Pa_2 • खोज] $Kh_{ed}Pa_1$ • सरोजमुखी] Kh_{ed}, सरोज Pa_1, शरोजमुखी Pa_2 • जहं] Kh_{ed}, हं (eyeskip) Pa_1, जंहा Pa_2 • भेठ] Kh_{ed}, भेट Pa_1, भेटि Pa_2 • ह्वै] $Kh_{ed}Pa_1$, हे Pa_2 • वीर] Kh_{ed}, बीर Pa_1Pa_2 • स्पोत सुवात] Kh_{ed}, सुबात Pa_1, शुबात Pa_2 • सुनाये] $Kh_{ed}Pa_1$, शुनाए Pa_2

When, having killed the antelope, Rāma gave him his own [heavenly] abode, then Rāvaṇa took Sītā on the chariot and ran away.
After fighting [with Rāvaṇa] Jaṭāyu's glance fell on the Lord, and as [if he were Rāma's] father he obtained Rāma's own form.[10]
[Rāma] killed Vālin, gave his kingdom to the monkey

[9] Cf. *Rāmcaritmānas, Ayodhyākāṇḍa* 116–117, in: *Rāmcaritmānas,* ed. tr. R.C. Prasad, Motilal Banarsidass, Delhi, 1991, pp. 325–326.

[10] Rāma himself performed the last ceremonies of Jaṭāyu and bestowed his own heavenly form on the heroic bird according to the *Rāmcaritmānas* (*Araṇyakāṇḍa* 32. op.cit. pp. 496-497).

> [Sugrīva], sent out Hanumān, knowing him as his good servant.
> Searching for the lotus-faced Jānakī, where [Hanumān] met her, the hero said nice words.

This *savaiyā* evokes the most important events in the *Araṇyakāṇḍa* and the *Kiṣkindhākāṇḍa* emphasizing Rāma's grace and generosity towards those whom he meets.

In Khidirpur and Pa_1 it is broken into two parts of two lines each. After the first two lines the *Araṇyakāṇḍa* ends and the other two lines open the *Kiṣkindhākāṇḍa.* In Pa_2 the *savaiyā* is kept as one and it is the last poem in the *Araṇyakāṇḍa.*

The *Araṇya-* and *Kiṣkindhākāṇḍa* both contain only one poem each in the *Granthāvalī* edition. In this quatrain there is an attempt to summarize the story in order to fill the gap. In spite of the fact that the author's name is missing from this poem it can be authentic. Tulsī did not aim at writing the full story in *Kavitāvalī*, and if some other poet had added the poem he would have probably elaborated more details.

4.1 जामवंत आदि कपि...

जामवंत आदि कपि चले खोज लेन फिरि
चंद्रप्रभा देखि राम वद्रिका को सो गई।
सिंधु तट लखे महाबीर विनु पक्ष रहे
भय ते भभरि भागे सोभा बहुते हई।
तुलशी कहत गुण जटा वंधु करणी सो
जमे पंख जस राम कृपादृष्टि सोभई।
राम के प्रताप गश वल गुण सुर लागि
कहै ऋक्षपति लखि आवो मातु को जई॥

---

1 जामवंत ... वहुरि] Σ, खोजनि वहोरी जामवंन्त कपि आदि चल्यौ Pa_2 • खोज] Kh_{ed}, खोजन Pa_1 • लेन] Kh_{ed}, *om.* Pa_1 • फिरि] *em.* वहुरि (hypermetrical) Kh_{ed}, बहुरि (hypermetrical) Pa_1 • चंद्रप्रभा] $Kh_{ed}Pa_1$, चंन्दप्रभा Pa_2 • देखि] $Kh_{ed}Pa_1$, देखी Pa_2 • वद्रिका] Kh_{ed}, पद्रिका Pa_1, बद्रीका Pa_2 • सो] $Kh_{ed}Pa_1$, वो Pa_2

2 सिंधु] $Kh_{ed}Pa_1$, शींधु Pa_2 • तट] $Kh_{ed}Pa_2$, तद Pa_1 • लखे] $Kh_{ed}Pa_1$, लखै Pa_2 • महाबीर] Kh_{ed}, महावीर Pa_1, माहावीर Pa_2 • विनु] Kh_{ed}, बिनु Pa_1, बीनु Pa_2 • पक्ष] $Kh_{ed}Pa_1$, पछ Pa_2 • भय] $Kh_{ed}Pa_1$, भए Pa_2 • ते] $Kh_{ed}Pa_1$, तें Pa_2 • भभरि] $Kh_{ed}Pa_1$, भभरी Pa_2 • भागे] $Kh_{ed}Pa_1$, चले Pa_2 • सोभा] $Kh_{ed}Pa_1$, शोभा Pa_2 • बहुते] Pa_1, हुते Kh_{ed}, बहुतें Pa_2 • हई] $Kh_{ed}Pa_1$, गइ Pa_2
3 गुण] $Kh_{ed}Pa_1$, गुन Pa_2 • जटा] Pa_2, जटायु $Kh_{ed}Pa_1$ • वंधु] Kh_{ed}, बंधु Pa_1Pa_2 • करणी] $Kh_{ed}Pa_1$, करनी Pa_2 • सो] $Kh_{ed}Pa_1$, शों Pa_2 • पंख] $Kh_{ed}Pa_1$, पछ Pa_2 • जस] $Kh_{ed}Pa_1$, जश Pa_2 • कृपादृष्टि] $Kh_{ed}Pa_1$, क्रीपाद्रीस्टी Pa_2 • सोभई] $Kh_{ed}Pa_1$, शोभइ Pa_2
4 राम] $Kh_{ed}Pa_1$, नाम Pa_2 • यश] $Kh_{ed}Pa_1$, जश Pa_2 • वल] Kh_{ed}, बल Pa_1Pa_2 • गुण] $Kh_{ed}Pa_1$, गुन Pa_2 • सुर] $Kh_{ed}Pa_1$, शुर Pa_2 • लागि] $Kh_{ed}Pa_1$, लागी Pa_2 • कहै] $Kh_{ed}Pa_1$, कहैं Pa_2 • ऋक्षपति] $Kh_{ed}Pa_1$, रीछपति पति (hypermetrical) Pa_2 • लखि] $Kh_{ed}Pa_1$, ल<खी> Pa_2 • आवो] Kh_{ed}, आबो Pa_1, *om.* Pa_2 • मातु] $Kh_{ed}Pa_1$, मातुं Pa_2 • जई] $Kh_{ed}Pa_1$, <व>इ Pa_2

Jāmavanta[11] and other monkeys went out again to search. Candraprabhā,[12] after seeing Rāma, proceeded to Badrīnāth.[13]
On the shore of the ocean [the monkeys] saw the great hero (Sampāti) who was without wings. Confused from fear they ran away—from his radiance they[14] were destroyed.
He[15] —and Tulsī—talk of the good qualities and of that act of his brother, Jaṭāyu. No sooner has Rāma's glance of grace shone [on Sampāti] than his wings were fixed.
He speaks of Rāma's majesty, glory, power, virtue [reaching] up to the deities, to the lord of the bears, and that he saw mother Sītā going [being taken away].

---

[11] Jāmavanta (Jāmbavān) is the king of the bears and minister of Sugrīva.

[12] In the *Rāmāyaṇa* of Vālmīki she is called Svayamprabhā. (Pur. Enc. p. 635 s.v. Rāma and also v. *Rāmcaritmānas Kiṣkindhākāṇḍa* 24-25, op.cit. pp. 528–529.)

[13] Badarikāśrama or Badaryāśrama, comprises Badrivana in the Himalayas (Pur. Enc. p. 97).

[14] This line can be interpreted as a reference to the story of Sampāti loosing his wings. But this event took place long time ago, so it seems to be not well fitted in the plot here. The other interpretation might be that the monkeys are scared because of the radiance of the hero.

[15] According to the *Rāmcaritmānas* Jāmavanta is the one who starts praising Jaṭāyu.

This *kavitta* refers to two events from the Rāma story. The first one is the story of Candraprabhā who is an ascetic woman living in a cave. The monkeys enter her abode, and she helps them to find Sītā by sending them to the seashore. She meets Rāma and then goes to Badrināth. The other story is that of Sampāti. He is Jaṭāyu's elder brother, who wants to eat the monkeys but when Jāmavanta mentions the deeds of Jaṭāyu, he becomes very happy realizing that the time of his *mokṣa* arrived. He had lost his wings long years before when flying too high to the sun, they were burnt. Now from the grace of Rāma he gets back his wings. He explains to the monkeys where is Sītā jailed.[16]

It is poem nr. 54 in the Khidirpur edition, where *Kiṣkindhākāṇḍa* along with this poem contains only the last two lines of the apocryphal #3.1. It is separated by a wavy line to mark the end of the previous *Araṇyakāṇḍa*. The half poem is also followed by a line of dots, and #4.1 starts after it. In $Patna_1$ similarly *Kiṣkindhākāṇḍa* contains the same half poem (the 3–4. lines of #3.1) followed by # 4.1. In $Patna_2$ this verse is nr. 55 as the first poem of *Kiṣkindhākāṇḍa*, the previous #3.1 is not broken in halves. The second poem of the *kāṇḍa (jaba aṅgadādina)* is the *savaiyā* published in *Granthāvalī* as the only poem of the section.

7.1 सासना सक्र अधीन...

सासना सक्र अधीन अधीन हतो दशकंट सो जानत जान्यौ।
जाके हे छाजत कोटिन कोटि सो वाजत है किधो कोटि
निसान्यो।
लंक कि पंक भई छन माह प्रजंत कि मीचु छुटी नियरान्यो।
भू को प्रभाव इहै तुलसी जो फरा सो झरा जो वरा सो
वुतान्यो॥

1 सासना] Kh_{ed}, शाशना Pa_2 • सक्र] Kh_{ed}, शक्र Pa_2 • अधीन ... हतो] Kh_{ed}, अधीन हुं तो Pa_2 • दशकंट] Kh_{ed}, दशकंधर Pa_2 • सो] Kh_{ed}, शो रीपु Pa_2 • जान्यौ] Kh_{ed}, उंनों Pa_2
2 कोटि] Kh_{ed}, कोटी Pa_2 • सो] Kh_{ed}, शो Pa_2 • किधो कोटि] Kh_{ed},

[16] Cf. *Rāmcaritmānas Kiṣkindhākāṇḍa* 27–28. op. cit. pp. 530–531.

कीधौ कोटी Pa_2 • निसान्यो] Kh_{ed}, नीशान्यौ Pa_2
3 कि] Kh_{ed}, की Pa_2 • पंक] Kh_{ed}, एक Pa_2 • भई] Kh_{ed}, भइ Pa_2 • छन] Kh_{ed}, छीन Pa_2 • माह] Kh_{ed}, मांह Pa_2 • प्रजंत कि] Kh_{ed}, प्रजंत की Pa_2 • नियरान्यो] Kh_{ed}, <ती>एरान्यौ Pa_2
4 भू को . . . तुलसी] Kh_{ed}, एह जग की है एहि करनी Pa_2 • सो] Kh_{ed}, शो Pa_2 • झरा] Kh_{ed}, हरा Pa_2 • वरा सो] Kh_{ed}, बरा शो Pa_2 • वुतान्यो] Kh_{ed}, बुतान्यौ Pa_2

Sovereignty, [first] submitted to Indra, was [then] submitted to the ten-headed Rāvaṇa—[everyone] is fully aware [of this]—,
who is decorated by crores of forts, while crores of kettledrums resound his fame,
and Lankā turned into a swamp within a moment, and death approached as a shot arrow.
This is the power of the world—Tulsī [says]—: whatever had yielded fruit fell down, whatever had burnt was extinguished.

This *savaiyā* is about the ways of the fate. The effect of the earth can change the good for bad and the bad for good.

It is poem nr. 235 in Khidirpur, nr. 237 in $Patna_2$, but it is omitted in $Patna_1$. In *Uttarakāṇḍa* of $Patna_1$ the order of the poems follows the *Granthāvalī* up to 90 but the 91–96 are omitted.

These four lines might be a later interpolation. The poem seems to be out of context since it does not belong to the group describing the majesty of Rāma's name (*Uttara* 89–110). In $Patna_2$ the last line does not contain Tulsī's name. It is rather to state the inevitable changes in the world: whatever flourishes will come to an end, no matter how powerful we are, within a moment we can loose everything.

7.7 कानन की पतुकी. . .

कानन की पतुकी करिकै गुरु की वतिआं सुनि दूध दुहावै।
या घट की मटुकी करिकै तव साधु की संगति जांवन लावै।
धीरज खंभ धरे तुलसी तहां अवगुण तीनि सो जारि वहावै।
ज्ञान रई लै मथै मन तक्र कों तौ नवनीत निरंजन पावै॥

1 करिकै] $Kh_{ed}Pa_1$, करिके Pa_2, करीकै Pa_3 • गुरु] Pa_2, गुर Kh_{ed}, गुण Pa_1, गुन Pa_3 • वतिआं] Kh_{ed}, बतिआं Pa_1Pa_3, बतिआ Pa_2 • सुनि] $Kh_{ed}Pa_1Pa_3$, शुनि Pa_2 • दूध] $Kh_{ed}Pa_1$, दुध Pa_2Pa_3 • दुहावै] $Kh_{ed}Pa_2Pa_3$, दुहाबै Pa_1
2 या] $Kh_{ed}Pa_1Pa_2$, जा Pa_3 • करिकै] $Kh_{ed}Pa_1$, करिके Pa_2, करीकै Pa_3 • तव] Kh_{ed}, तब $Pa_1Pa_2Pa_3$ • साधु] $Kh_{ed}Pa_1Pa_3$, शाधु Pa_2 • संगति] $Kh_{ed}Pa_1$, शंघति Pa_2, संघती Pa_3 • जांवन] Kh_{ed}, जांबन Pa_1, जावन Pa_2Pa_3 • लावै] $Kh_{ed}Pa_2Pa_3$, लाबै Pa_1
3 खंभ] $Pa_1Pa_2Pa_3$, खंम Kh_{ed} • तुलसी] $Kh_{ed}Pa_3$, तुलशी Pa_1Pa_2 • तहां] Kh_{ed}, तहा Pa_2, तब Pa_1Pa_3 • अवगुण] Kh_{ed}, अबगुण Pa_1, औगुन Pa_2, अवगुन Pa_3 • तीनि] $Kh_{ed}Pa_1Pa_2$, तीनी Pa_3 • सो] $Kh_{ed}Pa_1Pa_3$, को Pa_2 • जारि] $Kh_{ed}Pa_1$, दाम Pa_2, जारी Pa_3 • वहावै] Kh_{ed}, बहाबै Pa_1, बनावे Pa_2, बहावै Pa_3
4 लै] $Kh_{ed}Pa_1Pa_3$, ले Pa_2 • मथै] $Kh_{ed}Pa_1$, मथे Pa_2 Pa_3 • मन] $Kh_{ed}Pa_1Pa_3$, तन Pa_2 • कों] Kh_{ed}, को $Pa_1Pa_2Pa_3$ • नवनीत] Kh_{ed}, नबनीत Pa_1Pa_3, नवनीत्त Pa_2 • निरंजन] $Kh_{ed}Pa_1Pa_3$, नीरंजन Pa_2 • पावै] $Kh_{ed}Pa_3$, पाबै Pa_1, पावे Pa_2

Making a vessel of your ears listen to the guru's words
and get the milk;
then making an earthen pot of this body take the co-
agulator, the company of *sādhūs*;
grabbing the pole of steadfastness there—Tulsī [says]—
let the three defects burn[17] and flow away
taking the staff of wisdom churn the soul's buttermilk,
and then get the fresh butter, the Pure One.[18]

This *savaiyā* is an allegory of reaching the untainted God using the imagery of churning and getting pure butter. It is nr. 287 in the Khidirpur edition. It is nr. 23 on the folio 92 recto of Pa_1 and nr. 290 in Pa_2. It follows nr. 7.148 in Pa_3.

The use of the expression "the Pure One" might be the reason that this *savaiyā* was excluded from the *Granthāvalī* and from several manuscripts. The word *niraṃjana* "Pure, untainted One" suggests that the influence of the *niraṃjani* school and this poem may have been written by its most prominent poet, Tulsīdās.[19]

[17] *jār* in poetical language means 'burning', 'destroying', 'evaporating'.
[18] The word *niraṃjana* means pure, and also the Ultimate Being.
[19] See BANGHA op. cit.

7.8 काम...

काम तज्यौ अरु क्रोध तज्यौ अरु लोभ तज्यौ तौ कहा
भयो भाई।
भूष तज्यौ अरु प्यास तज्यौ घरवार तज्यौ जन जाति
सगाई।
देश तज्यौ अरु भेष तज्यौ अरु लाज तज्यौ तन की सुख-
दाई।
एते तज्यो तौ कहा तुलसी जो पै जानकीनाथ सो प्रीति न
लाई॥

---

1 तज्यौ ... तौ] Kh$_{ed}$Pa$_1$Pa$_3$, तेजो और लोभ तेजो और मोह तेजो तो Pa$_2$ • कहा] Kh$_{ed}$Pa$_1$Pa$_3$, कहां Pa$_2$ • भाई] Kh$_{ed}$Pa$_1$Pa$_3$, भाए Pa$_2$
2 भूष ... प्यास तज्यौ] Kh$_{ed}$, भूष तजी अरु प्यास तजी Pa$_1$, भुष तेजो और प्याश तेजो Pa$_2$, भुष तजी अरु प्यास तजी Pa$_3$ • घरवार] घरबार Pa$_2$Pa$_3$ • तज्यौ जन] Kh$_{ed}$, तेजौ जनि Pa$_2$, तजी जन Pa$_1$Pa$_3$ • जाति] Kh$_{ed}$Pa$_1$Pa$_3$, जानी Pa$_2$ • सगाई] Kh$_{ed}$Pa$_1$Pa$_3$, सगायौ Pa$_2$
3 देश तज्यौ] Kh$_{ed}$Pa$_1$, देश तेजो Pa$_2$, देस तज्यौ Pa$_3$ • अरु भेष तज्यौ] अरु भेस तज्यौ Pa$_1$Pa$_3$, और भेस तेजो Pa$_2$ • अरु लाज तज्यौ] *em.* औ लाज तज्यौ Kh$_{ed}$Pa$_1$Pa$_3$, <अ>चार[न/ज] तेजो Pa$_2$ • की] Kh$_{ed}$Pa$_1$Pa$_3$, को Pa$_2$ • सुखदाई] Kh$_{ed}$Pa$_1$, शुषधायौ Pa$_2$, सुषदाई Pa$_3$
4 एते] Kh$_{ed}$Pa$_1$Pa$_2$, ऐते Pa$_3$ • तज्यो] Kh$_{ed}$, तजो Pa$_2$, तजे Pa$_1$Pa$_3$ • तौ] Kh$_{ed}$Pa$_1$Pa$_3$, तो Pa$_2$ • कहा] Kh$_{ed}$Pa$_1$Pa$_3$, कहां Pa$_2$ • तुलसी] Kh$_{ed}$Pa$_3$, तुलशी Pa$_1$Pa$_2$ • जो] Kh$_{ed}$Pa$_1$ Pa$_3$, जों Pa$_2$ • जानकी-नाथ] Kh$_{ed}$Pa$_2$Pa$_3$, पानकीनाथ Pa$_1$ • सो] Kh$_{ed}$Pa$_1$Pa$_3$, शों Pa$_2$ • प्रीति] Kh$_{ed}$Pa$_1$, नेह Pa$_2$, प्रीती Pa$_3$ • लाई] Kh$_{ed}$Pa$_1$Pa$_3$, लायौ Pa$_2$

You have given up love and anger and greed, then what happened, my brother?
You have given up hunger and thirst, you have given up household, people, community and relatives;
you have given up your homeland and your garments and you have given up shame and the comforts of the body;
If you have given up so many things, then what?—Tulsī [says]—when you have no love for the Lord of Jānakī.

This *savaiyā* is about the superiority of devotion to Rama over all kinds of renunciation. In the Khidirpur edition it is nr. 288.

In $Patna_1$ it is written on folio 92 verso, nr. 24. In the $Patna_2$ it is numbered as 291, and in $Patna_3$ it follows #7.7, as the second poem after 148.

The last line is similar to that of 7.44. The poem may have been considered to be a *samasyāpūrti* on that given last line and omitted as inauthentic.

Conclusion

This article is the first attempt to bring into the light some unknown poems that were part of the textual tradition of Tulsī. It also tries to find some of the reasons why these poems were considered interpolations and later on left out from the standard modern editions.

Our survey of the manuscripts demonstrates that scribes in Bihar introduced features of their dialect into the copying process such as the *śa* like pronuntiation of *sa*, the loss of the short/long distinction in the wovels. These features rather suggest a passive knowledge of Brajbhāṣā in Bihar, in the periphery of the Hindi belt.

Our brief survey shows that further studies of medieval manuscripts are necessary even in the case of Tulsīdās's *Kavitāvalī*, a widely read and well known text.

We hope that we were able to show that the close examination of manuscript material can reveal some aspects how the *Kavitāvalī* was considered and received in premodern times.

Ten

Courtly and Religious Communities as Centres of Literary Activity in Eighteenth-Century India:

Ānandghan's Contacts with the Princely Court of Kishangarh-Rupnagar and with the Maṭh of the Nimbārka Sampradāy in Salemabad

Imre Bangha*

Some of the most fascinating works of old Hindi poetry originate from the princely states of Rajasthan, which because of its long tradition of patronage was one of the most important regions for literature during the Mughal era. Reconstructing the literary life of specific courts in Rajasthan is, however, a challenging task. In spite of the large amount of academic research on the history and culture of the region, material about the literary life of individual

*I am indebted to Prof. Govind Sharma for his help in interpreting the Braj texts, to Śrījī Mahārāj for his hospitality in Salemabad, as well as to Mr. Peter Diggle for his comments.

courts is uneven. A lot of research has been done on great court poets like Bihari or Matiram but far from being acquainted with the major authors of all the courts, today we are not even in a position to say which languages were used for literature in a particular court at a certain period. Many centres are famous for patronising Braj, Sanskrit or Urdu poets but were all these languages present in each court? Did they have specific roles or hierarchy? In what measure did literature in one language influence the other?

Hindi high literature of the eighteenth century was chiefly the literature of patronage. Literary activity was, therefore, centred on individuals or institutions that were able to patronise it. The secular centres were mainly the royal and princely courts, while the religious centres were the monasteries[1] of the various sects. It will be interesting to ascertain to what extent political and other interaction between these two types of centre influenced literature. We are going to see in the example of an individual poet that there was a subtle interplay between different languages and also between courts and monasteries. There was, however, a line that could not be transgressed and the finest poet of his time, Ānandghan, who violated this convention, had to pay a high price.

In my Hindi book *Saneh ko mārag* I argued that Ānandghan had lived in the Nimbārkī monastery in Salemabad and was in all probability in contact with the princely court of Kishangarh-Rupnagar. In this paper I am going to consider the cultural atmosphere of these centres of learning within the Kishangarh state and discuss Ānandghan's relationship with them.

Kishangarh-Rupnagar

The princely state of Kishangarh was founded in 1609 by Maharaja Kiśan Singh Rāṭhor[2] (r. 1609–1615), the younger son of

[1] I am using the word monastery in a broad sence to denote any institution (*maṭha, pīṭha, āśrama* etc.) where ascetics live together.

[2] Names that have a long established spelling in English will be spelt according to it (thus Singh instead of Siṃha). The inherent *a* in Hindi words will not be dropped in Braj quotations or in names with a prominent Sanskritic componenet. Thus the name Nāgrīdās will be written as Nāgarīdās and Parśurām as Paraśurām etc. It may also be retained after clusters of consonants as in Nandadās.

Udai Singh of Jodhpur who had been sent to the Mughal court and made friends with prince Salim, the later Jahangir (r. 1605–1627). His grandson Rūp Singh (r. 1643–1658)[3] founded the town of Rupnagar in 1648 and moved his court there. The golden period of the state was during the reigns of Mān Singh (r. 1658–1706) and his successor, Rāj Singh (r. 1706–1748). Mān Singh's family had also marital bonds with Aurangzeb (r. 1658–1707).[4] Both he and his son were frequent visitors to Delhi, which must have left a definite mark on their cultural tastes.

Rāj Singh's son, Sāvant Singh 'Nāgarīdās' was made *yuvarāj* 'prince regent', successor to the throne already in 1725.[5] The state was too small and barren to take part in the many struggles that characterised the eighteenth century. It also had immunity from the payment of tribute to the Mughals and to the Marathas alike.[6] So this peaceful atmosphere allowed Nāgarīdās to be involved more in his aesthetic pursuits than in the affairs of the state. This must be one of the principal reasons why after the death of Rāj Singh, Nāgarīdās's younger brother Bahādur Singh was successful in taking power in Kishangarh. Sāvant Singh did not return to Kishangarh until 1757 when he abdicated in favour of his son, Sardār Singh (r. 1757–1767) and the state was divided: Sardār Singh ruled the north of the country from Rupnagar and Bahādur Singh the south from Kishangarh. The state was united again when Sardār Singh died without offspring. Since the time of Bahādur Singh the capital has become Kishangarh again.

Contact with the Mughals

The name of Kishangarh has acquired world-fame because of the Kishangarh school of painting. Like most Rajasthani court painting this school combines indigenous elements with the achieve-

[3]SHARMA (1990:83).

[4]According to CELER (1973:9.) Mān Singh gave his daughter, Cārumatī, in marriage to Aurangzeb. HAIDAR(1995:26) also examines this question that embarrassed later Hindu chroniclers. According to her Cārumatī was not the daughter but the elder sister of Mān Singh and she was married to Mahārāṇā Rāj Singh of Udaipur while a younger sister was married to Aurangzeb's son Prince Mu'azzam.

[5]KHAN (1974:6).

[6]MALLESON (1875:89).

ments of the Mughal miniature. This combination was facilitated by the contacts of the Kishangarh court with the Mughals in Delhi. These contacts were both political and cultural. The Kishangarh rulers, like the other maharajas, not only visited the imperial capital frequently but also invited artists from Delhi to their courts.

One of the two most famous painters, Bhavānīdās, came to Kishangarh in 1719 straight from the Mughal capital.[7] The other one, Nihal Cand, also had connections with Delhi, since his great-grandfather, a minister under Maharaja Mān Singh, (1658–1706)[8] came from there. Some other painters, like Amar Cand, were trained in Delhi.[9] It was, however, not only the painters who were responsible for the spread of the Mughal taste. As has been mentioned members of the ruling family used to visit the Mughal court and their ideas were influenced by its culture. As Navina Haidar wrote:

> In the forty years of his reign, Raj Singh spent a considerable amount of time at Delhi, as did his son, Savant Singh. As with many of the Rajput princes from the early seventeenth century onwards, the time spent in Delhi by Raj Singh and Savant Singh must have had a strong effect on their artistic sensibilities, as they would probably have seen Mughal paintings in the reigns of Farrukh Siyar and Muhammad Shah, both of whom were active patrons. Certain stylistic and thematic developments at the Delhi court were thus reflected at Kishangarh...[10]

Apart from the Delhi artists and the regular visits to the Mughal court the use of Persian as one of the languages of diplomacy and administration in Rajasthan also helped to infiltrate Mughal culture into the Kishangarh court. Even some works in Persian were composed at such courts as Jaipur and Jodhpur.

---

[7] RANDHAWA and RANDHAWA 1980. (The authors quote Faiyaz Ali KHAN but do not give a precise reference.)

[8] DICKINSON and KHANDALAVALA (1959:14–5).

[9] DICKINSON and KHANDALAVALA (1959:16).

[10] HAIDAR (1996:56).

For example, in 1728 Maharaja Savāī Jai Singh and his team of astrologers compiled for the Mughal ruler Muhammad Śāh (r. 1719–1748) the *Zīj-i-Jadīd-i-Muhammad Śāhī*, one of the most important astronomical works of their times.[11] The Jodhpur epistolographer Munshi Madhū Rām (died 1732) wrote in 1708 the *Inśā'i Mādhū Rām*, a guide-book for the instruction of young students.[12]

At the same time the presence of Muslim musicians might also have contributed to the complexity of the court culture. A famous miniature of the Kishangarh court[13] from around 1760–66 shows among several courtiers the Delhi musicians Ustād Yār Muhammad and Ustād Nūr Muhammad together with singers Āmin Khān, Kiśanrām and Pokhrāj. Mīr Muhammad Umār, a dignity from the Ajmer dargāh, is also portrayed. Probably several Muslim religious authorities were present in the state and influenced the development of ideas. Rupnagar, for example, was also the seat of a Sufi saint known as Malang Śāh in the eighteenth century. According to legend the rulers used to ask his advice before military enterprises.[14]

There were courts where Persian poetry was appreciated,[15] and Braj authors like Nāgarīdās experimented also with Urdu, or rather Rekhtā, '(language) interspersed (with Persian and Arabic words)',[16] as it was called at that time. Themes of Persian poetry like that of the love of Laila and Majnun also appeared both in painting[17] and in poetry.[18] The courts, however, did not follow entirely what was seen in the imperial centre. Rajasthani court culture is a mixture of both Muslim and local Hindu elements. In spite of the works mentioned above it seems that comparatively

[11]KHAN (1981:47); HADI (1995:275).

[12]KHAN (1981:59); HADI (1995:327).

[13]Published in DICKINSON and KHANDALAVALA (1959:38–9).

[14]HAIDAR (1995:15) relying on Rose, H.A. 1883. *A Glossary of Tribes and Castes in the Punjab and the North-West Province Based on the census report for the Punjab*. Reprinted in Delhi, 1980.

[15]KHAN (1981:43, 58).

[16]Nāgarīdās's Rekhtā is Urdu with some Braj features. His works in Rekhtā are the collection of songs called *Rekhtā* (GUPTA 1965 I: 498-512) and the *Iśk-caman* (GUPTA 1965 II:48–52) written in *dohāo*.

[17]HAIDAR (1995:137–8)

[18]In the same *Iśk-caman*. See GUPTA (1965 II.51). For a translation of couplets 33–35 see HAIDAR (1995:138).

little genuine Persian literature was produced in the courts of Rajasthan. The dominant literary languages were Braj, Rajasthani and Sanskrit.[19]

Poets at the court

Works on Kishangarh miniatures do not fail to mention that the most important connoisseur patron, Nāgarīdās, was also a renowned poet. In fact, though he tried his hand at painting,[20] it is rather poetry that constituted his artistic production. It is also clear that he was not the only poet in Kishangarh-Rupnagar. In fact poetry as well as music and dance played a prominent role in the life of the courts of contemporary Rajasthan.

The high position that poetry enjoyed can be glimpsed from the fact that in many courts poets were heavily rewarded[21] and that poetry was part of the daily routine of the rulers. The 19th century poet Navīn for example put into verse what he received for the composition of his *Raṅgataṅga.*

> रीझ चतुर महराज वर गुन निधि मूरति काम।
> दीने अब तिह मौज में साज बाज धन धाम॥ 26॥
> बसन दिए भूषन दिए दिए मतंग उतंग।
> ग्राम दिए निज नाम हित सुनि करि रंगतरंग॥ 27॥[22]

> The excellent and intelligent king, who is a treasury of virtues and the [living] form of the God of Love, was pleased and in his delight gave me materials, riches and abode.
>
> He gave clothes, gave ornaments and gave big elephants. He gave villages when he heard the *Raṅgataraṅga* [written] for his name.

---

[19]For a survey of Rajasthani court literature in these languages in the 18th century see KATHURIA (1987:196–215).

[20]DICKINSON and KHANDALAVALA (1959:7, 19) and HAIDAR (2000:89).

[21]Some documents of payment of land and money to Vṛnd are published in CELER (1973:337–40).

[22]Quoted in NAGENDRA (1964:411)

Similarly, it can be supposed that with small variations daily routine must have been the same in all the courts in the neighbouring Rajput states. The *Pratāp prakās*, a work about Maharaja Pratāp Singh of Jaipur (r. 1778–1803), describes the daily routine of the Prince. Although it has a tendency to idealise, this description shows how important a place arts occupied in the life of the ruler and hence in the court. According to the *Pratāp prakās*,

> The minstrels *(bandījan)* start singing in praise of the family at four *ghaṛī* at night. The king, having heard it, rises in the period shortly before dawn *(brahmāmuhūrta)*. He meditates on his guru and after having a *darśan* of a cow and performing *chāyādān*-ceremony places his foot on the earth. Then he sits on a stool studded with jewels and washes his mouth. The petitioners submit their appeals and the artistes give performance to the devotional songs composed by him in *Vibhāsa* and *Bhairavī* (*rāgiṇīs*). He then attends to his daily morning duties. Arrangements for his bath are made... Having taken his bath, he attends to the *Pancāyatan* worship with Vedic hymns... Then he distributes the regular daily gifts among Brahmins and pandits *(nityadān)*... [He dresses himself] and starts for Śrī Govindadev's temple. Chiefs from different places, his kinsmen, *tāzīm* and *khāscaukī* nobles *(sardārs)*, scholars *(paṇḍits)*, poets *(kabīsvar)* and bards *(bhāṭ* and *cāraṇ)* stand in rows to pay respect and offer blessings to the king who sets out seated in a handcart... [*Then he visits the department of elephants where an elephant fight is arranged and visits the royal stables and retires to his palace where he takes rest, has lunch and then he gives a public audience where*] he attends to state business and petitions submitted by representatives of different states. He then turns to the artists *(guṇījan)*. The scholars have their discussions on the six schools of philosophy, the poets recite their eulogical poems *(kabīsvar jas paṛhaĩ)*, the bards recite the glory of the family *(bhāṭ, cāraṇ birada paṛhaĩ)*, the musicians *(kalāvat)* perform the six *rāgas* and thirty

> *rāgiṇīs*. [After the public audience he retires again for three hours and then practices archery, takes a bath; changes his dress, plays chess and attends a performance of dance.] The artists *(guṇījan)* come and after salutation they set their instruments...and the dancers *(naṭvā̃)* begin to show their feats...Thus having pleased the king with their performances they receive heavy rewards. The programme ends about midnight.[23]

This passage may give a picture of the life in the court with different groups of artist such as *bandījan, kabīsvar, bhāṭ, cāraṇ, guṇījan* and *naṭvā̃*. Its idealising tendency, however, does not let it show the complexity of poetry enjoyed at the court. As the editor of the text noted the *Pratāp prakās* does not mention certain important aspects of Pratāp Singh such as he himself being an excellent poet and a pioneer in Rekhtā poetry.[24] From this passage it seems that poetry either served as a vehicle of religious thought or of praise of the family or simply as text for the songs. The same idealising tendency may account for the fact that the text does not seem to give any place to non political secular poetry, namely *rīti*-poetry that was the most popular literature at that time.

One of our main interests in this article is the poetic atmosphere in Kishangarh-Rupnagar. How much of it can be reconstructed?Apart from Nāgarīdās who were the major poets?

Some of the most famous poets of the court belonged to the family of the ruler. This certainly testifies to the deep interest in poetry of the rulers but also suggests that members of the royal family received better recognition and probably more material support for spreading their manuscripts than others. Already Maharaja Rūp Singh has some stray devotional *pad*s to his credit.[25] Haidar claims that Mān Singh wrote *Sampradāy Kalpadrum*, a

[23]Based on passages from BAHURA (1983 [Hindi section]:5–12) and on their translation by BAHURA (1983 [English section]:3–7).

[24]BAHURA (1983 [English section]:15)

[25]Two songs are quoted in GUPTA (1965 I:28-29). HAIDAR (1995:24) also quoted and translated a *pad*, which she had taken from BRAJVALLABHŚARAṆ (1966:10).

work on the genealogy of the gurus of the *Puṣṭimārga*.[26] His successor, Rāj Singh is the author of longer works such as *Subāhuvilās* and *Rukmiṇī vivāh caritra* as well as of some stray *pads*.[27] He married twice and his second wife, Bāṅkāvatī (Brajdāsī) produced a complete Braj translation of the *Bhāgavata Purāṇa*, which is today called the *Brajdāsī Bhāgavata*. As late as 1734 Queen Bāṃkāvatī had a daughter who was called Sundar Kuṃvari. Princess Sundar Kuṃvari, author of twelve poetic works on bhakti themes,[28] was a poetess whose style, according to Kiśorīlāl Gupta,[29] is close to that of Ānandghan and of Nāgarīdās. The overwhelming majority of her poetic output consists in longer poems on bhakti themes, but she also wrote some *muktaks*, independent quatrains, that can be interpreted as expressions of both mundane and divine love. The two following *savaiyās* are cries of an abandoned beloved, which in their passionate description of feelings, instead of the outer signs of the sentiments, as was customary, remind one of Ānandghan's poems.

प्याय महा मदिरा निज माधुरी लोचन लोभिन लायो
हवेषो।
चेटक ज्यों सुखस्वाद लुभाय बढ़ाय बिसास हुलास बिसेषो।
लै ललचाय भुराय दुराय सु हाय बिहाय जुगौ अब मेषो।
जान परी निठुरान की बान पै रीझ के आगे न सूझै
परेखो॥[30]

[26]HAIDAR (1995:12). However, her reference to GUPTA (1965 I:30) is incorrect.

[27]GUPTA (1965 I:29–30). BRAJVALLABHŚARAṆ (1966:17.) seems to know about more works and gives the list as *Sukh Samīp*, *Bāhuvilās*, *Rukmiṇī haran*, *Rājpaṃcak kathā varṇan* and *Vīrsimhasāgar*. He also mentions a manuscript of *Rājsiṃhajī kī vāṇī* in the Sarasvatī Bhaṇḍār of Kishangarh which contains 176 folios (note 3).

[28]For a list of her works see BRAJVALLABHŚARAṆ (1966:17) and GUPTA (1965 I:30). Her earliest dated composition was from 1760 and the last work from 1803. Her works have been edited by Brajvallabhaśaraṇ (1983–84).

[29]GUPTA (1965 I:30)

[30]BIHARIŚARAṆ (1930:600) and GUPTA (1965 I:31).

You have made me drink the liquor of your sweetness
and brought intense longing into my covetous eyes.
Like a miracle with the taste of happiness you aroused
my desire and confidence and increased my joy.
You tantalized me, bewildered me and disappeared;
alas, even a moment passes like an aeon.
I have learnt the customs of the cruel ones but face to
face with delight there is no remorse.[31]

चौंकत ही चित कानन में उररै जब जो कोऊ नाव ले यातें।
आस सौं सास बिसास गहै रहै प्रेम प्रतीत वहै सुध आतें।
दै दै सँतोषन रोषन सों अब सोषन मोष ज्यों की हित घातें।
आहि सहै अस है पै चहै सु कहै कोऊ वाही बिसासी की बातें॥[32]

My ears are affected as soon as my mind startles that
somebody has taken his name.[33]
My breath keeps clutching at confidence out of hope
when I remember that trust in love.
Again and again you pleased me with contentment and
pleasure but now by giving dryness it is as if you
have smashed and abandoned your affection.
Either one bears it or not but one wants to talk about
that treacherous one.

She also tried her hand at writing in Rekhta. The choice of this style also brings the poem closer to the sentiments of one-sided love as expressed in Persian and Urdu ghazals:

---

[31]The word *parekho* means 'remorse' in Braj. The 'face to face' phrase suggests a simultaneous action and its original Sanskrit *par-īkṣ* 'examining' meaning cannot be excluded.

[32]BIHĀRĪŚARAṆ (1930:599) AND BRAJVALLABHAŚARAṆ (1983–84 II:95).

[33]The loose grammar of the poem, as much expressive of an agitated state of mind as of spontaneity of the style, cannot be retained in translation.

कृष्ण तो पियाले पिये चस्म मतवाले हैफ
कैफ उसी चले मुझ रोम रोम छाइयां।
बस्मौं करि बांधा लट तस्मौ चित खूब ख्याली
गस्मौं मै न जान दिलदारि यों भुराइयां।
वैसी करि ऐसी करी आफित असह परी
हाय रुह चोरी इस ख्यांमित बिताइयां।
कहना रह्या न अब सहना सलाह सब
यारी दा कुपेच मैडे नैनों दी कमाइयां॥[34]

Having drunk your cup, oh Krishna, alas, my eyes became intoxicated;[35] its exhilaration spread in my each and every pore.
Having subjugated my mind you have splendidly bound it with the strap of your tresses. In my unconsciousness I did not know that my sweetheart would thus beguile me.[36]
By your behaving this way and that way unbearable disaster befell me; Oh, because of this theft of heart I have to live this doomsday.
Nothing remains to say now, I have to forbear the advice of all—It is my eyes that earned this turn of affection for the worse.

Thousands of poems were also written by Nāgarīdās[37] both in Kishangarh and in Vrindaban and his beloved, Banī Ṭhanī, wrote bhakti-poetry under the pen-name 'Rasik Bihārī'. The following song is about Holī, the festival of colours in the month of Phālgun. The reference of the first line to the grove palace evokes the atmosphere of Kishangarh art.

कुंज महल में आज रंग होरी हो।
फाग खेल में बना बनी की ह्वै रही गठजोरी हो।

[34] BIHĀRĪŚARAṆ (1930:598) and BRAJVALLABHAŚARAṆ (1983–84 II:94).

[35] Or 'It is pity, oh Krishna, to have drunk the cup of your intoxicating eyes (since)...'

[36] Or 'would forgot me'.

[37] His earliest dated work is his *Manorath mañjarī* from 1723.

मुदित ह्वै नारि गुलाल उड़ावैं गावैं गारि दुहुँ ओरी हो।
दूलह रसिकबिहारी सुंदर दुलहिनि नवल किसोरी हो॥[38]

Today it is the merriment of the festival of colours in the grove palace:
In [this] sport of Phalgun the bridegroom and the bride are tying the [marriage] knot.
Delighted, the women throw red powder and sing mocking songs on both sides.
The bridegroom is the beautiful connoisseur Krishna and the bride is the young Radha.

It is important to note that the poets belonging to the royal family wrote overwhelmingly on devotional themes and produced very little overtly secular poetry. Just as in the miniatures of Nihal Cand, the most celebrated of the Kishangarh painters, secular activities and sentiments were rather projected into the divine plays of Radha and Krishna.

Comparatively little is known about other poets who lived in the court in the 18th century.[39] The most famous of them was Vṛnd[40] (1643–1723), who before settling in Kishangarh lived in the court of Aurangzeb as a tutor or guardian of the emperor's grandson, prince Azim-uś-Śān. Maharaja Mān Singh seems to have been so much moved by his poetry that he gave him gifts already in Delhi. The poet was finally brought to Kishangarh by Rāj Singh who in return of his support to Bahādur Śāh in the succession war in 1707 was permitted to take Vṛnd to his court.[41] Since that time the poet's family has become attached to the court of Kishangarh. His son, Vallabh, was in the service of Maharaja Rāj Singh and his grandson, Sanehīrām, served Maharaja Bahādur Singh.[42] Vṛnd's most famous work, the *Nīti-satsaī* (1704), is not on bhakti themes but on morals. Just as most court poets of his time he wrote chiefly about secular themes.

[38]Quoted in ŚARMĀ and SNĀTAK (1974:213).

[39]DICKINSON and KHANDALAVALA (1959:7); see also GUPTA (1965:35).

[40]On Vṛnd see CELER (1971) and CELER (1973). He is also quoted by Nāgarīdās in manuscript 'ya' of his *Chūṭak kabitta*. GUPTA (1965:7).

[41]CELER (1973:53). See also HAIDAR (1996:57) relying on *Chiefs and Leading Families in Rajputana*. (1894) Calcutta. Reprinted in Gurgaon (1992:25).

[42]CELER (1973:12) and DĪKṢIT (1993:3–5).

Another well-known poet is Haricaraṇdās Tripāṭhī (also known as Hari Kavi)[43] who lived under the patronage of Bahādur Singh. His works are not only independent compositions like *Sabhā-prakās* (1757), *Kavivallabh* and *Rāmāyansār* but also commentaries on the most celebrated works of the rītikāl: on Bihārī's *Satsaī* (1777), on Jasvant Singh's *Bhāṣābhūṣan* and on Kesavdās's *Kavipriyā* (c. 1778).

The case of 'Uncle' Hit Vṛndāvandās illustrates the point that princely courts gave shelter to poets who had strong sectarian affiliation and because of inimical circumstances had to leave their monasteries. Vṛndāvandās was a poet of the Rādhāvallabhī sect, who in 1757, at the time of the massacre in Braj, fled to Farrukhabad[44] and then to Bharatpur to the shelter of Maharaja Sūraj Mal (1757–1763),[45] later he spent the years 1774–78 in Kishangarh in the court of Bahādur Singh.[46]

Apart from Vṛnd and Haricarandās Dickinson and Khandalavala[47] mentioned the names of Hīrālāl,[48] Munshi Kanhīrām,[49] Pannālāl,[50] Vaiṣṇav Vijaycand[51] and Dāhivā̃ Vijayrām[52] who were present in Nāgarīdās's court although no source was given for this list. With the exception of stray verses by Munshi Kanhīrām[53]

---

[43] MIŚRA (1972:421). GAUṚ (1964:619). MIŚRA and MIŚRA (1913:780–781). Nāgarīdās knew about his poetry, since he is quoted in *Srīmad-Bhāgavat-parāyan-nidhi-prakās* 19.

[44] *Harikalā Belī* 4 quoted in BANGHA (1997:236).

[45] *Harikalā Belī* 191 quoted in BANGHA (1997:231).

[46] MCGREGOR (1984:162).

[47] DICKINSON and KHANDALAVALA (1959:7).

[48] Hīrālāl Sanādhya is quoted in *Śrīmad-Bhāgavat-parāyaṇ-nidhi-prakās* 17 and 30. He is different from Hīrālāl Kāyastha (son of Hemrāj) who lived a century earlier and wrote his *Rukmiṇīmaṅgal* in 1647.

[49] Quoted in *Śrīmad-Bhāgavat-parāyaṇ-nidhi-prakās* 31.

[50] Probably identical with Kalha Pannā quoted in *Śrīmad-Bhāgavat-parāyaṇ-nidhi-prakās* 29 and 16.

[51] Probably identical with Binaicand *(Vaiṣṇavī nām Carandās)* quoted in *Śrīmad-Bhāgavat-parāyaṇ-nidhi-prakās* 18, 32, 33 and 34 as well as in manuscript 'ya' of *Cūṭak kabitta* (GUPTA 1965:7).

[52] Quoted in manuscript 'ya' of *Chūṭak kabitta* (GUPTA 1965:7) and in *Śrīmad-Bhāgavat-parāyaṇ-nidhi-prakās* 14, 15 and 28. The *kabittas* of Vijayrām (!) are also quoted in a manuscript dated from VS 1814 (1757 AD) [Rajasthan Oriental Research Institute, Jodhpur 14137(3)3].

[53] Cf. MIŚRA and MIŚRA (1913:1020).

found in some manuscripts or quoted by Nāgarīdās elsewhere,[54] very little seems to be known about the literary activities of the rest. The best available source about them is a poetic compilation mentioning all these names along with those of Rasik Bihārī (Banī Ṭhanī), Haricaraṇdās, Purohit Brajlāl and Bhaṭṭa Brajnāth. This work is the *Srīmad-Bhāgavat-parāyaṇ-nidhi-prakās* compiled and partly written by Nāgarīdās in 1742. It contains poems by the above mentioned poets in praise of the *Bhāgavata Purāṇa*. Banī Ṭhanī was present in the court at that time. Brajnāth Bhaṭṭa, the teacher, *vidyāguru*, of Nāgaridās' step-mother, as well as Haricarandās, who was reported to be in the court of Bahādur Singh in later years, might well have been there in 1742. From their presence we can suppose that the rest were also in the court at that time. This seems to be corroborated by the prose passages between the poems of the *Srīmad-Bhāgavat-parāyaṇ-nidhi-prakās* suggesting that the verses were composed for a religious gathering. These lesser known authors, however, were not professional court poets; otherwise there would have been further literary traces. They were probably employed in the court as priests or scribes as their names suggest.

The literary ideals

The literary atmosphere in the court of Kishangarh partly corresponded to what is seen on the Kishangarh miniatures. The Kishangarh-school of painting infused the achievements of Mughal art into the already popular Krishna-bhakti themes. We can observe a development from the overtly secular approach of earlier art as illustrated in Bhavānīdās's miniatures and Vṛnd's poetry towards an art dressed in religious ideas in Nāgarīdās and Nihal Cand. While Bhavānīdās and Vṛnd came from Delhi, Nāgarīdās and Nihal Cand were born in Kishangarh. In this second phase bhakti gained prominence over overtly secular themes like hunting, court scenes etc.

Two most popular themes of the later phase—the celebration of the feminine ideal and the representation of the love-games of

[54] Kanhīrām's song *Kīra uṭhi bolyo ika ...* is quoted in *Pad muktāvalī* 142.

Radha and Krishna in sophisticated royal surroundings—can be abundantly observed also in the poetry.

घूंघट झीनैं दुकूल को झूलैं झुके दृग बंकित कानन छ्वै।
जुग भौंहनि बीच थक्यो मन गौंहन होठन लाल रह्यो रँग च्वै।
मंद हँसै सुख नागर कौं मुख चौंपन की उपमा तब ह्वै।
तिमिरावली साँवरे दंतनि कैं हित मैंन धरे मनौं दीपक द्वै॥[55]

Her fine veil of *dukūla* is swinging: she lowers her curved eyes that touch her ears.
My mind, transfixed with her red lips oozing beauty, languished on her eyebrows.
In her gentle smile is Krishna's (and Nāgarīdās's) joy and her face is a simile of desires.
As if the God of Love held two lamps for the thread of darkness of her black teeth.[56]

The description of the divine couple also gives an excellent occasion to celebrate nature.

लहकि लहकि जात लगि कैं पवन लता
महकि महकि उठै मालती सुवास है।
गहकि गहकि गावैं कोकिला तरुन चढ़ी
कुंज छबि पुंज काम सेवत निवास है।
नागरिया स्यामा स्याम सोहैं सुख सैनी पर
देखैं द्रुम रंध्रनि न कोऊ सखी पास है।
दोऊ मन हरैं दोऊ रीझि रीझि अंक भरैं
अंगनि अनंग बाढ्यौ रंग मैं बिलास है॥[57]

Rising and rising the wind moves the creepers and the scent of the blossoms is wafted again and again.

[55]GUPTA (1965 II:123).

[56]The image behind this line is that black antimony was applied to the teeth while gold dots decorated the two front teeth.

[57]GUPTA (1965 II:93).

Exhilarated the cuckoos on the trees sing; in the grove
Kāma serves the dwelling-place with a plenitude of beauty.
[Nāgarīdās says how] the dark Krishna and Radha
shine with joy on a bed; they watch through the branches of the trees if no companion is around.
The two capture the mind and embrace each other
with joy—in their limbs the God of Love has grown and in their pleasure love.

How did these two aspects gain prominence in Kishangarh at that time? There were three types of major forces working behind the increased emphasis on the feminine: religious, literary and personal. The religious force is the rise of Radha, Krishna's beloved, to the status of an independent goddess. She was different from all Hindu goddesses in that for long she had not had a role independent from Krishna. In painting it is not until the eighteenth century that a strong iconographical development of Radha can be seen in India. At Kishangarh the Radha image started to be painted not only as Krishna's consort but also as a subject in its own right.[58] Among the bhakti sects, however, it was not the Puṣṭimārga, as suggested by some scholars[59] that put Radha in such a high position. Although the Puṣṭimārga recognises Radha as Krishna's Śakti, divine energy, and thus entitles her to worship in her own right, Vallabhan devotees rather worship Krishna alone or with Radha in a subordinate position.[60]

The emergence of Radha in Kishangarh cannot be examined without taking into the picture the tenets of the other influential sect within the state, the Nimbārka Sampradāy. Since the 16th century Radha has been awarded a prominent place in this sect as one of the four major elements of its theology, Radha, Krishna, Vrindaban and the *sakhīs*, Radha's female companions. The human being aspires to the position of *sakhī* and delights in

[58]About the emergence of the Radha-image in miniature painting see HAIDAR (forthcoming).

[59]HAIDAR (1995:106).

[60]Only three of the eleven chief Vallabhan deity-images have consorts and even these three have Radha in a subordinate position. Cf. VAUDEVILLE (1982:329 note 26).

witnessing and serving the love-games of the ever newly wed divine couple. The fact that the devotee perceives himself or herself as a companion of Radha rather than as a male companion of Krishna, a *sakhā*, indicates that in this school Radha has become the focus of attention.[61]

In eighteenth-century Braj literature, however, Radha was given a prominent place sometimes inextricably connected to the secular presentation of woman categorised under different behavioural patterns in love. This genre was called *nāyikā-bheda*, 'categories of heroine'. Another popular literary theme was the *nakh-śikh-varṇan*, the description of a heroine from tip to toe.

Experts on the Kishangarh painting do not fail to mention that the most outstanding patron, Nāgarīdās, drew his inspiration not only from religious ideas of the Radha-Krishna theme, but also from his mundane affection to a living woman known as Banī Ṭhanī. Banī Ṭhanī, originally named as Viṣṇupriyā,[62] had been purchased as a slave by Rāj Singh in 1727, at the age of 10. She was taken into the employ of Queen Bāṃkāvatī in 1731 where she became an accomplished poet and singer. She also spent some time in Delhi with the queen. Nāgarīdās became enamoured of her probably around 1739 when she returned from Delhi and she became the prince's mistress.[63] In fact it was Banī Ṭhanī and not his wife who accompanied Nāgarīdās into his self-imposed retirement in Braj.[64] Some scholars went so far as to conjecture that she also provided inspiration for the invention of Kishangarh facial formula.[65] Although this hypothesis can be seriously questioned[66] it must be accepted that Nāgarīdās's secular love and the literary ideals current in Kishangarh cannot be detached from each other.

As far as the other thematic peculiarity of the Kishangarh school, the love games of Radha and Krishna, is concerned, Dickin-

---

[61] About the development of the theology of Radha in the Nimbārka school see CLÉMENTIN-OJHA (1990: 327–76).

[62] KHAN (1986:9) suggests this name on the basis of *bahī*-documents.

[63] DICKINSON and KHANDALAWALA (1959:8–9); HAIDAR (1995:128).

[64] DICKINSON and KHANDALAWALA (1959:11–12).

[65] DICKINSON and KHANDALAWALA (1959:9–10); RANDHAWA and RANDHAWA (1980:9).

[66] HAIDAR (1995:126–8) relying on KHAN, Faiyaz Ali 1979. 'Kishangarh Painting and Banī Thani' in *Roop Lekha* Vol. XL, pp. 83–88 and on KHAN (1986:9).

son and Khandalavala wrote in the context of the Kishangarh miniatures:

> "Their theme takes life and substance from the most consecrated of all themes, the shining of the feminine ideal recreated in the amours of Radha and Krishna. These, as it were, form a passionate breviary of the customs of lovers in the eternal kingdom of love. Quarrels and sweet reconciliations, momentary desertion followed by abject submission, wounded pride and then unutterable longing. Running through the idyllic themes of the pastorale of a cowherd and his maid, the true devotee identifies himself with Radha only to realise that pride, vanity, waywardness are of no avail to win the love of the almighty. Only an absolute devotion can reveal to the devotee the way of the grace of God. It is true, the feminine element predominates in the paintings; it is an art consecrated to beauty [...] and yet if one withdraws the mystical element hovering alike over silent forest groves and marble palaces, there is left only the lover and his lass. For the divine bridegroom and his bride have vanished from our ken."[67]

This 'mystical element' or rather the bhakti themes in Kishangarh, however, were more than a pretext for depicting secular themes. In poetry for example an essential part of Nāgarīdās's oeuvre is preoccupied with the individual's search for the divinity. In fact it was during the time of his active patronage that bhakti themes gained prominence in the Kishangarh paintings.[68] It was also at that time that the royal family built a temple in Braj known as Nāgarī Kunj, which is still in the custody of the Nimbārka sect.[69] According to the Nimbārkī scholar Brajvallabhśaraṇ one of the main impulses for the construction of this temple may have been the poetess-queen Bāṃkāvatī.[70] The

---

[67] DICKINSON and KHANDALAVALA (1959:18).

[68] HAIDAR (1995:101) states that bhakti themes appeared after 1725.

[69] ENTWISTLE (1987:210).

[70] BRAJVALLABHŚARAṆ (1966:15).

emergence of bhakti themes in miniatures and in poetry after the more secular approach of the Delhi artists is an interesting feature in the Kishangarh court. Already Navina Haidar noted that within a Rajasthani context, Kishangarh was unusual in developing a full blown bhakti idiom as late as the mid-eighteenth century.[71] Factors like self assertion on a spiritual ground against a weakening Delhi power, the increasing contact with Braj or an energetic pious queen's getting more prominence after the death of the first queen, Caturkuṃvarī in 1719 may account for this development.

Some scholars have tried to show that Nāgarīdās derived the driving force of his art and patronage from his affiliation to the Vallabh Sampradāy.[72] The question of the inspiration for his poetry and patronage is, however, far more complex. Nāgarīdās may well have been initiated into the Vallabh Sampradāy because the sect has been associated with the royal court since the time of Rūp Singh (r. 1629–43) till the present day. Rūp Singh symbolically dedicated his state to Śrī Kalyān Rāy, the deity of the Puṣṭimārga at Kishangarh.[73] However the religious interests of a princely state in Rajasthan in the eighteenth century are unlikely to be extended only towards one sect. In neighbouring Jaipur for example there were three protective deities belonging to different sects[74] and other sects like the Puṣṭimārga or the Nimbārkīs who did not have an important deity in the capital were not necessarily less influential than the others.[75] Similarly in Kishangarh royal patronage seems to have been extended to the Nimbārkīs after the time of Kiśan Singh.[76]

Nāgarīdās's poetry was not limited to sectarian tenets and he

[71]HAIDAR (1995:56).

[72]DICKINSON and KHANDALAWALA (1959:18–19); GUPTA (1965:37–57); RANDHAWA and RANDHAWA(1980:10); HAIDAR (1996:12). BRAJVALLABHŚARAṆ (1966) tried to present Nāgarīdās as a follower of the Nimbārka sect but his ideas were refused by KHAN (1974:9–16).

[73]HAIDAR (1995:5–6) based on KHAN (1986:35).

[74]Jamvāīmātā, the domestic deity of the royal family, was taken over from the Mīnās, Govindadev belonged to the Gauḍīy sect and Sītārām to the Rāmānandī sect. See CLÉMENTIN-OJHA (1999:25–27).

[75]CLÉMENTIN-OJHA (1999:76, 86–94).

[76]As claimed by BRAJVALLABHŚARAṆ (1966:9) though he did not quote any source material for this assertion.

seems to be influenced more by later bhakti poetry that emphasises the love plays of Radha and Krishna than by the Vallabh school. This attitude would also be encouraged by the Nimbārkīs who had their headquarters in the vicinity of Kishangarh, in Salemabad, and where at that time lived one of the most respected religious authorities of Rajasthan, Vṛndāvandev, the guru of Queen Bāṃkāvatī.

Nāgarīdās's liberal religious approach is well illustrated in the *maṅgalācaran* of the *Pad prabodh mālā*:

मेरे येई वेदव्यास।
श्री हरिवंश ऽरु व्यास गदाधर परमानंद नंददास॥
श्री हरिदास बिहारिनिदास बिट्ठल बिपुल सुजान।
रामदास नाभा दामोदर अलि भगवान सखी भगवान॥
चतुर्भुजदास दास मेहा पुनि श्रीभट चतुर बिहारी।
प्रीतम रसिक रसिक वल्लभ अरु ध्रुव रस रीति उचारि॥
तुलसीदास मीराँ माधव अरु उभै नागरीदास।
आसकरन नरसी वृंदावन रुचि माधुरी सुख रास॥
कृष्णदास सूर गोविंद अरु कुंभन छीत स्वामि अनुरक्ता।
श्रुति पुरान मेरैं इनके पद हौं श्रोता ए वक्ता॥
तजि इनके पद अर्थ सुनै को नाना मत बिभचार।
मूल सास्त्र सिध क्यौं हेरैं पद छाड़ि अमृत फल सार॥
रसना श्रवननि मैं इनके पद रहो हिय मैं निर्दूषन।
'नागरिया' इनकी पद रज सो होहु भाल भूषन॥ 1॥[77]

These are the authors of the Vedas for me:
Śrī Harivaṃśa and [Harirām] Vyās, Gadādhar [Bhaṭṭ],
Paramānanda[dās], Nandadās;

Śrī Haridās, Bihārinīdās, the intelligent Biṭṭhal Bipul;
Rāmdās, Nābhā[dās], Dāmodar ['Sevak'], [Ananya] Ali
Bhagavān, Sakhī Bhagavān;

[77] GUPTA (1965 I:1).

Caturbhujdās, Mehā Dās then Srībhaṭṭa [and] the clever Bihārī;
Prītam Rasik, Rasik Vallabh and Dhruv[dās] proclaimed the correct usage of the rasa.

Tulsīdās, Mīrā [Bāī], Mādhav[dās] and both Nāgarīdās;[78]

Āskaran, Narsī [Mehtā], Vṛndāvan[dās?] [and] Mādhurī-[dās] are interested in the joy of the *rāsa*-dance.

Kṛṣṇadās, Sūr[dās], Govinda[svāmī] and Kumbhan[dās], the loving Chītsvāmī
For me their songs are the Vedas and the Purāṇas, I am the listener, they the speaker;

Who will abandon their songs and meaning[79] and listen to diverse opinions and deviations?
Why should we look at the root texts or at the feet of [accomplished] siddhas giving up the essence of the fruits of immortality?

Their songs are on my tongue, in my ears and I remain unpolluted in my heart.
Nāgarīdās [says:] the dust of their feet[80] should be the ornament of my forehead.

This list gives an idea of which devotee-poets' works Nāgarīdās was acquainted with. He recognised devotees with different sectarian affiliation to be his masters. There are bhaktas from among the *Aṣṭachāp*, 'the eight seals', of Vallabhācārya's Puṣṭimārga (Paramānandadās, Nandadās, Caturbhujdās,[81] Kṛṣṇadās, Sūrdās,

[78]GUPTA (1965 I:14) argues that one of the two Nāgarīdās is identical with Nāgardev, a religious leader in Svāmī Haridās's lineage, and the second with 'Nehī' Nāgarīdās, a follower of Hit Harivaṃśa. This may also be a reference to two brothers who were the pupils of Bihārinīdās: Nāgarīdās and Sarasdās (d. 1626). Cf. MCGREGOR (1984:93).

[79]There is a double meaning here with the words *pad* 'foot, song', *artha* 'meaning, aim' and with *padārtha* 'gem'.

[80]There is a conventional pun here with the double meaning of *pad* 'foot' and 'song'.

[81]Apart from the Caturbhujdās of the *Aṣṭachāp* there is also a famous

Govindasvāmī, Kumbhandās, and Chītsvāmī). Apart from them Āskaran 'Kachvāhā' Maharaja Kiśan Singh's uncle[82] and the Gujarati Narsī Mehṭā were also considered to be Pusṭimārgīs. There are devotees from Caitanya's Gauḍīy Sampradāy (Gadādhar Bhaṭṭa and Mādhavdās 'Jagannāthī'), the Haridāsī Sampradāy (Svāmī Haridās, Bihārinīdās, Biṭṭhal Bipul, Srībhaṭṭ and Nāgarīdās), the Rādhāvallabhī Sampradāy of Hit Harivaṃśa (Harivaṃśa, Harirām Vyās, Dāmodar 'Sevak', Rasikdās (?), 'Nehī' Nāgarīdās (?) and Dhruvdās). Some poets without sectarian affiliation (Mīrā Bāī) are also mentioned as well as non Krishna bhaktas (Nābhādās and Tulsīdās).

Salemabad

Many of the Rajasthan states had influential deities and hence influential religious centres within their precincts. Nāthdvārā in the Mewar state for example is the home of the principal Pusṭimārgī deity, Srīnāthjī and Jaipur gave shelter to Govindadev of the Gauḍīy sect. The principal religious centre within the Kishangarh state was the monastery of Salemabad, the centre of the Nimbārka Sampradāy in Rajasthan and the seat of its leader, Srījī Mahārāj. In the past centuries the Nimbārka Sampradāy has been considered to be one of the four orthodox Vaishnava schools *(cauḥsampradāya)*. The sect states that it was started by Nimbārkāārya, who in his *Vedāntaparijātasaurabha* advocated the *bhedābheda* 'difference-and-nondifference' theory about the relationship etween the individual soul and the absolute. Today, however, is not the writings of Nimbārka but Harivyāsdev's *Mahāvānī* ıat Nimbārkīs hold in highest esteem. The *Mahāvānī* depicts the ve games of Radha and Krishna and in its approach is clearly fluenced by the concepts of Svāmī Haridās and Hit Harivaṃśa. imbārkī tradition puts the text back to the 16th century.

The seat at Salemabad was established in the 17th century by raśurāmdev one of Harivyāsdev's twelve disciples. The *mahant*, perior, of the seat is the spiritual leader of a community of

dhāvallabhī poet of this name: Caturbhujdās 'Murlīdhar'. It is not clear ch of them Nāgarīdās refers to.

[2]ENTWISTLE (1987:210 note 417).

ascetics and laics. Since the establishment of the Salemabad seat many of its superiors had literary activities. The most famous of them was the same Paraśurāmdev, whose Hindi *Paraśurāmsāgar* is close to *nirgun* poetry proclaiming the 'attributeless' God to be immanent in every being and emphasising the power of his name.

परसा दरपन नैन को उभय मिलाप अनूप।
जो देखे निज रूप को सो देखे हरि रूप॥ 53॥

ज्यों दर्पन पावक पड़े परसत ही रवि धूप।
परसुराम हरि नाम ते प्रगटे हरि निज रूप॥ 54॥[83]

The meeting of the mirror and the eye is extraordinary.
The one who sees his own form sees also the form of God.

As fire falls into the mirror when the sunshine touches it.
By the name of Hari, Paraśurām, God's own form becomes manifest.

In the eighteenth century the ascetic branch of the Haridāsī Sampradāy became associated with the Nimbārkīs. This event took place due to Savāī Jai Singh's regulatory endeavours in the field of religion. Jai Singh, Maharaja of Jaipur (r. 1699–1743), made an effort to ensure that only those sects get royal recognition that can trace back their origin to one of the classical Hindu sects. The ascetic branch of the Haridāsī Sampradāy took refuge in the older, prestigious Nimbārka sect. The Haridāsīs in turn enlivened it with their popular approach to the love-games of the divine couple Radha and Krishna. Acārya Vṛndāvandev's *Gītāmṛt Gaṅgā* is an excellent expression of devotion towards the divine couple.

[83] BIHĀRĪŚARAṆ (1930:78).

आज सुख लूटत लाल विहारी बैठे चित्र विचित्र अटारी।
ज्यौं ज्यौं पिय निरखत मुख त्यौं त्यौं हंसि हंसि उर लपटति पियारी।
चुंबन दै पुनि लै लज्जित ह्वै छिन ह्वै जाति नियारी।
वृंदावन प्रभु तब अंकन भरि रीझि प्रकासंत कामकला री ॥ 7, 19 ॥[84]

Today the dear Krishna riots in pleasure sitting in an ornamented upper room.
As her lover is watching her face the beloved one smilingly takes him into her embrace.
She gives and then takes kisses and ashamed[85] she separates herself for a moment.
Then Vrindaban's Lord embraces her rejoicingly—displays his art of love.

The Nimbārka sect was not confined to Salemabad. During Ānandghan's time, it had shrines in places like Mathura, Vrindaban, Jaipur and Rupnagar served by members of the sect. In Vrindaban for example it had a small temple at Baṃsī Baṭ,[86] the Banyan tree on the bank of the Yamuna under which Krishna is said to have played his flute. The seat in Rupnagar[87] was the place of religious discussions between Nimbārkīs and Vallabhans[88] and Vṛndāvandev also stayed in the town for some time.[89]

During the first half of the eighteenth century, the sect had excellent contacts with the court of Jaipur. The town had a high number of *Nimbārkīs* and even Vṛndāvandev the *mahant* of Salemabad (1697–1740) used to spend a part of the year there. It was at his times that serious royal patronage was given to his sect since documentation about it in the royal archives date back

[84] *Śrīsarveśvar* (1952–53:45).

[85] An alternative translation is 'giving a kiss she is ashamed to take it back and she separates herself for a moment'.

[86] ENTWISTLE (1987:414).

[87] This must be the 'Gopāl Dvārā' mentioned by BRAJVALLABHŚARAṆ (1966:10).

[88] HAIDAR (1996:15) (based on personal communication of Faiyaz Ali Khan).

[89] BRAJVALLABHŚARAṆ (1966:14).

as early as 1719. The centre in Salemabad received the revenues of some villages within the Jaipur state. Patronage was not extended because of an important *Nimbārkī* temple in Jaipur but because of the superior's good contacts with the palace and especially with the women's quarters.[90] Today only one *Nimbārkī* temple is known within the palace precincts, the *Srījī kī moṛī*, which was established in 1791 by the mother of Maharaja Savāī Pratāp Singh (1778–1803) for an image known as *Gopījanavallabh.* However there may have been *Nimbārkī* sites in the town already at the time of Vṛndāvandevācārya. Those years, according to Brajvallabhśaraṇ, a Benares paṇḍit, Jayrāmdās Śeṣ, and ācārya Brajānand were in charge of these sites.[91] The *mahant* was surrounded by several servants and had his horses, elephants and arms since he also controlled some groups of ascetic warriors *(nāgas)*. When he was staying in Jaipur he conducted a lavish life with great feasts. The grandest of them was in the early nineteenth century when 90 000 people were fed by the regent Bhaṭṭiyānī in a feast organised for her guru, Nimbārkaśaraṇ, for a *guru-pūrṇimā* festival.[92]

In the early eighteenth century the prestige that the leader of the sect enjoyed was partly due to Vṛndāvandevācārya's contacts with the princely courts. A Sanskrit poem in his praise is attributed to Maharaja Savāī Jai Singh.[93] Queen Bāṃkāvatī 'Brajdāsī' and princess Sundar Kuṃvarī of Kishangarh were among his disciples. Nāgarīdās must also have been in close contact with the ācārya residing within the territory of his state.

At the same time the rulers of the states wanted to have a voice not only in the tenets of the sect but also in its decisions about filling up posts in the hierarchy. On Vṛndāvandevācārya's death for example Savāī Jai Singh and some other maharajas filled the post of ācārya with Jayrāmdās Śeṣ. However, after Jai Singh's death three years later, Śeṣ was removed and a new ācārya, Govindadev, was declared by the ascetics.

[90]CLÉMENTIN-OJHA (1999:86). About Jaipur's contact with Nimbarkīs in the early nineteenth century see also CLÉMENTIN-OJHA (forthcoming).

[91]BRAJVALLABHŚARAṆ (1943:2) and BRAJVALLABHŚARAṆ (1966:18). Unfortunately no source for this information is mentioned.

[92]CLÉMENTIN-OJHA (1999:88).

[93]Published in *Śrīsarveśvar* (1952–53:ca).

If we can postulate that secular aspects of poetry written by religious personalities in monasteries are due to interaction with centres of secular literature then we can state that the interaction with the princely courts did not leave Vṛndāvandev's poetry untouched since it also has secular traits. Although all the poems of the *Gītāmṛt Gaṅgā* are classified under one of another *līlā*, 'divine game' of Radha or Krishna, if they are examined independently from this context, they will show an affinity to the refined mundane love poetry of the time:

तो मुख चन्द किधौं अरविंद ये मो दृग धोखैं परे ही रहैं
री।
देखन को अति आतुर हैं सु इन्हैं ऊ चकोर कै भौर कहैं
री।
ये सब प्रेम मनौं इन हीं बस मोहू लियें फोरैं गैल गहैं री।
वृंदावन प्रभु रोके रहैं नहीं धाय परैं जब तोहिं लहैं री
॥ 4, 40 ॥[94]

Is your face moon or lotus my eyes remain uncertain;
They are very eager to see it so shall they also be
[called] partridge or black bee?
As though all my love were in their hands; they roam
bedazzled taking their ways;
Vrindaban's Lord, they cannot be restrained; they start
to run as soon as they catch you.

This complex approach, however was given up by later *ācāryas* who again wrote poetry clearly about bhakti themes.[95]

[94] *Śrīsarveśvar* (1952–53:23).

[95] For specimens of the poetry of the later *mahants* see the relevant chapters in BIHĀRĪŚARAṆ 1930. GovindŚaraṇ Devācārya's poetry is also published in BRAJVALLABHŚARAṆ 1970.

Ānandghan

Ānanadghan's poetry in princely courts

Even though it is after all the literary outcome that decides a poet's place in the imaginary 'literary hierarchy' of an era, there are many instances when factors outside literature—fashion, patronage, politics etc.—influence reputation. The history of Ānandghan's standing is a striking example of this since his early fame in literature seems to have faded away when his name was denigrated. This was so much so that the traces of his sectarian and court affiliation were lost in oblivion or maybe consciously erased. Ānandghan was one of the finest Hindi poets of the eighteenth century but until recently he has not been counted among the celebrated authors of Indian literature. There are even Hindi literary histories with his name missing.[96]

In Ānandghan's case one encounters a strange situation. While on the one hand disrepute was attached to his name, on the other hand his poetry was enjoyed both in courts and religious centres. Ānandghan wrote two types of poetry. In the later part of his life when he was an ascetic he produced bhakti poetry abundantly. The high number of manuscripts of song-collections that include his poems shows that his religious songs were popular in the late eighteenth and in the nineteenth centuries. It is, however, clear that Ānandghan was even more celebrated for his quatrains with a secular tinge although it seems that they were often presented as bhakti poetry. His quatrains enjoyed popularity, and the best poets in the late eighteenth and in the nineteenth centuries were deeply influenced by his quatrains. It was his quatrains that were popular in princely courts and several rulers were well acquainted with them.

Maharaja Madho Singh (1750–1767) of Jaipur, for example, is said to have praised his songs when he met the poet in the temple of Govindadev in 1757.[97] Nāgarīdās included some of Ānandghan's devotional poems into his *Pad-muktāvalī*. There are Ānandghan manuscripts written in Bharatpur for Maharaja Ranjit Singh (1777–

[96] E.g. KEAY, F. E. *History of Hindi Literature*.

[97] ŚYĀMSUNDARDĀS (1937:173) based on the letter of Jaylāl.

1805) and in Jaipur for Maharaja Savāī Pratāp Singh 'Brajnidhi' (1778–1803).[98]

Indeed, Prince Javān Singh 'Brajrāj' of Udaipur was so much moved by Ānandghan's quatrains that he asked his court poet, Dayānidhi to write a cycle of eight poems, an *aṣṭaka*, based on a phrase from Ānandghan.

सुघर शिरोमनि श्री कुंवर जवान सिंघ
एक दिन बिरह कबित्त मो सों सुनि सुनि।
आय कब आनंद को घन बरसायहो या
कबित्त पै अष्टक बनै यों कहि पुनि पुनि॥[99]

One day, having heard from me [several] poems on separation, the crest-jewel of the accomplished ones, Prince Javān Singh
Insisted that a cycle of eight poems should be composed on the quatrain 'when will you come and rain down from the cloud of bliss?'

Prince Javān Singh was referring to the following quatrain by Ānandghan:

प्रीतम सुजान मेरे हित के निधान कहौ
कैसें रहैं प्रान जौ अनखि अरसायहौ।
तुम तौ उदार दीन हीन आनि पर्‌यौ द्वार
सुनिये पुकार याहि कौ लौं तरसायहौ।

---

[98]For a description of the Bharatpur manuscript see ŚUKLA (1950:269–79). At the end of manuscript 3469 in the Pothikhana of Jaipur the following couplet is found:

bānī ānandaghana daī nṛpa pratāpa ke hātha|
pāū̃ brajanidhi darasa nita bhajana sunāū̃ sātha||

I gave Anandghan's Vāṇī to king Pratāp's hands;
I have the sight of the 'Treasure of Braj' and sing *bhajans* with him forever.

[99]BANSAL and BANSAL (forthcoming:10). The *aṣṭaka* is on pp. 123–127.

चातक है रावरौ अनोखे मोह आवरौ
सुजान रूप बावरौ बदन दरसायहौ।
बिरह नसाय दया हिय मैं बसाय आय
हाय कब आनँद कौ घन बरसायहौ॥[100]

Tell me, my dear Sujān, treasury of my affection, how can my life remain if you tarry angrily?
You are generous [and] this destitute wretch came to your door. Listen to his call; how long are you going to torment him?
He is your pied cuckoo enclosed in unique passion, mad for the beauty of the Intelligent One; show him your face.
Destroying his separation, taking compassion into your heart, oh, when will you come and rain down from the cloud of bliss?

The popularity of Ānandghan's quatrains in princely courts shows that he was able to write poetry that was enjoyed at court. Although the possibility of some secular poetry reaching the monasteries cannot be denied, it is more probable that Ānandghan was well acquainted with court atmosphere and therefore he was able to produce literature that was enjoyed in princely courts. From this point of view the question of his association to a court needs special attention. The available legends suggest that a movement from a court to an ashram has been associated with his figure. An investigation into Ānandghan's contacts with monasteries and courts can also shed light on the interaction between these two centres of patronage.

The legend and the search for the historical figure

Ānandghan died in the year of the battle of Plassey, in 1757. His century is a more convenient era for research in Hindi literature than the previous ones from which we tend to have only legends about poets. In our case Ānandghan's silence about his own life is somewhat counterbalanced by having three manuscripts from

[100] *Sujānhit* 24. Published in MIŚRA (1952:9–10).

his lifetime and some contemporary references to him. Although scholars like Viśvanāth Prasād Miśra and Manoharlāl Gauṛ made efforts to trace the historical figure, they were not able to offer a view detached from nineteenth-century legends connecting the poet with the Mughal court in Delhi. The only scholar who mentioned Ānandghan's connection with Salemabad and Kishangarh was Brajvallabhśaraṇ Vedāntācārya from Salemabad.[101]

Today, however, it is not Brajvallabhśaran's idea that prevails. Ānandghan's quatrains are included in Hindi high school textbooks and usually his legend is taught along with them. Most people familiar with Hindi literature find Ānandghan's story set in the Mughal court very useful for understanding his poetry. According to this legend the poet was the chief scribe, Mir Munshi, of Muhammad Śāh of Delhi. He was so much in love with a courtesan whom he called Sujān that he made a vow that he would sing only to her and to no one else. When his enemies at court learnt about this, they plotted against him and told the emperor, who was known as *Raṅgīle* 'pleasure-loving', about Ānandghan's skill in singing. He was then summoned but declined to sing. Then the conspirators suggested ordering the courtesan to ask the Mir Munshi to do so. Then the scribe sang, but he turned towards his beloved and not the emperor. Although the song delighted everyone, the sultan was infuriated by the munshi's disrespect and ordered him to quit the court. When the poet asked Sujān to accompany him, she refused. Nevertheless, Ānandghan did not cease writing poems to his beloved, and until his death he used to address Sujān in them. In his exile he went to Vrindaban, became an ascetic of the Nimbārka Sampradāy, and the word *sujān* in his works came to mean Krishna himself or Radha and Krishna jointly. According to the legend quoted by Rāmcandra Śukla, he wrote his last quatrain to Sujān when he was mortally wounded.[102]

बहुत दिनान की अवधि आस पास परे
खरे अरबरनि भरे हैं उठि जान कौ।
कहि कहि आवन सँदेसो मनभावन कौ

[101] BRAJVALLABHŚARAṆ (1956:287) and BRAJVALLABHŚARAṆ (1966:13).
[102] ŚUKLA (1942:366).

गहि गहि राखति ही दै दै सनमान कौ।
झूठी बतियानि की पतियानि तें उदास ह्वै कै
अब न घिरत घन आनँद निदान कौ।
अधर लगे हैं आनि करिकै पयान प्रान
चाहत चलन ये सँदेसो लै सुजान कौ॥[103]

Fallen into the noose of hoping for an end to many days [of waiting], he is now full of real haste to get up and go.
I kept giving the message that the 'one who delights the heart' is coming and I kept catching at him holding him back with respectful attendance.
But now, disillusioned from trusting in the lying words, in the end he cannot be kept back from the Cloud of Bliss.
Setting out, my life has reached the [door] of my lips; he wants to go and take the message of Sujān.

Ānandghan's story described by Rāmcandra Śukla, as it is, is a mixture of legendary and real elements. This 'last' poem for example is already found in a manuscript from 1727.[104] The legend, however, refers to the poet-bhakta as someone who died in Braj. This fact is attested by 'Uncle' Vṛndāvandās who in his poem *Harikalābelī* deplored Ānandghan's death in the massacre of Braj in 1757.[105] At the end of the poem *Murlikā-mod*, Ānandghan seems to have given the date and place of composition as VS 1798 (1741 AD) Vrindaban.[106] Therefore it can be said that Ānandghan spent his last years in Braj.

One of his works called *Paramahaṃs Vaṃśāvalī* describes the lineage of his gurus in the Nimbārka Sampradāy. From the praise poured on Vṛndāvandevācārya, it can be inferred that he took

[103] *Sujānhit* 54. Published in MIŚRA (1952:18–19).

[104] Pothikhana, Jaipur, *Khāsmohar Collection* Ms Nr. 2437 (4) poem Nr. 40.

[105] About the *Harikalā Belī* and Anandghan's death see BANGHA (1997:231–41).

[106] It is only given like that in Miśra's edition. In ŚUKLA (1950:269-279) these line are reported to follow the colophon and thus not being part of the poem.

initiation from him. A further sign of Ānandghan's affiliation to the Nimbarkīs is that the most complete manuscript of his works is preserved in the Nimbārka Sampradāy.[107]

Although Viśvanāth Prasād Miśra argued that the poet took initiation in Vrindaban and Vṛndāvandev may have visited Vrindaban several times, there is no reason to exclude the possibility that Ānandghan took his initiation from him elsewhere, most probably in Salemabad, and lived his early religious life outside Vrindaban.

Two out of the three manuscripts dated from Ānandghan's lifetime were written near Salemabad, in Rupnagar, the then capital of the Kishangarh State. Ānandghan's earliest dated manuscript is from here and was written by the circle of a certain Svetāmbar Hemrāj. The two other manuscripts largely rely on this one. The peculiarity of this manuscript is that it tries to get rid of the suspicious word Sujān, the alleged name of the poet's beloved, and tries to substitute it with names that show either a clear bhakti context like Radha or Krishna, or with names that have a secular connotation like *su priya* 'that/good beloved' etc. These changes seem to be the result of an awkward effort to protect the poet's name.[108] The quatrains lose their soul, their multiple layers of meaning, by these changes. It becomes difficult to explain these changes, if one argues that it is not the poet's fame that was involved somehow in them. We can, therefore, state with almost certainty that Ānandghan was personally known in Rupnagar and probably lived in that area.

There are some indications that Ānandghan and Nāgarīdās were closely acquainted with each other. A picture shows Ānandghan and Nāgarīdās together with Brajānand sitting in front of Vṛndāvandev. There is mention of this picture already at the end of the nineteenth century. At that time the picture was kept in the royal archives of Kishangarh as attested by the court poet Jaylāl, who was an advocate of Nāgarīdās's contact with the Vallabh Sampradāy. After the death of Vṛndāvandev there would have been no need to forge a similar picture in the Kishangarh court

[107] MIŚRA (1952 *'Prastut granthāvalī'*:3), (1952 *'Vānmukh'*:72). At the time of the edition the manuscript was in the Śrījī kī baṛī kuñj, the Nimbārkī centre in Vrindaban, today it is in Salemabad.

[108] BANGHA (1999:49–58).

showing Nāgarīdās's contact with the Nimbārkīs. The Vallabhan affiliation of the royal family seemed to be more prominent. Therefore there is not any reason to question the originality of this picture. The court poet Jaylāl told of Nāgarīdās's journey to Kishangarh in 1757 together with Ānandghan. According to Jaylāl, Ānandghan did not go as far as Kishangarh but returned from Jaipur and consequently was killed in the massacre of Braj.[109]

Ānandghan's quatrains

Ānandghan's poetic oeuvre can be divided into two main groups. The first is relatively simple religious poetry, namely some one thousand songs (*pads*) and thirty-odd long poems in praise of Radha, Krishna or Braj. These poems fit well into the flow of devotional poetry that had been written in North India since the 16th century. The other group is his quatrains (*kabittas*), the overwhelming majority of which is not overtly devotional. Here devotional quatrains alternate with poems that are secular or that can be read in either way. It was Ānandghan's *kabittas* that earned him fame and they also seem to be instrumental in his bad reputation. The poet was condemned because one reading of his poetry was that he was using the name of his mundane beloved, the Muslim dancer Sujān, to denote the divinity. Other Hindu poets like Nāgarīdās were cautious not to identify the beloved overtly with God. In his *Iśk-caman*, another example of Rekhtā poetry, where he speaks about love with Islamic imagery and vocabulary, Nāgarīdās's interpretation is different from that of the sufi mystics since he considers lover, God and the beloved to be three different entities while in sufism *Khudā*, God, and *mahbūb*, the beloved, are the same.[110]

> आसिक पीर हमेस दिल लगें चस्म के तीर।
> किया खुदा महबूब कौं सदा सखत बेपीर॥ 15॥[111]

---

[109] ŚYĀMSUNDARDĀS (1937:173) based on the letter of Jaylāl.
[110] Cf. KHAN (1974:24).
[111] GUPTA (1965 II:49).

The lover's heart is always tormented struck by the arrow of the glance;
[But] God made the beloved to be continuously hard and unfeeling.

The larger part of Ānandghan's quatrains can be read as relating also to secular love, as was done by the scribe who tried to change the word for the beloved, *sujān* into expressions like *ju syāma* to make sure that it is not read as mundane. However, when the quatrain was too overtly mundane, then *sujān* was changed into *su pyārī* and the like to make sure that this 'secular' poem does not have any religious reference. It never happened in Hindi literature before Ānandghan that the human beloved was identified with the absolute as Ānandghan's double usage of the word *sujān* suggests. This twofold reading of the poems was peculiar rather to Persian and then to Urdu. I quote a quatrain to illustrate this:

झलकै अति सुंदर आनन गौर छके दृग राजत काननि छ्वै।
हँसि बोलनि मैं छबि फूलनि की बरषा उर ऊपर जाति है ह्वै।
लट लोल कपोल कलोल करै कल कंठ बनी जलजावली द्वै।
अँग अंग तरंग उठै दुति की परिहै मनौ रूप अबै धर च्वै॥
प्रकीर्णक ॥ 2॥

Her very charming fair face shines [and] her ear-touching intoxicated eyes are bright;
In her smiling speech flowers of grace are showered on her breast;
On her temple a fickle lock of hair is gambolling, [as does] the well-made double pearl-necklace on her beautiful neck;
A wave of lustre emerges from her every limb; it seems as if beauty [itself] is now pouring down on the earth.

In quatrains like this the description could be either that of Radha or of Ānandghan's mundane beloved.

Today critics link Ānandghan's approach to the Sufi theory that his excessive mundane love led to love divine. They also try to show that his *kabittas* draw on Persian poetry in their preference for idiomatic usage and for strong contrast *(virodh)*.[112] Moreover, love brought to such an extreme that someone dies with the name of the beloved who has long abandoned him, is rather Persian than Indian. Indian aesthetic theories do not even know about completely unrequited love. Scholars take refuge in the Sufi ideology to demonstrate the deepest bhakti in Ānandghan and draw a parallel between him and Raskhān who also reached Vaishnava bhakti through his mundane love.

However, if we forget about the nineteenth-century legend quoted above it is more difficult to interpret his poetry. It seems that his contemporary critics took just the opposite of the modern view: it is degrading to the divine to be called by the name of a human being let alone that of a Muslim courtesan.

It is however not so easy to detect direct Persian influence in Ānandghan. Many of the features that one is tempted to consider alien to traditional Hindu literature, are in fact present in Sanskrit. As is the case with drinking alcohol:

दृग छाकत हैं छबि ताकत ही मृगनैनी जबै मधुपान छकै।
घन आनँद भीजि हँसै सु लसै झुकि झूमति घूमति चौंकि
चकै।
पत्ल खोलि ढकै लगि जात जकै न सम्हारि सकै बलकै 'रु
बकै।
अलबेलि सुजान के कौतुक पै अति रीझि इकौसी ह्वै लाज
थकै॥ 100॥

The eyes become drunk looking at the beauty when
the gazelle-eyed one is drunk with alcohol.
Soaked in a 'cloud of bliss' she laughs, shines, bend-

---

[112]For discussion of possible Persian influence on Ānandghan see Miśra's *'Paricay'* in GAUṚ (1958:0–16) as well as GAUṚ (1958 153–4, 159–60).

ing she staggers and feels dizzy, [then] becomes startled and alert.
She opens and closes her eyelids, dozes off and wakes up, she can't restrain herself, babbles and talks nonsense.
Utmostly delighted by the wonder of the beautiful Sujān, the shame left alone loses its strength.

Scenes of drunkenness, if not common, were not alien to Sanskrit literature. It is enough to think of the drunken women in the beginning of Harṣa's *Ratnāvalī*. Or to quote another example from the *Pānagoṣṭhīpaddhati* chapter of the *Sūktimuktāvalī*:

पिपि प्रिय सस स्वयं मुमु मुखासवं देहि मे
तत त्यज दुदु द्रुतं भभज भाजनं काञ्चनम् ।
इति स्खलितजल्पितं मदवशात्कुरङ्गीदृशः
प्रगे हसितहेतवे सहचरीभिरध्यायत ॥[113]

'De-de-dear, give me the nectar of your lips yourself;
le-le-leave quickly the golden vessel'
This talk of the gazelle-eyed one stammering from the force of alcohol
was repeated by her companions in the morning to laugh at.

Whatever may be the origin of such ideas, it is difficult to interpret similar poems in a bhakti context. The secularisation of religious themes as observed in Vṛndāvandev and Nāgarīdās prepared the ground for Ānandghan's poetry, and probably it was also responsible for the change in Hindi Poetry in which it became more open to absorb Persian influences. One aspect of Ānandghan's secular *kabitta*s can certainly derive from that of his guru, Vṛndāvandevācārya, who already wrote poetry that taken out of its bhakti context can be interpreted as mundane. Ānandghan went further: he not only wrote ambivalent quatrains but in many of them the mundane aspect overshadowed every Vaishnava aspiration.

[113] *Pānagoṣṭhīpaddhati* 3. Published in VYAS (1991:266). I am indebted to Dr Harunaga Isaacson for drawing my attention to this poem.

According to the legend and to an early source Ānandghan belonged to the *kāyastha* (scribe) cast and therefore was probably well acquainted with Persian, the language of administration. It is not unlikely that directly or indirectly his poetry was influenced by the ideals of Persian or Urdu ghazals. It can be supposed that to be receptive to such ideals was not learnt in a Hindu religious community but rather in a royal or princely court, where both Hindu and Muslim ideas were more naturally mixed in the culture. The popularity of Ānandghan's *kabitta*s in princely courts also indicates that he was acquainted with the taste cultivated there. We do not possess enough evidence to tell whether he lived originally in Delhi as legend says or whether he was connected to a court later, when he was already an ascetic.

It is clear that Ānandghan was not a court poet in Kishangarh since his name is missing from the Persian or Rajasthani *bahī*s (records of payments, commissions, dates and places of work) in Kishangarh,[114] where the name of poets like Vṛnd is several times present.[115] No poem of Ānandghan praises any mundane patron as was usual for court poets. If this acquaintance with court poetry does not originate from an initial life in a royal or princely court then it can be said that it was of a type similar to that of Vṛndāvandev since the ascetics of one of the most influential monastery in Rajasthan had to keep the connection with the courts. While Ānandghan's connection with Salemabad seems to be very probable, the type of his relationship with Kishangarh-Rupnagar needs further investigation.

The debate about Ānandghan's poetry

Ānandghan's approach to Sujān as both human and divine infuriated some religious circles. We can glimpse the views of the opponents in the lines of certain *bhaṛauā chand* (mocking verses),[116] which according to Gauṛ, were probably composed before 1755

[114]Personal communication of Faiyaz Ali Khan in March 1997.
[115]For payments to Vṛnd see CELER (1973:337–340)
[116]First published in MIŚRA (1952 '*Vaṃmukh*' :66–67).

AD[117] but with all probability in circles that knew Ānandghan well.

> कायथ आनंदघन महा हरामजादा हो। सु ब्रज की कटा मैं आयौ परंतु अपजस वकौ थिर है। ताकौ बर्नन।
>
> The *kāyastha* Ānandghan was a great rogue. Although he came to the district of Braj, his bad reputation remains. [This is] his description:

> डफरी बजावै डौम डाढ़ी सम गावै काहू
> तुरकैं रिझावै तब पाव झूठौ नाम है।
> हुरकिनी तुरकिनी सुजान को सेवक है
> तजि राम नाम वाकौं पूजै काम धाम है।
> ... ॥ 3 ॥

> He beats the tambourine, sings like a Ḍom or a Ḍhāṛhī,
> pleases a Muslim and then gets false fame;
> He is the servant of the prostitute Muslim Sujān; he leaves the name of Rām and worships[118] her abode of desire.

Such verses mock not only Ānandghan's physical contact with Muslims but also suggest literary interaction.[119] In other words the person and his poetry were considered alien to orthodox Vaishnavism. It should be mentioned that this example of inter-communal distrust is not an isolated case in Vaishnava context. The author of Raskhān's *vārtā* in the *Do so bāvan vaiṣṇavan kī vārtā* distances himself from Raskhān's Muslim background by mocking at it.[120]

[117] GAUṚ (1958:7–8). Unfortunately Gauṛ did not give any justification for this date. The poems were taken from a book called *Jas kabitta*. In a personal communication in 1996 he said that *Jas kabitta* was in the *Yājñik*-collection of the Nāgarīpracāriṇī Sabhā in Benares; however I was not able to find it there. Bhavānīśaṅkar Yājñik was a priest at the Gokulnāth temple in Gokul, which suggests that the manuscript came from Braj.

[118] The word *pūjai* is an obscene pun with a secondary meaning of 'he fills'.

[119] For a more detailed discussion of these mocking verses see BANGHA (1999:44–46, 115) and BANGHA (2000:529–531).

[120] SNELL (1989:29–37).

The blame on Ānandghan was so strong that not even his beautiful composition, the *Kṛpākand*, 'The Root of Grace', on divine grace as opposed to the rituals as advocated by the earlier Nimbārkī *ācāryas*[121] redeemed him. Eventually he had to give up not only writing complex poetry but had to abandon the quatrain form since it was so closely associated with Sujān, the dancer. He began to write simple bhakti poetry in a conventional style.

रसना गुपाल के गुन उरझी।
बहुत भँति छल छंद बंद बकवाद फंद तें सुरझी॥[122]

My tongue is entangled in Gopāl's virtues;
[and] disentangled from the various bonds of false poems
[and] traps of twaddle.

Research done by Heidi Pauwels shows that Nāgarīdās also wrote about his mundane beloved in a religious context.[123] As has been mentioned, Nāgarīdās was more cautious in his approach to themes associated with Muslims than Ānandghan. Moreover, Ānandghan lacked the royal power to ward off similar attacks.

We have noted above that some of Sundar Kuṃvarī's quatrain bear close resemblance to those of Ānandghan. It is interesting to observe that three of them (including one quoted above, *pyāya mahā*, and two others with the word 'sujān' in them) that seem to be the closest to Ānandghan are missing from the manuscript that served as the basis of Brajvallabhaśaraṇ's edition although they are present in the *Nimbārka mādhurī*.[124] Considering the amount of change Ānandghan's anthologies underwent because of the ambiguous usage of Sujān, it may not be a coincidence in this case either.

Probably it was also his bad reputation that made him decide to take up a new home in Vrindaban. His quatrains continued to be both blamed and popular. Nevertheless, there were people who wanted to reach 'the original Ānandghan' and get rid of the

[121] Cf. dohā 30 of the *Siddhānta Sukh* in the *Yugal Śatak* referred to in CLÉMENTIN-OJHA (1990:371).
[122] *Padāvalī* 687. MISRA (1952:493–4)
[123] PAUWELS, 2005
[124] Nrs. 23-25 in BIHĀRĪŚARAṆ (1930:600)

changes that were introduced by scribes like Svetāmbar Hemrāj. One of them was Brajnāth, who with all probability is identical with the Sanskrit poet Brajnāth Bhaṭṭa a courtier and friend of Savāī Jai Singh of Jaipur (r. 1697-1743).[125] In his Sanskrit *Padyataraṃginī*,[126] Brajnāth Bhaṭṭa praises both Savāī Jai Singh and Savāī Madho Singh (r. 1750-1767) but not Savāī Īśvarī Singh (r. 1743-1750). During the reign of Īśvarī Singh Brajnāth lived in Rupnagar in the Kishangarh state of his disciple, the poetess-queen Bāṃkāvatī who mentioned him as her *vidyāguru* at the end of her Braj translation of the Bhāgavata Purāṇa.[127] It was in Rupnagar in 1748 that he composed his Braj work on aesthetics, the *Sāhitya-sār*.[128] Brajnāth also prepared a new collection of Ānandghan's quatrains that did not show Ānandghan as a religious poet but as a 'great lover (who is) skilled in Brajbhāṣā'. He even discarded most of Ānandghan's openly religious quatrains and inserted eight poems at the beginning and the end of his collection explaining that Ānandghan was misunderstood:

स्वाद महा खर दाखनि चाखत ज्यौं जन नैननि रोष बढ़ावै।
ज्यौं तरुनी तन रूप निहारत षंद बढ़ै हिय सोच उपावै।
चित्र बिचित्र के भेद सराहत ज्यौं दृगमंद न काहू सुहावै।
त्यौं घन आनँद बानि बखानत मूढ़ सुजाननि आनि सतावै॥

As it angers the eyes of the people when an ass relishes the great taste of the grape,
As it perturbs the heart when a eunuch, staring at the beauty of a girl's body, approaches her,
As it pleases no one when the short-sighted praise the secrets of a wonderful painting,
So it disturbs the intelligent ones when the stupid expound Ānandghan's words.

According to Brajnāth, Ānandghan should be read as a *nehī mahā brajabhāṣā-prabina*, 'a great lover [who is] skilled in Bra-

[125] BANGHA (1999:121–8).

[126] ŚĀSTRĪ 1996.

[127] ŚARMĀ (1996:1266).

[128] A manuscript of this unpublished work can be found at the Rajasthan Oriental Research Institute in Jodhpur (Nr 2264).

jbhāṣā' and this should be done 'with a cautious mind'. The blame attached to Ānandghan was so strong that expounding his poems cost Brajnāth his prestige:

> मैं अति कष्ट सों लीने कबित्त ये लाज बड़ाई सुभाय कों
> खोय कै।
> सो दुख मेरो न जानै कोऊ लै बखानै लिखाइयै मोहू कों
> गोय कै।
> कैसी करौं अब जाहुँ कितै बिताए हैं रैनि दिना सब भोय
> कै।
> प्रेम की चोट लगी जिन आँखिन सोई लहै कहा पंडित होय
> कै॥ 8॥

> I have taken these kabittas with a lot of trouble losing
> my honour, prestige (and) character.
> Nobody knows my suffering; 'Take' they say '[and]
> write them down secretly for me, too'.
> What shall I do, where shall I go now? I have spent
> my days and nights immersed [in it].
> What is the use of being a scholar for one whose eyes
> have been wounded by love?

The censure of Ānandghan may be the reason why neither Salemabad nor Rupnagar claimed the poet with pride in the eighteenth and nineteenth centuries and his connection with the Rajasthan state was lost in oblivion.

Conclusion

As has been seen both the court of Kishangarh-Rupnagar and the monastery at Salemabad were home to both secular and religious poetry to a varying extent. Although Kishangarh-Rupnagar court culture was open to Mughal and Muslim influences there was a movement from a secular approach towards a more religious one at the time of Queen Bāṃkāvatī and Prince Sāvant Singh. At the same time secular poetry was not alien to the Nimbārkī monastery at Salemabad either. In the first half of the eighteenth century the Nimbārka sect was influential not only in courts like Jaipur but through a pious queen also in Rupnagar. It should be the Nimbārkīs rather than the Vallabha sect that influenced the development of a feminine ideal in the court through their increased emphasis on the divine figure of Radha.

The culture of Rupnagar and Salemabad were dynamic cultures experimenting with novel approaches and generating literary debates. The best example of these debates is the one about Ānandghan's quatrains. The most outstanding quatrains of this poet are found at the meeting point of the cultures of the courtly and of the religious communities and can be read as expressing love both for a worldly beloved and for the divinity. The overt identification of the mundane beloved with the divinity was, however, too much for certain religious circles and they rejected Ānanadghan's twofold approach as a Muslim idea. To protect Ānandghan's fame Hemrāj of Rupnagar and his circle mutilated the text of his poems in order to reject the doublefold interpretation. The scholar Brajnāth, who in all probability is identical with Brajnāth Bhaṭṭ of Jaipur, tried to rescue Ānandghan's quatrains on the basis of their literary merit. Although he 'lost his honour' in the process, his approach prevailed and till the present day people read Ānandghan's quatrains through his eyes being moved by the love expressed in them both in its divine and mundane aspects.

Bibliography

BAHURA, Gopal Narayan. 1983. *Pratapa Prakasa: Life in Jaipur Court in Late 18th Century*. Jaipur: Maharaja Sawai Man Singh II Museum.

BANGHA, Imre. 1997. 'The Harikalā Belī and Ānandghan's Death' in *Annali* (Istituto Universitario Orientale, Napoli) Vol. 57, pp. 231-241.

BANGHA, Imre. 1999. *Saneh ko mārag: Ānandghan kā jīvanvṛtt.* New Delhi: Vāṇī Prakāśan.

BANGHA, Imre. 2001. 'Lover and Saint: The Early History of Ānandghan's Reputation' in *Journal of the Royal Asiatic Society* Vol. 11/2, pp. 175–90.

BANSAL, Umārānī and BANSAL, Nareścandra. (forthcoming). *Dayānidhi Granthāvalī.* Kasganj: Madhulikā Prakāśan.

BIHĀRĪŚARAṆ, Brahmacārī, ed. 1930. *'Nimbārka mādhurī.* Vrindaban: Brahmacārī Bihārīśaraṇ.

BRAJVALLABHŚARAṆ, ed. 1943. *Srī Jayśāh Sujas Prakās: Racayitā Devarṣivar Maṇḍan kavi.* Vrindaban and Jaipur: Śrī Nimbārka Mahāsabhā and Śrī Nimbārka Satsaṅg Maṇḍal.

BRAJVALLABHŚARAṆ. 1956. 'Bhakta kavivar śrī Ānandghanjī' in *Śrīsarveśvar (Vṛndāvanāṃka).* Vol. V, p. 287.

BRAJVALLABHŚARAṆ. 1966. *Śrī Nāgarīdās kī vāṇī.* Vrindaban: Śrī Sarveśvar Pres, Vrindaban.

BRAJVALLABHAŚARAṆ, ed. 1970. 'Śrī Govind Śaraṇ Devācārya jī kī vāṇī.' *Śrīsarveśvar* 18/1–3.

BRAJVALLABHAŚARAṆ, ed. 1983–84. 'Śrīsundarāṅka I–II.' *Śrīsarveśvar* 31/1–2, 32/1–2.

BROWN, C. Mackenzie. 1982. 'The Theology of Radha in the Purāṇas' in *The Divine Consort: Radha and the goddesses of India* ed. Hawley, John Stratton and Wulff, Donna Marie. Berkeley: Graduate Theological Union (Berkeley Religious Studies Series), pp. 57-71.

CELER, Janārdan Rāv. 1973. *Vṛnd aur unkā sāhitya.* Agra: Vinod Pustak Mandir.

CELER, Janārdan Rāv. 1971. *Vṛnd granthāvalī.* Agra: Vinod Pustak Mandir.

CLÉMENTIN-OJHA, Catherine. 1990. 'La renaissance du Nimbārka Sampradāya au XVIe siècle: Contribution à l'étude d'une secte kṛṣṇaïte' *Journal Asiatique.* CCLXXVIII pp. 327–376.

CLÉMENTIN-OJHA, Catherine. 1999. *Le trident sur le palais: Une cabale anti-vishnouite dans un royaume hindou a l'époque coloniale.* Paris: Presses de l'École Française d'Extrême-Orient.

CLÉMENTIN-OJHA, Catherine. (forthcoming). 'Ascetics' rights in early 19th century Jaipur (Rajasthan)' In *Asceticism and Power in Asia* ed. Flugel, Peter and Hartman, Gustaaf. London: Curzon Press.

DICKINSON, Eric and KHANDALAVALA, Karl. 1959. *Kishangarh Painting.* New Delhi: Lalit Kala Akademi.

DĪKṢIT, Ānandprakāś. 1993. *Daulat kavi granthāvalī.* Pūṇe: Anusandhān Sanstān.

ENTWISTLE, Alain. 1987. *Braj: Centre of Krishna Pilgrimage.* Groningen: Egbert Forsten.

ENTWISTLE, Alain. 1991. 'The cult of Krishna-Gopala as a version of the Pastoral' in *Devotion Divine: Bhakti traditions from the regions of India* ed. Eck, Diana and Mallison, Françoise. Groningen and Paris: Egbert Forsten and École Française d'Extrême-Orient. pp. 73–90.

GAUṚ, Kṛṣṇdevprasād et als., ed. 1964. *Hastalikhit hindī granthõ kā saṃkṣipt vivaraṇ II.* Benares: Nāgarīpracāriṇī Sabhā.

GAUṚ, Manoharlāl. 1972. *Ghanānand aur svacchand kāvyadhārā.* Second edition. Benares: Nāgarīpracāriṇī Sabhā.

GOSVĀMĪ, Saraṇbihārī. 1966. *Kṛṣṇabhakti kāvya mẽ sakhībhāv.* Benares: Caukhambhā Vidyābhavan.

GUPTA, Kiśorīlāl, ed. 1965. *Nāgarīdās granthāvalī I–II.* Benares: Nāgarīpracāriṇī Sabhā.

HADI, Nabi. 1995. *Dictionary of Indo-Persian Literature.* New Delhi: Indira Gandhi National Centre for Arts.

HAIDAR, Navina Najat. 1996. *The Kishangarh School of Painting c. 1680–1850.* D. Phil. thesis, University of Oxford.

HAIDAR, Navina Najat. 2000. 'Satire and Humour in Kishangarh Painting' in *Court Painting in Rajasthan* ed. Topsfield, Andrew. Bombay: Mārg Publications. pp. 78–91.

HAIDAR, Navina Najat. (forthcoming). 'Radha in Kishangarh Painting: Cultural, Literary and Artistic aspects.' in *The Romantic Heroine* ed. Dehijia. India: Roli Books.

KATHURIA, Ramdev P. 1987. *Life in the Courts of Rajasthan During the Eighteenth Century.* New Delhi: S. Chand and Co.

KHAN (Khā̃), Faiyaz (Faiyāz) Ali, ed. 1974. *Nāgarīdās granthāvalī.* New Delhi: Kendrīy Hindī Nideśālay.

KHAN, Faiyaz Ali. 1986. *The Kishangarh School of Painting.* Doctoral Thesis, The University of Rajasthan, Jaipur.

KHAN, Shaukat Ali. 1981. *History and Historians of Rajasthan.* Delhi: Triveni Publications.

KEAY, Frank E. 1980. *History of Hindi Literature.* (first edition: 1920) New Delhi: Award Publishing House.

MALLESON, G. B. 1875. *An Historical Sketch of the Native States of India.* London: Longmans, Green & Co.

MCGREGOR, Ronald Stuart. 1984. *Hindi Literature from its beginnings to the nineteenth century.* Wiesbaden: Otto Harrassowitz.

MIŚRA and MIŚRA. 1913. *Miśrabandhu Vinod I-III.* Allahabad: Hindī Granth Pracārak Samiti.

MIŚRA, Bhagīrath, ed. 1972. *Hindī Sāhitya kā Bṛhat Itihās VII (Rītimukt).* Benares: Nāgarīpracāriṇī Sabhā.

MIŚRA, Viśvanāth Prasād, ed. 1945. *Ghanaānand aur Ānandghan (granthāvalī).* Benares: Vāṇī Vitān.

MIŚRA, Viśvanāth Prasād, ed. 1952. *Ghanaānand (granthāvalī).* Benares: Vāṇī Vitān.

NAGENDRA, ed. 1964. *Hindī sāhitya kā bṛhat itihās VI: Rītikāl: rītibaddha*. Benares: Nāgarīpracāriṇī Sabhā.

PAUWELS, Heidi. 2005. 'Romancing Radha: Nāgrīdās' Appropriation of Bhakti Themes' in *South Asia Research* vol. 25, nr. 1, pp. 55-78.

RANDHAWA, Mohinder Singh and RANDHAWA, Doris Schreier. 1980. *Kishangarh Painting*. Bombay: Vakils, Feffer and Simons Ltd.

ŚARMĀ, Devendranāth and SNĀTAK, Vijayendra, ed. 1974. *Hindī sāhitya kā bṛhat itihās V: Bhaktikāl (Saguṇ bhakti)*. Benares: Nāgarīpracāriṇī Sabhā.

ŚARMĀ Rāmprasād, ed. 1996. *Śrī Brajdāsī Bhāgavat*. Salemabad: Śrī Nimbārktīrtha.

SĀSTRĪ, Kalānāth. 1996. 'Bhāgavat ke amar kathāvācak Brajnāth Bhaṭṭa' in *Rājasthān* 5th December 1996.

SHARMA, Gopi Nath. 1990. *Rajasthan Through the Ages II (From 1300 to 1761 AD)*. Bikaner: Rajasthan State Archives.

SNELL, Rupert. 1989. 'Raskhān the neophite' in *Urdu and Muslim South Asia* ed. Shackle, Christopher. London: School of Oriental and African Studies, University of London. pp. 29-37.

Śrīsarveśvar. 1952–53. (Salemabad) Vol. I/3-9.

ŚUKLA, Kesarīnārāyaṇ. 1950. 'Ānandghan kī ek hastalikhit prati' in *Sampūrṇānand abhinandan granth* ed. Narendradava and als. Benares: Nāgarīpracāriṇī Sabhā pp. 269-279.

ŚUKLA, Rāmcandra. 1942. *Hindī sāhitya kā ithās*. Benares: Nāgarīpracāriṇī Sabhā.

ŚYĀMSUNDARDĀS, ed. 1937. *Rādhākṛṣṇadās granthāvalī*. Allahabad: Indian Press.

VAUDEVILLE, Charlotte. 1982. 'Krishna, Gopāla, Rādhā and the Great Goddess' in *The Divine Consort: Radha and the Goddesses of India* ed. Hawley, John Stratton and Wulff, Donna

Marie. Berkeley: Graduate Theological Union (Berkeley Religious Studies Series). pp. 1–12.

VYAS, R. T., ed. 1991. *The Sūktimuktāvalī of Bhagadatta Jalhana.* Vadodara: Oriental Institute.

Eleven

The Question of Sufism in Khwājah Mīr Dard's Urdu Poetry

Hajnalka Kovács

phūlēgī is zabāṇ mēṇ bhī gulzār-e maʿrifat
yāṇ maeṇ zamīn-e šiʿr mēṇ yah tuḫm bō gayā

"The rose-garden of wisdom will bloom in this language as well.
Here, I have planted the seed in the soil of verse"[1]

Khwājah Mīr Dard (1721-1785) is one of the greatest poets and mystics of 18th-century Delhi. Son and spiritual successor of Muḥammad Nāṣir 'Andalīb, a Naqshbandi Mujaddidi Sufi who envisaged a unique mystical path that would unite all Sufi paths

[1] *Dīwān* 25/4. References to Rašīd Ḥasan Khān's edition of *Dīwān-e Dard* are given in brackets in the main body of the text, the first number referring to the page while the second to the number of the *šiʿr* (couplet) on the given page. Other works of Dard are referred by their titles and page numbers. The transliteration follows the default transliteration for Urdu provided in the ArabTEX packege of the LaTEX typesetting system (roughly the ZDMG conventions, except that I use "kh" for *ḫ* if it is the first letter of personal names. Technical terms are transliterated except for the ones that have become accepted in English. Translations are mine unless indicated otherwise.

through the spiritual guidance of the Prophet Muḥammad,[2] Dard is the author of several mystical treatises in Persian which illustrate his deep insight into the problems of Sufi thought and reflect his own mystical experiences.[3] In contemporary sources, however, he is displayed not only as a mystic respected by all but also as an excellent poet.[4] In the literary histories he is counted as one of the "four pillars of Urdu" (the other three being Mīr, Saudā and Maẓhar): poets who transformed the Urdu language into a powerful vehicle of poetic expression and laid the foundation of the Classical Urdu ghazal.[5]

Dard owes his father not only his inclination to Sufism but also his literary aspirations. 'Andalīb organized monthly *mušāʿirahs*, gatherings of poets,[6] a practice that was continued by Dard until he passed over this responsibility to Mīr.[7] 'Andalīb, however, is known not for his poetry but for a long allegorical–mystical tale titled *Nālah-ye ʿAndalīb*, which he composed allegedly "in Hindi"[8] but wrote down in Persian, and which continued to be the main source of inspiration for Dard throughout his life.

Notwithstanding Dard's reputation in his own times as a mystic and a poet, today neither his mystical works nor his poetry is very well known for the Urdu-speaking audience, except that he is respectfully referred to as "Sufi poet" and a few of his couplets circulate as proverbs. In the literary histories he received much less weight than his more famous contemporaries, Mīr and Saudā. For the Western world Annemarie Schimmel's *Pain and Grace* introduced Dard's mystic thought and poetry. In the Indian subcontinent a few serious scholarly works (AḪTAR 1971, QADĪR 1964,

---

[2]Therefore named *ṭarīqah muḥammadiyyah*; for a study of some aspect of this path see SCHIMMEL 1976.

[3]The most important ones are *ʿIlm al-kitāb* and *Čahār risālāt* (i.e *Nālah-ye dard*, *Āh-e sard*, *Dard-e dil*, and *Šamʿ-e maḥfil*).

[4]E.g. MĪR 1984:61, QĀ'IM 1966:103, MĪR ḤASAN 1985:74; cf. DA'ŪDĪ 1962:43-67.

[5]ĀZĀD 2001:138,174.

[6]In that time it was possibly known as *maǧlis* or *maḥfil*, the term *mušāʿirah* gained prominence later. Mīr used the expression *maǧlis-e rēḫtah*; NAIM 1999:180. Cf. NAIM 1989 and RAHMAN 1983.

[7]MĪR 1984:61, also see NAIM 1999:181 and PRITCHETT 1994:70.

[8]Before the end of the 19th century Urdu language was called *hindī* or *rēḫtah*; see FARUQI 1991, Chapter 1.

and BARĒLWĪ 1983) were devoted to Dard's oeuvre, but in general Dard's poetry has received attention only inasmuch as it provided material for the illustration of his mystic thought.

Literary critics of the last decades of the 20th century, however, started to realize that in the shadow of Dard's fame as a mystic, justice had not been done to his literary achievements.[9] Arguing that Dard's poetry cannot be evaluated without taking into consideration the literary milieu in which he worked, and the literary and generic conventions that he, similarly to his fellow poets, observed, they proposed that the peculiarities and outstanding features of Dard's poetry should be pointed out with the methods of literary criticism.[10] A few critics even expressed their doubts concerning the accepted notion that Dard was a Sufi poet.

The controversy over whether Dard was a Sufi poet became the focus of my attention years ago when I started working on Dard's poetry. Although today I find it much less relevant for the appreciation of Dard's poetry than, for example, acquaintance with the poetics of Classical Urdu ghazal and with the poetry of the poets of the same period, the problem of the relationship of mysticism and poetry in general, and with regard to Dard's oeuvre in particular, is worth considering. Therefore, I think, a short discussion of the related issues as well as an overview of the reception, evaluation, and interpretation of Dard's poetry could serve as a preliminary study before any thorough study of Dard's poetry is attempted.

I. The problem of defining mystical poetry

The question what is mystical poetry and how can it be defined poses difficulties. While defining mystical poetry as poetry that should "concern union in some way with a single and transcendent supernatural", Lowry Nelson limits it to the communication

[9]See AḤMAD–ṢIDDĪQĪ 1989:11. Some of the articles in the same volume and the forewords to the different editions of Dard's *dīwān* address the literary aspects of Dard's poetry. Recently, the International Ġālib Seminar in 2002 (Delhi) was devoted to Dard; the papers were promised to be published in a forthcoming issue of the *Ġālibnāmah*, but to my knowledge they have not come out so far.

[10]E. g. FĀRUQI 1989, and RAŠĪD ḤASAN KHĀN 1989.

of the mystical experience, and excludes the wider categories of "religious", "devotional", or "meditative" poetry.[11] Further, he observes that since mystical experiences are "of their very nature inexpressible", "mystical poetry is fraught with a basic paradox—the impossibility of expression and, though doomed to fail it, the attempt at it."[12]

One may wonder as to what extent can Nelson's definition be made with regard to Persian Sufi poetry,[13] in which mystical and philosophical, homiletic and didactic often overlap.[14] In Persian poetry the two main genres that were employed for expressing mystical ideas were the longer narrative *maṯnawī* and the shorter lyrical ghazal. The *maṯnawīs* are usually categorized as heroic, romantic, didactic, but the individual poems often belong to more than one categories. For example, didactic *maṯnawīs* have been permeated by philosophical and mystical notions, while romantic *maṯnawīs* were employed for expressing the mystical quest and the ultimate union in the form of allegorical love stories.

Ghazal, a genre of love poetry, on the other hand, has been widely cultivated for expressing the emotional aspect of Sufism.[15] The vocabulary and imagery of secular love made it possible to express the longing for the Divine beloved, or the experience of the *unio mystica*, in erotic terms. As a consequence, in the ghazal the two have become more or less indistinguishable. Moreover, since in the medieval societies poetry was an art and a profession that could be learned, any poet who had sufficient knowledge of rhetorical and poetical devices, the prosody system, and the network of accepted themes could compose ghazals on mystical themes.[16] As de Bruin points out, "The decision whether a given poem should

---

[11] NELSON 1956:324.

[12] NELSON 1956:325.

[13] Marshall Hodgson coined the term 'Persianate' (along with 'Islamicate') "to embrace the broader cultural traditions associated with the Islamic religion and the Persian language."(cf. HODGSON 1974, I:57–60 and II:293–94.) Christopher Shackle further suggested using the adjective 'Suficate' for indicating "the problematic of disentangling the relationships between Sufism and Sufi poetry and the poetry which uses Sufism"(SHACKLE 1999:436.).

[14] Cf. DE BRUIN 1983:145–47, 164–68.

[15] For a good overview of Persian Sufi ghazal and *maṯnawī*, see DE BRUIN 1997:51-83, 84-127.

[16] Cf. ISLAM AND RUSSELL 1998:7, 10, 206, 214; FARUQI 2001:98-101; for a detailed discussion with examples, see PRITCHETT 1994:63-122.

be called a Sufi ghazal or a profane love song very often does not depend so much on the poem itself, but on what we know about its writer, that is the answer to the question: does the life of the poet provide us with clues of mystical affiliation, or is the poet only known as a court poet?"[17]

The most salient feature of the ghazal, polysemy, arises partly from its thematic and partly from its structural characteristics. Being a short lyrical genre, in a ghazal only certain aspects, themes, or moods of love—be it mundane or mystical—can be presented or evoked, as opposed to a detailed description of the whole experience. The situation became further complicated as the connection between the lines of the ghazal became gradually loser. In the Indo-Persian and Urdu ghazal each line (couplet) is practically an independent semantic unit, and it is only the formal characteristics—meter, rhyme and the *radīf* (repetative element after the rhyme)—that bestow a formal unity on the ghazal.[18] It follows that in one single line of the ghazal the theme has to be presented in an extremely condensed way. Allusion, ellipsis, metaphors and other figures of speech all serve the purpose of the condensation of the narrative. A compact line of poetry, in turn, allows for interpretation on more than one level.

In addition, the way poetry was put to use by the Sufis themselves further complicates the situation. In Sufi circles it was seldom investigated whether a poem was about earthly or Divine love. If it brought about a transformation in the heart of the seekers, it was regarded mystical. Similarly, poems that do not seem to us mystical have been extensively quoted in Sufi treatises, albeit they were often commented upon in the mystical sense, a practice which naturally narrowed the range of possible interpretations. Here, I think, distinction should be made between mystical poetry and the mystical use of poetry.

Dard's oeuvre is a case in point. His main work, *ʿIlm al-kitāb* is in fact a mystical commentary on 111 of his Persian quatrains (*rubāʿīs*), called *Wāridāt*.[19] The fact that he felt necessary to comment on the poems and to bring their meanings in accordance

[17] DE BRUIJN 1997:55.

[18] Cf. PRITCHETT 1994:77–90.

[19] The term is often used in Sufi literature for short poems or rhymed prose that "descend upon the heart" of the seeker from the Divine realms.

with his general mystic thought indicates that he was aware of their inherent ambiguity.[20]

Dard, moreover, is one of the few Sufi writers in whose mystical thought the importance of speech and writing, and the relationship of poetry and the communication of mystic thought occupies a prominent place.[21] On the one hand, he claimed to have written only by inspiration, on the other, he attributed as much value to the beauty of expression as to the content. In his view, mystical works of poetical beauty have the quality to exercise effect on and bring about a transformation in the hearts of those who hear or read them.[22] He consequently equally despised mystical works that, except for meter and rhyme, lack the characteristics of poetry,[23] and poetry that merely displays the technical perfection of its authors:

> The poems which come from the master poets who are not acquainted with the Reality and which show purely perfection of poetical technique—those are mostly completely made of metaphors and are bare of any reality; (they are) only exaggerations and lies...[24]

As far as Dard's Urdu poetry is concerned, however, we face another problem. In his Persian writings Dard never referred specifically to his Urdu poetry.[25] Did his claims to Divine inspiration include all of his poetry, or just his *Wāridāt*? Why was he silent about his Urdu poetry? Given the important role he played in contemporary literary life, how can his silence be explained?

---

[20] He was nevertheless not the first Sufi to realize this—one may recall Ibn al-ʻArabī's example who, in order to avoid criticism from the orthodox circles, wrote a commentary to his collection of apparently sensuous love poetry, entitled *Tarǧumān al-ašwāq*.

[21] For a detailed discussion of the question see SCHIMMEL 1976, Chapter 3, and ZIAD 2005.

[22] *ʻIlm al-kitāb*:148-149; cf. SCHIMMEL 1976:108.

[23] Cf. *ʻIlm al-kitāb*: 288-289 and SCHIMMEL 1976:111, 118, 121–22.

[24] *ʻIlm al-kitāb*, quoted and translated by SCHIMMEL 1976:122. Here Dard refers to rhetoric techniques and figures of speech, as well as to the famous Arabic saying "*aḥsan al-šiʻr akḏabuhu*" (the most beautiful verse is which contains the biggest lie), subject of numerous treatises on poetics, see e.g. QĀSIMĪ 1992:64.

[25] SCHIMMEL 1976:57.

One of the reasons why Dard does not refer to his Urdu poetry might lie within the Indian Sufi tradition itself. Quoting Persian poetry in Sufi prose works has long been an established practice. The same, however, is not true about Urdu poetry, at least in North India, where Urdu literature began only a generation before Dard's time. Dard possibly did not know any Sufi work that contained samples of poetry in the vernaculars, and Urdu poetry did not bear the same mystical connotations for him as Persian did. With the traditional learning that he received, it must have definitely been much easier for him to express his mystical experiences and thoughts in Persian.[26]

Or, Dard's silence about his Urdu poetry may indicate that he did not consider it worthy of mentioning. Writing poetry was a part of the social demeanor expected from youths of an aristocratic descent, but in the early 18th century Urdu poetry was still considered of a lower quality than Persian.[27] The verse quoted at the beginning of this article, however, seems to contradict this. Dard's boasting of having laid the foundations of Sufi poetry in Urdu may in fact indicate such a desire on his part, and is wholly in harmony with his religious claims, exposed in the *ʿIlm al-kitāb* and his other mystic works.

Dard, however, differed from his fellow-poets in one important respect: he did not consider himself a professional poet and did not live like one, inasmuch as he did not attach himself to any patron and refrained from composing any panegyric or satire.[28] It is understandable that he came to be known as a Sufi poet. But is there any proof that would bolster the widely held view that Urdu poetry for Dard was a means to convey his mystic message?[29]

---

[26]Maẓhar, Dard's contemporary fellow-poet and Sufi master of the Naqshbandi-Mujaddidi order, is reported to have quoted his Persian poetry in his discourses, but was equally silent about his Urdu poetry. See GHULĀM ʿALĪ DIHLAVĪ 1983.

[27]See FARUQI 2001, Chapter 7.

[28]Āzad's famous anecdote about Dard as 'half a poet'(ĀZAD 2001:175, 197) might have originally meant this; Qāḍī 'Abdul Wadūd at least traced the story in a *qaṣīdah* of Muṣḥafī where the author calls Dard 'half a poet' because he has not written any *qaṣīdah*. See 'ABDUL WADŪD 1989:42; cf. DA'ŪDĪ 1971:42-43 and QADĪR 1964:37.

[29]For example ṢIDDĪQĪ 1971:30 and DA'ŪDĪ 1962:89. Da'ūdī, one of the editors of Dard's *dīwān* credited Dard with leading Urdu poetry back to "Is-

II. The reception of Dard's poetry

The earliest sources that contain information about Dard's poetry are the *tadkiras* that were written in his lifetime. *Tadkiras* are anthologies of poetry, with biographical information about the poets, and critical remarks regarding their poetry. The organization, content, and tone of the *tadkiras* varies widely in accordance with the proclivities of their writers and the information available to them: while some of them provide only the barest biographical remarks about the poets, others are garnished with anecdotes.

Compiling anthologies of Persian poetry has been a common practice in Muslim India for many centuries, but *tadkiras* of Urdu poetry began to be written simultaneously with the consolidation of Urdu as a literary language of North India, thus in the time of Mīr, Saudā, and Dard. Dard, as a poet in both Persian and Urdu, is included in both types of the *tadkiras*. While the authors living in Dard's time knew him or met him, later *tadkirah*-writers compiled their works relying on the earlier ones as well as orally transmitted stories and anecdotes. They had more information at their disposal, but were less critical in their selection. The *tadkiras* thus are not the most reliable sources for biographical information, but tell much about the reception and evaluation of Dard's poetry.

Because of space consideration, here I will examine only a few of the earliest *tadkiras*. The *Tadkirah-ye nikāt aš-šuʿarā* (1752)[30] was written by Mīr (1722–1810), perhaps the best known poet of the 18th century and a friend of Dard, when Dard was in his thirties. Therefore his evaluation of Dard's poetry is an interesting instance of the literary taste of 18th-century literati. It also indicates what kind of difficulties we face when we try to make

lamic Sufism" from the deviation of "Persian Sufism", which Urdu inherited from Persian poetry! Da'ūdī apparently reads Dard's poetry in the light of his mystic thought; moreover, his judgment simply reflects the aversion that the majority of 20th-century Islamic thinkers of India have to Ibn al-ʿArabī's system of metaphysics (known as *waḥdat al-wuǧūd*, 'unity of existence'), which has been dominant in Persian and Indian Sufism.

[30]The dates given for the *tadkiras* reflect the date of completion. In reality, however, they were composed over years and often even after the "publication" additions and corrections were made to many entries. Farmān Fathpūrī gives the following dates for the composition of Mīr's *tadkirah*: 1161–1165 A. H. (1748–1752); see FATHPŪRĪ 1972:30–31.

sense of such sources. Mīr's convoluted Persian prose, filled with poetic metaphors, is not easy to translate and even less easy to understand:

> Mr. Khwājah Mīr, may God the Most Exalted protect him, with the pen name Dard: for the rose-garden of speech he is the efflorescence of the spring, for the flower-bed of this art he is the sweet-voiced nightingale. The language of his discourse untwists the twists of the tresses of the night of longing, his line of poetry on the sheet of paper is more pleasing than the ringlet of the dawn. His eloquent genius is a gracefully moving cypress in the garden of style. At times he is pleased to take the trouble of entering the garden of search by way of an evening stroll. In the flower-bed of his poetry colorful words are scattered all over, and flowers of meaning fill the skirt of his flower-picking imagination. Being a powerful poet of *rēḫtah*, in his perfection he is free from the need of others. He is a man of good disposition and humility, and a great companion. He composes poetry in Persian too, but mainly *rubāʿīs*. The briskness of the market is within the compass of his manner of living.[31] In short, he only has to do with friendship. A citizen of Shāhjahānābād, he is a Sufi as well as the son of a Sufi. He is virtuous and God-fearing, he has his full share of Sufism. This humble person is devoted to his service in a special way, although he is well-disposed towards everyone. He embraced this conduct, and removed all pride from the corners of his heart[...][32]

Mīr apparently accords much more space to Dard's poetry than to his mystical life, praising the elegance of Dard's style, his powerful and choice words, and his imaginativeness. He mentions Dard's saintly character and upright conduct, and in the rest of the paragraph describes how Dard's father predicted Mīr's

[31] Neither the syntax, nor the meaning of the last sentence is very clear.
[32] Mīr 1984:60–61

future greatness, and how he was entrusted with the organization of *mušāʿiras*.

Let us compare Mīr's account with a *tadkirah* that was written about twenty years later, but still in Dard's lifetime.[33] Its author, Mīr Ḥasan (1727–1786) is a noted poet of Urdu, best known for his masnavi *Siḥr al-bayān*. He too had a special relationship with Dard: although he is not counted among Dard's disciples, he admitted that his poetry was greatly influenced by Dard's. He praises Dard in hyperboles:

> Traveler on the paths of unveiling the secrets of religion, wayfarer of the roads of the spiritual struggle towards certainty, one of the high-ranking gnostics and of the revered doctors of law, on the heaven of speech like a sole sun: Ḥazrat Khwājah Mīr, with the pen-name Dard. One of the blessed scholars and of the virtuous Sufis, the echo of his excellence and perfection and the fame of his dignity and grandeur have reached heaven, and the ropes of the tent of his elevated thought, like the rays of the sun, are tautened from East to West. The sea of his mind is full of unbored pearls [i.e. unexpressed ideas], while the intellect said 'well done!' for what he has expressed. Spiritual guide to the valley of Reality, escort on the field of Law, his vigilant heart is a treasury of Divine secrets, the purity of his inner self is intimate with the Kaba of Divine majesty. King of the realms of *ḥāl* and *qāl* [spiritual states and utterances], he unites in himself the attributes of Divine beauty and Divine majesty. Son of Ḥazrat Khwājah Nāṣir, may God sanctify his secret. He is from Shāhjahānābād [Delhi]. He is a poet of both Persian and Hindi—nay, how would this be worthy of him? 'Poetry is beneath his lofty rank'[...]His *dīwān*, albeit short, is altogether choice. [34]

Mīr Ḥasan's language clearly recalls that of the hagiographies. He devotes almost the whole entry to the description of Dard's

[33] Between 1774–78, according to Farmān Fathpūrī 1184–1191 A. H. (1770–1777). Cf. FATHPŪRĪ 1972:155.

[34] MĪR ḤASAN 1985:74.

excellence in spirituality, and alludes to his poetry as a pastime which is insignificant in comparison with his spiritual achievements. His entry is almost like the mirror image of that of Mīr. The difference between the two may partly be explained with the difference of the time in which the respective *tadkiras* were written. At the time of the compilation of Mīr's *tadkirah* Dard was a young man who—if we are to believe his autobiographical confessions—just entered the mystical path. Twenty years later he was a revered Sufi, author of mystical treatises. Qā'im Čāndpūrī (1722/25–1794), who wrote his *tadkirah Mahzan-e nikāt* in 1755 (thus roughly at the same time as Mīr),[35] seems to confirm this. He too describes Dard's station in spirituality in hyperboles, but he also mentions that he entered the path not long ago, and since that time his constant remembrance of God leaves much less time for him to compose poetry.[36] The third of the earliest *tadkirah*-writers, Gardezī (*Tadkirah-ye rēhtah gōyāṇ*, 1752),[37] is extremely succinct: he only praises Dard's eloquence and lofty thought.[38]

What is common in all these *tadkiras* is that their authors treat Dard's poetry and his mysticism separately. They praise both, but do not mix them. None of them calls Dard a "Sufi poet", or refers to his poetry as a mirror of Sufism. In later *tadkiras* such expressions as "he often composes verses of a Sufi flavor",[39] or that "the smell of Sufism and of inner purity is apparent in the style of his utterance (*guftār*)"[40] do appear, but even these cannot be taken in support of the notion that they regarded Dard a Sufi poet. On the other hand, many of the popular anecdotes about Dard originate in these *tadkiras*.[41]

Criticism of Urdu literature in the subcontinent, paradoxic-

[35]Dates of composition: 1157–1168 A. H. (1744–1755); additions up to 1172 A. H. (1759) see FATHPŪRĪ 1972:30–31.

[36]QĀ'IM 1985:104–5.

[37]Dates of composition: 1156–1166 A. H. (1743–1752); additions up to 1168 A. H. (1754); see FATHPŪRĪ 1972:30–31.

[38]GARDEZI 1995:85.

[39]ŠORIŠ-'IŠQĪ:251.

[40]ŠAWQ RĀMPŪRĪ 1978:172; for quotations from more *tadkiras* see DA'ŪDĪ 1962: 43-67.

[41]A thorough study of the reception of Dard's poetry in the later *tadkira*-tradition is beyond the scope of the present paper; see e.g. MUṢHAFĪ 1933:92–93.

ally, has been heavily influenced by a work that, despite its being regarded the first history of Urdu literature, has much in common with the *tadkiras*.[42] Scanty in biographical details and critical remarks but abounding in anecdotes, Muḥammad Ḥusain Āzād's *Āb-e ḥayāt* (1883) has been serving as a storehouse of information not only for the Urdu-speaking public, but also for literary critics.

Āzād places Dard in his self-defined third era of Urdu poetry (the period of "the builders of the edifice of Urdu")[43]. Following a short biographical account and a list of his works, he introduces Dard's Urdu *dīwan*:

> His Urdu volume is short; there is nothing in it except ghazals, repeated-line poems, and quatrains. The odes, masnavis, and so on that poets normally write, he did not compose. Still, the ghazals 'on' ghazals of Saudā and Mīr Taqī that he did write are by no means inferior to theirs. There is also a small volume of Persian ghazals[...] The ghazals of Ḳhvājah Mīr Dard Sahib are normally seven to nine verses long; but each is a selection. Especially in the short meters, which he has used very often—it's as if he compressed the sharpness of a sword into a lancet. His ideas are serious and sober. No satire about anyone ever pollutes his tongue. No one has ever put Sufism into Urdu as he has[...] Mīr Sahib has counted him half a poet. If you want to hear the speech of his time, look at his volume. His language is the same as that of Mīr and Mirzā [Saudā].[44]

The rest of the entry consists of some objections to the orthography current in Dard's times, and anecdotes, followed by a se-

[42] For a detailed analysis of *Āb-e ḥayāt* see PRITCHETT 1994, Chapter 5.
[43] ĀZĀD 2001:138.
[44] Transliteration and translation are Pritchett's, ĀZĀD 2001:174–75.

lection of eight ghazals,[45] three of the which are among Dard's best known ghazals.[46]

The overall impression is that what Āzād appreciates most in Dard's ghazals is rather their emotional than mystical overtone. He refers to Dard's ability to compress potent and poignant words into his short meters (i.e. ghazals in short meters) in such a way that they evoke an emotional storm in the audience. Moreover, he draws the attention to the fact that the ghazals Dard composed in the same metrical and rhyme pattern (*zamīn*) as Saudā and Mīr did are of the same high quality.[47]

On the other hand, the sentence "his ideas are serious and sober" seems to imply that Dard's choice of themes excludes anything worldly, antinomian, or frivolous. The paragraph is reinforced by Āzād's remark, "no one has ever put Sufism into Urdu as he has", and by a great number of anecdotes that probably contributed more to Dard's fame as a Sufi than his critical observations.

Āzād was living in a time when, due to the rapid changes in the political situation and social life following the Mutiny, the "old world" was disappearing. He felt that changes are underway in literary taste too, and while in his work he intended to capture the now lost glory of Urdu poetry, at the same time he proposed a new path, on European patterns, for Urdu poetry. Āzād's friend, Ḥālī, in his influential *Muqaddimah* ("Introduction to poetry and poetics") laid down the principles for reforming the "decadent and artificial" Urdu poetry, embodied in his slogan "simplicity, naturalness, and emotion". He argued that while the Persian mystic poets described their real mystical experiences in simple and emotional terms, this quality is found in very few Urdu poets. He denounced the "sensual love" of Urdu poets, and argued that only "spiritual love" is worthy to become the subject matter of ghazal.[48]

---

[45]Even the number of the lines in Dard's ghazals in Āzād's selection do not conform his description: three of the ghazals exceed the limits, the longest of them has as much as 16 lines. The philologist Qāḍī 'Abdul Wadūd put Āzād's entry on Dard to scrutiny; see 'ABDUL WADŪD 1989.

[46]Or the other way around: they might have become popular because they are included in the *Ab-e ḥayāt*.

[47]For "composing ghazals 'on' ghazals see below.

[48]ḤĀLĪ 2001:101-3.

While Ḥālī did not discuss Dard's poetry in particular, his voice is clearly echoed in the portrayal of Dard's poetry in the first history of Urdu literature in English, written by Ram Babu Saksena:

> Dard's style is very eloquent, clear, intelligible, and perspicuous. It is polished and poignant, full of fire and pathos. His ghazals are marked by apt idioms, lofty thoughts, chastened emotions and refined diction. He is the best exponent of Sufism and he shows great skill in developing the theme of spiritualism. His verses are equal to Mir in simplicity and directness and the effect is enhanced and beauty heightened by the introduction of spiritualism. [...] His conception of worldly love is very high. He does not confound worldly love 'Ishk Majazi' with sensuality 'Bulhavasi', neither does he believe that sensual love would lead one to love spiritual. He identifies worldly love with his love for his Pir or for his real intimate friends. He does not believe in the ordinary 'Bazar love'. Similarly his conception of poetry is sublime. He deprecates its being made a means of self-advacement. Likewise he advises the writing of poetry in inspired moment in the very white heat of emotion.[49]

We can clearly see how the Romantic notions of poetry operate in Saksena's account, reinforced with Dard's autobiographical confessions. We may wonder, however, why Saksena gives no examples from Dard's poetry.

Muḥammad Ṣādiq, author of the other popular literary history in English, begins his account in the same venue:

> He is the first and last poet, in Urdu poetry before the Indian Mutiny, to strike an authentic mystic note. The others only amused themselves by versifying mystical thought. The vanity and unreality of life and its joys and sorrows, unity of existence, the greatness of man in the hierarchy of life, the mirage of

[49] SAXENA 1940:57–8.

> the intellect, praise of intuition, the extinction of self and suspicion of worldly life, pietism, contentment, resignation—these are some of the important topics of his mystical verse. Nearly one-third of his poetry is devoted to these ideas.

Having paid in this way due respect to Dard the Sufi (but without giving any example of his mystical poetry), he continues in a different venue:[50]

> The other two-thirds is erotic. There is much in it that is merely conventional. But like Mīr he has the saving grace of sincerity, and is more intent on expressing his feelings than on mere fanciful elaborations. There are some who read a mystical meaning into his amatory verses, but the result is seldom convincing. Dard was not a sour-faced theologian, hostile to earthly love and beauty. The poet and aesthete in him overcame the theologian, as his love of and proficiency of music show. His poetry reveals a mind keen-edged and sensuous, delighting in physical beauty for its own sake and not treating it as a mere stepping-stone to the supersensible. He was a man first and a theologian afterwards, and to refine him away into a spiritual abstraction is to ignore the sensuous side of his mind.

Ṣādiq was not alone with his dilemma. Other critics too, puzzled by the great number of verses that could be interpreted in the mystical sense only with great difficulty, attempted to solve the problem by dividing Dard's poetry into two or three categories: verses undoubtedly on Sufi topics, purely profane verses, and verses that can be interpreted in both mystical and profane sense.[51] Since the large number and the high quality of the profane verses in Dard's oeuvre cannot be easily overlooked, they struggled to find excuses for Dard, saying for example, that sometimes he yielded to the fashion of his age, the spirit of *mušāʿiras*, and composed a few conventional poems.[52]

[50] Ṣādiq 1984:140-41.
[51] See for example Ṣiddīqī 1971:67, 80 and Abdullah 1989:239-40.
[52] Ṣiddīqī 1971:92.

In this approach, in reality, two distinct approaches are combined: the division of the verses according to the thematic content, and according to the possibilities of interpretation. This approach is not easy to avoid, perhaps because in the case of such an intricate genre as the ghazal, it is the first to offer itself. In most works on Dard written on the subcontinent we find long lists of quotations from Dard's poetry, divided under such subheadings as 'Oneness of God', 'Divine love', 'Purity of the heart', 'Reliance on God's will', 'Transcendence and immanence' (for the mystical themes), and 'Love affair', 'Libertinism', 'Wine-poems', and 'Pederastry' (for the non-mystical).[53]

Ṣādiq's observations about Dard's "erotic" poetry were reinforced in Khalīlur Raḫmān A'ẓamī's article. A'ẓamī finds it strange that Dard's name is never mentioned in connection with love poetry, although his poetry is loaded with powerful expressions of "true longing and passion" and is not merely "a conventional treatment of the theme 'love'".[54] He sees no reason to interpret the object of Dard's longing as the Divine beloved, or at least his spiritual master;[55] on the contrary, he detects "an earthly, flesh and blood beloved hiding behind many of Dard's verses"[56] like the following:[57]

maeṇ sāmnē sē ǧō muskarāyā
hōṇṫh us kā bhī dard hil gayā thā (26/7)

When I smiled at her,
O Dard! her lips also moved.

kahā ǧab maeṇ tērā būsah tō ǧaesē qand hae pyārē
lagā tab kahnē par qand-e mukarrar hō nahīṇ saktā
(29/7)

[53]E.g. DA'ŪDĪ 1962:149-60, AḪTAR 1971:312–37.

[54]A'ẒAMĪ 1989:218.

[55]Cf. Dard's confession that he has never had intimacy with any beloved and that he considered the love for one's *pīr* (spiritual guide) as the only justifiable worldly love; quoted e.g. in AḤMAD-ṢIDDĪQĪ 1989:21.

[56]A'ẒAMĪ 1989:219, cf. RAŠĪD ḤASAN KHĀN 1989:177 and AḪTAR 1971:435.

[57]These examples has been selected from Dard's *dīwān*, and not from A'ẓamī's article. For his examples see A'ẒAMĪ 1989:221-225.

When I said, "your kiss is like sugar, my dear,"
She said, "but this sugar cannot be refined."[58]

čāhē kih bāt ğī kī muṇh par nah āʾē mērē
apnē dahan kō lā kar rakh dē mērē dahāṇ par (39/2)

If you don't want me to declare my heartfelt desire,
Come and place your lips on my lips.

The next step seemed logical: to look for real love experience in Dard's life that could have inspired such verses. This he found in Dard's confession that he had lived as a worldly person before he entered the Sufi path at the age of 29.[59] A'ẓamī found this period to have been enough for a person with such a sensitive mind and soft heart like Dard to fall in love. He regretted that the date of compositions of Dard's 'worldly' ghazals cannot be determined because of the lack of reliable evidence, but argued that conclusions can be drawn from the meanings the ghazals suggest. He went as far as deriving the basic characteristics of Dard's beloved from his ghazals.[60]

A'ẓamī's assumption that the ghazal can be read as an autobiographical document can be questioned from several points of view. First, in the case of Indian poets of the Classical period, it would be very difficult to establish any chronology and would not be of much use, since they started recording their poetry only after having reached a certain level of mastery in it.[61] Second, it takes no notice of the conventions that gave shape to it. In the ghazal the conventional speaker is the lover, whose persona the poet assumes. "The ghazal as a love lyric presents the various states and stages of a fictionalized, idealized experience of love, an underlying narrative from whose episodes the poet selects his topic."[62] Third, singling out one meaning out of the possible meanings greatly narrows the possibilities of interpretation.

[58] A play on *qand-e mukarrar*, which literally means "refined sugar", while metaphorically the lips of the mistress. Moreover, *mukarrar* means "repeated".

[59] Quoted in some *tadkiras*; cf. SCHIMMEL 1976:43, 47-48. Schimmel, however, interprets these as expressions of *tawbah*, repentance, which marks the beginning of the mystical path. See SCHIMMEL 1975:170.

[60] A'ẒAMĪ 1989:225.

[61] S. R. Faruqi, personal communication.

[62] MEISAMI 1990:134.

A'ẓamī's greatest merit, however, is that he drew attention to one of the conventional voices in Dard's poetry that has generally been marginalized or allegorized.

While A'ẓamī reads Dard's poetry as being powerful expression of a real love experience, Shamsur Rahman Faruqi, the most versatile critic of Urdu poetry points out another feature that has hitherto seldom been noticed in Dard's poetry: the intellectual complexity of Dard's thought, which manifests itself in his preoccupation with existential and metaphysical questions on the one hand, and in the way of using the conventional imagery of the ghazal on the other. Some examples for the former:

ʿālam hō qadīm ḫāh ḥādiṯ
ǧis dam nahīṇ ham ǧahāṇ nahīṇ hae (99/3)

Eternal it may be, or transient,
The moment we are not, the world is not.[63]

is hastī-ye ḫarāb sē kyā kām thā hamēṇ
ay naššah-ye ẓuhūr yah tērī tarang hae (80/5)

What use was this wretched existence of us?
Oh intoxication of manifestation, all this is your whim.[64]

zindagī hae yā kōʾī ṭūfān hae
ham tō is ǧīnē kē hāthōṇ mar čalē (103/8)

Is this life, or is it some storm?
Anyway, we have been destroyed by living.[65]

thā ʿadam mēṇ bhī muǧhē ik pēč-ō tāb
muḏtarib hō ǧis ṭaraḥ mawǧ-e sarāb (36/2)

Even in non-existence I was perturbed
by the way the waves of the mirage were agitated.

Such verses of Dard are usually interpreted as Sufi poetry, but Faruqi argues that such a view should be reconsidered. His

---

[63]Translation by Faruqi, in FARUQI 1981:20.

[64]Translation by Matthews and Shackle, in MATTHEWS AND SHACKLE 1972:54.

[65]Translation by Matthews and Shackle, in MATTHEWS AND SHACKLE 1972:56.

criteria for true Sufi poetry are that it should be concerned with the union with a higher reality; it should not accept any material intermediary between the two; it should confess the superiority of soul to matter and of nonexistence to existence; heart should have more role in it than mind, and "spiritual states" (*ḥāl*) than rational exposition of the mystical thought (*qāl*); there should be no place for sorrow, despair, or fear in it.[66] He argues that since reflection on existential questions and metaphysical speculation involve the rational faculty, Dard should rather be considered the first representative of the intellectual trend in Urdu poetry than the first Sufi poet.[67] He sees him especially close to Ġālib, not only in their inclination to metaphysical speculations, but also in the striking similarity in their use of language and imagery.[68]

Faruqi draws attention to another characteristic of Dard's poetry that, in his view, tells against Dard's being a Sufi poet. He notices that in Dard's ghazals expressions of sorrow, despair, doubt, and feeling of constraint abound, while the moods of joy, ecstasy, expansion and tranquillity that we would expect from a Sufi master of high station are largely missing. These qualities, in Faruqi's view, have to do with the "world of I", or at best, are characteristics of a beginner on the path.[69] In his words: one can feel "the piercing of the scorpion-sting of a personal grief and sorrow hidden in the chamber of his heart" in his verses like these:[70]

---

[66] FĀRŪQĪ 1989:180.

[67] Elsewhere he himself acknowledges that existential and metaphysical speculations are in general among the peculiarities of Indo-Persian, and Urdu, ghazal. Cf. FARUQI 1981:11–34.

[68] FĀRŪQĪ 1989:196-198, 202. Wahīd Aḫtar had earlier drawn attention to the parallels between Dard and Ġālib. He argued that Dard is the only poet of Urdu whose poetry could have served as a model for Ġālib's reflective poetry. He gave examples of the ghazals of Dard and Ġālib that are in the same *zamīns* (AḪTAR 1971:514–18.), but remarks that since Mīr and Saudā too have ghazals in these *zamīns*, it cannot be said with certainty that Ġālib had Dard's ghazals in mind when composed his. He notes that, on the other hand, even many of the *shi'rs* of Dard and Ġālib that do not share the same *zamīn* are strikingly similar in diction and imagery (examples: AḪTAR 1971:518–20). He nevertheless sees a profound difference between the intellectual attraction that Ġālib has towards Sufism, and Sufism as experienced and expressed by Dard. See AḪTAR 1971:515, 521.

[69] FĀRŪQĪ 1989:186, examples 191–94. Cf. RAŠĪD ḤASAN KHĀN 1989:173, 177.

[70] FĀRŪQĪ 1989:193.

sīnah-ō dil ḥasratōn̤ sē čhā gayā
bas huğūm-e yās ğī ghabrā gayā (24/4)

My chest and heart are overwhelmed with grief.
Enough, o swarm of despair! My soul is already bewildered.

mirā ġunčah-ye dil hae wah dil-giriftah
kih ğis kō kisū nē kabhū wā nah dēkhā (25/8)

The bud of my heart is the heart in grip
that has never been seen open by anyone.

gō salāmat hūn̤ maen̤ ẓāhir mēn̤ pih dil kē ḫaṭrāt
rāt din ghun kī ṭaraḥ mērē ta'īn̤ khātē haen̤ (49/4)

Although I am quite well from outside, the fears in my heart
eat me like a woodworm day and night.

Here I think Faruqi is mistaken in equating the above mentioned qualities with the spiritual states of *basṭ* and *qabḍ*.[71] One's inner states or his station in spirituality can no more justifiably be ascertained on the basis of some samples from his ghazal poetry than the identity or the characteristics of his beloveds.

Faruqi's study of Dard's poetry, however, is ground-breaking in many respect. His is perhaps the first study in which peculiarities of Dard's poetry are pointed out with the methods of literary criticism.

III. A few examples for Dard's use of the ghazal imagery

In the course of the discussion of the various views about Dard's poetry examples we have seen examples of poetry on the themes of love, on metaphysical themes, and on the theme or sorrow and suffering. In the last part of the paper I will attempt to show through a detailed analysis of a few chosen examples *how* Dard

[71] For an overview of the states and stations in Sufism see ARBERRY 1960 (*basṭ*), GARDET 1971 (*ḥāl*), LINGS 1978 (*qabḍ*), and NASR 1972:68-83.

uses the conventional imagery of the ghazal. The themes of the first three couplets may be characterized as "non-Sufi", while of the latter three as "Sufi"—although there is some overlap between the two.

mōṙiyō muṇh nah abhī sōzan-e mižgāṇ ham sē
t́āṇkē zaḫmōṇ mēṇ tō haeṇ kitnē hī darkār hanōz (40/12)

Do not turn away from us yet, o needles of eyelashes:
our wounds still need so many stitches.

The leitmotif of the couplet is that though the beloved's glances cause pain, the lover longs for them: for him they have a healing effect on his wounds. At the same time he knows that they will inflict yet more wounds. He, however, gladly undertakes that suffering, since it is a sign of the beloved's attention.

In ghazal poetry the eyelashes of the beloved are often compared to arrows, with which she wounds the lover. While this identification is also in the background, in the present couplet the eyelashes are compared to needles. Needles are needed to stitch wounds, but since they are pointed, they cause pain and even more wounds. The idea is further supported with a phonetic coincidence: the word *sōzan* ("needle") calls to mind a couple of words associated with burning, pain, or suffering (*sōz*, *sōziš*).

In the couplet the similarity between the form of the eye and of the wound (*dāġ*), and, on the other hand, between the eyelashes and the needles, is exploited. Moreover, the wound with the stitches looks like the eye with the eyelashes. This couplet is a good example not only of rare and striking imagery, but also of powerful emotional load.

harčand saʿī mēṇ hae sadā nāḫun-e hilāl
khultī hae par sipihr kī kōʾī kuhan girah (73/6)

No matter how much the nail of the crescent strives,
can it unravel any of the the mysteries of fate?

In this couplet, the protagonist is reflecting upon the mysteries of fate, never solved by anyone. This simple idea is supported with a double metaphor, containing an extremely graphic image. First, on the basis of shape, the crescent moon is likened to a nail, and the stars to knots. The image of the crescent on the sky running after the stars recalls the image of the nail, as it is trying to untie the knots. Second, the word "sky" (*sipihr*) traditionally stands for destiny or fate; in this context, *girah* refers to a knotty problem, a mystery, a puzzle. The rhetoric question implies a negative answer: just as the crescent can never get closer to stars, no human effort will meet success in solving the mysteries of life.

Besides the graphic imagery, the appropriate choice of words also contributes to the beauty of the *šiʿr*. The verbal root of *saʿī*, here used for the crescent's strife, also means running to and fro; in Arabic it is specifically used for the movement of the moon. Besides, it refers to a ritual during the *haǧǧ*, when the pilgrims, in commemoration of Hagar's search for water, run seven times between the two hills Safa and Marva. The first two meanings—running and strife—are present simultaneously, and the third one—the *ḥaǧǧ* ritual—is evoked by analogy. No word other than *saʿī* could convey such range of meanings and implications.

> *zamānē kī nah dēkhī ǧurʿah-rēzī dard kučh tū nē*
> *milāyā miṯl-e mīnā ḫāk mēṇ ḫūn har šarābī kā* (15/1)
>
> Dard! Don't you see how fate, like a goblet, drop by drop,
> spills the blood of all drunkards, mixing it with the soil?

The theme of the couplet is that fate is essentially unfavorable to those who dare to love: the outcome of love is death. The expression *ḫāk mēṇ milānā* implies not only destruction, but also waste: the precious blood of the lovers is spilt in vain, since it will not stop love. The addressee—the poet-lover—knows that he will meet the same fate if he continues to love, but it is not in question for even a moment what he will do. The pivotal word of the couplet is *mīnā*, which with its double meanings (heaven and goblet) underscores the graphic comparison between wine-spilling and blood-shedding. On the other hand, if we can believe the numerous examples documented in Persian poetry, it was a custom during the drinking parties to pour some wine on the ground for those who can no longer drink.

arḍ-ō samā kahāṇ tirī wusʿat kō pā sakē
mērā hī dil hae wah kih ǧahāṇ tū samā sakē (84/7)

How could earth and heaven embrace your vastness?
It is only my heart where You can be contained.

This couplet, the opening verse of one of Dard's most famous ghazals, has often been quoted to illustrate his mystic thought. It refers to the unique place of human being in the hierarchy of created beings. If the heart is purified from the contaminations that arise from his carnal self, it will be able to reflect the Divine. Metaphorically: the human heart is the throne of God. The first line is a direct allusion to the Koran: "We offered our trust to the heavens, to the earth and to the mountains, but they refused the burden and were afraid to receive it. Man undertook to bear it, but he has proved a sinner and a fool."[72] The second line alludes to a *ḥadīṯ*: "Neither My heavens nor My earth encompass Me, but the heart of My servant with faith does encompass Me."[73]

It is, however, not only the mystical content and meaning but also the tight structure as well as the elaborate and yet smoothly fitting rhetorical devices that make this couplet so appealing. Alliterations too reinforce the meaning. To list just a few, the Arabic noun *samā* (heaven) and the Hindi/Urdu verb *samā sakē* ("can be contained") have the same written form and pronouncation. The verbal root of the noun *wusʿat*, moreover, also means "to contain", and even "to be able". The former meaning is also present in the Hindi/Urdu verbs *pā sakē* and *samā sakē*, while the latter in the auxiliary verb *saknā* that stands at the end of both lines. Another verbal noun that derives from the same root is *wusʿ*, "ability, capability, power, strength", further enforces the meaning of the verse: only the human heart is able to contain God. Despite its apparent simplicity, the word choice, the semantic and phonetic correspondences of the words, and its fluency make this couplet a masterpiece of 18th century Urdu poetry.

[72]Koran 33:72, translated by N. J. Dawood.
[73]Quoted in CHITTICK 1994:69.

ahl-e fanā kō nām sē hastī kē nang hae
lawḥ-e mazār bhī mirī čhātī pih sang hae (80/2)

Those who have annihilated themselves are ashamed
of any sign of existence:
even the tombstone lies heavy on my chest.

Fanā is a central concept in Sufism; it refers to the annihilation of the individual (base) self, followed by subsistence in God. The temporary worldly existence (*hastī*) is viewed as an obstacle to complete annihilation (in mystical love, or in God's will). The point of the couplet is that although with physical death the last veil that stood between the mystic and God disappeared, the name engraved on the tombstone still recalls man's worldly existence. It is a burden for the mystic, just as the tombstone is a burden for the dead body. The pivotal word in the couplet is *sang* with the primary meaning "stone", but it also means "tombstone" and "weight". With the former it refers back to *lawḥ-e ma*, "tombstone", and with the second it supports the claim expressed in the first line. Moreover, the expression *čhātī pih sang hae* recalls the idiom *čhātī pih patthar hae*, which refers to the taking of a burden on one's self unwillingly.

patthar talē kā hāth hae ġaflat kē hāth dil
sang-e girāṇ huʾī hae yah ḫāb-e girāṇ muǧhē (93/11)

In the hands of negligence, heart is like a hand stuck
under a stone:
this heavy sleep lies heavy on me.

According to the Sufi teaching, negligence (*ġaflat*) is the main cause of human suffering, because it keeps human beings veiled from the reality of their selves and of God. Worldly life itself is a dream (*ḫāb*), because it separates human being from the World of Spirit. Thus, drunk with worldly life, human beings are asleep. In reality, such a life is a spiritual death for the soul. It is like the gravestone (*sang*), which lies heavy on the dead body.

Similarly, heart in the hands of *ġaflat* is no more than a dead organ. It is helpless, just as a hand that is stuck under a stone. The expression of the hand stuck under a stone (*patthar talē kā hāth*) is a direct translation of the Persian proverb *dast tah-e sang*, "to be entangled in difficulties, to be defeated", whereas in Urdu it is rather used in the sense "to be helpless, forced".[74]

The two circles of poetic identifications are complete: on the one hand, heart (real self)–hand struck under stone–dead body; on the other, *ġaflat*–stone–gravestone–worldly existence/heavy sleep. In this couplet, mystic ideas are expressed with extremely graphic images and powerful metaphors.

Conclusion

Having chosen as my point of departure the question whether Dard was a Sufi poet, in this paper I attempted to provide a preliminary review of some of the views current in the literature about Dard's poetry.

What we can possibly learn from such a review is that reliance on too many factors outside poetry, such as the poet's personality, life, or his Sufi ideas, can easily lead to narrowing the possible interpretations of poetry itself. Dard's *dīwān* is definitely not the place where one could look for either his spiritual autobiography,[75] or for his doctrine. For estimating and appreciating Dard's Sufi doctrine we had better turn to his Persian treatises, and I agree with Shamsur Rahman Faruqi that it is more suitable to talk about Dard as "a Sufi who wrote poetry too".[76]

Dard's poetry can be approached from two directions. I believe that, from the point of view of literary criticism, the outstanding features of Dard's poetry should be pointed out in the context of the poetic tradition to which it belonged: the 18th-century Urdu ghazal.

If, on the other hand, it carries mystical meaning for the reader, for him it will be mystic poetry. But it belongs to another category: that of interpretation. Moreover, it is often the context or the occasion that invests secular poetry with the quality of the "mystical". Here it might not be out of place to quote During's conclusion of his discussion of Sufi music:[77]

---

[74] FĀRŪQĪ 1997a:I/267.

[75] There have been such attempts, e.g. 'AẒMATULLĀH KHĀN 1942.

[76] FĀRŪQĪ 1989:179.

[77] DURING 1992:283-284.

...without the active participation of the subject who performs or listens to the music, no music is *per se* mystical...all music, even though it possesses all the derived mystical qualities, will be efficient only by virtue of the intention of the listener and/or performer. Inversely, the true Sufi may interpret the most mundane of melodies as 'music of the spheres'.

Bibliography

Works in English

ARBERRY, A. J. 1960. "Basṭ". *Encyclopedia of Islam*, ed. H. A. R. Gibb et al. 2nd edition. Leiden: Brill. Vol. I:1088.

ĀZĀD, Muḥammad Husain. 2001. *Āb-e ḥayāt :shaping the canon of Urdu poetry.* Translated and edited by Frances Pritchett in association with Shamsur Rahman Faruqi. Delhi: Oxford University Press.

DE BRUIN, J. T. P. 1983. *Of Pietry and Poetry: The Interaction of Religion and Literature in the Life and Works of Ḥakīm Sanā'ī of Ghazna.* Leiden: E.J. Brill.

DE BRUIN, J. T. P. 1997. *Persian Sufi Poetry. An Introduction to the Mystical Use of Classical Poems.* Curzon Sufi Series.

BÜRGEL, Johann Christoph. 1988. *The Feather of Simurgh. The "Licit Magic" of the Arts in Medieval Islam.* New York and London: New York University Press.

CHITTICK, William C. 1994. *Imaginal worlds: Ibn al-'Arabī and the problem of religious diversity.* Albany: State University of New York Press.

DURING, Jean. 1992. *What is Sufi Music?* In: *The Legacy of Medieval Persian Sufism*, ed. by. Lewisohn, Leonard. London: Khaniqahi Nimatullahi Publications.

FARUQI, Shamsur Rahman. 1981. *The Secret Mirror. Essays on Urdu Poetry.* Delhi: Academic Literature.

FARUQI, Shamsur Rahman. 1999. "Conventions of Love, Love of Conventions: Urdu Love Poetry in the Eighteenth Century", *Annual of Urdu Studies*, Vol 14. (1999), pp. 1–32.

FARUQI, Shamsur Rahman. 2001. *Early Urdu Literary Culture and History*. Delhi: Oxford University Press.

GARDET, L. 1965. "Ḏh̲ikr". *Encyclopedia of Islam*, ed. B. Lewis et al. 2nd edition. Leiden: Brill. Vol. II:223-7.

GARDET, L. 1971. "Ḥāl". *Encyclopedia of Islam*, ed. B. Lewis et al. 2nd edition. Leiden: Brill. Vol. III:83-85.

HODGSON, Marshall G. S. 1974. *The Venture of Islam. Conscience and History in a World Civilization*. Chicago: The University of Chicago Press.

ISLAM, Khurshidul and RUSSELL, Ralph. 1998. *Three Mughal Poets. Mir–Sauda–Mir Hasan*. Delhi: Oxford University Press.

The Koran. 1999. Translated with notes by N. J. Dawood. Penguin Books.

LINGS, M. 1978. "Ḳabḍ". *Encyclopedia of Islam*, ed. van Donzel at al. 2nd edition. Leiden: Brill. Vol. IV:325-6.

MATTHEWS, D.J. and SHACKLE, C. 1972. *An Anthology of Classical Urdu Love Lyrics. Text and translation*. Delhi: Oxford University Press.

MEISAMI, Julie Scott. 1990. "Persona and generic conventions in medieval Persian lyric." *Comparative Criticism* 12 (1990), pp. 125–34.

NAIM, C. M. 1989. "Poet-audience interaction at Urdu mushairas". In: *Urdu and Muslim South Asia. Studies in honour of Ralph Russell*. Edited by Christopher Shackle. London: School of Oriental and African Studies, pp. 167-73.

NAIM, C. M., translated, annotated and with an introduction by. 1999. *Zikr-i Mir. The Autobiography of the Eighteenth Century Mughal Poet: Mir Muhammad Taqi 'Mir'*. New Delhi: Oxford University Press.

NASR, Seyyed Hossein. 1972. *The Spiritul States in Sufism.* In: *Sufi Essays.* London: Edgar Allen and Unwin.

NELSON Jr, Lowry. 1956. "The Rhetoric of Ineffability: Toward a Definition of Mystical Poetry", *Comparative Literature* 8 (1956), pp. 326-36.

PRITCHETT, Frances W. 1994. *Nets of Awareness. Urdu Poetry and Its Critics.* Berkeley and Los Angeles: University of California Press.

PRITCHETT, Frances W. 2003. "A Long History of Urdu Literary Culture, Part 2: Histories, Performances, and Masters", in: *Literary Cultures in History. Reconstructions from South Asia.* Ed. S. Pollock. University of California Press, Berkeley–Los Angeles–London, pp. 864-911.

RAHMAN, Munibur. 1983. "The Mushairah". *Annual of Urdu Studies*, Vol 3. (1983), pp. 75–84.

SADIQ, Muhammad. 1984. *A History of Urdu Literature.* Delhi: Oxford University Press.

SAXENA, Ram Babu. 1940. *A History of Urdu Literature.* Allahabad: R. N. Lal.

SCHIMMEL, Annemarie. 1975. *Classical Urdu Literature from the Beginning to Iqbal.* In: *History of Indian Literature*, ed. J. Gonda. Wiesbaden: Otto Harrasowitz.

SCHIMMEL, Annemarie. 1976. *Pain and Grace. A Study of Two Mystical Writers of Eighteen Century Muslim India.* Leiden: Brill.

SHACKLE, Christopher. 1999. "Persian Poetry and Qadiri sufism in Later Mughal India: Ghanīmat Kunjāhī and his *Mathnawī-yi Nayrang-i 'ishq.*" In: *The Heritage of Sufism. Volume III. Late Classical Persianate Sufism (1501–1750). The Safavid and Mughal Period.* Ed. by Leonard Lewisohn and David Morgan. Oxford: Oneworld, pp. 435–463.

ZIAD, Homayra. 2005. "The Nature and Art of Discourse in the Religious Writings of Khvaja Mir Dard". *Annual of Urdu Studies*, Vol. 20 (2005), pp. 145–165.

Works in Urdu and Persian

'ABDUL WADŪD, Qāḍī. 1989. "*Dard aor āb-e ḥayāt*". In *Ḫǎǧah Mīr Dard. Tanqīdī-ō taḥqīqī muṭālaʿah.* Edited by Anīs Aḥmad and Ṯāqib Ṣiddīqī. Delhi: S. A. Publications, pp. 29–48.

'ABDULLĀH, Sayyid. 1989. "*Dard kī šāʿirī kā ṣūfiyānah lab-ō-lahǧah*". In *Ḫǎǧah Mīr Dard. Tanqīdī-ō taḥqīqī muṭālaʿah.* Edited by Anīs Aḥmad and Ṯāqib Ṣiddīqī. Delhi: S. A. Publications, pp. 231-245.

AḤMAD, Anīs and ṢIDDĪQĪ, Ṯāqib, eds. 1989. *Ḫǎǧah Mīr Dard. Tanqīdī-ō taḥqīqī muṭālaʿah.* Delhi: S. A. Publications.

AḪTAR Wahīd. 1971. *Ḫǎǧah Mīr Dard.* 'Alīgarh: Anjuman-e Taraqqī-ye Hind.

ĀZĀD, Muḥammad Husain. 2001b. *Āb-e ḥayāt.* Ed. Muḥammad Naḏīr and Ṭāhir Naḏīr. Lahore: Khazīnah-ye 'Ilm-o Adab.

'AẒMATULLĀH KHĀN, Muḥammad. 1942. *Maḍāmīn-e ʿAẓmat.* Part 2. Haydarābād.

A'ẒAMĪ, Khalīlur Raḥmān. 1989. "*Ḫǎǧah Mīr Dard ʿišqiyyah šāʿirī kī āʾinē mēṉ*". In *Ḫǎǧah Mīr Dard. Tanqīdī-ō taḥqīqī-muṭālaʿah.* Edited by Anīs Aḥmad and Ṯāqib Ṣiddīqī. Delhi: S. A. Publications, pp. 217–229.

BARĒLWĪ, 'Ibādat. 1983. *Ḫǎǧah Mīr Dard Dihlawī.* Lāhaor: Idārah-ye Adab o Tanqīd.

DARD, Khwājah Mīr. 1891. *ʿIlm al-kitāb.* Delhi, Maṭba'-e Anṣārī.

DA'ŪDĪ, Khalīlur Raḥmān, ed. and foreword. 1962. *Dīwān-e Dard* (*urdū*). Lāhaor: Majlis-e Taraqqī-e Adab.

FATHPURĪ, Farmān. 1972. *Urdū šuʿarā kē taḏkirē aor taḏkirah-nigārī.* Lahore: Majlis-e Taraqqī-ye Adab.

FĀRŪQĪ, Šamsur Raḥmān. 1989. "*Sayyid Ḫāǧah Mīr Dard*". In *Ḫāǧah Mīr Dard. Tanqīdī-ō taḥqīqī muṭālaʿah.* Edited by Anīs Aḥmad and Ṯāqib Ṣiddīqī. Delhi: S. A. Publications, pp. 179–216.

FĀRŪQĪ, Šamsur Raḥmān. 1997a. *Šiʿr-e šōr angez. Ġazaliyyāt-e Mīr kā intiḫāb-ō tafṣīlī muṭālaʿah.* 4 volumes. Delhi: Taraqqī-ye Urdū Bureau.

GARDĒZĪ, Fatḥ 'Alī Ḥusaynī. 1995. *Taḏkirah-ye rēḫtah gōyāṇ.* Ed. by Akbar Ḥaydarī Kašmīrī from MS dated 1760. Lucknow: Uttar Pradesh Urdu Academy.

GHULĀM 'ALĪ DIHLAVĪ 1983. *Maqāmāt-i Maẓharī: aḥvāl o malfūẓāt o maktūbāt-i Ḥazrat Mīrzā Maẓhar Jān-i Jānān shahīd.* Taḥqīq o ta'līq o tarjumah, Muḥammad Iqbāl Mujaddidī. Silsilah-yi matbū'āt (Urdū Sā'ins Borḍ, Lahore, Pakistan) 175. Lāhaur: Urdū Sā'ins Borḍ.

ḤĀLĪ, Alṭāf Ḥusayn. 2001. *Muqaddamah-ye šiʿr-ō šāʿirī.* Lāhaor: Khazīnah-ye 'Ilm-o Adab.

MĪR, Taqī Mīr. 1984. *Taḏkirah-ye Nikāt aš-šuʿarā.* Ed. Maḥmūd Ilāhī. Lucknow: Uttar Pradesh Urdu Academy.

MĪR ḤASAN Dihlawī. 1985. *Taḏkirah-ye šuʿarā-ye urdū.* Lucknow: Uttar Pradesh Urdu Academy.

MUṢḤAFĪ, Ġulām Hamadānī. 1933. *Taḏkirah-ye hindī.* Ed. Maulvī Abdul Ḥaqq. Aurangābād, Dakan: Anjuman-e Taraqqī-ye Urdū.

QADĪR Aḥmad. 1964. *Ḫāǧah Mīr Dard aor un kā ḏikr-ō fikr.* Delhi: Maktabah Šāhrāh.

QĀ'IM Čāndpūrī. 1966. *Maḫzan-e nikāt.* Ed. Dr. Iqtidā Ḥasan. Lahore: Majlis-e Taraqqī-ye Adab.

QĀSIMĪ, Abul Kalām. 1992. *Mašriqī šiʿriyāt aor urdū tanqīdī-rivāyat.* Delhi: Maktabah Jāmi'ah Limited.

RAŠĪD ḤASAN KHĀN. 1989. "*Ḫ̆āǧah Mīr Dard kyā ṣūfī šāʿir thē?*" In *Ḫ̆āǧah Mīr Dard. Tanqīdī-ō taḥqīqī muṭālaʿah.* Edited by Anīs Aḥmad and Ṯāqib Ṣiddīqī. Delhi: S. A. Publications, pp. 169–178.

RAŠĪD ḤASAN KHĀN, ed. and foreword. 1997. *Dīwān-e Dard.* Mi'yārī Adab No. 13. Delhi: Maktabah Jāmi'ah Limited.

ŠORIŠ-'IŠQĪ. n. d. *Dō taḏkirē.* Ed. by Kalīmuddīn Aḥmad. S. l.

ŠAWQ RĀMPŪRĪ, Qudratullāh. 1978. *Ṭabaqāt aš-šuʿarā.* Ed. by Niṯār Aḥmad Fārūqī. Lahore.

ṢIDDĪQĪ, Ẓahīr Aḥmad, ed. and foreword. 1971. *Dīwān-e Ḫ̆āǧah Mīr Dard.* Delhi: Maktabah Šāhrāh.